Gossip

Gossip

Patricia Meyer Spacks

THE UNIVERSITY OF CHICAGO PRESS

Chicago and London

The University of Chicago Press, Chicago 60637
The University of Chicago Press, Ltd., London

Published by arrangement with Alfred A. Knopf Inc.

Portions of this work were previously published in *The Hudson Review* and *The Yale Review*. "Borderlands" was first published in *The Georgia Review*. "The Talent of Ready Utterance" was first published in *Women and Society in the Eighteenth Century*, edited by Ian P. H. Duffy, published by the Lawrence Henry Gipson Institute.

Owing to limitations of space, all other acknowledgments for permission to print previously published material will be found following the index.

Library of Congress Cataloging in Publication Data

Spacks, Patricia Ann Meyer.
  Gossip.

  Bibliography: p.
  Includes index.
  1. English literature—History and criticism.
2. Gossip in literature. 3. Gossip. 4. American
fiction—History and criticism. I. Title.
PR408.G66S6 1986   820'.9'353   86–11359
ISBN 0–225–76844–9 (pbk.)

For Aubrey Williams

The best of life is conversation,
and the greatest success is confidence,
or perfect understanding between
sincere people.

EMERSON

Contents

Preface

My decision to write a study of gossip originated in two personal experiences. One, sustained over some years, involved a close friend, a woman colleague. Beleaguered though we both felt, trying to sustain families and careers, we met early every morning for half an hour of coffee and reinvigorating conversation. Sometimes a male colleague would come in, his expression conveying—or so we fancied—contempt at our verbal trivialities as our talk moved from details of our own lives to speculation about others, or from discussion of novels to contemplation of friends' love affairs. Our husbands couldn't understand why, considering our frequently proclaimed, desperate need for more time, we counted those morning minutes sacred: only dire emergency interfered with them. Both married to unusually sensitive, understanding men, we felt shocked to discover their incomprehension of this essential part of our lives. But we couldn't explain to them; nor did we ever fully explain to ourselves.

The other experience had little in common with the first. In the spring of 1980, I went to China with a group of professional women, several of them social workers or psychiatrists with a special interest in adolescence. We met Chinese mental health workers and asked questions. One recurrent inquiry—recurrent because long unanswered—concerned adolescent pregnancy. There *is* no adolescent pregnancy in China, we would be told. Persistence, however, elicited a more satisfactory response. China in fact has little adolescent pregnancy because "a neighborhood of voluntary spies" (Jane Austen's phrase from *Northanger Abbey*: referring to late-eighteenth-century England) customarily prevents such outcomes for early attachment. At the time of our trip, Chinese men had to retire at 55,

ix

women at 50; the life expectancy had risen—so we were told—to 75. The huge resultant population without paid work found various socially accept-able occupations: among them, watching and discussing individual activ-ities of neighbors, to forestall as well as to criticize impermissible deviation.

Gossip as an instrument of social control: I thought of the Salem witchcraft trials. And I thought back to those treasured daily conversations, which, in self-condemning moments, we referred to as gossip. If gossip could have useful public functions, it also appeared to have useful private ones. Yet the very word, to my ear, implied severe derogation. I looked it up in the dictionary, to discover that official definitions suggest triviality as a concomitant of gossip, but nothing worse. How had the word acquired such negative overtones? Why did my friend and I feel faint guilt about what we did every morning? Why were we so addicted to it? What was the relation between gossip as public and as private instrument? Such ques-tions inspired my investigation. I started giving public lectures about gossip, and found that the subject elicited general interest. But almost every time I held forth, someone in the audience would suggest, helpfully, that I find another word to designate the kind of talk that preoccupied me—a term without such bad connotations. My mission began to define itself as a rescue operation: to restore positive meaning to a word that had once held it, and to celebrate a set of values and assumptions particularly associated with women, as well as with gossip.

Yet the subject would not have preoccupied me so long or so intensely without the important literary issues that gradually attached themselves to it. The daily conversations that first turned my attention to gossip always involved books as wells as people: we would invoke George Eliot to help us think about whether a friend's psychoanalysis had really changed her as profoundly as she claimed. Eliot and James and Austen and Joyce wrote, we knew, about the concerns we found it so absorbing to talk about. The subject matter of gossip and that of the realistic English novel largely duplicate one another. This recognition—self-evident as soon as formu-lated—led to further questions. Why didn't the novel as genre attract the same kind of denunciation leveled at gossip? In fact, as I soon realized, eighteenth-century moralistic objections to the newly developing novel—objections by writers as distinguished as Dr. Johnson—had the same tone and thrust as published condemnation of gossip. Such objections no longer often find their way into print, yet they may underlie the common view that poetry is a more "serious" literary form than prose fiction.

I gradually came to understand that connections between gossip and the novel encompass more than subject matter. Trying to define those connections led me to think about relations of speech to writing, about the nexus of narrator and reader, and about genres besides the novel. Biography, drama, and published personal letters all share material with gossip. All specify and play upon intricate and intimate relationships between imagined and real persons; all, like gossip, encourage reflections about the boundaries of the actual, the necessities of imagination. This book tries to delineate the links between literature and gossip in order to locate the positive power of both. It therefore engages itself along the way with some crucial issues of contemporary criticism.

Gossip is news in a red silk dress. A friend slid under my apartment door a newspaper clipping (about the Academy Awards) containing that definition. A red silk dress: A slattern's dress, making the news tawdry, claiming false seductiveness? Or an assertively feminine garment focusing attention on details that might otherwise go unnoticed? The ambiguities, the perplexities, associated with gossip appear endless. To explore them has been great fun.

P. M. S.

Acknowledgments

To write a book about conversation appears to generate conversation. Many people have talked with me about gossip; many have supplied me with references, to texts and to pictures; many have read and commented on my manuscript. They have made it, at times, a happy communal experience to work on this subject of communal talk. To acknowledge the abundant help I have received therefore gives me special pleasure: sharing ideas on the subject of gossip has supplied much of the gratification of writing this book.

A year at the National Humanities Center in Research Triangle Park, North Carolina, provided an ideally communicative atmosphere for my work. I am grateful to my fellow Fellows and to the staff, particularly to Rebecca Sutton and Alan Tuttle, who found the books I needed, and to Margaret Bockting, who typed the entire manuscript. A Faculty Fellowship from Yale University also helped to support this project.

The book has been enriched by suggestions from Houston Baker, Richard Bjornson, Frank Brady, Harriet Chessman, James Dalsimer, Pamela Daniels, Teri Edelstein, Elizabeth Ermarth, Jo Ann Fineman, Christine Froula, Joseph Gordon, James Baker Hall, Jerome Handler, Barbara Harman, Myra Jehlen, Paula Johnson, Deborah Kaplan, Elizabeth Long, Adrienne Munich, Maggie O'Connor, Darius Ornston, Thomas Pavel, Mary Poovey, Ernst Prelinger, Mary Price, Leslie Rado, Gail Reimer, Joyce Root, Margery Sabin, Judith Spacks, Lance Stell, Joan Stewart, Mark Taylor, Larry Thomas, Robert Thompson, Thomas Vargish, Thomas Whitaker, Carolyn Williams, and Bryan Wolf. All of them have helped to make this work better than it would otherwise have been, and have added to my pleasure in writing it.

Five people in particular devoted time, attention, and wisdom to large portions of my manuscript: Margaret Bockting, Werner Dannhauser, Margaret Ferguson, Carol Gilligan, and Aubrey Williams. They have enlarged my comprehension of more than gossip; to thank them adequately exceeds my capacities.

Gossip

1

Its Problematics

Think of gossip as a version of pastoral. Not just any gossip: the kind that involves two people, leisure, intimate revelation and commentary, ease and confidence. It may manifest malice, it may promulgate fiction in the guise of fact, but its participants do not value it for such reasons; they cherish, rather, the opportunity it affords for "emotional speculation."[1] Temporarily isolated from the larger social world, having created for themselves a psychic space like that of Arden or Thessaly, they weave their web of story. Their "art," like other oral forms, endures only briefly; its transience heightens its value. Like the fictions of Spenser's shepherds or Virgil's, such gossip may comment both obliquely (by its implicit assertion of opposed values) and directly on society's corruptions.

Or think of it as drama. Two characters more cheerful than Beckett's, but testifying their closeness like Vladimir and Estragon in *Waiting for Godot*, speaking the language of shared experience, revealing themselves as they talk of others, constructing a joint narrative—a narrative that conjures up yet other actors, offstage, playing out their own private dramas.

Or as fiction: fragments of lives transformed into story.

Gossip diverges, of course, from these and all other forms of art in lacking a conceivable audience (as well as a consciously structured form), and in spilling over, sometimes dangerously, into the real world. No spectator watches, no reader pursues a printed or written text, no auditor listens. Indeed, the privacy of the dyad or small group involved in this kind of talk largely determines its special tone. The presence of even a single observer would

3

change the conversation's character: no longer true gossip, only a simulacrum. Gossip is not literature—not pastoral or drama or even fiction. On
the other hand, to dwell on its analogies to literature both focuses attention
on gossip's positive aspects and illuminates the dynamics of real texts. If I
speculate here about gossip's problematics, I do so partly in the hope of
finding new ways to think about perplexities of narrative and voice and subject
in realistic fiction, new ways to understand historical and proximate forces
generating the novel, new ways to read biography and published letters. To
think about gossip and literature also provides a vantage point from which
to take gossip itself seriously. Gossip is not fiction, but both as oral tradition
and in such written transformations as memoirs and collections of letters it
embodies the fictional.

It would seem logical to begin with a definition. Instead, I shall begin
with a quotation. "The actual practices of the English linguistic community
with regard to the wordform *poetry* have been and remain so divergent and
inconsistent that any resolution or answer would constitute merely one more
ad hoc and essentially arbitrary definition of the term, with no greater claim
than any other to descriptive accuracy. It would not, then, be at all unreasonable or frivolous to conclude that *poetry* simply cannot be usefully
defined."[2] Even less unreasonable, less frivolous, to come to a similar conclusion about *gossip*, which means many things to many people and even,
at different times and in different contexts, to a single person. Always it
involves talk about one or more absent figures; always such talk occurs in a
relatively small group. As a group expands, the level of its gossip usually
deteriorates: no more than two or possibly three at a time can engage in what
I call "serious" gossip.

Let me isolate two typical modes, at opposite ends of a continuum, by
way of description if not definition. At one extreme, gossip manifests itself
as distilled malice. It plays with reputations, circulating truths and half-truths
and falsehoods about the activities, sometimes about the motives and feelings,
of others. Often it serves serious (possibly unconscious) purposes for the
gossipers, whose manipulations of reputation can further political or social
ambitions by damaging competitors or enemies, gratify envy and rage by
diminishing another, generate an immediately satisfying sense of power,
although the talkers acknowledge no such intent. Supplying a powerful
weapon in the politics of large groups and small, gossip can effect incalculable
harm. Iago typifies the purposefully malicious gossip at his worst, sowing
insinuations which generate tragedy.

But Iago has seemed to many critics less than, worse than, human in
his "motiveless malignancy." In practice, the gossip that seeks to damage

others is probably relatively rare—easy to imagine as an activity of the faceless figures who inhabit dark recesses of our minds, but infrequently evident in our living rooms. More common is gossip issuing not from purposeful malice but, as Kierkegaard and Heidegger suggest, from lack of thought, the kind of gossip accurately characterized as "idle talk." It derives from unconsidered desire to say something without having to ponder too deeply. Without purposeful intent, gossipers bandy words and anecdotes about other people, thus protecting themselves from serious engagement with one another. When I tell people I am writing about gossip, they often associate the term with this sort of talk. The most "public" form of a private mode, such gossip takes place before and after (not to say during) department meetings and business meetings, at cocktail parties and dinner parties, around the office coffee machine. Who has been sleeping with whom, who is considering what job? It can slide in and out of the purposeful, involving deliberate circulation of information, deliberate testing of opinion, without necessary malice. Of course, it too damages reputations and hurts feelings, its consequences uncontrollable and incalculable. Like other forms of gossip, it can also solidify a group's sense of itself by heightening consciousness of "outside" (inhabited by those talked about) and "inside" (the temporarily secure territory of the talkers). Blunted awareness marks such gossip; involving little real consideration of the issues its discourse touches, it constitutes moral avoidance. Often it sounds competitive, measuring who's up, who's down. My examples of it all belong to Western middle-class life; it reveals complacencies of groups in power, groups whose members, when they gather, feel no need to question themselves or their assumptions.

At the opposite end of the continuum lies the gossip I call "serious," which exists only as a function of intimacy. It takes place in private, at leisure, in a context of trust, usually among no more than two or three people. Its participants use talk about others to reflect about themselves, to express wonder and uncertainty and locate certainties, to enlarge their knowledge of one another. Such gossip, like the other forms, may use the stuff of scandal, but its purposes bear little on the world beyond the talkers except inasmuch as that world impinges on them. It provides a resource for the subordinated (anyone can *talk*; with a trusted listener, anyone can say anything), a crucial means of self-expression, a crucial form of solidarity. (An account of women in the Muslim harem reports that they "exchange experience and information, and critically analyze . . . the world of men. The general tone . . . is one of satire, ridicule, and disrespect for males and the ideals of the male world."[3] That's what I mean about "the subordinated.") The relationship such gossip expresses and sustains matters more than the

information it promulgates; and in the sustaining of that relationship, interpretation counts more than the facts or pseudo-facts on which it works.

This crude taxonomy omits complex combinations lying along the continuum; and even so general a division of types risks misleading by isolating
characteristics of a verbal mode marked above all by its fluidity. One form
of gossip changes readily to another, changes back again, modulates into a
third. Moreover, the forms may overlap: genuinely malicious talk can generate close alliance. But the classification at least suggests gossip's range of
functions and emphasizes that these functions can involve those talking,
those talked about, and/or persons not mentioned at all.

My characterization of the varieties of gossip raises the question of purpose. Gossip insists on its own frivolity. Even the most destructive gossip
does not announce destructive intent; the talk's alleged "idleness" protects
its participants. Like children's play and joking, however (see Chapter Three),
gossip in fact expresses a range of purpose. The classification I have just
offered differentiates most importantly in terms of real rather than announced
goals: destructiveness at one extreme, avoidance and competition in cocktail-
party gossip, intimacy and moral investigation at the "serious" end of the
spectrum. And these distinctions of purpose have yet greater significance
because conventional assumptions about gossip obscure them.

The terms *public* and *private*, which recur in my account, in themselves
suggest certain perplexities. The sharp differentiation of public and private
belongs to a relatively recent moment in history. Richard Sennett, for instance, locates the delineation of separate spheres as beginning in the late
seventeenth century. In the eighteenth century, he says, citizens "attempted
to define both what public life was and what it was not. The line drawn
between public and private was essentially one on which the claims of
civility—epitomized by cosmopolitan, public behavior—were balanced against
the claims of nature—epitomized by the family."[4] On which side of this
dichotomy does gossip belong? I have called it "a private mode," but the
matter is not so simple. Another troubling aspect of gossip is its blurring of
a line that we prefer to keep distinct. Even the most "private" forms of gossip,
the kitchen-table variety, often have effects in the larger world. The anxiety
aroused by gossip derives partly from its incalculable scope. One can never
know quite where it goes, whom it reaches, how it changes in transmission,
how and by whom it is understood. Whether or not gossipers hope to create
important effects, their talk may travel, may change opinion, may have
unforeseen consequences. Gossip belongs to the realm of private, "natural,"
discourse, it often violates "the claims of civility," but it incorporates the

possibility that people utterly lacking in public power may affect the views of figures who make things happen in the public sphere.

Both paradigmatic extremes in my classification—gossip as malice, gossip as intimacy—and the middle range as well, help to clarify aspects of the novel. Gossip proves relevant to considerations both of content and of form in English and American realistic fiction. Without detailed demonstration for the moment, I shall suggest aspects of the verbal mode which may prove useful for literary purposes, sketching an aesthetic, a morality, and an economics of gossip. Succeeding chapters will provide a history of the word *gossip* and of articulated attitudes toward the phenomena it describes and an inquiry into gossip's psychological meanings before moving on to more extensive literary investigation. The literary analysis, necessarily arbitrary in its selection of texts from the enormous range of possibilities, begins with collections of published letters, moves on to consider the problem of biography, contemplates gossip as an issue in Restoration and eighteenth-century comedy, and finally concentrates, for several chapters, on the English and American novel, particularly on narrator-reader relationships. Such investigation both exposes inner workings of literary modes and provides further insight into gossip's peculiar power.

As subject matter, gossip impels plots. It differs from other sorts of subject— love or war or man's struggle against fate—in almost always serving instrumental purposes, illuminating the psychological and social dynamics of love, war, or whatever. Rarely does it occupy the foreground more than briefly. In the background, however, it figures in ways corresponding to its full spectrum of real-life possibility. One thinks most readily of gossip in fiction as the circulation of scandal, an activity of obvious value for plot construction. The literary importance of such gossip depends on its symbolic function as voice of "the world"—the amorphous social organization that enforces its own standards and disciplines those who go astray. Most often, specific verbal exchange of this kind of gossip, as rendered in novels, involves groups mulling over information or pseudo-information that has already passed through many ears, many mouths, acquiring authority and heightening in the process. Anne Brontë's novel *The Tenant of Wildfell Hall* comes to mind. The plot shapes itself around intensifying gossip about a mysterious woman who has entered the community. The gossip both derives from and generates a need to know the facts of the case—generates that need in the reader as well as in the fictional society. Out of such need develops the pattern of revelation.

In fictional uses of this sort, gossip consists more importantly of what is said than of the act of saying. Given the emphasis on content rather than process, the purveyors of gossip often lack fictional "character," existing for the sake of their utterance, not defined by it. Indeed, they may not appear at all—in Restoration comedy, for example, where what "the world" says becomes an issue for many characters but "the world" itself can never be located. (Chapter Six will enlarge on this point.) Nonetheless, that social entity called "the world" vibrates with significance, not only in drama but most particularly in the novel, a genre defining its space as the intersection of the social and the individual. Gossip occurs at the same intersection, serving social purposes, defining social opinion, embodying social power (the power of opinion), but issuing from individual mouths and tracing psychic agendas as well. Characters in realistic fiction locate themselves within or against a social context. Gossip declares their status: inside, outside, indeterminate, or struggling to get or stay in. It epitomizes social dramas, not only reporting happenings but often speaking in the voice of an individual's imagined opponent: gossip labels as degraded the woman struggling for respectability, thus embodying the force she fears. Often fictional uses of malicious or otherwise dangerous gossip stress its distortions or actual falsehood, emblems of its transforming power. Spenser invented a "Blattant Beast," a malice-circulating monster, "The which did seeme a thousand tongues to haue, / That all in spight and malice did agree" (*Faerie Queene*, 6.1.75–6). The beast speaks with the tongues of dogs, cats, bears, tigers, and serpents, but most of all with "tongues of mortall men, / Which spake reprochfully, not caring where or when" (6.12.242–3); the chivalric adventurer must muzzle and chain him, but the narrative reports that he subsequently breaks his chain. No one has again managed to capture him, we are told; he threatens even poets. Chaucer evoked the goddess Fame, who heightens or demolishes reputations at whim ("The House of Fame"). These ancient embodiments objectify the power of "idle talk." In new forms, they continue to populate our fictions, now voices rather than monsters or deities, yet still possessing potencies which our predecessors expressed in more concrete terms.

Novelistic uses of gossip as substance also take benign forms, however, forms revealing its protean possibilities as a thematic device. If malicious and frivolous gossip destroys reputations, all gossip also circulates information (duly mixed, of course, with misinformation). A novel can build its plot from the accumulation of such data. "To understand just one life, you have to swallow the world," says the narrator of an Indian novel.[5] Gossip speaks in the world's voice and elucidates the world's operations. It thus calls attention to ambiguities of facticity and of interpretation—useful stuff for the novelist—and to the crucial importance and complexity of context. When information comes by means of gossip, one can hardly avoid noting that it has been filtered through multiple consciousnesses. The problem of assessing its value inheres in the act of receiving it.

Joseph Conrad's novel *Chance* exemplifies the text built by accumulation of something much like gossip, although never quite called that. The vaguely defined "I" of the narrative inquires of Marlow, the cryptic wise man in several Conrad fictions, why some human beings have the capacity to understand "what is happening to others." "Is it," he asks, "that we may amuse ourselves gossiping about each other's affairs? You for instance seem—" Marlow does not let him say that he, Marlow, seems an incorrigible gossip. Instead Marlow shifts vocabulary. "It would be still a very respectable provision if it were only for that end [i.e., gossip]. But from that same provision of understanding, there springs in us compassion, charity, indignation, the sense of solidarity; and in minds of any largeness an inclination to that indulgence which is next door to affection."[6] He might have added that from it spring novels. *Chance* tells of a woman whose experience drives her repeatedly to the edge of suicide. When a man falls passionately in love with her, she cannot believe in his devotion because she feels unlovable. Afflicted with his own self-doubt, her husband avoids consummating the marriage; he thinks she does not love him. This intimate chronicle emerges through second-hand and third-hand testimony from observers most of whom know relatively little about their subject's life. Marlow assembles the details and establishes their meaning.

The set of virtues Marlow associates with interest in and understanding of others precisely opposes the vices usually linked with gossip: malice, sense of superiority, lack of solidarity with the talk's victim. Marlow also accepts the connection of understanding and gossiping, since he assumes that information provides understanding's necessary foundation. He describes himself as "an investigator—a man of deductions," engaged in "the old-maiden-lady-like occupation of putting two and two together" (341). The association of knowledge, understanding, and charity controls the novel as a whole, an exercise in creative gossip that generates interest less by the substance of the woman's experience than by the texture of narrative: we read a story not only of a marriage but of what that marriage means to Marlow, who creates the tale he tells. The implicit definition of gossip as discovery generates a valuable resource for fiction. Novels less centrally concerned than *Chance* with gossip—think of Agatha Christie's Miss Marple—can also make use of that resource, examining the transmission of information as it takes place in "idle talk," asserting the importance of the odds and ends of knowledge thus accumulated.

Marlow's interest in the intricate manifestations of human nature helps to characterize him. Many writers employ gossip as characterizing speech. Few have mastered the technique so completely as Eudora Welty, whose post-office dwellers and beauticians, by talking of human trivia, reveal themselves utterly, but Jane Austen and Henry James among others also know that in gossip's relaxed rhythms speakers expose themselves. For fiction, gossip serves better than conversation ostensibly concerned with more "important" matters the end of human revelation. To imagine gossip in its specificity, what people say to one another and how they say it, as opposed to mere paraphrasable content ("Susie Jones must be having an affair")—to imagine gossip thus, with all its detail about Susie's dress and facial expression and what she said to the milkman, implicitly acknowledges that conventional triviality may allow the articulation of intense human feeling. Thus, gossip fully imagined in tone and substance conveys fictional personality. It can also suggest the dimensions of close relationship, particularly between or among women.

But of course it doesn't mean much to point out that novels use gossip as subject matter—novels, after all, use just about everything. What interests me more is the way that subject, in the case of gossip, can penetrate method. Indeed, the methods of gossip often control even novels employing no such subject matter. "Much fiction operates in the spirit of inspired gossip," Margaret Drabble has written; "it speculates on little evidence, inventing elaborate and artistic explanations of little incidents and overheard remarks that often leave the evidence far behind."[7] Novelistic narrators often arouse in readers the kind of intense interest in personal detail that gossip generates, and they may attempt to establish with their readers a kind of relationship approximating that of gossip (see Chapter Seven and Chapter Nine). *Chance* provides a rich case in point, a novel using gossip as subject and as narrative technique. As Marlow builds his narrative, piece by piece, from scraps he sees and hears, he generates a novel, not just an interrupted oral tale. This obvious fact has important implications. Marlow's listener engages in dialogue with him, breaks in, asks questions; the reader has no such freedom. Yet the reader's fascination approximates that of hearing an extended and absorbing piece of gossip: interest not only in the persons spoken of but in the speaker's sensibility.

I have said nothing so far about gossip's special fascination. Most people appear to feel it, as horror or as attraction. The fact that many who disapprove of gossip find themselves engaging in it testifies to its emotional power. Its fascination bears some relation to that of pornography, although many feel gossip's pull who loathe pornography. Gossip, even when it avoids the sexual, bears about it a faint flavor of the erotic. (Of course, sexual activities and emotions supply the most familiar staple of gossip—as of the Western realistic novel.) The atmosphere of erotic titillation suggests gossip's implicit voyeurism. Surely everyone feels—although some suppress—the same prurient interest in others' privacies, what goes on behind closed doors. Poring over fragments of other people's lives, peering into their bedrooms when they don't know we're there, we thrill to the glamour and the power of secret knowledge, partly detoxified but also heightened by being shared. A relatively innocent form of the erotics of power (we mostly don't expect to affect the course of people's lives by talking about them—or we don't consciously acknowledge any such expectation), this excitement includes the heady experience of imaginative control: gossip claims other people's experience by interpreting it into story. Voyeurism, shared secrets, story-telling: these private forms of power supplement the more public ones involved in circulating rumor and shaping reputation.

But I do not feel entirely satisfied with these explanations of gossip's fascination, the faint excitement inhering in the very idea. Voyeurism, secrets, stories; one might add the special thrill of the forbidden (we know it's wrong, but it doesn't *kill* anyone)—but is this all? Perhaps the concept of gossip subliminally recalls ancient belief in the magic of language. "Sticks and stones can break my bones, but words will never hurt me," children chant, verbally claiming dominion over the verbal force they rightly fear. They know quite well, we all know, how much words can hurt. The anthropologist Victor Turner reports tribal leveling rituals which avert disaster by allowing weak or low-status members to insult their social superiors; Robert Elliott speculates about the origins of satire in ancient rituals of magical reviling.[8] The idea of talking in secret—i.e., without the subject's knowledge—about someone recalls old conceptions of words as dangerous weapons. Once rats were rhymed to death, and maids to love; now, telling stories takes possession of others' experience: a form of magic no less potent for being familiar. Gossip means more in our communal imagination than we can sensibly explain.

Some of gossip's magic finds its way into realistic fiction; I hope here to explain how and imagine why. To say that gossip provides a model for many operations of the novel opens the way for a kind of interpretation that defines aspects of the text's relation to the reader and locates its roots in ordinary social discourse. *Chance*, for example, involves the reader in a process of accretion and interpretation and sharing which duplicates Marlow's functioning within the novel; Conrad forces attention to the problem of meaning by implicating the reader in the action of creating meaning. To think about gossip calls attention to such important aspects of the fiction.

I shall be using *gossip* in shifting senses corresponding to the word's fluidity in general usage, and I shall use it with full awareness of both negative and positive associations. The protean implications of gossip as a verbal mode enable its application in many literary contexts; the possibility of viewing its operations in multiple forms emphasizes its diverse manifestations in non-literary experience. My interest focuses both on literature and on the life outside it, on gossip as a social and psychological fact and as a hermeneutic resource in literary and non-literary contexts. I shall seek examples of gossip's operations largely in printed texts (imaginative, descriptive, polemical, didactic), investigating its uses as a mode of oral discourse articulating values often otherwise unspoken, and as a model for types of written discourse. A hidden life of language emerges.

To take gossip seriously as a model of verbal relationship helps define the importance of relationship as an issue of literary interpretation, not only for non-canonical genres such as personal letters and biography, but for novels and drama as well. Fictional characters relate to one another in ways sometimes analogous to those generating gossip, and readers relate to characters, to narrators, to biographical subjects, to recipients and senders of letters. Gossip as a phenomenon raises questions about boundaries, authority, distance, the nature of knowledge; it demands answers quite at odds with what we assume as our culture's dominant values. The subversive implications both of literal gossip and of its printed transformations will gradually manifest themselves through this study.

Let me return to my initial, quickly abandoned suggestions about gossip as pastoral, drama, fiction, in order to survey aspects of the mode that will prove useful in detailed literary analysis. Gossip's aesthetic manifestations provide an obvious starting point. Gossip is not pastoral, fiction, etc.; but observers literary and non-literary have noted analogies between gossip and the novel, without developing them. I have already quoted Margaret Drabble. Then there was the visitor to Alabama in the 1930s who observed that "the main diversions of the Alabamians are lovemaking and gossip." Their gossip, he continued, does not include an undue proportion of malice. "The majority of Alabamian gentlefolk take a strong interest in people that is not unlike that of a novelist. They are entertained and instructed by the antics of their fellow beings—they like to speculate on motivations." A literary critic writing about her own experience parenthetically remarks, "Gossip, like novels, is a way of turning life into story. Good gossip approximates art."⁹ The nature of the approximation may be suggested by Clifford Geertz's remarks on the Balinese cockfight, which also, in his view, approximates art. "Cultural forms," Geertz maintains, "can be treated as texts, as imaginative works built out of social materials." He adds that real art works and the cultural forms that analogize them share a crucial property: they "are not merely reflections of a pre-existing sensibility analogically represented; they are positive agents in the creation and maintenance of such a sensibility."¹⁰

Only in a vague sense can gossip be called a cultural form. The vague sense, however, matters, for it calls attention to continuities of structure between one episode of gossip and the next. Narrative, interpretation, judgment: this sequence dominates gossip, with varying proportions of each component. Together they generate a characteristic rhythm of investigation. And—more to the immediate point—they create story: story which, like the cockfight, both expresses and helps to sustain, even to modify, sensibility.

Here is an example of the kind of story gossip transmits. A youngish man—I'll call him Baxter—sets out to spend a summer on Martha's Vineyard. On the ferry to the island, he meets a beautiful young woman (Clarissa, let's say), the recently acquired daughter-in-law of an aggressive middle-aged woman whom he knows well and rather dislikes. Clarissa's husband, it develops, is away on business; her mother-in-law soon leaves. Twice divorced, at loose ends, captivated by Clarissa's unfamiliar beauty, Baxter sets out to seduce the bride. She proves resistant, committed to marital fidelity, suspicious of men, apparently too stupid to find Baxter captivating. Finally, however, he succeeds: he discovers and exploits Clarissa's longing that someone should believe her intelligent, although in fact her incapacity for lucid thought is staggering.

I have tried to summarize this story in more or less neutral terms, but of course even the bare account contains judgments: of Clarissa's response to attempted seduction, of Baxter's technique. Added details would make judgment more obvious. For example: Baxter realized that Clarissa liked to get presents, but he was too stingy to get her anything sufficiently lavish to serve his ends. An ungenerous interpretation of an ungenerous man, the kind of interpretation many people readily associate with gossip. Such an assertion of motivation, in intimate conversation, would elicit counter-hypotheses. Maybe Baxter didn't buy Clarissa presents because his narcissism impeded his imagination: he couldn't think of what she might want. Or—

a fresh access of information—you know he never carries credit cards, and his girlfriend keeps track of his cash. Or, he claims to be anti-materialistic: he doesn't believe in presents.

Each new suggestion enriches the story and adds to our imagined talkers' pleasure in it. The basic form of the anecdote, however, belongs to tradition and derives from social and aesthetic expectation. Gossip on the whole fits its material into established structures, interpreting happening first by perceiving it in familiar patterns. The unarguable facts of the Baxter-Clarissa case are simple: an unmarried man and a married woman go to bed together. The elaboration—stupid woman, wily man; motives for attack and resistance—largely determines attributed meaning. Characterization and motive alike conform to structures of cultural assumption. These structures generate obvious sources of satisfaction in gossip: both the universal delight in story and particular pleasure in the kind of story our culture makes immediately comprehensible.

I did not invent the Baxter-Clarissa episode. It summarizes the action of a published story by John Cheever, "The Chaste Clarissa."[11] Not only the plot but the detail about Baxter's stinginess originates in Cheever's text. Both plot and detail might, however, with equal probability emerge in a sequence of gossip, which builds up stories—conflict, characterization, elaboration—as a writer of fiction might. The aesthetic pleasure of gossip begins here, in the fundamental structure of story, which creates the most apparent link between gossip and the novel.

One might, in fact, wish to inquire how Cheever's story *differs* from gossip. In being written down, first of all: stabilized: made safe. This apparently simple fact (to which subsequent chapters will return) in itself helps to free the reader of fiction from the guilt likely to afflict not only the retailer of gossip but even the passive recipient. Far less dangerous than its oral equivalent, gossip converted to fiction keeps its place on the page—not in the air between two speakers, not subject to incalculable elaboration or speculation. And a short story concerns itself (or so comforting convention has it) with invented rather than actual characters. And its language and form, products presumably of artistic care, invite examination for their own sakes. We can think of a story, if we like, as aesthetic patterning; we have no pre-existent relation with its characters; we need not trouble ourselves with them after the story's end. None of these differences amounts to much in itself, but the reader's aesthetic and moral response to reading Cheever will, as a result of them, diverge from his/her reaction to a juicy bit of gossip.

The oral mode of gossip supplies also less obvious, perhaps less inevitable, analogues to literature. The Clarissa story in its concern with sexual conduct exemplifies a familiar aspect of gossip's preoccupations. Gossipers do not, however, require episodes of adultery to create their narratives. The color and cut of Janet's new dress, the tone of voice in which Bob responded when the boss asked him to go to Dubuque: much of gossip's narrative generates itself out of trivia. "Surfaces are not superficial," the theologian Reinhold Niebuhr is said to have said. Much gossip delights by an aesthetic of surfaces. It dwells on specific personal particulars. People and their concerns preoccupy gossipers, by definition, but the special way in which they matter evolves from belief in the importance of the small particular. Janet's dress, Bob's voice yield their import in discussion. They engage talkers not simply because of the significance they can claim, but in themselves, with the special shimmer of meaning that envelops detail for those interested in it. As we shall see, the assumed triviality of gossip has constituted one basis for attack on the activity. It might equally well supply a ground for defense. To make something out of nothing is gossip's special creativity.

The final aesthetic aspect of gossip that I shall mention at the moment is its self-containment. Gossip creates its own territory (equivalent, as I suggested earlier, to Arden or Thessaly), using materials from the world at large to construct a new oral artifact. Its special value as a resource for the oppressed or dispossessed derives partly from this fact. The remaking that takes place as gossipers pool and interpret their observations expresses a world view. I suggested earlier that gossip resembles in some respects what Geertz calls a "cultural form"; one may wish to inquire from what culture, exactly, it emanates. Such elements of gossip as the shape of the stories it tells come, in our society, from ancient traditions of Western culture at large. But other manifestations of gossip reflect, on occasion, the beliefs of quiet sub-cultures. Inasmuch as gossip—and I am speaking here of what I earlier called "serious" gossip—inhabits a space of intimacy, it builds on and implicitly articulates shared values of intimates. If its plots take familiar forms, its interpretations may prove less commonplace. I heard a story once about a woman who had for ten years persisted in a love affair with a married man who showed no intention of leaving his wife. The story gained interest from its characters; as a mere plot, it suffered from banality. More compelling still was the commentary offered by the small group of women participating in this particular sequence of gossip. Without divulging what still, at considerable distance in time, seem "private" observations—observations belonging entirely to the immediate context—I can say that the communal conclusion emphasized the psychic advantages, for a woman pursuing a career, of this conventionally distressing situation. The lover had another woman to sew on his buttons and take care of his colds; his mistress could organize her life neatly to include love and work, since love demanded of her only limited, if intense, commitment. The narrative itself, as emended by the women's talk, assumed a new shape—not the shape it would have had in the *Ladies' Home Journal* version or, perhaps, in most gatherings of both sexes. Conversation's creativity generated a fable with special meaning in the group. In the normal course of events, it probably would never have moved outside. Its value belonged to the moment. It told the talkers about themselves, what they felt and believed.

If gossip's aesthetic of self-containment, concentration on surface, valorizing of story, partly accounts for its value as a literary resource, its moral problematics calls attention to ambiguities also useful to the novelist. The long-standing moralistic attack on gossip as frivolous and/or malicious will supply the subject of my next chapter. For the moment, I shall focus on modern philosophers' re-articulation of the old objections. Heidegger and Kierkegaard can help define the peculiar moral status of gossip. Although both condemn "idle talk," they inadvertently clarify the possibility of claiming for gossip a special kind of moral penetration.

Heidegger announces that he intends no disparaging signification for the term translated as "idle talk," but his discussion implies at least deprecation. He apparently alludes to the kind of discourse based more on hearsay than on observation or first-hand interpretation. It need not involve talking specifically about other people, but it would include such talk. "Idle talk" communicates what has been said rather than the nature of "the entity talked about." "Things are so because one says so."

> The average understanding of the reader will *never be able* to decide what has been drawn from primordial sources with a struggle and how much is just gossip. The average understanding, moreover, will not want any such distinction, and does not need it, because, of course, it understands everything. . . . Idle talk is the possibility of understanding everything without previously making the thing one's own. . . . Idle talk is something which anyone can rake up; it not only releases one from the task of genuinely understanding, but develops an undifferentiated kind of intelligibility, for which nothing is closed off any longer.[12]

The trivial, in Heidegger's apparent view, can never achieve intelligibility because its articulation occurs at a distance from the true grounds of being. Lack of struggle marks gossip, as opposed to the authentic discourse which wrenches meaning from profound sources. Gossip's assertions exist for their own sake, referring to nothing beneath the apparent. Anyone can gossip. People like to do so because they thus achieve an effortless illusion of understanding.

Heidegger hardly distinguishes between speech and writing as far as "idle talk" is concerned. "This idle talk," he says, "is not confined to vocal gossip, but even spreads to what we write, where it takes the form of 'scribbling' " (212). He moves back and forth between literal talk and its written equivalent without acknowledging significant differences. Earlier, he has spoken of "Being-with," which "develops in listening to one another" (206). And he has specified "the items constitutive for discourse": namely, "what the discourse is about (what is talked about); what is said-in-the-talk, as such; the communication; and the making-known" (206). Both formulations suggest a passive role for the listener: at most, two people take turns "listening to one another." Communication appears to involve transmission from mouth to ear, not an action of exchange and mutual modification. "Discourse" implies a speaker (who does or does not struggle to articulate the profundities of his being) and a listener (who does or does not struggle to understand the "primordial" grounds of what he hears). Heidegger's account never acknowledges the possibility of genuine dialogue, of meaning emerging gradually and cooperatively, or of meaning not articulated yet mutually understood.

The "average understanding," in Heidegger's view, merits contempt because of its inability to discriminate between the trivial and the profound and its reluctance to struggle for its own profundities. The philosopher does not, in this context, define *trivial* except by his suggestion that "talking extensively about something, covers it up and brings what is understood to a sham clarity—the unintelligibility of the trivial" (208). Abundant talk, then, tends to trivialize; silence, on the other hand, can be profound. The case against "idle talk" deprecates its nominal subject matter without acknowledging the possibility that the true preoccupations of apparently aimless conversation may lie elsewhere, and it concerns itself with avowed content ("the trivial") to the exclusion of form: the form of mutual conversational modification. Surfaces are not superficial: talk that dwells on the surfaces of life, even talk that sounds like mere chatter, may constitute a form of intimate relationship.

Of course, it *need* not constitute anything of the sort. I would not wish to claim that Heidegger is necessarily wrong about the idleness of "idle talk": only that he ignores a set of possibilities crucial to full understanding of gossip.

Kierkegaard's objections to gossip, more passionately expressed than Heidegger's, focus even more emphatically on avowed subject matter. He opposes gossip to "real talk" and identifies it with "talkativeness . . . afraid of the silence which reveals its emptiness." He worries about obliteration of the "vital distinction between what is private and what is public" as gossips, in speech and writing, circulate news of "the most private concerns" to large audiences. Most important, he claims that the subject of gossip

> is non-existent from the ideal point of view. It always consists of some trivial fact such as that Mr. Marsden is engaged and has given his fiancée a Persian shawl; that Petersen, the poet, is going to write some new poems, or that Marcussen, the actor, mispronounced a certain word last night. If we could suppose for a moment that there was a law which did not forbid people talking, but simply ordered that everything that was spoken about should be treated as though it had happened fifty years ago, the gossips would be done for, they would be in despair. On the other hand, it would not really interfere with any one who could really talk.[13]

"Real talk," it seems, concerns the inner life—specifically the inner *religious* life—the spiritual as opposed to the intellectual, the "important" (69). Like Heidegger, Kierkegaard objects to the "triviality" of gossip and to its blurring of distinctions. He knows the nature of the important: Mr. Marsden's fiancée's shawl does not qualify.

Inasmuch as Kierkegaard describes gossip, he does so more or less accurately, although he does not describe it completely. His assumption, in this instance, that "the ideal point of view" constitutes the appropriate standard for discourse necessitates his condemnation of what he describes, although not, perhaps, the tone of disgust with which he evokes the kind of detail that interests gossipers. Like Heidegger, he fails to acknowledge dialogue as gossip's necessary component; he sounds as though gossip's point and purpose consisted in the transmission of news about a shawl or a forgotten line.

Both philosophers supply moral grounds for their condemnation of frivolous and trivial talk. Kierkegaard, invoking "the ideal point of view," suggests the superiority of ideas to happenings as matters for reflection; Heidegger implies that "struggle" necessarily marks the process eventuating in meaningful discourse. Both obviously wish to condemn a mode of chatter more inclusive than even my large category of "gossip": all talk that constitutes avoidance rather than engagement. But they would define "avoidance" and "engagement" as involving the speaker's relation to ideas; "serious" gossip would locate such concepts in relation to people. The value of gossip at its highest level involves its capacity to create and intensify human connection and to enlarge self-knowledge predicated more on emotion than on thought. The philosophic position that condemns much genuinely meaningless talk also excludes the large body of conversation based on personal rather than public values—conversation that may or may not be "meaningless."

I am claiming an inadvertent moralistic narrowness in these treatments of discourse—a narrowness which oddly (and, I think, significantly) corresponds to that in certain eighteenth-century responses to the novel as genre. Many early commentators expressed anxiety about the novel's potential for contaminating particularly such vulnerable readers as women and adolescents. Dr. Johnson, for instance, argued that novels, as imitations of life, should confine themselves to models of virtue. "If the world be promiscuously described, I cannot see of what use it can be to read the account."[14] Characters who mingled virtue and vice might endanger the reader's powers of moral discrimination, suggesting that vice could be condoned for the sake of the virtue that accompanied it. Fiction, like other literary forms, must aspire to please and to instruct, with emphasis on the latter function.

Like Kierkegaard, Dr. Johnson assumes that subject determines meaning. Yet one can argue that the moral impact of such novels as *Tom Jones* derives specifically from their refusal to evoke a universe defined exclusively in moral terms. To contemplate an attractive character who apparently sleeps with his mother will not automatically encourage the reader to go and do likewise. Indeed, being forced to dwell on inadvertencies and small happenings that lead to and issue from such an event may arguably heighten the reader's consciousness of moral complexity in ways that would intensify his/her capacity to make informed choices. Awareness of specific complexities of human behavior, enlarging perceptions of personal and social contingency, declare the ramifications of minute events. The novel, from its beginnings, dwelt on life's surfaces in order to penetrate its depths. It trained readers to take surfaces seriously as means of reaching the profound.

Heidegger's distaste for gossip, and Kierkegaard's, deny the moral possibilities of trivia. The realistic novel depends for its existence on the assumed importance of the concrete personal particular in all its revelatory power. So does gossip. The shawl Mr. Marsden gave his fiancée possesses untold narrative possibilities: in the giving lie all the moral intricacies of exchange. If the initial revelation of the gift conveys none of these intricacies, the fact remains: gossip consists not in revelation but in extended interchange. Kierkegaard and Heidegger alike appear to assume that "discourse" involves the making of a statement and its reception by a hearer. Their sweeping judgments of the triviality and inauthenticity of gossip suggest their deafness to the possible moral overtones of dialogue and of attention to personal detail. Dr. Johnson pointed out (without naming names) that novels like Richardson's, with their clear moral intent, have less dangerous possibilities for the reader than do novels like Fielding's, which may confuse the young and naïve. We may grant the large point—not without a smile about the particular instance, since Richardson seems morally ambiguous (as, indeed, he seemed also to some of our eighteenth-century forebears). Similarly, we may acknowledge that Heidegger and Kierkegaard accurately locate the moral insufficiency of gossip in its frivolous modes, and still complain that they betray ears dead to the power, aesthetic and moral, of "serious" gossip: gossip as dialogue, gossip as the loving contemplation of detail, gossip which (in ways we will explore more fully) provides a model for one range of moral possibility in the realistic novel as a genre.

"Speech," Norbert Elias asserts, ". . . is nothing else but human relations turned into sound." Art, science, politics, and economics likewise function as "substantializations of human relations and human behavior"; indeed, all "human phenomena" can be so described.[15] The realistic novel, human relations as printed words and as plot, epitomizes a morality of attentiveness to human (as well as, often, non-human) detail. We have learned to value in the poetry of William Carlos Williams the diction and the perception of specificity: revelations of physical detail that interpret experience not by abstractions of freedom or will but by red wheelbarrows and chickens. Fernand Braudel has argued the value of anthropological and geographical specificity as historical explanation. Long before either of them, novelists showed that a young man's pulling a muff out of the fire could uncover the state of his soul (*Tom Jones*), that a married couple's way of driving their chaise expresses their marital balance and harmony (*Persuasion*), that the redness of a room confining a rebellious child speaks to her deepest consciousness (*Jane Eyre*). Novels insist on the need to pay attention. Regardless of their specific content (which may, of course, partake of the immoral), they suggest the moral value of a special kind of knowledge, the kind they inculcate: minute awareness of human behavior in all its bearings, knowledge that develops discrimination and the capacity to value difference.

Gossip inculcates the same knowledge and, at its best, the same morality. (At its worst, it uses its knowledge for meretricious purposes and violates the respect for multiplicity implicit in the novel.) Like the novel, it "substantializes" human relations by exploring them. Like the novel, it thrives on the sound of the human voice and on dramas of personal exchange.

If gossip has moral and aesthetic aspects, both of which fiction transforms and exploits, gossip also reveals an economics. The subject of dialogue calls attention to it. A mode of exchange, gossip involves the giving and receiving of more than information.

I am not referring now to novelistic subject matter. As I have already suggested, gossip's concealments and revelations, its manipulations of power relations, offer rich material to move a plot along, to convey vital information, to characterize. But gossip also supplies a form analogizing the exchange between narrator and reader: the novel's basic economics. The reader brings to this relationship a body of general knowledge and of personal experience; the narrator brings particularized knowledge of the story being told. Of course, no literal exchange takes place: the reader can't talk back. But the idea of exchange expresses the *activity* involved in reading as a process.

To think of reading as verbal exchange does not simply imply Barthes's view that the reader modifies the text by reading it. The act of interpretation central to reading involves imposition on the literary object by the reader's sensibility and experience; it also includes the converse imposition of the narrator's sensibility on the reader. Bakhtin's account of dialogue, although he does not turn it to these ends, applies usefully here. Bakhtin points out that all rhetorical forms implicitly take into account the concrete listener. "An active understanding, one that assimilates the word under consideration into a new conceptual system, that of the one trying to understand, establishes a series of complex interrelationships, consonances and dissonances with the word and enriches it with new elements." And again: "Discourse lives, as it were, on the boundary between its own context and another, alien, context."[16] In other words, the implicit presence of a listener—or, by extension, a reader—would affect the dynamics of language even in the process of composition. The energies of "active understanding," however, work in both directions. The double context of literary language, no longer entirely the narrator's property, never entirely the reader's, generates much of that language's power.

In the contest over this linguistic property, "understanding" is at stake. The reader alone must win "understanding," in the dialogue between narrator and reader; the narrator's "understanding" inheres in the text. Yet that previously achieved mastery creates its own illusion of activity. Even James's magisterial "central intelligence," looking over a character's shoulder, offering its utterances in the voice of wisdom, even George Eliot's moralizing asides, may evoke implicitly the struggle to assert meaning in the face of competing assertions, actual or potential.

More insistently than other forms of conversation, gossip involves exchange not merely, not even mainly, of information, and not solely of understanding, but of point of view. (Again, I am referring to my category of "serious" gossip.) For this reason, as well as because of its concern with specific personal detail, it provides a more precise model than does conversation in general for the dialogic aspect of realistic fiction. Of course, fiction's "dialogue" of narrator and reader involves not distinctly alternating but virtually simultaneous contributions—an oscillation so rapid as to be undiscernible. To think of it in relation to gossip calls attention not only to the intense intimacy of the narrator-reader relationship—an absolute privacy of two—but to their mutual contribution to an understanding generated by exchange.[17]

What, in the economics of gossip, is offered, what received? Point of view, information; also reassurance. Participants assure one another of what they share: one of gossip's important purposes. Gossip may involve a torrent of talk, yet its most vital claims remain silent. Seldom does anyone articulate the bonding that it generates or intensifies. The sensibility that gossip helps to create is dual: a mode of feeling and of apprehending which rises, as it were, in the space between the talkers, enveloping both. The comparable experience associated with reading fiction helps to account for cases of youthful (or mature) addiction. Nights of concentration with the bedclothes pulled over your head so your mother won't catch you, evenings of private gratification before the fire: the faint guilt associated with such pastimes results partly from the exclusionary alliance formed in the act of reading. More than other sorts of literary activity, reading novels establishes a tie resembling that of gossip, since what reader and narrator share is a set of responses to the private doings of richly imagined individuals.

In this preliminary sketch of analogies between gossip and fiction, I am largely ignoring differences. It goes without saying that the fictional status of novelistic characters matters. The meaning of a human connection formed through speculating about such figures differs from that of a relationship formed by discussing living people. The material of gossip in writing implies something different from that evoked in speech; the silent alliance of storyteller and reader differs from that of two talkers. Such differences will emerge more fully in the detailed examination of texts which demonstrates and tests the theory's implications. For the moment, it suffices to map the general terrain.

One more thing. Social scientists explain how gossip consolidates and uses social power to affect status and opinion in a community. The literary equivalent of the gossip relationship also generates power. To what end? I have already suggested that gossip gets its power by the illusion of mastery gained through taking imaginative possession of another's experience. People use this pseudo-mastery for their own purposes: to manipulate the subject's reputation, to generate feelings of superiority, to provide evidence for argument. Fiction creates its own sense of mastery by making us feel we understand its characters, having participated in the imaginative exchange with the narrator whose purpose is achieved understanding. Gossip, Walter Benjamin suggests, "comes about only because people do not wish to be misunderstood."[18] So, it might be argued, does the novel. "We perform verbal acts as well as other acts . . . in order to extend our control over a world that is not naturally disposed to serve our interests."[19] Barbara Herrnstein Smith refers, in that sentence, to the meaning of speech; the reading of fiction serves as psychological enlargement of speech. We extend our control over the recalcitrant world by strengthening our intellectual and psychological grasp. Fictional characters and actions, comprehended, may teach us to understand better—or to believe that we do so—the less distinctly defined characters and actions that comprise our real-life experience. The private act of reading creates a private sense of power with effects in the world.

The theory of literature implied by my interest in placing gossip and printed texts side by side as objects of contemplation depends on the notion that literature originates in the life outside the text and has for the reader consequences also extending outward. To insist on gossip's positive value, as I shall do, even while acknowledging its possible negative impact, implies acknowledgment of comparable (although not identical) ambivalences in literature's effects. An 1821 defense of gossip justifies the activity finally on the grounds of its essential *humanness*. "We are all gossips by nature. Why do men associate? Some say it is owing to our weakness, and our wants, but it would be more correct to attribute it to the delights afforded us by the sound of the human voice. . . . Those only who amuse, amend, and instruct others, are really wise and pious."[20] Literature and gossip alike amuse, amend, and instruct. Literature translates the sound of the human voice to the printed page. To think of gossip helps to clarify strategies of discourse shaped by intimate talkers and imaginative writers.

First, though, we may take a look at how other people have thought of gossip.

2

Its Reputation

People keep supplying me with references to gossip from unlikely sources. My favorite of these allusions comes from a publication called TWENTY YEARS AFTER: *Results of the Ivy Passages Poll of the Smith, Yale, and Williams Class of 1962.* A preliminary section before the actual questionnaire tests respondents' "Tendency to Give Socially-Desirable Answers." " 'True' answers to #3 and #4," the surveyors explain, "indicate candor." Statement #4 reads, "I like to gossip at times." Eighty percent of Smith respondents, 73 percent from Yale, and 62 percent from Williams declared it "true." The rest, presumably, were lying.

The other test statement, #3, "I sometimes feel resentful when I don't get my way," received a higher percentage of "true" responses (85, 87, 87): people feel more willing to acknowledge emotions than actions. The test questions and their interpretation imply that everyone gossips, everyone sometimes feels resentful, and everyone is ashamed of uncontrolled talk and uncontrolled feeling. The matter of resentment lies beyond my immediate scope; as for gossip, considerable evidence suggests that for several centuries everyone has gossiped and has felt ashamed of doing so. In religious and secular contexts, by standards of morality and of decorum, loose talk about people is deplorable. Few activities so nearly universal have been the object of such sustained and passionate attack.

One analogy, however, comes readily to mind: the unanimous official condemnation over the centuries of unlicensed sexual activity, a condemnation persisting, at least in religious contexts, even in periods like our own when such activity openly flourishes. Politicians whose less than respectable sex lives come to public attention still find themselves in trouble at the polls. "Loose living," like "loose talk," meets disapproval; unbridled lust and unbridled tongues, we are told, cause trouble. Norbert Elias describes in historical terms the process by which the ideal of sexual restraint develops. "Control [of sexual expression] grows ever stricter. The instinct is slowly but progressively suppressed from the public life of society. . . . And this restraint . . . is cultivated in the individual from an early age as habitual self-restraint by the structure of social life, by the pressure of social institutions in general, and by certain executive organs of society (above all, the family) in particular. Thereby the social commands and prohibitions become increasingly a part of the self, a strictly regulated superego."[1]

Elias' description of the suppression of sexual instinct, or at least of its public manifestations, tells only some of the truth. With equal accuracy, one might say that blatant sexual activity has become essential to certain public roles. Entertainers, for instance, rock stars and movie stars, use their sex lives, or a fantasized version of them, as part of their glamorous self-projection. Correspondingly, the activity of gossip, suppressed by official morality, flourishes in specified contexts: magazines, television. A character in a recent novel observes, "It's the great age of gossip. And *that*, truth to tell, David, is where my loneliness comes from. The magazine faces, the guests on the talk shows—they mean nothing to me. Who *are* these people? With their teeth? Their breasts? Rock stars! Actors on TV series! When their names are announced the audience howls!"[2] Instead of fostering closeness, as the "serious" gossip I spoke of in the last chapter does, this kind of gossip, like publicized sex, creates loneliness: a sense that people have nothing to do with one another except to look and be looked at.

Public sex, public gossip may on occasion generate lawsuits, but such stylized transformations of impulse are not really dangerous; indeed, they exist to direct dangerous impulse into channels of vicarious gratification. The moralistic castigation of private gossip over several centuries suggests continuing vivid perception of its social threat—a threat equivalent in certain respects to that of unrestrained lust. Yet gossip, like sex, embodies positive force. Its energies, as I suggested in the last chapter and will argue more fully in the next, lend themselves simultaneously to the destruction and the sustenance of human ties. The very history of the word incorporates this paradox. Etymologically, *gossip* means "god-related." As a noun, the word originally designated a godparent, of either sex; then its meaning enlarged to include any close friend—someone belonging to the group from which godparents would naturally be chosen. But the word undergoes a process of degradation. Dr. Johnson, in the middle of the eighteenth century, offered a second meaning of "tippling companion" and a third definition for the first time connecting gossip unambiguously and officially with women: "One who runs about tattling like women at a lying-in." Not until 1811, according to the *Oxford English Dictionary*, did the noun designate a mode of conversation rather than a kind of person: "idle talk, trifling or groundless rumour; tittle-tattle."

In the late twentieth century, *gossip*, as noun and as verb, appears to have lost all dignity in its dictionary definitions. The *O.E.D.* acknowledges one "more favourable sense: Easy, unrestrained talk or writing, esp. about persons or social incidents," but offers only a single trivial example, from 1879, a reference to "topographical gossip." (Gossip about mountains?) *Webster's New International Dictionary* mentions "chat or light familiar writing" as a meaning for the noun and "To write in a light familiar way" as a sense for the verb. Even these "more favourable" elucidations implicitly stress triviality. They convey no vestige of the emphasis on close human association that earlier definitions reveal.

Webster's first current meaning of *gossip* as a verb draws on Dr. Johnson, although it avoids his allusion to women: "To run about and tattle; to tell idle, esp. personal, tales." Idle, personal, frivolous, often malicious: gossip hardly sounds like a serious activity for grown-up persons. When the Englishman Simon Raven refers to ours as "The Age of the Gossip Column," he conveys contempt.[3] The process of degradation has obscured the energy it distorts. On the other hand, the sheer bulk of five centuries' commentary on gossip suggests a phenomenon worth taking seriously. If gossip is merely contemptible, why have so many people said so much about it? A survey of what they have said over the past six centuries reveals mostly fierce castigation, with occasional acknowledgments of gossip's value. Almost never does the same commentator call attention to both positive and negative aspects. Those understanding gossip as fellowship typically deny its malice; those stressing its destructiveness ignore its bonding. I propose to summarize a large body of observations about gossip, considering first the mass of negative criticism, then the much smaller group of texts calling attention to positive possibilities. Finally I will consider the historical association of gossip with women, speculate about reasons for it, and try to define the moral assumptions justifying certain sorts of gossip.

A minimal definition of gossip: "idle talk about other persons not present." ("Idle" implies lack of announced purpose: talk in a personnel committee about the behavior of a candidate for promotion presumably does not qualify as gossip—although it can get mighty close.) Since before the early nineteenth century the noun designated not a kind of talk but a kind of person, earlier commentary reveals attitudes toward gossip through other key terms. From the Middle Ages on, moralists perceived clear dangers in talk about people. Malice (or "detraction"), the betraying of secrets, idle curiosity, triviality: these possibilities preoccupied many who wrote about the moral pitfalls of everyday life.

Detraction, even now, worries almost everyone who thinks about gossip: the likelihood that those talking in private about others may invent or promulgate socially destructive slanders. From early times, metaphors of murder associated themselves with such activity. Words may kill souls, a medieval writer explains, as many souls as hear them. People who attack the good names of others are more cruel than hell. They act like sows, which bite men; wasps, which flee flowers and love dung; mythical birds ("huppe") that make their nests in ordure. To call their words "idle" only obscures the desperate danger they embody. Backbiters eat a man whole, or eat him piece by piece; they resemble the scorpion, which makes a good appearance with his face while spurting venom from his tail. To harm the good name of another betrays a "fiendly appetite." Backbiters are mad dogs; they engage in a form of manslaughter.[4] Such observations dominated English discussion of "detraction" through the fifteenth century.

At the end of the sixteenth century, a minor poet wrote, "Backbiters do kill, more men with a word, / Then souldiers in field, destroyes with their sword."[5] The perception of derogatory talk as mortally destructive continued unchanged from the Middle Ages to the Renaissance, as did the lurid imagery associated with it. Venomous serpents, fire, a branch of a wild plant, a torrent drowning many good wits: such metaphors characterize backbiting.[6] "What is there that envy hath not defamed, or malice left undefiled? Truly no good thing," one moral philosopher concludes.[7] Through the seventeenth century, the theme remained the same. Backbiters are asps' tongues, spiders, leeches, worms; detraction is the basest activity possible to man; the very word *backbiting*, we are told, suggests the cowardice of an activity which attacks only the unprepared or absent and involves serious robbery; the viperous tongue of the malicious gossip recalls the dog who will tear a dead boar's skin although he dare not look upon the living animal.[8]

The eighteenth century continued the assault. Detraction exposes its practitioner to the contempt of all humane and considerate people; a robbery committed on your neighbor, it is one of the most unkind things one man can do to another; it is the meanest and most ungenerous of vices; envious tongues kill like an arrow shot from a dark hiding place, the speakers concealing their foul intentions.[9] The metaphors still suggest the danger of malicious talk, but important changes had occurred in the attitudes of those expounding its evils. The medieval texts I have cited, and the fifteenth-, sixteenth-, and early seventeenth-century examples, all derive from a clear religious context. The Bible had warned of the dangers of backbiting (as well as of tattling and curiosity); moralists' commentary drew on Biblical authority, expanding hints into doctrine. One can hardly overstate the seriousness of sixteenth- and seventeenth-century attacks on malicious gossip. The seven deadly sins, sins of the heart, lead to deadly action. Belonging as they do to man's natural depravity, they defy extirpation. Only by subordinating one's will to God could one hope to control their manifestations. Early moralizing linked detraction with three of the seven sins: it could originate in pride, anger, or envy. Moreover, in its perversion of the uniquely human capacity of speech, that gift which links man by analogy to the Articulator of the original creative Word, it symbolizes man's tragically fallen nature.

In the late seventeenth century, works begin to appear with titles such as *Humane Prudence, or the Art By which a Man May Raise Himself and his Fortune to Grandeur*, and *Moral Gallantry*, a book arguing that morality makes a man socially attractive. My last paragraph cites, among other texts, a work called *The Polite Philosopher: Or, An Essay on that Art which Makes a Man Happy in Himself, and Agreeable to Others*, published in 1734. Moralists still draw on the Bible and on Christian rhetoric, they still talk mainly to the upper classes, but they increasingly assume a secular social context. "We live upon the Credit and Reports of others," William De Britaine writes, in a work published in 1680[10]; a century earlier, we would have been assumed to live by the grace of God. Given a world of other people, rather than one whose meaning depends on its membership in a divinely ordained hierarchy of creation, gossip becomes both more and less significant. What other people say about us, what we say about them, matters more, from one point of view, if the human community defines our being. On the other hand, gossip was changing status from sin to solecism.

The change rapidly intensified through the eighteenth and nineteenth centuries, as the audience for moral instruction became increasingly middle-class. Moralists did not abandon the language of Christian reference, but their increasing shrillness suggests that readers could no longer automatically be expected to assume the primacy of their Christian obligations. An American book published in 1880 contains this indignant observation: "The black slandering tongue is constantly preying upon the rose buds of innocence and virtue, the foliage of merit, worth, genius, and talent; and poisons, with its filth of innuendoes and scum of falsehood, the most brilliant flowers, the most useful shrubs, and the most valuable trees, in the garden of private and public reputation."[11] Such rhetorical overkill belongs to a work offering "Aims and Aids to Success and Happiness": to blight rosebuds might interfere with one's rise in the world (or one's rise might be interfered with by other people's black slandering tongues). Fourteen years later, in London, an English writer named Edna Lyall published a piece of fiction called *The Autobiography of a Slander.*[12] Its rather hysterical plot concerns a Polish émigré in an English village, Sigismund Zaluski, who woos a local girl named Gertrude Morley. Old Mrs. O'Reilly, whose "love of gossip amounted almost to a passion" (4), suggests, on the basis of the Pole's vehement distaste for Russian tyranny, that the foreigner is a nihilist. This suggestion expands in its transmission from mouth to mouth until the news reaches Russia that Zaluski has been involved in the assassination of the Czar. Arrested during a visit, the young man dies in a Russian prison of tuberculosis. The book's elaborate illustrations record the growth of the Slander from infancy to a full-grown, manifestly diabolical state, true son of his father, Mephistopheles (3). Finally the narrator evokes the Last Judgment, "when those self-satisfied ones, whose hands are all the time steeped in blood, . . . shall realise to the full all that their idle words have brought about" (145), suffering appropriate "shame, and horror, and remorse" (146). Gossips are murderers.

The paranoid aspects of this fiction, emphasized by its establishment of a political context for moral doctrine, call attention to similar elements in other attacks on malicious gossip. Not what we hear but what we don't hear fills us with alarm. We rarely know, we only imagine, what other people say of us; the figure of Iago inhabits the Western imagination. The idea of gossip readily inspires paranoia because of its unmeasurable threat to reputation, to what others think about us, and because one can do little to counter circulated slander, however unfair. The sense of barely acknowledged terror often underlying attacks on detraction depends less on verifiable fact (although striking case histories do exist) than on fantasy. Social scientists now study gossip instead of condemn it, but virulent condemnation of gossip's destructiveness persists into our own time, condemnation based less on evidence than on surmise. In 1912, a popular magazine article suggested that prejudice against Jews and witches is the product of gossip, that "race-hatred is undoubtedly nine-tenths the heritage of ancient gossip," that "the poison in the death-cup of Socrates was not so much the juice of the hemlock as the venom of the gossips of Athens," that gossip is a vast serpent encircling the world and producing noisome spawn which grow into dragons or multiply "a million a minute, in the covered cesspools of private life."[13] Later twentieth-century writers show rather more restraint, but the sociologist Samuel Heilman speaks of gossip as "surreptitious aggression which enables one to wrest power, manipulate, and strike out at another without the other's being able to strike back"; Roland Barthes associates gossip with "murder by language"; psychoanalytic theorists connect it with "the unconscious wish for father murder."[14] Ann Landers regularly prints diatribes against gossip. When I was quoted in newspapers as saying that gossip is good for you, I received an indignant letter informing me that gossip is a lethal instrument and another asking me if I knew how God feels about gossip. (God, it turns out, takes a very dim view.)

From Biblical times to the present, in other words, persistent opinion insists that negative comment about the absent constitutes a deadly weapon. Those promulgating this judgment rarely support it by reference to fact, although fictive accounts of gossip's destructiveness recur with some frequency. It is as difficult to call to mind anyone killed by gossip as to find someone murdered by a negative book review, but beliefs in language's lethal force require no evidence. Like the notion that taking a photograph of someone endangers his spirit, the view that saying something bad has the force of *doing* something bad wells from pre-rational depths. (Often, of course, the view is quite accurate.) Anyone can invoke the dangerous magic of language: a weapon for the otherwise powerless, a weapon (as many have noted) usable from dark corners.

The vocabulary of that last sentence, alluding to weapons and to power, hints an ideological dimension in the attack on backbiting. Malicious talk supplies for under classes an outlet impossible to shut off. Graduate students gossip about teachers, servants gossip about employers, women gossip about men. These propositions may operate also in reverse, but teachers have more direct methods of imposing their standards on students; from the students' point of view, private talk provides the most socially acceptable (and sensible) expression for anger and resentment. Malicious gossip becomes an increasingly vital resource as other avenues of aggression are closed; and gossip as a means of solidarity also has special importance for the subordinated. It follows that those nominally in control, the moralists who articulate society's view of itself, may feel nervous about what by definition they cannot govern. The ferocity of several centuries' attack on derogatory conversation about others probably reflects justifiable anxiety of the dominant about the aggressive impulses of the submissive.

Tattling—unconsidered talk, frequently involving betrayal of secrets—provides another focus of denunciation by moralizers, although they express themselves more moderately about this less uncontrollable form of discourse, a subject treated from the beginning largely in prudential terms. Unlike the attacks on backbiting, those on tattling focus (at least in discussions addressed to predominantly male audiences) on the danger of victimization by other people's indiscretion rather than on experienced temptation. Like other people's "detraction," other people's loose tongues violate the integrity of the self. Be careful what you say, medieval courtesy books prescribe; if you reveal yourself to anyone, you risk his spreading your secrets far and wide. A man may appear to be your friend while really being your foe; what you say to him you will hear again. You may tell a private tale to someone; after a few drinks, he will betray you, making whatever you said sound worse. It is dangerous to trust anyone; better keep what you know like treasure in a chest. At the beginning of the seventeenth century, the same doctrine survived. Trust no man with what you would not have publicly known; once you tell a friend anything, you run the danger that he will change his mind about your friendship and blazon your secrets to the world. And in the eighteenth century: foolish prattlers will tell any secret, public or private; whoever confides in them risks ruin. Indeed, most people have trouble keeping secrets, finding them an insupportable burden.[15]

The implicit standard of conduct is silence and solitude. One should be extremely wary about friendship, since all intimacy involves risk, and about marriage, where risk is intensified, given the talkative nature of women. Words kept to oneself can do no harm; words shared make one vulnerable. Every lapse into companionship and communication intensifies danger. The passion of attacks on backbiting partly reflects the impossibility of protecting oneself from slander of unknown origin and form. Against tattling, on the other hand, obvious defensive measures present themselves, since only revealed secrets can be transmitted. Perfect silence, perfect solitude, would violate the human condition, yet one can approach self-protective isolation, imagined almost as a state of transcendence.

Tattling, like detraction, threatens a tender and valued aspect of social beings: their reputations. Reputation matters equally (though for different reasons) to men and to women. "As the soule is more precious than the bodie; so it is greater offence to take away any mans good name, which refresheth the soule, then to defraude him of his foode, that sustaineth but the bodie."[16] The importance of a man's good name derives partly from his need to function in public. Reputation is social currency. Public men have always known that conspicuousness invites calumny ("From Fame to Infamy is a beaten Roade," writes the seventeenth-century essayist Francis Quarles[17]), but their continued opportunities for action may allow them to restore or remodel their reputations—a fact which does not prevent worry lest a wound to honor prove mortal, as sometimes it metaphorically does.

Women have no way to wipe out stains to their good names. Filling roles, before the twentieth century, mainly in private rather than public life, women depended vitally on their reputations. As late as 1880, moralists observed that a wound to a person's name, however frivolously originated, lasts forever. "Especially is this true of the fair sex, many of whom have, from this cause, withered and melted in their youth like snow in the spring."[18] In the sixteenth century, Castiglione had pointed out that a woman must always be more circumspect than a man, taking care to give no occasion for ill report, behaving so that no suspicion can touch her, because she lacks a man's ways to defend herself against slander. A good name is a woman's halo, a seventeenth-century aristocrat explains to his daughter. Much earlier, Geoffrey Chaucer, in his poem on reputation ("The House of Fame"), characterizes Dido as mourning not for the loss of Aeneas, who has seduced and abandoned her, but for the loss of her good name: though she lived forever, she says, she could not recover it. (Virgil, telling the Dido-and-Aeneas story, does not emphasize this point.) Later in the same poem, a group of men appeal to the Goddess Fame to give them reputations as seducers even though they cannot in fact win the women they want; the name, they say, serves as well as the reality. A medieval knight warns his daughters that any woman who looks lovingly at a man risks being thought and called an adulteress; her husband will come to hate her because of what people say about her. For men, the unearned reputation of sexual activity sometimes aggrandizes social position; for women, before very recent times, it would prove devastating to status in respectable society. In the late eighteenth century, a writer purporting to offer a *History of Women, from the Earliest Antiquity, to the Present Time* points out that women risk too much in allowing themselves sexual deviation: the resulting scandal will destroy their reputations and exclude them "from more than half the joys of life."[19]

Reputation for women, the literature suggests, is sexual reputation. A man's good name concerns behavior in many situations; a woman's sexual conduct is definitive. Detraction and tattling alike victimize women more seriously than they do men partly because of the special fragility of sexual reputation. Yet, as we shall see, women are imagined as their chief agents as well as their principal victims.

The more active role of "busy body," on the other hand, although often associated with women, invites a metaphor of male sexuality. "Adultery is nothing else but the Curiosity of discovering another Man's secret Pleasures, and the Itch of knowing what is hidden; and Curiosity is (as it were) a Rape and Violence committed upon other Peoples Privacies. I have observed that the same Curiosity which is thus inquisitive to know, is generally no less intemperate in talking too, and must needs be as ill-spoken, as it is ill-

natured."[20] Pandora, a woman, mythically exemplifies the dangers of curiosity; but the attack over several centuries on curiosity about one's neighbor's
actions implicates men and women alike. It draws on the theological tradition
of excessive curiosity as presumption, but emphasizes the danger implicit in
the imagined use busybodies make of what they learn. A sixteenth-century
Frenchman who also employs the analogy of adultery (attributing it to Plu-
tarch) adds that those curious about other people usually wish to know the
bad rather than the good, resembling snakes which seek infected and stinking
places. Once they know, they tell, converting the corruptions of others into
stories to sport with. They rely on their memories to register other men's
vices, failing to investigate their own.[21]

For three centuries, no one added appreciably to this indictment. Its
accusations occur repeatedly, with varying emphasis. Trying to know about
others is thought to preclude knowing oneself; the information gained by the
investigation can only cause trouble, to governments and to families. No
one values the busybody, whose tongue carries firebrands to set the whole
world aflame. The baseness of curiosity is both assumed and reiterated; people
would be ashamed, we are told, to have anyone think they spend their time
so meanly as to try to ferret out what others are doing. People ought to think
about higher things. Most especially, they should *talk* about higher things.
"To slip upon a pavement is better than to slip with your Tongue," John
Evelyn, writing at the age of eighty-four, tells his grandson, after warning
him against curiosity and more specifically against talking of other men's
lives and faults. By the late nineteenth century, when readers showed avid
interest in published police reports, news of divorce cases, even lists of births,
marriages, and deaths, a guide to good manners could argue that much of
the world's trouble came from people talking about people instead of about
things—adding that such talk is indulged in only by persons "devoid of brains,
education, and culture." The terminology of disapproval had changed; the
fact remained the same.[22]

The three aspects of gossip condemned by the moralists I have summarized—its circulation of slander, its betrayal of secrets, its penetration of
privacy—all embody threats to those made the objects of gossip's discourse.
Whether the commentators invoke religious or social sanctions, they imply
that the self can be damaged by being discussed. If other people handle my
secrets, discuss my character, describe me as worse than I hope I am, they
threaten my integrity. Indeed, as Roland Barthes has pointed out, the idea
of being talked about implies threat, regardless of what specifically is said.
"Gossip reduces the other to *he/she*, and this reduction is intolerable to me.
. . . The third-person pronoun is a wicked pronoun: it is the pronoun of the

non-person, it absents, it annuls."[23] Even "innocent" forms of gossip objectify the person considered; those talking communicate at the cost of another, whom they reduce to a kind of fiction.

These indictments of gossip, passionate, powerful, persuasive, may leave one wondering about the possibility of a counter-case. Indeed, the "counter-case" does not counter allegations of gossip's destructiveness and danger; it only suggests that even malicious gossip may possess positive value. Like the denunciations, the defenses of gossip draw more on intuitive than on objective evidence. Social scientists, however, produce solid data as a basis for their claims of gossip's social value, the political and personal purposes it serves. Gossip, they tell us, is a catalyst of social process. It provides groups with means of self-control and emotional stability. It circulates both information and evaluation, supplies a mode of socialization and social control, facilitates self-knowledge by offering bases for comparison, creates catharsis for guilt, constitutes a form of wish-fulfillment, helps to control competition, facilitates the selection of leaders, and generates power. It provides opportunity for self-disclosure and for examination of moral decisions.[24] Such accounts of gossip's functions avoid moral judgment. Their insistence on social and psychological purposes served by this mode of talk bypasses ancient problems of propriety and of virtue.

To summarize thus in a few sentences complex arguments by contemporary sociologists, anthropologists, and psychologists hardly does them justice. My cursory treatment simply acknowledges my awareness of a body of thought about gossip which takes such talk seriously as a social phenomenon and suggests grounds for defending it. But I am myself interested in possibilities that do not interest social scientists; they emerge in the "intuitive" defenses of gossip, occurring mainly in imaginative literature. Such defenses suggest gossip's positive moral value by privileging the moral system it implies. I shall return to this complicated hypothesis after summarizing a few texts that hint a positive view of gossip and after examining the traditional association of gossip with women.

To take a positive view involves suspending consciousness of gossip's destructive force and considering what besides animus against others it may involve. Apologies for this mode of discourse take advantage of the range of meanings connected with gossip, stressing such facts as these: its talk may be devoid of malicious intent; it often involves close and emotionally fruitful human association; reflecting intense interest in the personal, it may include subtle judgment and discrimination. Two medieval poems, for instance, suggest gossip's intricate relation to questions of human obligation. Chaucer's

Wife of Bath feels neither guilt nor shame about her propensity for verbal gossip and her commitment to her female gossip, which apparently surpasses her devotion to her fourth husband. My gossip, she says, knew my heart better than did the parish priest. If my husband pissed against a wall, or if he did something that would cost his life if known, I would tell my gossip about it—and another woman as well, and my niece. Indeed, often I *did* tell them his secrets: my husband would blush with shame that he had confided in me. The Wife herself does not blush. On the contrary, she celebrates her small community of women and values her participation in it: a participation which depends partly on the sharing of other people's secrets.[25]

A fifteenth-century poem to which a later editor gave the title *The Gossips* suggests men's sense of mystery in such associations of women. A male narrator tries to imagine how women behave when they spend time together without male company. He sounds timid: first he offers to explain what gossips do together, then he modifies his promise by confessing that he dares not reveal all that they say. He tells an inconsequential tale. The women meet in the street and agree to gather in a tavern, to which all bring food. They drink wine and talk of their husbands, one of whom beats his wife. One woman says she would not tolerate such treatment. Another leaves, putting down a penny for the reckoning: not enough. The others talk about her: who is she, anyhow? with whom did she come? Finally the gathering ends, the participants returning to domestic responsibilities. The narrator appeals to his presumably male audience: now fill the cups and drink to me and we shall all be good fellows together; we will leave off talking in this way and speak only good of women.[26]

Both these texts evoke a female alliance at least partly antipathetic to men. The women's intimacy depends on, or is reflected in, their discussion of their husbands. Women tell one another, in these male evocations, about their spouses' weaknesses and faults. They incite one another to insubordination. Their association violates traditional hierarchy: women, in concert with their gossips, may criticize or mock those on whom their economic and social welfare depends. Like the anxieties about "detraction," the worry about what women say to one another stems more from imagination than from experience. When the reporter of the women's tavern conversation ends by promising to speak only good of women, his placating tone conveys fear lest women speak evil of men.

On the other hand, the Wife of Bath's guiltless pleasure in her own reminiscences and the atmosphere of excitement in *The Gossips* over the discovery of female secrets both declare an imperfectly realized sense of richness in intimate conversation. Nothing the Wife says fully explains the high value she places on her relation to her gossip, but she makes it clear that something important takes place between them—something sufficiently vital to justify betraying her husband for its sake. The account of gossips in the tavern leaves out, the narrator confesses, "half the substance" of what they say, thus sustaining the mystery about why it matters to them. Yet an uneasy perception that something significant happens in gatherings of gossips permeates both texts.

Shakespeare resolves *The Comedy of Errors* in "a gossips' feast," playing on shifting meanings of the word. At the end of the final act, a woman who has just discovered her long-lost twin sons, now grown to adulthood, invites the assembled company to "Go to a gossips' feast, and go with me: / After so long grief such festivity!" "With all my heart I'll gossip at this feast," responds the duke who governs the city. One of the twin slaves who have also found one another asks his brother, "Will you walk in to see their gossiping?" and the action concludes with the two slaves preparing to enter hand in hand. [27]

The mother plays with a metaphor of delayed childbirth: for the years of her sons' absence, she says, she has been in labor; now, with their discovery, she is delivered. She therefore welcomes her companions to a feast of metaphorical godparents, baptismal sponsors: those originally designated as *gossips*. The duke declares his eagerness to "gossip" as a good companion, participating in communal merrymaking: a later definition of the verb. The slave refers to a gossiping as generalized companionship, implying talk as its chief activity; he thus foretells yet another meaning (from 1630): an assembly where idle talk is the chief occupation. Shakespeare's usage stresses positive implications: the gossiping, in all its meanings, declares happiness and closeness, an end to misery, an appropriate resolution for comedy.

The activity evoked by Shakespeare's comedy is *inclusive* rather than, like that of the Wife of Bath and the fifteenth-century gossips, *exclusive*. Perhaps as a consequence, the prospect of people talking together in *The Comedy of Errors* has only affirmative value. Moreover, the lines contain no implication that talk at the feast will specifically concern other people; the conversation can therefore be more readily imagined as innocent. At the end of the seventeenth century, Mary Astell made one of the first attempts to argue explicitly the positive value of talking about others. Commenting on the stereotypically female social activity of paying visits, which most moralists stigmatized as a pretext for malicious and trivial talk, Astell writes, "The only use we can make of that Time which the World borrows of us and necessary Civility exacts, is to lay in Matter of Observation. I do not mean that we shou'd make Ill-natur'd Remarks, or Uncharitable Reflections on Particular Persons, but only that we take notice of the several workings of Human Nature, the little turns and distinctions of Various Tempers; there being somewhat peculiar almost in every one, which *cannot be learn'd but by Conversation* and the Reflections it Occasions."[28]

Astell's hopeful fantasy postulates the possibility of separating gossip's moral virtues from its defects. Her imagined conversationalists think fruitfully about other people without saying anything bad about them; in practice, of course, taking notice of the detailed workings of human nature and of the minute distinctions of temperament will often generate uncharitable verbal observations. Astell clearly does not consider herself to be defending gossip. Her sense of morality, as well as her consciousness of her own victimization by detraction, would keep her from doing anything of the sort. But she suggests cogent grounds for defense.

The few writers who have purposefully attested gossip's value typically isolate its positive aspects. The nineteenth-century English periodical *The Gossip*, quoted in the last chapter, contains a full and eloquent panegyric: gossip enriches the mind as well as expresses the essential human impulse to share and communicate by voice. The anonymous apologist explicitly excludes malice, insisting that it belongs to slander, not gossip. Although trivial, gossip should not be thought useless; its bad reputation has obscured its true moral, social, and psychological worth. Less elaborately, later in the century, a woman named Julia Byrne eliminates malice and frivolity from her definition of gossip and celebrates the mode as a basis for truths on which historians build. The well-known Victorian writer Henry Morley entitled a collection of his essays *Gossip* and explained in his preface that he valued the tone, substance, and flexibility of such discourse. More recently, *Moralities of Everyday Life* has deprecated gossip's destructive possibilities and insisted on its ethical weight: "Gossip brings ethics home by introducing abstract morality to the mundane."[29]

Even if one includes among the apologia for gossip imaginative evocations of ambiguous tone, attacks far outnumber defenses. Moreover, the passionate intensity of denunciations finds little counterpart in the relatively few celebrations of gossip, which typically sound at least faintly defensive. To choose definitions that avoid gossip's use of people as subject, as Shakespeare does, or, like Julia Byrne and the magazine called *The Gossip*, to exclude malice as a component, makes it easy to uphold gossip's value. Yet not even gossip's alleged malice fully accounts for the ferocity of diatribes against it. A partial

explanation for that ferocity may lie in the traditional connections of gossip
with women.

My daughter recently sent me a comic strip from a Boston newspaper.
In the first frame, a man leans against a woman's desk. The balloon next to
his smugly smiling head reads, "Say, did you hear about Shirley? They say
she's got something going with that guy from . . ." The woman responds,
"I've got to run, Ralph . . . I'm afraid I don't have time to gossip." The
second frame shows the man responding to the silent woman: "*Gossip?* Men
don't gossip! I was merely analyzing her shortcomings."

That comic strip contains a lot of history. For centuries, commentators
have pointed out that men gossip too: combating the folk myth that gossip
belongs mainly to women. No one ever says that women gossip *too*.

A more dignified version of the comic strip: observations by a social
anthropologist studying a village in the French Alps called Valloire.

> Housewives in Valloire avoid being seen talking to one another. In
> the winter, when the snow lies deep and one can walk only along
> narrow cleared pathways, these women stay indoors. If they need
> something from the shops, they try to find a child who will run the
> errand for them. There is no reason why the husbands should not
> go to do the shopping, and if they happen to be around, they do
> so: being men, they combine the shopping with a visit to a café.
> . . . For men to sit around in public and gossip is quite acceptable
> since, it is generally assumed, this exchange is . . . a friendly,
> sociable, light-hearted, good-natured, altruistic exchange of news,
> information and opinion. But if women are seen talking together,
> then something quite different is happening: very likely they are
> indulging in . . . gossip, malice, "character assassination."[30]

The anthropologist describing this situation does not reveal the actual subjects
of either men's or women's conversation; he concerns himself with its interpretations. What, after all, *could* women be talking about? Lacking public
occupation, with no responsibility for the world's important affairs, they must
be discussing other people. And what they say must be dangerous: the ancient
metaphor of "character assassination" reflects that conviction.

Few writers have asserted that *only* women gossip, but many have assumed
the natural, or at least the socialized, connection between women and trivial
or malicious talk about other people. Sir Thomas Overbury's early seventeenth-century character of "A Very Woman, Her Next Part" epitomizes the

contemptuous tone reserved for female verbosity. "She travels to and among, and so becomes a woman of good entertainment, for all the folly in the country comes in cleane linnen to visit her: she breaks to them her griefe in sugar cakes, and receives from their mouths in exchange, many stories that conclude to no purpose." John Evelyn warns his grandson to keep his wife and daughter out of London, because they will there spend their time in visiting, dressing, playgoing, gossiping, and other forms of vanity. Obadiah Walker, writing late in the seventeenth century, relegates women to a parenthesis, so casual is his assumption that women talk about people. "In *Discourse* concerning *other persons* (familiar amongst Women) *Backbiting*, and *calumny* is most frequent." A late eighteenth-century periodical adopts a more judicious tone: "It gives me pain to observe, that, in ancient as well as modern times, the reproach of this gossiping mania has principally fallen upon the women, whose natural bias towards tenderness and mercy would make this a very unaccountable particularity, unless we looked for the cause of it in the narrower compass of their education, and the more circumscribed range of their lives and employments. The love of scandal is generally in proportion to the deficiency of other topics."[31]

Attacks on tattling addressed to female audiences, unlike those for males, which stress the danger of victimization, emphasize women's tendency to indiscretion. The medieval knight offering counsel to his unmarried daughters uses his final chapter for a tale about a man nearly executed because his wife betrays his confidence. A seventeenth-century emblem book presents a leaking barrel as the type of the babbling as well as of the whorish woman. Thomas Fuller, writing of *The Holy State*, characterizes the good wife as one who preserves her husband's confidence, the good husband as keeping his wife ignorant of unnecessary secrets. A father's versified advice to his daughter, late in the seventeenth century, repeats the image of leaking vessels, warning the girl against disclosing what a friend tells her. The amount of space the poem dedicates to this theme equals that lavished on advice about how to choose a husband. Richard Allestree, a clergyman whose work *The Ladies Calling* was widely read in the late seventeenth and early eighteenth centuries, comments on the general reproach that women cannot keep confidences, urging his readers to vindicate themselves and their sex from the charge, "this blabbing humour being a symptom of a loose, impotent soul, a kind of incontinence of the mind, that can retain nothing committed to it."[32]

The reproach expresses itself as strongly in the eighteenth century, when Eliza Haywood, journalist and popular novelist, attributes women's delight in scandalmongering to "a weak and degenerate mind." She points out the fault is generally attributed to women: "with but too much Justice," she adds. "Some will have it, that this unlucky Propensity in us proceeds from a greater Share of Envy and Malice in our Natures; others, less severe, ascribe it meerly to a Want of something else wherewith to employ ourselves." Haywood herself prefers the latter explanation.[33] Accepting the negative stereotype, she denounces her sisters with intensity comparable to that of any male moralist.

During the sixteenth and seventeenth centuries, when moralists most insistently declared women's verbal indiscretion, female lasciviousness was also almost universally assumed; women could read endless warnings of their need for internal and external controls on their sexuality. Women's share in the fallen condition of humankind emphasized sins of talk and of lust— perversions of primary modes of human connectedness. As we have seen, some writers about gossip suggest analogies between sins of sex and of speech: George Wither's suggestion that the whorish woman and the blabber have something in common, Allestree's description of verbal incontinence as resembling its sexual equivalent. Moreover, the violence of typical denun- ciations calls to mind that of sexual warnings. In both cases, commentators imagine the consequences they fear—or that, perhaps, they ambivalently desire. In both cases, they posit a secret female life. Female sexuality should be concealed, they believe, as well as controlled. If you allow yourselves to dance freely, an eighteenth-century clergyman warns an audience of young women, you may inadvertently reveal your sexuality; no man will wish to marry you in that case.[34] (Social life worked differently in the eighteenth century!) Like the disastrous consequences of exposed female sexuality, the dreadful outcomes of gossip inhabit the imagination. Gossip, like sexual intercourse, belongs to a hidden life. Sex and gossip alike comprise modes of intimate communication; both epitomize the unpredictable and uncon- trollable. Like sex, gossip serves impulse and has explosive potential. Pas- sionate attacks on the secret life of words parallel warnings about the secret life of the body. The eighteenth-century clergyman, one may suspect, watches a girl dancing, finds his own imagination inflamed, and projects his distur- bance onto her: she must guard herself more carefully. Just so, the sight of two or three women closely engaged in verbal exchanges which the observer cannot hear—the very possibility of such a conjunction—may arouse fan- tasies of the talk's destructiveness or indiscretion. Verbal, like sexual, expres- sion may rise from passion; the story of Midas' wife telling his secret to the reeds perhaps draws as deeply on essential female nature as does the legend of Isolde's love for Tristan; or perhaps both stories stem from male fantasy, male fear.

Two explanations for the association of gossip with women emerge explicitly and one tacitly from early discussions. Christian denunciation implicitly assumes that Eve, a woman, brought sin into the world by unwise speaking and unwise listening; women's propensity for foolish talk declares their ancestry. Few commentators spell out this point, but the tradition helps to explain the intensity of sixteenth- and seventeenth-century attacks on female garrulity. A second explanation which may only disguise the first emphasizes the natural weakness of women's minds. "Women being for the most part of a Constitution naturally feeble, because their Blood and Humours hold more from the Nature of Water than any other Principle, and their brain is of a soft consistence, because their Fibres are fine and slender, their Animal Spirits which in Truth are agitated enough, but feeble, weak and light, and by consequence very easily dissipated. . . . The Difficulty they have to give a serious Attention to any thing abstracted and above the Senses, the dislike they conceive for all solid Reasoning, fully proves the Delicateness of their Imagination, or, what is here much the same thing, the Weakness of their Minds."[35] That sort of thing passed for science in the late seventeenth century. By the mid-nineteenth century, the charge of mental weakness had been slightly obscured: someone named Ezra Sampson, for instance, declared himself unsure whether women's "greater volubility of tongue" derived from the superior flexibility of their organs of speech or the heightened volatility of their animal spirits, but he concludes that they not only talk more than men, they possess more "small talk," which lends itself readily to "the evil of petty scandal."[36] A third, more generous, way of accounting for the female inclination to gossip manifests itself only in the late seventeenth and early eighteenth centuries, as an increasing number of upper-class women found themselves deprived of significant economic function. Several commentators in this period suggest that women gossip because they have nothing better to do, lacking good education and meaningful occupation; we have already encountered examples of this view.[37]

All such attempts to relate the habit of gossip to the nature of women rest on the manifest assumption that to gossip involves reprehensible weakness or actual sin. Even now, women remain sensitive to the stereotype of female gossip, and men casually invoke that stereotype, even when they know better, as they might refer to the notion that women are bad drivers. A well-known politician visiting an institution that I frequented chatted with me about gossip. We agreed about its importance in Washington life. Soon my interlocutor informed me that, although he recognized the value of gossip's information, he never gossiped himself, that kind of thing didn't interest him. His *wife* gossiped, he said, and told him what he needed to know. A

few minutes later, his wife responded indignantly to the suggestion that
she might do such a thing, even for her husband's sake. She didn't enjoy
gossip at all, she insisted, and she never participated. Nor did she find
any interest in the idea of a book on the subject: a subject hardly worthy of
consideration.

I know nothing about the actual verbal habits of the politician or his
wife, but I recognize the impulse to reject allegations that one might engage
in this variety of frivolous conversation, particularly if one is a woman.
As my survey of several centuries' commentary suggests, many notions
about gossip fit all too neatly with standard derogatory assumptions about
females. But one can also postulate more dignified reasons for the
assumed link between gossip and women: which brings me back to the
question of the value system implicit in the alleged female propensity to
gossip.

A passage from the works of Immanuel Kant that outlines an ideal of
friendship suggests the kind of positive value one might attribute to intimate
gossip.

> Moral friendship . . . is the complete confidence of two persons
> in the mutual openness of their private judgments and sensations,
> as far as such openness can subsist with mutual respect for one
> another.
>
> Man is a being intended for society (even though he is also
> unsociable). In the cultivation of the social state he strongly feels
> the need to open himself up to others. . . . But, on the other hand,
> he is also constrained and admonished by his fear of the abuse which
> others might make of this disclosure of his thoughts; and he therefore
> sees himself compelled to lock up within himself a good part of his
> judgments (particularly those concerning other people). He might
> like to talk with someone about what he thinks of the people with
> whom he associates . . . ; but he must not risk it because others,
> by cautiously holding back their own judgment, might make use of
> his remarks to his own detriment. . . .
>
> But if one finds a man of good disposition and understanding to
> whom he can open his heart with complete confidence, without
> having to worry about such dangers, and moreover with whom his
> opinions about things are in accord, then he can give vent to his
> thoughts. Then he is not completely alone with his thoughts, as if
> in prison, but enjoys a freedom which he misses in the mass of men,
> among whom he must keep himself to himself.[38]

The fear that those a man confides in might use his secrets to his disadvantage recalls earlier moralists' admonitions to silence and solitude. But the vision of a friendship of shared and mutually discovered opinion, in which one can say what he thinks of the people with whom he associates, can give vent to his thoughts—this vision identifies the freedom of intimate gossip. Kant would not, of course, call it that. Still, the kind of relationship he describes suggests that of the Wife of Bath with her female friends, that of the women who meet in a tavern to talk about their husbands: a relationship allowing the expression of thoughts and feelings about others, one releasing people from the prison of their own thoughts.

Another philosopher, Hannah Arendt, writing of Greek political ideals, comments, "We humanize what is going on in the world and in ourselves only by speaking of it, and in the course of speaking of it we learn to be human. The Greeks called this humanness which is achieved in the discourse of friendship *philanthropia*, 'love of man,' since it manifests itself in a readiness to share the world with other men."[39] Arendt's implied ideal resembles Kant's. Both are illuminated by the work of the psychologist Carol Gilligan, who, studying people's ways of thinking about themselves and of formulating their sense of moral obligation, has discovered widespread reference to a moral system at odds with traditional assumptions about Western values. Instead of declaring justice the standard of morality, those operating within this system assert themselves to value a concept of responsibility. They talk about relationship and about particularities, declaring themselves unable to arrive at moral decisions without knowing individual circumstances, specific facts. The people whose moral talk conforms to this pattern are mainly, although not entirely, women.[40]

The assumptions governing the best kind of gossip correspond quite precisely to those invoked by the people Gilligan considers representative of a counter-system to that generally proposed. "Serious" gossip assumes the importance of particularities, but also of relationship. (The worst kind of gossip, on the other hand, manifests interest in particulars but *not* in relationship: intimate information prized for its own sake, or for the power it provides, does not serve the purpose of alliance.) Like the moral system Gilligan outlines, gossip does not conform to the official values of our society; like the operations of that system, it frequently has a subversive effect. On the other hand, the passages from Kant and Arendt suggest that humanizing attention to the world, freedom in relationship, both aspects of the best kind of gossip, also fulfill important social and personal purposes. Gossip, in this reading, exemplifies what Arendt describes as a lost ideal.

To interpret two early texts from this point of view will illustrate more precisely what I mean. A story from *The Book of the Knight of La Tour–Landry*, translated into English in the late fifteenth century, epitomizes a large body of narrative material about gossip. (Different versions of the tale exist in German, Spanish, Arab, and Jewish lore as well as in Hungarian, Serbo-Croatian, and Indian tradition.) A squire marries a young wife and worries about whether he can trust her. He tells her he has a secret to share with her, but she must promise never to pass it on. When she agrees, he informs her that he has just laid two eggs. His reputation, he says, depends on keeping this news quiet. His wife thinks about the matter a bit and then goes to her gossip, swears her to secrecy, and confides that her husband has laid—three eggs. In due time, the news gets back to the husband that he has laid five eggs. He calls together family and friends in the great hall of the castle and shames his wife before them all. She presumably sins—that is to say, gossips—no more.[41]

The story belongs to the familiar genre of cautionary tales. Its themes resurface for the next five centuries: the linkage of loose talk with women, suggestions that gossip implies credulity, betrayal, and exaggeration, that it flourishes in intimate female associations, and that the best thing to do about it is to shame women who indulge in it. The meaning and moral are unambiguous. By this example, the narrator concludes, we learn that the good woman should be careful not to reveal her husband's secrets, but always to keep his confidence and fulfill his commandments. You're supposed to feel outrage at the wife's betrayal, satisfaction at her eventual humiliation.

But is the matter really so simple? What about the story's specific content: why does it involve a man's claim to lay eggs? (In versions in other languages, he sometimes claims that a crow has flown out of his belly.) From the wife's point of view, her husband has suddenly claimed not only the male power he obviously possesses—quite enough, she might think, for any man—but the unique female procreative power as well. If the woman keeps the news to herself, she meekly accepts the man's superiority in female as well as in male accomplishment. She chooses, rather, to assert her own kind of authority: the authority of talk, and of female association. The man still triumphs by his social and moral dominance, but the woman has performed a self-assertive act. By sharing her husband's secret, she has turned a troubling event into a story; she has drawn on female community; she has asserted both the interest of the fact and the necessity of sharing.

I would not seriously argue that this subversive interpretation of a moral exemplum as a fable of domestic politics should replace the obvious reading of the tale: only that the abundant moral literature about gossip often has an underside. Neither participant in this little story emerges as an attractive figure: the husband is mean, the wife spiteful. Nor is the tale an effort at realism. Nonetheless, it reveals not one but two sets of standards. If the man values, and has a right to value, secrecy, the woman values, and has a right to value, community. She needs such community in order to resist an imposition of power. She resists by subverting: as gossip often subverts.

History testifies to the persistence and the power of gossip as a social mode. Moralizers have taken gossip seriously even when they declared its lack of seriousness. It supplies a weapon for outsiders—a weapon appropriately directed at the façade of reputation people construct around themselves. And the weapon can be converted to a bond: a means of alliance, a way of feeling united as insiders. The story about the man who laid eggs expresses the double aspect of gossip: its capacity to damage reputation, its reliance on and creation of alliance through shared delight in story and in character. It conveys also the repressive impulse which responds to gossip's subversions. But gossip will not be repressed: hence its danger and its insistent force.

Four centuries ago, an Italian named Steeven Guazzo offered a written example of one kind of gossip:

> Let us nowe come to ill tongued Hypocrites, who under the colour of griefe and compassion, to be the better beleeved, lamentably rehearse the ill haps of other; which vice, though it bee common to manie, yet it is most familiar with certaine women, who meeting with other of their Gossips, after the first greetings, they foorthwith breake into these speeches, Have you not hearde the hard hap of my unfortunate neighbour: and thereupon making the storie, they rehearse howe the husbande by meanes of his servant, took her tardie in her hastie business. Then they tell [about] the wall, and the way whereby her lover got downe: next, how cruelly her husbande beate her, and her maid, and thinke not that they leave any thing behind untolde, but rather will put too somewhat of their own devise. After this, another beginneth to say, And I will quite [i.e., requite] your tale with the like chaunce that happened within this six dayes in our streete, but I pray you in any wise let it go no further.[42]

Four hundred years after the fact, the vitality of that summary still declares not only the moral dubiousness of gossip but its indestructible human energy and the pleasurable association that energy can generate. The joy in narrative detail and in personality infusing Guazzo's account of what he condemns suggests gossip's positive essence—inextricably mingled with its destructive potential. The paradox of that mingling creates the dilemma gossip continues to embody.

By citing texts which suggest the connection of women and gossip and by associating gossip myself with values often identified as female, I do not mean to imply a belief that only women gossip: merely to insist on the traditional link and to speculate about reasons for it. If gossip in its positive aspects indeed reflects moral assumptions different from those of the dominant culture, that fact suggests, as I have already argued, its special usefulness for subordinated classes. It embodies an alternative discourse to that of public life, and a discourse potentially challenging to public assumptions; it provides language for an alternative culture. Gossip's way of telling can project a different understanding of reality from that of society at large, even though gossip may claim to articulate the voice of the community. A rhetoric of inquiry, gossip questions the established. These observations apply on occasion even to malicious gossip, but they particularly concern the exploratory, intimate form of talk which need not express itself in malice. Women, even now, have more social freedom for such talk than men do—if only because several centuries' stereotyping makes it seem "natural" that they should band together to gossip.

But the bonding of gossip, its interest in human detail, the speculative atmosphere it fosters—such aspects, as Kant and Arendt indicate, have even wider social bearings than the connection with women might suggest, and broader literary implications. To insist on gossip's primary concern with relationship and with particularity hints ways it will prove useful as implicit model and subject for novelists, biographers, and letter-writers. It also suggests a yet more important claim: that gossip epitomizes a way of knowing as well as of telling. I shall turn first, however, to gossip as a way of feeling.

3

How It Feels

"We might call it a free activity standing quite consciously outside 'ordinary' life as being 'not serious,' but at the same time absorbing the player intensely and utterly. It is an activity connected with no material interest, and no profit can be gained by it. It proceeds within its own proper boundaries of time and space according to fixed rules and in an orderly manner. It promotes the formation of social groupings which tend to surround themselves with secrecy."[1]

So J. Huizinga summarizes his view of play. Subsequent commentators have challenged and modified it; it remains, however, a remarkably precise, if inadvertent, characterization of gossip. From outside, as the opinions adduced in the previous chapter reveal, gossip often looks dangerous. It ferrets out secrets, harms other people, reveals human nature's worst propensities. Within the group of participants, gossip can feel otherwise. Freed from ordinary social inhibitions, seeking no material benefits, proceeding by established rules, forging bonds within their group, talkers pursue a game which, like all absorbing games, expresses impulse and satisfies need.

In Richland Park, Saint Vincent, British West Indies, peasants believe that gossip involves an "art" comparable to that demonstrated in composing stories or speeches. The behavior involved in gossip, they feel, is potentially disruptive but vital to individual and community life. They categorize gossip as a "nonsense" performance, unlike the "sensible" behavior which demonstrates order and decorum, products of knowledge. Gossip's "nonsense" displays the energetic, licentious atmosphere associated with lies.[2]

Like the cultural text of Clifford Geertz's Balinese cockfight, gossip provides specific content varying from one occasion to the next, though its large forms—inquiry, assertion, speculation, judgment—remain constant. Geertz's allegation about "quartets, still lifes, and cockfights"—they "are not merely reflections of a pre-existing sensibility analogically represented; they are positive agents in the creation and maintenance of such a sensibility"—might be enlarged to include gossip.[3] Yet the instability and the privacy of its manifestations protect it from observation. A participant-observer could not take notes; and memory does not preserve the evanescences of such talk—partly because its substance often has less importance than its complex, hard-to-define tone. Ever shifting in mood and subject, dependent on an atmosphere of confidentiality and secrecy for its very existence, playful and anarchic in impulse although it may serve the interests of the community, gossip would instantly change shape under the microscope, curbing itself toward decorum. Even anthropologists hear what people say *about* gossip far more often than what they say *in* it; and if those people gossip with the anthropologist, the observer could yet never know how they gossip among themselves.

Huizinga's description of play and Roger Abrahams' account of what goes on in the West Indies tell of fruitful and joyous aspects of gossip and suggest compelling motives for engaging in the activity. Other theorists about gossip's motivation have, however, taken a far darker view. The psychoanalyst Stanley Olinick suggests envy, isolation, curiosity, voyeurism, exhibitionism, and orality as feelings, conditions, or pathologies accounting for gossip. Samuel Heilman sticks to aggression. "Gossip . . . provides the gossiper (as well as the enthusiastic and willing recipient) with a means of expressing aggressive feelings toward another with a minimum of interpersonal risk and anxiety." The gossip, in other words, refuses to stand up and fight like a man—a far from random choice of simile, given the insistent association of women with gossip. Not only does gossip derive from aggression, in this and other characterizations of it—not only does it derive from aggression, it involves *sneaky* aggression and ugly collusion by the "enthusiastic and willing recipient."[4]

If life does not readily supply sufficient data to resolve discrepancies between the opposed views of gossip—as white and as black magic—literature provides useful evidence. The effects of gossip, as we have seen, encourage two kinds of interpretation: gossip in its modes of backbiting, tattle, and betrayal proves destructive; inasmuch as it supports close alliance, it becomes sustaining. Comparable duality must govern any attempt to describe gossip's psychological dynamics. One can find literary demonstration of gossip's origins in aggression, and data to insist on the originary yearning for intimacy. I want to examine both sides, speculating about how to describe the psychological forces at work in gossip's contrasted modes and looking at texts that illuminate their workings.

As published commentary about gossip overwhelmingly concentrates on its dark side, so does imaginative literature, emphasizing the aggressive component readily apparent in even unmalicious gossip through the will to control always implicit. To transmit a narrative about other people briefly takes possession of their lives, although the story in its outlines may express no hostility. Aggression disguises itself in information-sharing, with the relevant information falling into recognizable patterns. The categories for gossip, like those for more public forms of news, derive from cultural history. If a middle-aged man leaves his wife in order to share bed and board with an undergraduate, that fact becomes "news"—information of widespread public concern—only when it leads to the divorce court; it provokes instant gossip. Its interest (apart from the personalities involved) depends partly on the very familiarity of its form. We have heard this story before; to embed people we know in the hackneyed narrative emphasizes our freedom, their subjection to ineluctable pattern. The bizarre, which may provide substance for gossip, is quickly assimilated into comprehensible forms. Gossip expresses aggression partly by making other people into personae, actors in the talker's play.

Roger Abrahams, in his account of West Indian gossip, suggests important analogies between gossip and joking in the culture he surveys. Both take place only between individuals who stand in special relationships to each other. "Furthermore, like joking, both the content and forms of gossip are traditional, and it is these conventional aspects which define and restrict the communicative situation" (290). Such observations cannot necessarily survive transfer from one culture to another, but Abrahams' remarks suggest an approach to analyzing gossip's dynamics. Gossip and joking share not only intimate context and conventional form but the aggressive content which Freud has declared essential to jokes. Freud's well-known account of jokes hints specific ways that gossip's aggression too may operate.[5]

Freud divides jokes into two categories, "innocent" and "tendentious," thus distinguishing those which constitute ends in themselves, serving no particular aim, from those filling a definable purpose.[6] Two possible purposes emerge: a joke "is either a *hostile* joke (serving the purpose of aggressiveness, satire, or defence) or an *obscene* joke (serving the purpose of exposure)" (97). Civilization demands that we "renounce the expression of hostility by deeds," but allows indirect expression in words. "By making our enemy small, inferior, despicable or comic, we achieve in a roundabout way the enjoyment of overcoming him—to which the third person, who has made no effort, bears witness by his laughter. . . . A joke will allow us to exploit something ridiculous in our enemy which we could not, on account of obstruction in the way, bring forward openly or consciously; once again, then, the joke *will evade restrictions and open sources of pleasure that have become inaccessible.* It will further bribe the hearer with its yield of pleasure into taking sides with us without any very close investigation" (103). This hearer plays an important part in the production of jokes; "no one can be content," Freud points out, "with having made a joke for himself alone" (143). Every joke demands a special "public," and "laughing at the same jokes is evidence of far-reaching psychical conformity" (131). "A joke . . . is the most social of all the mental functions that aim at a yield of pleasure. It often calls for three persons and its completion requires the participation of someone else in the mutual process it starts" (179).

Each of Freud's comments adapts itself readily to description of gossip. By all definitions, gossip implies a social context: at least two participants. It too often serves purposes of aggression or exposure; it too may prove "innocent" or purposeful. Moreover, the pleasure it provides emerges from a genetic sequence comparable to that Freud outlines for jokes. Freud discusses the inhibitions often applying, in our culture, to open personal insult. Even if one wished to insult an enemy, no pleasure would accrue to such an act because too many social prohibitions interfere. A clever joke, however, may disguise the desired insult enough to make it permissible. To utter the joke, in such a case, will generate not only the delight appropriate to its wit and energy, but an extra charge of pleasure as a result of the newly possible insult (136–7).

Looked at in the perspective of Freud's explanation of jokes, gossip's distortions become more comprehensible. Given the hypothesis that gossip originates in aggression, the subject of a given piece of gossip need not coincide literally with the original object of hostility. A gossiper may displace aggression onto a beautiful woman, an arrogant man, who shares salient characteristics with the "enemy." Inasmuch as aggressive wishes control the discourse, the narrative that initiates the gossip interchange may alter form or content to serve the reporter's needs. Gossip thus often partakes of fiction (some people would say *lies*), less because of the inevitable distortions of its passage from mouth to mouth than because of the purposes it serves for the retailer, who forms the story to fill unconscious needs. The pleasure of its sharing, like that of jokes, intensifies as it makes the impermissible acceptable. The gossiper's dominance over the hated or feared object assumes the guise of moral speculation or even of sympathy. "Isn't it awful?" one speaker says to another. "How can she stand it? I don't see why she puts up with him." Such questions, such sympathy declare a covert sense of superiority and of the anger that justifies it. The listener responds not, as to a joke, with laughter; sometimes, indeed, with professed horror. But the response includes pleasure—the pleasure of voyeurism, often, as well as of aggression: forms of "hard to achieve" satisfaction.

The idea of joking arouses no outrage, that of gossip often does; why does gossip seem so much worse? For one thing, it attaches the names of real people to its characters; therefore, it has potential effects in the real world. The indeterminacy of those effects intensifies ominous possibility, as the ferocious commentary on gossip makes clear. Rarely can one locate with precision the damage gossip causes, yet the chance of damage always remains, part of our social mythology as well as, perhaps, of our experience. Only reluctantly do most people confess pleasure in discussing other people's private affairs. Even lacking consciousness of immediate aggressive impulse, they may partake in infantile fantasies about language's magical power of destruction; to gossip can evoke the terror of the self as agent or as victim of such power. If I talk about them, perhaps they will talk about me; if I expose, may I not be exposed? We all experience or imagine the aggressiveness of other people's gossip, whether or not we feel the aggressiveness of our own. Primitive terror of reprisal underlies part of gossip's guilt. Our superegos warn us what others might find to say of us; we dread an all too readily imagined danger.

Unlike joking, in other words, the idea of gossip involves unconcealed threat. If gossip evades restriction less successfully than joking, we might expect it to generate less unalloyed pleasure. And indeed aggressive gossip provides only qualified pleasure, but it also serves more complex purposes than those fulfilled by joking. Imaginative literature elucidates gossip's functions; the idea of gossip, in turn, illuminates the dynamics of fiction. A case in point is George Meredith's little-read 1885 novel, *Diana of the Crossways*, a work that maps gossip's intricate connections with aggression. The novel illustrates how powerful and painful gossip can feel to its victim, suggests complex psychic forces contributing to gossip's promulgation, and illuminates gossip's social functions. But no novel consists merely of a set of social and psychological data for the literary anthropologist. To look at the operations of gossip in *Diana of the Crossways* calls attention to the work's concentration on linguistic process and helps to locate the energy of the book considered as a verbal complex. The text reminds us that gossip inhabits a continuum of discourse. Novels belong to the same continuum. Although the distinction between oral and written discourse becomes important in *Diana*, finally the work hints significant analogies between gossip and fiction.

"Gossip," the heroine of Meredith's novel observes, "is a beast of prey that does not wait for the death of the creature it devours."[7] Verbally acknowledging the virulence of such talk, she yet refuses to accept its power over her. Her story, initially, takes a familiar form. A beautiful Irish girl, Diana Merion, orphaned but of high social class (daughter of a general), comes to England to establish herself in the world, necessarily through marriage. Her resources include not only beauty but great intelligence and verbal wit; she has one close female friend, a prosperous married woman. Suitors abound, but all goes awry when her friend's husband makes a sexual overture to her. Wishing to visit no longer at the friend's home, Diana marries the next man who presents himself. The marriage proves disastrous.

At this point, the plot becomes less predictable. Diana's energy, wit, and brains demand outlet; she interests herself in politics. Pursuing her concerns in the only way open to her, she gives select dinner parties which become famous for quality of conversation and wine. Her husband, jealous of the most persistent habitué, Lord Dannisburgh, a distinguished statesman who drops in on Diana every evening on his way home from the House of Lords, sues her for divorce, but loses the suit, unable to prove non-existent adultery. The unendurable marriage must endure, at least in name. Diana refuses to cohabit with her husband or to accept his money. She subsists as a novelist, living increasingly beyond her means, partly because her political aspirations now center on Lord Dannisburgh's nephew, Percy Dacier (the old lord has died), whom she educates in the ways of politics and whose career she furthers by her luxurious, intimate, sparkling, expensive dinners. Desperate for money, and motivated in ways not altogether apparent to herself, she sells to a newspaper a secret Percy has told her. Percy, rejecting her contemptuously, marries an heiress. Diana's husband dies, she virtually expires from sheer despair; eventually she marries Redworth, the faithful, solid, unpretentious Englishman who has loved her since her girlhood.

Gossip's function in the novel depends partly on that of other uses of language. Gossip belongs to the same spectrum as rumor, news, dinner-table conversation, story, and aphorism—forms of discourse characterized by their greater or lesser degree of individual intellectual control. All these linguistic modes share, in varying proportions, three crucial functions: they provide concealment or protection, serve as media of exchange, and generate power. Moreover, all both reflect and comment on existing social realities.

Some forms of language protect against others. The novel opens with lavish citation of Diana's aphorisms, emblems and evidence of the wit which, the narrator declares, provides armor against slander. That wit, though valued by those who hear it, often derives from desperation. "The witty Mrs. [Diana] Warwick, of whom wit was expected, had many incitements to be guilty of cheap wit; and the beautiful Mrs. Warwick, being able to pass anything she uttered, gave good and bad alike, under the impulsion to give out something, that the stripped and shivering Mrs. Warwick might find a cover in applause" (124). She needs a cover against what "the world" says: against gossip. In fact her wit provokes verbal aggression against her. She inadvertently offends a rather stupid middle-class woman, Mrs. Wathin, by making too clever a joke; the applause she wins further exposes her stripped and shivering self. Mrs. Wathin becomes a tireless source and agent of gossip against Diana. The beautiful woman's linguistic expertise releases a flood of uncontrolled utterance which threatens to overwhelm her.

Diana attempts to use aphorisms and sophisticated dinner-table conversation as social currency. No scandal contaminates the talk at her gatherings: she will not stoop to gossip or tolerate it in her setting. Yet gossip remains a more widely current medium of exchange than wit; eventually Diana too employs it. She learns to exploit her knowledge of others to generate social success. Having left London for a time, however, she loses that knowledge. One maker and breaker of fame inquires how she could "expect to be his Queen of the London Salon if she lost touch of the topics" (264). A newspaper editor pronounces her no longer useful. "Everything she knew of men and affairs was to him stale" (264). These powerful men expect of her a form of gossip. She has never understood that she deals in such a commodity, in her fiction, popular largely for its evocation of recognizable real personalities, or in her conversation, but the assessment of her diminished value foretells her literary decline: her commodity value has decreased. Exchange of gossip, at various levels, fuels her society.

It also fuels fiction, and not only Diana's. (Meredith's novel too is a *roman à clef.*) In the opening chapter of *Diana*, the narrator distinguishes among forms of written discourse. History and even philosophy, in his apparent view, are inferior to fiction, which takes as its province the inner life. The superior "realism" of fiction, a later digression argues, exposes hidden truth. Gossip deals with surfaces, draws facile conclusions from often misinterpreted evidence, purveys evidence with no conclusions at all: activities opposed to those of fiction as the novel has characterized it. Yet Meredith's narrative relies on a gossipy relationship between narrator and reader. The book opens with scraps of evidence about Diana, hearsay from other people's diaries. The narrator adds his own scraps. He tacitly invites the reader to wish further information and to speculate on the knowledge gained. For story-teller and reader too, then, gossip serves as currency. One can learn to value and to use different currency, as Diana comes to do, finally giving up the social world which has condemned her; the reader too, presumably, eventually desires hidden rather than manifest truth—but only after first utilizing the lesser truths of gossip.

Language as power has yet more importance than language as protection or as currency. Diana confuses power and love. Only by talk, in her view, can she "preserve" the "ascendancy" she wishes over Percy, and by talk, reaching for greater power, she forfeits all. Percy comes to her at midnight and in revealing crucial political information exposes also his sense of sexual dominance as he demands that she allow their relationship physical consummation. She temporizes; when he leaves, she feels degraded. He has treated her, she feels, as the woman that gossip—"the world"—declares her to be. "She felt humiliated, plucked violently from the throne where she had long been sitting securely, very proudly" (311). Trying to regain her power, she goes, late at night, to the editor, who will make her feel important for what she can tell.

Diana admires soldiers like her father. She has trouble valuing men of less forceful occupation. Her own aggressive impulses conceal themselves behind a screen of language; language hides them from herself in this instance too—although not, presumably, from the reader. Her secret, told, protects her humiliated self, as wit had protected her earlier. The exchange of secret for money underlines the second use of gossip, as exchange medium; but the most serious work of gossip, as power, remains paramount. Diana finally fails because she wants not only power but love; she cannot have both. Rejected by her lover, she sinks to muteness and submission, accepting Redworth finally because "His poverty in the pleading language melted her" (405). She yields to the inarticulate, now unwilling, she says, "to be seated on a throne" (405). Relinquishing linguistic and social dominion, she finds passion and, presumably, contentment.

The plot of *Diana of the Crossways* thus communicates, even depends upon, a set of perceptions about gossip's uses for the individual. Gossip as concealment, exchange, power: such associations shed light on the world outside as well as inside the novel. The book also reminds us of the degree to which our ideas about gossip often involve fantasies about ill-defined "others." The energy of gossip in *Diana*, far greater than that of any Mrs. Wathin, derives from its invisibility, involving the power of language without locatable personal control or responsibility. And despite gossip's moral ambiguity, the invisible Other who promulgates it speaks in the moralistic voice of a civilization generating its discontents.

The fantasy of gossip as representing both the out-of-control and the controlling—what the individual knows herself powerless to manage and what she imagines as trying to manage her—dominates *Diana of the Crossways*. "Crossways" designates Diana's house, her treasured inheritance; it also means a place where roads intersect—a duality of significance causing some confusion when Redworth tries to find his beloved early in the story. Diana says of her relations with her husband, "we walked a dozen steps in stupefied union, and hit upon crossways" (131); again, of Redworth, "I am always at crossways, and he rescues me" (259). The same word, then, common or proper noun, means security (the place Diana loves) or confusion or conflict or multiple possibility. Its ambiguous force images that of language in general. Language and its sub-species, gossip, depend upon convention, but lack stability. The novel concerns "crossways," points of choice; at every crux—Diana's "stupefied union" with her husband, her effort to achieve political influence, her decisions about her lovers—convention exerts its inescapable force.

Convention, as exemplified by social gossip, has the effect of aggression with no necessary individual will behind it: the more powerful and unpredictable for that reason. Diana defies social custom; at her dinner parties, men and women leave the table together, the men not allowed to linger over port. Yet all happens in her life as the social world wills. Gossip says her husband will die, lacking her care; he dies—from an accident, not disease, but precisely as foretold. Gossip deplores Percy Dacier's defection from the young woman who wishes to marry him; he returns to her. Gossip disapproves Diana's freedom and power; she gives them up. Nothing works out quite along conventional lines, yet everything resolves itself as convention would have it.

Finally the narrator himself, who has maintained an elevated, faintly acerbic tone, succumbs to that mysterious power. At the novel's beginning, he has declared the meretriciousness of sham decency and sentimentality because both reflect convention and oppose not only history's truth but fiction's greater truth. At the end, he reports, without apparent irony, Diana's friend Emma's musings about the heroine's marriage. "Thence it grew that one thought in her breast became a desire for such extension of days as would give her the blessedness to clasp in her lap—if those kind heavens would grant it—a child of the marriage of the two noblest of human souls, one the dearest; and so have proof at heart that her country and our earth are fruitful in the good, for a glowing future" (414). Sentimentalism with a vengeance—an utter capitulation to stereotypical social convention. The highly original plot, the individual tone of the fiction—both have yielded to the power of Mrs. Wathin and her kind. Meredith thus inadvertently emphasizes potencies his fiction set out imaginatively to oppose. The capitulation emphasizes the awesome energy of that voice often articulated in gossip, the voice of convention: a kind of collective superego, equally severe, equally difficult to evade.

Generalized gossip trivializes Diana, interpreting her actions reductively in order to condemn them. The narrator, at the end, glorifies rather than condemns. But to glorify only as a prospective mother this woman who has sought independence and power also reduces her. Gossip exemplifies the novel's central concern with formulation as determining meaning, and it epitomizes the way that "the world" diminishes those who defy it. Gossip contaminates history by judging it; it weakens individuals in the same way. Diana's meaning changes even for herself; for all her resistance, she succumbs to what people say.

Such internalization of gossip's judgments emphasizes once more the analogy between gossip and superego as punitive embodiments of authority. The imagined gossip of others derives partly from projected aggressive feelings of the self. The gossip of the self, apparently under the individual's conscious control, perhaps embodies equally unconscious wishes. So, at any rate, Diana's career allows one to speculate. Diana would not allow herself the vulgarity of a Mrs. Wathin, would not stoop to malicious speculation about her acquaintance. Yet her succession of popular novels and her culminating betrayal suggest her moral decline into a purveyor of gossip. Her form of aggression implies desire not to hurt but to dominate; gossip provides the means of fulfillment.

The structure of Meredith's novel, in other words, supports the view that gossip emanates from aggression. *Diana of the Crossways* explores the problematics of gossip as social and as verbal fact. It outlines gossip's work: aggression and defense, self-assertion and communal repression, social exchange. The novel charts the intricacies of gossip's social functioning; and always—even when the narrator exploits its appeal—the fiction implicitly deplores the activity. Gossip, as here represented and employed, reveals itself as superficial, hence false, and as complexly aggressive. It provides alternative affective experiences, depending on one's relation to it: self-righteous power or victimization. Serving always an end beyond itself—some form of control—it generates pleasure mainly from what it accomplishes. We learn from this novel what we already suspected: gossip is A Bad Thing. To be sure, we may find ourselves reminded also that it helps individuals function in society, that its reliance on human curiosity provides a resource for fiction-writers, and that its verbal possibilities bear some relation to those of aphorism at one end of a continuum, the novel at the other end. *Diana of the Crossways*, however, retreats from fully endorsing such potential positive values.

But other novelists have imagined gossip in other ways: as a form of dialogue, for example, full of feeling in itself. If one directs attention more closely to form as well as content—the way gossipers articulate their views, the psychological setting in which they operate—new issues emerge. Gossip as a verbal engagement depends upon and fosters intimacy. It exemplifies the power of one-to-one talk: a mode not of domination but of linkage.

Jane Austen in *Persuasion* provides an exchange clarifying this point. Anne Elliot, the protagonist, has befriended a poor, sick widow, Mrs. Smith, who demonstrates her human excellence by remaining cheerful in adversity. During one of Anne's visits, Mrs. Smith speaks of her sustaining contacts with Nurse Rooke, who brings reports from the outside world. "Call it gossip if you will; but when nurse Rooke has half an hour's leisure to bestow on me, she is sure to have something to relate that is entertaining and profitable, something that makes one know one's species better." Anne, full of sympathy for her friend, enthusiastically remarks that such women have the opportunity of seeing "all the conflicts and all the sacrifices that ennoble us most," the best of human nature. Mrs. Smith reacts doubtingly. "Here and there, human nature may be great in times of trial, but generally speaking it is its weakness and not its strength that appears in a sick chamber; it is selfishness and impatience rather than generosity and fortitude, that one hears of." Nurse Rooke's gossip provides pleasure, in other words, by its recitals of base rather than noble manifestations.[8]

A psychoanalyst friend of mine defines gossip as *healing talk*. The exchange from *Persuasion* exemplifies Austen's bracing realism in its awareness of the satisfaction involved in dwelling on the worst aspects of human nature, but it also suggests the sustaining and enlivening force of conversation focused on "emotional speculation": using details of someone else's experience to stimulate expression of responses and beliefs, to affirm and strengthen alliance. Healing comes from sharing.

Indeed, in the most common paradigm of gossip—two people talking about a third—aggression becomes in effect a function of sharing. The gossiping pair establish their alliance at the expense of another, displacing hostility onto the absent third. Reduced to means rather than ends, aggression serves alliance.

This statement suggests a way of reversing Freud's argument about jokes. Freud notes but hardly investigates joking's mutuality; the mutuality of gossip has more far-reaching implications. More than joke-telling, gossiping implies confidentiality. Secrets supply its substance, the level of secrecy involved often measuring the participants' intimacy. Gossipers confide not only information but, more importantly, judgments. The atmosphere of intimacy allows the freedom to venture exploratory judgments and to exchange risky information.

Let me offer another text. It comes from fiction, from Muriel Spark's *The Prime of Miss Jean Brodie,* but for the moment I will consider it not as part of a novelistic action but as an example of a familiar kind of human interchange. The speakers are eleven-year-old girls, close friends.

> "Do you think Miss Brodie ever had sexual intercourse with Hugh?" said Jenny.
> "She would have had a baby, wouldn't she?"
> "I don't know."
> "I don't think they did anything like that," said Sandy. "Their love was above all that."
> "Miss Brodie said they clung to each other with passionate abandon on his last leave."
> "I don't think they took their clothes off, though," Sandy said. "Do you?"
> "No. I can't see it," said Jenny.
> "I wouldn't like to have sexual intercourse," Sandy said.
> "Neither would I. I'm going to marry a pure person."
> "Have a toffee."[9]

Depending on the kind and level of interpretation one prefers, one could ignore the comedy and make a good deal of the substance of this exchange. Clearly it derives from the sexual anxiety of pre-pubescent girls. It depends on the girls' complex relationship to their teacher; it expresses aggression as well as affection and dependency toward Miss Brodie. It also conveys the trust between the speakers: they can take risks with one another.

Each of these observations lends itself to elaboration, but none of them defines the spirit of the interchange. Aggression and voyeurism emerge, but neither anger nor lubriciousness characterizes the tone. Perhaps this is "innocent" gossip, the counterpart of Freud's innocent joking. It exemplifies a kind of exchange that takes place, at more sophisticated levels, between adults as well.

In the *Miss Jean Brodie* encounter, the atmosphere which, from one point of view, disguises the gossipers' real concerns also reveals an important truth of feeling: not aggression but playfulness—we return to Huizinga's description. This kind of play, according to D. W. Winnicott, makes culture; it enables discovery. Contemplating Roger Abrahams' characterization of West Indian gossip and its conceivable connections to the "idle talk" of England and North America raises the further possibility of contradicting the implications of *Diana of the Crossways*. The set of associations Abrahams establishes—the energetic, licentious, lying—suggests that, far from supporting convention, gossip exercises subversive force.

And not only in the West Indies. The little girls discussing sex come out unequivocally in favor of "purity." They declare their own disinclination to experiment; they implicitly condemn the activity of anyone so crude as to undress in the presence of a member of the opposite sex. Older girls, who knew more about what they discussed, might deplore the misconduct of a peer or an elder indiscreet enough to betray her sexual indulgence. Imagine the gossipers older still; we can imagine them condemning the younger generation for sexual looseness—condemning Diana for failures of discretion. Gossip reinforces established mores.

Yet to take the conversation of Sandy and Jenny as a series of statements in favor of purity would miss the point. As they deny Miss Brodie's misbehavior ("I don't think they took their clothes off"), they vividly imagine it; as they deny their own interest in sexual intercourse, they test that interest. Indeed, the scene's comedy depends on the disjunction of apparent and latent content. By questioning stories they hear, relating them to their own actual and vicarious experience, the little girls establish a subversive context. Their anti-sexual conformity only faintly obscures the truth of their feelings. "I'm going to marry a pure person" neither describes what Jenny will do nor what she intends. She uses the verbal form of commitment to protect her internal space of experimentation. Moreover, the formulae of interrogation— "Do you think?" "wouldn't she?"—establish an air of intellectual inquiry which can mask from the participants their erotic involvement with one another. As they declare their opposition to heterosexual engagement, they foster the homosexual attachment that allows their freedom of speculation. The daring of their mutual wondering is itself a form of sexual experimentation: the form appropriate for eleven-year-olds.

The experimental quality of gossip for grown-ups as well inheres more in its form of inquiring exchange than in its content of often dogmatic-sounding judgment. To perceive that form demands concentration on the specific verbal exchange, on utterance and response. Dyadic gossip, I would hypothesize, depends as much on the desire for alliance and for moral exploration as on open or hidden purposes of aggression. More helpful than Freud for a tentative understanding of what actually happens when two persons talk intimately about others are Winnicott, with his discussion of play and culture, and Erik Erikson, writing about play and ritual.

By now, many theorists have argued for play as serious occupation. Its seriousness, however, often disguises itself. Professed purposes of adult play rarely reflect actual ones. For this reason among others, play offers a revealing model for gossip. The little girls might have used their dolls to convey the same preoccupations that emerge through their wonderings about Miss Brodie's sex life. Those of us who presumably know more about sex also have our wonderings; gossip provides indirect means to express and perhaps to gratify them. Why the indirection, why not talk about oneself instead of other people? Gossip makes fuller investigation possible, partly through its aspect of ritualization; and in the same way, it may facilitate a saving escape from self-absorption.

Erikson, associating play and ritual, lists several characteristics of ritualization. He understands it as involving formalized, repeated acts of "recognition." "All such meetings at their best," he writes, "embody seeming paradoxes; they are *playful* and yet *formalized*; quite *familiar* through repetition, they yet renew the *surprise* of recognition. And while the ethologists will tell us that ritualization in the animal world must, above all, be *unambiguous* sets of signals which avoid the arousal of conflicting instinctive patterns, we suspect that in man the overcoming of *ambivalence* (as well as of ambiguity) is one of the prime functions of ritualization."[10] Anyone who has ever gossiped (in the serious sense which interests me most) will recognize these hallmarks of the experience. Gossip follows its own familiar forms and rhythms, combining surprise over content with recognition of formal pattern, and it deals with the stuff of ambivalence. As a personal interchange, it partakes of the pleasure and the enlightenment of play.

"Play," Winnicott writes, "*is in fact neither a matter of inner psychic reality nor a matter of external reality.*" It takes place somewhere else, in a kind of space between, belonging in origin to the infant's transition from total identification with the mother to full participation in a world outside. "I have located this important area of *experience* in the potential space between the individual and the environment, that which initially both joins and separates the baby and the mother when the mother's love, displayed in human reliability, does in fact give the baby a sense of trust, or of confidence in the environmental factor."[11] If gossip belongs to the genre of play, it harks back to—perhaps embodies an attempt to recapture—the primal experience of intimacy and trust. From this point of view, its subject matter, however trivial or malicious, facilitates not aggression or voyeurism but human association.

The opening and closing pages of Doris Lessing's *The Golden Notebook* provide rare documentation of what this special kind of human association sounds like. Molly and Anna, unmarried forty-year-old women, meet for conversation. "Well, what's the gossip?" Molly inquires, just as the phone rings to interrupt them. They discuss Molly's ex-husband and his current wife. "Odd, isn't it?" Molly comments, and the narrator observes, "This *odd, isn't it?* was the characteristic note of the intimate conversation they designated gossip."[12] Such a remark exemplifies the assumed identity of values, the freedom to wonder, the ease that make such talk valuable to the participants. Lessing offers a fairly extended sample of the conversation—which ends, inevitably, when a third person arrives, a man. Taken in isolation, the talk strikes an appealing note of openness. But it introduces a novel in which such conversation, felt as an important psychic resource by the women who engage in it, cannot help them. Realities of the larger world impinge; the possibilities of free talk diminish as each woman makes her necessary compromises. The value of gossip inheres in its small sphere of intimacy. Enlarged perspective makes it hard to keep such value in view. Lessing demonstrates the difficulty of affirming playfulness in a universe of pain.

The Prime of Miss Jean Brodie, like *Diana of the Crossways* and *The Golden Notebook*, creates a fictional structure predicated on interchanges and tensions between personal and public politics. In *The Golden Notebook*, the large world contaminates and finally diminishes the small. *The Prime of Miss Jean Brodie* depicts a more ambiguous relationship, in which large domain and small intricately reflect and modulate one another. It provides not only exemplary vignettes of gossip but a plot predicated on gossip's positive and negative possibilities. For the fiction's ironic narrator, gossip means relationship; but relationship can assume malignant as well as benign forms. Ties between pairs of females energize the action. Miss Brodie seeks to establish powerful individual connections with several of her group; her links with each girl depend on her talking with one at a time about other girls (as well as about members of the school's faculty). The girls counteract Miss Brodie's force by forming alliances between themselves, and by talking about Miss Brodie. The substance of their talk, and, in a superficial sense, of the novel, includes little besides the trivial and the personal; yet the final revelation depends on an equation between Miss Brodie's confined mode of "fascism" and what Hitler and Mussolini are up to. The private and the public thus reveal themselves as a continuum.

Miss Brodie's girls know about "subjects irrelevant to the authorised curriculum, as the headmistress said, and useless to the school as a school. These girls were discovered to have heard of the Buchmanites and Mussolini, the Italian Renaissance painters, the advantages to the skin of cleansing cream and witchhazel over honest soap and water, and the word 'menarche'; the interior decoration of the London house of the author of *Winnie the Pooh* had been described to them, as had the love lives of Charlotte Brontë and of Miss Brodie herself" (8). Politics, art, sex, beauty hints—and gossip: all share a place in Miss Brodie's mind. But her pedagogical gift depends partly on her capacity to convert official information to gossip. Who is the greatest Italian painter? Leonardo, someone answers. Miss Brodie responds, "That is incorrect. The answer is Giotto, he is my favourite" (14). Thus, the teacher's mind becomes the measure of all things, and the little girls can gossip about her preference in painters as about the varying size of her bosom and her curious relation to male teachers; only the personal matters.

Miss Brodie's most powerful mode of gossip is the prophetic. "Sandy will make an excellent Secret Service agent, a great spy. . . . Rose will be a great lover. She is above the common moral code, it does not apply to her" (139). Her technique calls attention to the close association between gossip and story. Her talk about the girls partakes of myth-making, as does her talk about herself. Sandy comes more and more fully to understand Miss Brodie's gossip as power. Her talk takes possession of others; her sending the disturbed girl Joyce Emily to die for Franco reveals a danger implicit in all her verbal manipulations.

Sandy, grown-up, a nun, writes a book called *The Transfiguration of the Commonplace*. The novel that contains her could sustain the same title, though Sandy's book concerns spiritual change, whereas the transfigurations of *The Prime of Miss Jean Brodie* belong to the secular world. But the talk that forms the substance of fiction, the talk of the girls among themselves and of the students, individually and collectively, with Miss Brodie, dwells on and enlarges the commonplace. By making and telling stories about people, Miss Brodie wields power; and by only hinting a story about Miss Brodie, Sandy defeats her.

The novel touches also on the other, external, view of gossip as shaper of reputations, preserver of convention, the view which dominates *Diana of the Crossways*. The reputations of the Brodie set form their schoolday destinies; the reputation of Miss Brodie prepares for, although it does not precipitate, her downfall. When the housekeeper reports finding Miss Brodie's nightgown under a man's pillow, the faculty talk about the event and its perpetrator. But this outside view of gossip has far less importance than gossip as a direct, personal instrument of intimacy and power, rich alike in sinister and comforting possibility. Gossip's effects, however, matter less than its existence. The dramatic events of the novel reveal themselves in a series of asides which emphasize the relative insignificance of event in comparison to the dynamics of relationship. Through the intimate talk that fuels her relationships, Sandy (the only character whose mind we enter) grows; though her growth has not altogether attractive results, such development appears preferable to the prolonged childishness implicitly characteristic of those with more conventional educations. Acknowledging gossip's possible destructiveness, the novel yet insists on its educational function.

Both *The Golden Notebook* and *The Prime of Miss Jean Brodie* convey double views of gossip. It comforts, Lessing's novel suggests, but cannot finally sustain; it furthers moral and psychological investigation, says Spark's fiction, but creates its own betrayals. Relatively few texts illustrate gossip's fruitful intimacy: as though it were a secret, shared only by initiates. Those who tell the secret also disguise it. Or maybe they express their own ambivalence. The official fear and disapproval of gossip perhaps respond not only to gossip's aggression but also to its intimacy. Imagining gossip as an activity of the self can stimulate dread of its regressive appeal to closeness; imagining it as the action of others may rouse fear of the exclusion implicit in other people's intimacy. From both points of view—inside and outside—one may fear the lure of complicity in malice. Although gossip serves useful purposes for the ego—as diverse examples from fiction testify—it also provides cause for anxiety, by its nature as well as by its effects.

Gossip's freedom, the freedom of creative play, makes room for the socially and the psychically impermissible. But both its aggressive and its intimate aspects create problems. Play with language is play with power; the possibilities exemplified in *Diana of the Crossways* also operate in the real world. Whether or not gossip actually does harm, it unleashes potentially explosive forces. Gossipers may know the guilt of toying with such forces, the guilt of possessing great resources for aggression. Or they may experience the guilt of intimacy: two consciousnesses united by using happenings from other people's lives to engender the pleasure of shared response, jointly achieved judgment.

Gossip feels good: a form of closeness, a mode of power. And gossip feels bad: devious and treacherous power, potentially threatening attachment. In literature and in life, it signifies ambivalence. The metaphor of play, in its multiple senses, summarizes gossip's complexities of emotional meaning. Play as dramatic performance: a shadow-theater in which absent actors play their parts at the behest of talkers who direct or even dramatize the production. Play as musical performance: theme and variation, rhythms of interchange, patterns of improvisation. Play as game: partnership in the service of competition, competition in the service of partnership. As recreation: an alternative to the utilitarian, free, "licentious," responsible to no pre-ordained program. As parody or imitation of work: subversive commentary on or faithful support of established mores, like the child's "playing house," which may suddenly expose bourgeois convention from the underside even as the player tries to act just like Daddy (does Daddy *really* do nothing but drink martinis when he gets home?). Like other forms of play, gossip expresses both aggression and intimacy, sometimes simultaneously, sometimes in bewildering shifts. Its evocations in imaginative literature convey the rich range of its meanings and emotions.

4

Borderlands

Just as gossip inhabits the borderlands of socially sanctioned oral discourse, literary species difficult to assess in orthodox critical terms survive on the edges of what our culture agrees to call "literature." Biography, autobiography, published letters and diaries attract wide readership but rarely belong to any generally accepted canon. Only recently has a critic attempted to articulate aesthetic criteria for the eighteenth-century familiar letter; the larger question of appropriate literary standards for published letters of any period has not yet been confronted.[1] Collections of letters—written for one kind of audience, pre-empted by another—offer themselves readily for psychological analysis, but elude literary exegesis. More problematic still is the status of popular journalism. A work first published in *The New Yorker* or *Atlantic* and subsequently expanded into a book may receive serious critical attention. But what about "The Talk of the Town," brief narrative or commentary printed each week at the front of *The New Yorker?* If that be allowed appropriate substance for literary analysis, what of the ephemera in gossip magazines and the tabloid press? Where do we draw the line—and what line, exactly, do we draw?

I cannot hope entirely to resolve these perplexing problems, but the analogy between gossip and the more dubious literary genres provides a useful vantage point from which to contemplate what it means to publish private letters and to read them in published form. I start somewhat circuitously, with the twentieth century and *People* magazine; then I shall return to the eighteenth century—another great age of gossip—and the letters of Lady

Mary Wortley Montagu and Horace Walpole, concluding with brief consideration of the published twentieth-century letters of E. B. White.

Two randomly chosen issues of *People*, fourteen months apart (September 14, 1981; November 15, 1982), display many common elements. Their covers reflect rather different notions of "news": one depicts Princess Grace's sorrowing survivors, the other shows the actor Dudley Moore, 1981 star of *Arthur*, with "sexy Susan Anton." (The inside text focuses on the discrepancy in height between the two, the woman being ten inches taller than her lover, but the cover pose makes the man loom over his partner.) Inside, both issues purport to offer information about movies, sports, television, fashion, national and international affairs.

The *People* style relies heavily on denial. "The men of E-Ring [in the Pentagon] categorically deny that the Black Aces were sent up to pick a fight." "She angrily denies a rumor that her stepfather at first refused . . . " "His family denies reports that he carried a steel plate in his skull." The magazine thus avoids responsibility for its suggestions. Similarly, it employs ambiguous syntax and photographs to hint more than it states. More relevant to my concerns than these familiar techniques of innuendo is the subject matter they dubiously illuminate. The overwhelming mass of material in *People* involves three themes: sex, violence, and money.

Violence comes in two varieties: sanctioned aggression (dogfight over Libya, Vietnam veteran fights his toughest battles as a civilian, Tommy Hearns vows he'll pummel Sugar Ray Leonard, wounded vet remembers why he went, boxer Alexis Arguello stalks . . .) and its more private equivalents (someone killed town bully, a gun-toting nun on Broadway). No comparable dichotomy presents itself for the other two subjects: sex and money inhabit an indeterminate realm, neither public nor private, or mysteriously both at once. "Indians, feminists and Atari are on the warpath over an X-rated video game" (all three themes operative here). Naked General Custer, in the game at issue, throws himself on a bound Indian maiden to rape her repeatedly or, by another interpretation, to create "a fun sequence where the woman is enjoying a sexual act willingly." Public or private? People play the game, and entertain the fantasies it generates, in home living rooms. Other people picket in public protest; Atari has filed a public lawsuit against the company making X-rated cartridges for playing on Atari units. Or does everything really happen only in the pages of *People*? "Caroline Reed, 18, finds her actor-uncle Oliver [43 years old, and bulky] surprisingly agile in a pas de deux." Caroline is visiting her uncle on the isle of Guernsey, where he lives with his "17-year-old love." The photograph of uncle and niece manifestly substitutes for that of uncle and youthful girlfriend; Oliver Reed's asserted surprising agility—he looks comically *un*-agile in the picture —metonymizes deftness at more hidden forms of activity, the photograph's true subject. The unmentionable is mentioned, the unphotographable photographed, by skillful deflection. *Nothing* remains really private.

As for money: a story labeled in the table of contents "Ex-Traffic cop Steve Winwood is cultivating rock as a cash crop" begins, "Standing in the doorway of his 17th-century manor house, Steve Winwood looks every inch the gentleman farmer." From another article: "He is unembarrassed by the family windfall, which can be hauled to the bank in any one of three jets, two Rolls-Royces and two Mercedeses." And another: "This year she stands to earn $100,000. 'Carmen is a long-distance runner,' explains Francesco Scavullo. . . . 'She is poetic—a Madonna.' " A sexy $100,000-a-year Madonna: just right for *People*. The subject of how much money people have, traditionally almost as absolute a conversational tabu as what they do in bed, becomes a journalistic staple.

People epitomizes gossip's journalistic mode at its most successful, by no means at its most tasteless. One can find stories similar to those to which I have alluded in virtually any newspaper, in many magazines, on television; and more damaging innuendo, cruder allusion, obvious and deliberate falsification. Journalistic gossip, making public what it insists is private, promulgates the illusion of being in the know, declares the universal comprehensibility of other people's lives. It both imitates and debases social functions of oral gossip. Often it usurps the place of real news, as information about the personal lives of people involved in important events substitutes for attempts to comprehend the events themselves. Such gossip, one must conclude, makes money—so much money that the baser tabloids can afford to lose well-publicized lawsuits and to pay damages to some of those they slander. It makes money, and often it makes money its subject.

Explanations for the popularity of this public form of gossip come fluently to mind. Demanding only automatic and superficial emotional response, an item about a five-foot-two man and his six-foot inamorata invites a slightly comic, slightly prurient reaction. News of larger matters becomes equally digestible: Israel's troubles on the West Bank or the woes of Social Security "personalized" (that is to say, often connected with sex and/or money as problems of individuals) and packaged for two- or three-page presentation. The reader can feel at once envious of and superior to the rich and famous: *they* may be rich and famous, *s/he* knows all about them. Reading, one gains a temporary conviction of possessing inside knowledge: that pleasure associated with gossip in all its forms. *People* traffics in what people represent.

The glamorous movie star, the frightening town bully, the rich rock singer: all inhabit pre-existent categories, comforting because known. They evoke and support a familiar scheme of things. That singer who gets rich buys a Mercedes or a manor house or beautiful women, just as the reader might expect. Although printed gossip of this sort thrives on surprises, its shock value matters less than its clichéd structure. Such gossip exists because it sells; it sells brief illusions of intimacy and power. It thus corresponds rather precisely to prostitution.

The "gossip" published in *People* (or, for that matter, in the New York *Post*) bears little obvious connection to the kind of gossip that concerns me most, the kind that thrives on genuine intimacy, and not much manifest analogy to the novel. In subject and tone, *People's* discourse somewhat resembles the familiar cocktail-party variety of gossip, but its commercialization divides it from that as well. If gossip possesses its own economics, its own system of exchange, these publications parody it. They reduce and parody as well gossip's aesthetics—its illusion of self-containment—and call into question any claims for gossip's morality; and the "knowledge" they promulgate is dubious indeed. Such texts cast lurid light on gossip as a phenomenon. I would find it in many ways more convenient for my argument simply to ignore *People* and its shady relatives.

On the other hand, the light shed by such publications exposes the importance of gossip's characteristic obsessive focus on a few themes and calls attention to the fact that gossip, at least in debased form, sells. Violence figures little in the other variety of published gossip that I shall consider shortly, but sex and money appear to matter at least as much to "private" writers—for example, those believing themselves to address an extremely limited audience: letter-writers—as to the audience for their "public" counterparts. Both sex and money, in modern Western society, represent particularly obvious forms of power. "Sexuality," Michel Foucault writes, "is tied to recent devices of power; . . . it has been linked from the outset with . . . [the body's] exploitation as an object of knowledge and an element in relations of power."[2] As for money, its function as a means of control hardly needs substantiation. Gossip, dwelling on both crucial devices for mastery, deals with what matters.

Gossip, however, constitutes not only a discourse about power but in itself a code of power. In commercialized form, dramatizing and enlarging and damaging reputations, it shapes images with dollars-and-cents value for rock stars and politicians and novelists and restaurateurs. People read the *National Enquirer* and the New York *Post* and *People* to learn how to feel about public figures whose fates they indirectly determine; the periodicals control popular fantasies through anecdote and innuendo. As I have already hinted, fundamental power inheres in the act of talking or writing about the personal. Such eighteenth-century novelists as Fielding and Sterne through their narrative personae called attention to the godlike power over characters exercised by fiction-makers, free to dispose of imagined lives. The gossiper has rather more responsibility to fact. Yet gossip of voice and print through allegation and judgment also handles lives, lives partly imagined though belonging to actual people. Readers of *People*, listeners to talk shows seek the vicarious experience of control through dwelling on what they like to fancy is somehow privileged information.

The salability of gossip extends to its "private" forms, when those forms are transcribed. The commercial viability of private letters, like that of gossip columns, became manifest in the eighteenth century, when Pope manipulated the publication of his own correspondence (carefully reworked), Boswell as a young man outraged his father and gratified his own need for notoriety by publishing letters between himself and a contemporary, Lady Mary Wortley Montagu's letters from Turkey appeared in print promptly after her death. Lady Mary's correspondence could claim the excitement of describing exotic places, Pope counted on his contemporaries' fascination with his literary persona, but Boswell in his narcissism simply assumed the intrinsic interest of what he and his friend said to one another. In our own time, a boundless audience, scholarly and popular, appears to exist for ever more recovered intimacies. Editions of letters from the distant and recent past proliferate; occasionally a living person publishes private letters with no claim for their public importance but with apparent faith—supported by commercial publishers—in their interest for other people.

The eighteenth-century flurry of published letters coincides chronologically with a proliferation of secular autobiography and with philosophic preoccupation about questions of identity. Lawrence Stone has argued for a shift in the nature of affective life in eighteenth-century England. One can with more certainty observe a change in conventions for expressing feelings—and for publicizing them. Even autobiographies as reticent as Edward Gibbon's, from very late in the century, convey latent valuation of personal emotive response. "I sighed as a lover, I obeyed as a son": no comment about the son's feelings, only a hint of the lover's—yet the famous sentence's energy depends on the emotion implicit in the tension between the verbs.

Whatever people of the period believed about the self and its feelings, one truth is manifest: the feeling self could now become a product. Letters differ from autobiographies partly in exerting less continuous control over the construction of a life-myth. Written for particular readers, they reveal a version of the self in relationship. Even letters carefully edited by their authors (like Pope's, and Lady Mary's Turkish letters) expose those authors in successive fragments, glimpse after glimpse, encouraging the reader's fantasy that real revelation may take place, that letters provide evidence of authentic personality. Yet letters transmit more than personality—as *People* does.

What more, exactly? One may claim, with some justification, that such letters as Boswell's or Lord Chesterfield's or George Eliot's or E. B. White's (the authors' names suggest the range of tone and reference implicit in the letter as genre) supply valuable material for the social historian. The distaste for history expressed by Catherine Morland, heroine of *Northanger Abbey*, hints the alternative kind of data letter-writers may supply—the kind that traditional historians have typically ignored. "I read it a little as a duty," Catherine says, of history, "but it tells me nothing that does not either vex or weary me. The quarrels of popes and kings, with wars or pestilences, in every page; the men all so good for nothing, and hardly any women at all— it is very tiresome."[3] Private letters include women and reduce wars and pestilence to manageable proportions. They may elucidate customs of visiting and child-rearing, the underside of politics, the assumptions governing public conduct. Yet their fundamental power derives from another sort of knowledge: a kind related to that gossip generates.

The obvious fact that letters often use gossip about others as raw material interests me less than the more subtle, more perplexing, more rewarding parallels between letters and gossip that emerge in epistolary uses of relationship and presentation of the self. Self and relationship change aspect when letters appear in print. Walter Benjamin has reflected on the altered aspect of art in an age of mechanical reproduction. Given easy reproduction, he points out, the art work no longer belongs in the same sense to its own time and place. It loses its "aura," its uniqueness, as versions of it proliferate.[4] The letters of Lady Mary Wortley Montagu or Horace Walpole, unlike the paintings of Rembrandt or Gauguin, appeal not to a mass audience but to a limited and on the whole academic readership. Nonetheless, once offered to anyone who happens to pick up the book, they lose what defined them in the first place: their existence as direct communications from one unique sensibility to another. As the will of her press agent or herself or the editors of *People* (or of all three) turns Elizabeth Taylor into a representation of the glamorous actress, so editorial or authorial purpose transforms into a character in a book, objectified in print, the Lady Mary who tentatively, with incomplete knowledge, wrote letters describing her life-in-process.

Rembrandt survives his reproductions; Aristotle contemplates the bust of Homer on the walls of the Metropolitan with mysterious power although his image also inhabited the pages of *Life* and of many a schoolbook. Lady Mary transcends her own objectification—not in spite of but because of the printing of her letters. The change that takes place when letters appear in print implies not only loss. The dynamics of that change clarify yet more fully the gratifications we seek in gossip; conversely, thinking about gossip provides an entry point into the literary problem of letters. And Lady Mary offers a useful case history.

In 1710, at the age of twenty-one, Lady Mary Pierrepont wrote a female confidante about a recent marriage, in an account worth quoting at length:

> Next to the great ball, what makes the most noise is the marriage of an old Maid that lives in this street, without a portion To a Man of £7,000 per Annum and they say £40,000 in ready money. Her Equipage and Liverys outshine any body's in Town. He has presented her with £3,000 in Jewells and never was man more smitten with these Charms, that had lain invisible this forty year. But with all this Glory, never Bride had fewer Envyers; the dear Beast of a Man is so filthy, frightful, odious and detestable I would turn away such a footman for fear of spoiling my Dinner while he waited at Table. They was marry'd friday and came to church en Parade Sunday. I happen'd to sit in the pue with them and had the honnour of seeing Mrs. Bride fall fast asleep in the middle of the Sermon and snore very comfortably, which made several women in the Church think the bridegroom not quite so ugly as they did before. Envious people say 'twas all counterfeited to oblige him, but I believe that's scandal, for she's so devout, I dare swear nothing but downright necessity could make her miss one Word of the Sermon. . . . I believe I have given you too much of this Couple, but they are not to be comprehended in few words.[5]

Six weeks later, she writes her first letter to Edward Wortley Montagu, whom she would marry ("Tis the first [letter] I ever writ to one of your sex and shall be the last. You must never expect another"). In it, she complains about Steele's mistaken notions of her sex, protests her own undying faithfulness ("when I say I love, it is for ever"), and insists that "Was I to chuse of £2,000 a year or twenty thousand, the first would be my choice. There is something of an unavoidable embarras in makeing what is calld a great figure in the world, [that] takes off from the happynesse of Life" ([28 March 1710], 1.25, 24). Both letters concern sex and money, with different forms

of disguise. Both provide written equivalents of gossip, in spite of the fact
that in the second instance Lady Mary's subject is herself.

In making this assertion, I am trying to suggest the curious relation of
writer to reader in a published letter. The letter to Frances Hewet straight-
forwardly presents itself as gossip, the staple of the women's epistolary relationship. Although Lady Mary intermittently protects herself by irony,
poignant seriousness of concern underlies surface comedy. The mystery of
sexual feeling controls the lines. An unattractive rich man and an old maid
marry. But the man apparently sees something in the woman that others
have failed to see; and the woman appears to have found abundant sexual
gratification from her unlikely spouse. Or does she merely pretend? The
privacy of the marriage bed eludes the observation of a churchful of watchers—
all interested, by Lady Mary's interpretation, in the same question: Is the
bride expressing or merely imitating sexual exhaustion?

Given its lack of immediate modification and response, written gossip
can never correspond precisely to the oral form it in some respects mimics.
Yet the letter from one woman to another brims with awareness of an
interlocutor. Lady Mary's tone and vocabulary ("dear Beast of a Man") suggest
a history of verbal exchange. Free from fear of being misunderstood, she
can hint her own anxiety: Will anyone find *me* attractive? Will I too fall in
love only after forty years of maidenhood, or never? Will I ever understand
the secrets this couple embodies? Although the narrative contains no syntactical questions, it reflects an investigatory spirit. Most of my hypotheses
about oral gossip would apply as accurately to this written counterpart. Here
too we find a strong note of aggression—toward bride and bridegroom, comically evoked, and toward envious onlookers who interpret what they see so
as to preserve their own comfort. The impulse toward verbal play clearly
shapes the story, in total form and in details. A sense of assumed intimacy
breathes from every line: only that makes possible this kind of sharing. Indeed,
the atmosphere and purpose of the implicit exchange almost precisely duplicate—with differences appropriate to the participants' differences in age—
the tone and intent of the dialogue of eleven-year-old girls from *The Prime
of Miss Jean Brodie* quoted in the last chapter—the one in which the children
speculate about whether Miss Brodie had sexual intercourse with Hugh.
Lady Mary's letter and the eleven-year-olds' conversation demonstrate the
same concern with the erotic (the older women add the financial) and the
same implicit inquiry into mysteries felt to be of pressing personal importance.
The letter, like the talk, serves purposes of alliance and of investigation.

Unlike the participants in the *Miss Jean Brodie* conversation, the pair
evoked by Lady Mary's letter lived once in an actual social world, although

their reality for us, twentieth-century readers, depends as completely as that of fictional characters on words on a page. One can hypothesize but never know Frances Hewet's response to receiving Lady Mary's account. What of our reaction as readers? To some extent, our situation duplicates that of the original recipient. We too read the story for the first time, we smile over the evoked scene and react to the emotional weight of Lady Mary's speculations as Mrs. Hewet may have done. But we have pre-empted the narrative intended for Mrs. Hewet, and the possibility of that pre-emption creates a new transaction.

Twenty-one-year-old Lady Mary did not consciously write for posterity when she described a neighborhood event for her friend. Unanticipated, undesired, we look over Mrs. Hewet's shoulder, responding not to the writer's wishes but to those of her excellent twentieth-century editor. And we read in a new context, not only the special circumstance of the late twentieth century but the special literary setting of Lady Mary's subsequent letters, more than fifty years of them. As an early letter in a lengthy existing series, the narrative of bride and bridegroom lends itself to different kinds of interpretation from that available to its original reader. Poised at the brink of her disastrous romance, about to embark on the course leading to her long, ungratifying marriage, Lady Mary acquires retrospective poignance. Although we do not know all that she knows, about herself or about what she has experienced, we yet from one point of view know far more about her than she can know about herself. She has been "placed," her words literally located in a book, her significance posited by the fact of her letters' collection. We are invited—by the three-volume format, the imprimatur of a distinguished university press, the apparatus of textual data and annotation—to take her seriously. Yet our relation to the Lady Mary evoked by her words on the page partakes of the gossip's delight in secret knowledge and of gossip's titillation.

To suggest an equivalence between these published letters and gossip implies no denigration. At the simplest level, that equivalence implies only that the reader who intrudes into the original intimacy of two, enlarging dyad to triad, duplicates the first reader's presumable pleasure in the malicious, comic, detailed, personal, evocative account of an unmomentous human event: the pleasure of gossip. But the analogy to gossip also clarifies some implications of publication in the case of private letters. To offer such letters for public readership involves no equivalent reductiveness to that of *People*. On the contrary, the satisfaction of the literary experience they supply comes partly from their evocation of genuine human complexity, like that achieved in the best kind of intimate gossip. Almost regardless of their specific subject matter, though, personal letters, published, function for the reader in ways analogous to *People*'s, as moral equivalents for gossip. We read them out of interest in their writer, they enable speculation about that writer. Thrust into exciting intimacy with someone we do not know, we savor secrets never intended for us, allowed to encounter aspects of another's experience not ordinarily divulged. Lady Mary serves both as partner in dialogue—the voice of the story-teller—and as subject of her own story, topic of gossip. The interposition of the third person, the editor or compiler, who transforms letters into something for public consumption, changes their meaning as documents.

The point becomes clearer in relation to the letters of Wortley's courtship. Even reading them with no knowledge of what happens later, one may sense emotional quicksand. Ardent, intelligent, self-willed, Lady Mary had met Wortley through his sister, Anne, with whom she had long corresponded. (The first letter in the collection of her correspondence, written perhaps at the age of seventeen, is addressed to Anne.) Her notes to Anne begin tentatively to reveal increasing interest in the brother; Anne encourages the romance by showing Lady Mary's letters to Wortley and by chiding her correspondent for displays of interest in other men. Finally the lovers address one another, from the beginning with mutual suspicion and mutual efforts at reassurance. Each worries about the authenticity of the other's love. Wortley expresses his anxiety with more specificity and detail. He fears that his beloved will prove unfaithful, that she will be unable to survive outside the world of high society, that she will want more money than he has. Her letters increasingly consist of protestations: she doesn't care where she lives, she will remain faithful to death, money matters not at all to her. Meanwhile, her correspondence with her closest female confidante, Philippa Mundy (by this time, 1711, Anne Wortley has died), reveals her fears about remaining unmarried. The two adopt a private vocabulary: *hell* designates an unhappy marriage; *paradise*, the man or marriage of one's choice; *limbo*, the average man and marriage. "I have a Mortal Aversion," Lady Mary writes, "to be an old Maid, and a decaid Oak before my Window, leavelesse, half rotten, and shaking its wither'd Top, puts me in Mind every morning of an Antiquated Virgin, Bald, with Rotten teeth, and shaking of the Palsie. Since therefore Hell must be, why not now?" (12 December [1711]; 1.112).

Hell comes closer. By April 1712, Lady Mary's father has engaged her, without her consent, to Clotworthy Skeffington, son and heir of an Irish peer. She tells Philippa Mundy that her reflections on male inconstancy derive from no personal experience. "I should be happyer than I am if I had not too much reason to think too well of one of them. I see no probable prospect of my ever entering Charming Paradice, but since I cannot convince him of the Necessity of what I do, I rack my selfe in giving him pain" ([April 1712]; 1.121). The correspondence with Wortley heats up, money and sex constant issues: he fears she will cuckold him, both worry over financial arrangements. Now that her father has committed himself to her marriage with another man, they can hope for no financial settlement from him. Lady Mary warns her lover not to expect her father's change of mind: he will never provide money for a marriage of which he disapproves. If they marry, she will be totally dependent on her husband for support. Wortley hesitates. He doesn't care about her money, the lover claims, although he had strongly resisted her father's suggestions about the kind of financial commitment a would-be husband should make. But he cannot credit her capacity for fidelity. Finally they agree to elope, after Lady Mary's father has discovered their correspondence, confined her closely, and taken her to the country—where Wortley follows her. "I shall go to meet you," he declares, "with more joy than I shoud to take possession of Riches, Honour or Power; nay, than I shoud to meet you if you brought 'em along with you because I coud not so well convince you how much I value you" ([11 August 1712]; 1.152).

The story, as Lady Mary would subsequently observe, bears strong re-semblances to that of Samuel Richardson's *Clarissa* (1747–8), although its ending achieved no such tragic dignity as the fictional version. The riches and power that Wortley declared irrelevant remained dominant issues. Lady Mary aspired to true alliance; Wortley asserted dominance. He refused to write his wife when they were apart, he remained away unnecessarily long. Wortley owned coal mines; they made him rich. His wealth and his avarice became part of eighteenth-century satiric mythology. Lady Mary, having married without parental approval, lacked financial protection—the protec-tion her father would have arranged in a marriage settlement. In her middle forties, she fell passionately in love with a much younger Italian man, who scorned her. She moved to Italy herself and lived the rest of her long life in isolation. When Wortley came to the Continent, he neglected to visit her. Deprived of riches, power, and love, she gratified herself by small domestic concerns and by intimate correspondence. Her son bitterly disappointed both her and his father; her daughter married Lord Bute, who became Prime Minister.

All this, of course, belonged to the distant future as the two fenced and parried in pre-marital correspondence. But the subsequent facts participate in the same "plot" as the early romance, and that romance's power over the reader's imagination reiterates the inherent power of narrative. Which brings us back to gossip: narratives about others, transmitted in intimate context,

made the object of interpretation. In the letters between Lady Mary and
Wortley, both participants speak only of themselves and of one another; other
people inhabit these pages as adjuncts to the protagonists' intents. Yet the
experience of reading the letters, more than two and a half centuries after
their writing, is for the reader one of encountering "other people" as objects
of narrative. Between the acts of writing and of reading, the fact of publication
has intervened. Like the processes of gossip, those of publication objectify
the thinking, feeling, composing subject. In effect, publication changes the
you and *I* of the letters into the *he* and *she* Barthes deplored ("The third-
person pronoun is a wicked pronoun"): for the reader, Lady Mary can be
neither *you* nor *I*. Her literary status resembles that of Clarissa, who also
declares herself a consciousness (within a fiction), yet is perceived by the
reader as a character. Even if the reader identifies with that character, the
person evoked by words on a page remains *other*, more distant than any
recipient of a letter.

The transformation into artifact converts individual letters composed in
diverse situations over an extended time-span into pieces of a story, sum-
marizable like that of a novel. Yet the reader's knowledge, extraneous to the
text, of the characters' historicity must affect the possible range of response.
We contemplate Lady Mary as a character. On the other hand, gossiper
(about her own life and others) as well as gossipee, she appears to invite the
contemplation—to invite us into the illusory intimacy of personal narrative,
into sequences of speculation like those that compose gossip. (Her editor, of
course, literally supplies this invitation, but the voice to which we imaginatively respond is Lady Mary's.) Such "gossip" analogizes the kind Kierkegaard imagined as morally acceptable, in which nothing can be talked
about except as though it had happened fifty years ago. We interest ourselves
in Lady Mary not because we know her but because she enforces herself as
a personality, a personality informing all she writes, manifest in her selection
of detail (women in the Turkish bath fingering her stays and concluding that
English men keep their wives thus armored in order to guard their chastity),
in her epistolary tone (astringent, loving, ironic, curious . . .), in her
insistence on the personal. Like someone one might enjoy gossiping with,
she participates in a duality of interpretation for which the reader provides
the other half.

To use gossip as model for the communicative exchange between reader
and writer in the special case of published personal letters helps to locate
the guilty pleasure associated with intrusion into privacies; it calls attention
to the objectification implicit in publication, even when publication implies
no reductiveness beyond that necessarily involved in reifying part of a human

life; and it suggests by analogy a crucial positive aspect of serious gossip in speech as well. Unlike the personalized news that *People* purveys, such published letters as these dignify small truths rather than trivialize large ones. Anecdotes like that about the old maid wedding a rich man, episodes of courtship as minute as Lady Mary's difficulties about finding a friendly drawing room where she might plausibly hope to encounter her lover—the reporting of such minutiae creates the texture of a life. The reader becomes vicariously absorbed in the kinds of small consideration that preoccupy most people every day; the literary experience of such absorption, unlike its literal counterpart, seems infused with meaning. An implicit conversational model often governs the familiar letter. This fact in itself invites attention to the particular variety of conversation imitated in specific instances. If, as I have argued, the mode of gossip frequently prevails, the attribution of meaning to the printed text might extend backward, to the model as well as its written and printed adaptations. When Lady Mary writes Wortley, "I go this Evening to Lady J[ekyll]. I am afraid you won't have this letter time enough to come" ([c. 24 July 1712]; 1.133), the reader feels the full momentousness of the fear. Gossip might well report just such emotion: "Mary hopes she'll see her lover at Sandra's party, but she's afraid he won't know that she's going to be there." Lady Mary's letters, taken seriously in full detail, can help the reader value the small remark—in life as well as on the page. They do not, like tragedy, for instance, emphasize the grandeur of the human spirit; they insist, rather, on the compelling persistence of personality.

Only the conversion of Lady Mary's letters into gossip, in the complex sense I have described, saves them, and her, for posterity. Although her relationship with Pope, her putative authorship of anonymously published poems, her advocacy of inoculation against smallpox, made her well known in her own time, Lady Mary did not present herself to the public mainly as an author. Her interest in the published letters of others (testified in the correspondence with her daughter) hints that she glimpsed the possibility of posthumous fame for her own epistolary gifts. She has won that fame by her transformation into metaphorical object as well as literal agent of gossip. The analogy between published letters and gossip may remind us of gossip's value as an agent of preservation, even of glorification (turning lives into stories declares their importance), as well as of reification.

One final point exemplified by Lady Mary's correspondence. Letters, even letters entirely by a single writer, offer their readers a view not only of a rendered self but of a relationship; gossip provides a precise metaphor for the nature of that relationship, reliant on the verbal exchange of confidences, in many personal letters. In reading other people's published letters, we seek reassurance not only about the stability of a continuous self but about the possibility of intimacy, of fruitful human exchange between members of the same sex as well as between men and women. *People* purveys the same reassurance in debased form, inviting its readers into brief, unstable alliance, creating a temporary *we*: a one-night stand rather than an extended relationship. The multiple *we*'s evoked by published letters substantiate what *People* cannot. Despite the objectification involved in reading letters, the text, by offering vicarious participation in a harmless simulacrum of gossip, provides comfort: as gossip does.

Lady Mary's letters represent only one of the many possible relations between published letters and gossip. Horace Walpole, another eighteenth-century master of the social letter (and one who loathed Lady Mary), makes talk about other people the substance of his correspondence. Sometimes this talk declares itself "important" by focusing on the conduct of political figures whose behavior even in private might have public consequences. Sometimes Walpole writes about other matters: about his estate at Strawberry Hill in all its slow development, about works of art; increasingly, as he aged, about his health. But discussions of politics and architecture and even health rarely stray far from the consuming interest in the multiplicity of human personality and action.

Writing at the age of seventy-two to young Mary Berry, Walpole introduces a narrative about Lady Luxborough in these words: "I have talked scandal from Richmond like its gossips, and now by your queries after Lady L. you are drawing me into more, which I do not love; but she is dead and forgotten, but on the shelves of an old library or on those of my old memory which you will be routing into." He then offers a delightful summary of the lady's amours, rich in literary allusion, and concludes: "This might be a fable, like that of her Cretan Highness [i.e., Ariadne]—no matter; the fry of little anecdotes are so numerous now, that throwing one more into the shoal is of no consequence if it entertains you for a moment, nor need you believe what I don't warrant."[6] "I have often said it of myself, and it is true, that nothing that has not a proper name of a man or a woman to it, affixes any idea upon my mind," he writes Sir Horace Mann.[7] And again, much later, to Mary Berry, "I never understood anything useful; and now that my time and connections are shrunk to so narrow a compass, what business have I with business?" (19 March 1791; 11.222). Finally, also to Mary Berry: "I am far from fond of dissertationary letters, which present themselves humbly, but hope to rank as essays—I must be in sad want of nonsense, when I talk seriously on general topics; and I hope that . . . you will not charge me with any gravity. I have gossipped to anybody's heart's wish; and the deuce is in it, if any letters are worth receiving; that have the fear of wisdom before their eyes" (31 March 1791; 11.234).

The terms of value, and of anti-value, emerge clearly. *Useful, business, dissertationary, seriously, general, wisdom:* the orthodox vocabulary of male seriousness elicits Walpole's disapproval. He prefers fables to dissertations, names of people to names of ideas, entertaining nonsense to pretentious wisdom. Although he deprecates his "old memory," he treasures it as a resource. To be sure, he strikes poses: like the Cambridge undergraduate who refuses to acknowledge ever studying, Walpole clings to a self-image of frivolity while writing, often, to serious purpose. The self-image itself reiterates standards and assumptions conveyed in the letters' diction and detail.

Despite all the gossip he reports, Walpole insists on his distaste for "scandal" and his contempt for those who promulgate it, partly because he believes them to make no distinction between truth and falsehood. If he acknowledges on occasion the problematic truth of his own narratives, the acknowledgment becomes part of the story; he never (or so he implies) knowingly misleads his reader. Life composes itself into fictions, to Walpole's perception. Over many months he reports to the Berry sisters the current history of Elizabeth Gunning, a young woman apparently making forged letters her principal means to an aristocratic marriage. "It is lost time," Walpole writes Mary Berry, "for people to write novels, who can compose such a romance as these good folks have invented" (18 February 1791; 11.205). In a slightly earlier letter to Agnes Berry (13 February 1791; 11.196), he contrasts the denouement of this "legend" with the endings of "other novels"—literal novels—by Miss Gunning's mother and aunt. Four decades earlier still, in a letter to George Montagu, he had offered a kind of apology for truth-telling as less formally satisfying than fiction: "If all the adventures don't conclude as you expect at the beginning of a paragraph, you must not wonder, for I am not making a history, but relating one strictly as it happened, and I think with full entertainment enough to content you."[8] Although the events of actuality violate literary expectation, they generate their own pseudo-fictional form: sufficiently entertaining.

The self-evident value of narrative provides an important item in Walpole's moral and aesthetic credo. To say of him, as many readers have said, that he excels in gossip acknowledges, among other things, his sensitivity to story—miniature and extended. "The Primate has hurt his leg, and keeps his room. He sits on the side of his bed in his nightgown, without breeches, and tallies at pharaoh to all comers. You never saw so good a figure. The Princess Borghese says, she is persuaded he will never recover now, since he has found out this expedient to play from morning to night."⁹ This short-short story, written by a twenty-one-year-old, with its sense of telling detail, of the intricacies of character, of the rich implications in what remains unsaid, reflects a mind capable of investing the minute with significance and of questioning conventional assumption. Such investment, such skepticism mark gossip's discourse.

The Primate as gambler, revealing his good figure: money at stake, sexual hints in the background. Both subjects recur in more open terms. In the youthful correspondence, Walpole indulges in abundant sexual joking. He also tells story after story about sex and money in conjunction. To Mann: "The former lost near fifteen thousand pounds to Janson, you know, a professed sharper; and the latter, on his pretty person and an opera girl, has spent about four thousand. Then he exposed himself in laying monstrous wagers . . . " (5 September 1741 N.S.; 17.126). "The Duke of Newcastle has lately given [Lord Vane] three-score thousand pounds to consent to cut off the entail of the Newcastle estate; the fool immediately wrote to his wife to beg she would return to him from Lord Berkeley, that he had got so much money, and now they might live *comfortably*: but she will not live *comfortably*: she is at Lord Berkeley's house; whither go divers after her" (23 November 1741 O.S.; 17.209–10). As an old man, he recounts the Gunning story in letter after letter; or he provides vignettes about others: "Scandal I hate, and would not send you what I thought so; but it is not doubted now but two of our finest ladies, sisters, have descended into the *basse cour* of the Alley with Jews and brokers, and waddled out with a large loss of feathers, though not so considerable as was said—yet 23 thousand makes a great gap in pin-money" (5 March 1791; 11.213). "Good Hannah More is killing herself by a new fit of benevolence about a young girl with a great fortune, who has been taken from school at Bristol to Gretna Green, and cannot be discovered, nor the apothecary who stole her" (23 April 1791; 11.253).

The first two passages come from letters to a male contemporary, written when both men were in their early twenties. The last two belong to the correspondence with Mary Berry, almost half a century younger than seventy-two-year-old Walpole. Despite the differences in the circumstances of the writer and the nature of the recipient, the four sequences have more in common than the sex-money linkage. They share a tone of superiority to the objects of discussion. Walpole's gently amused shaping of each episode distances him as observer and declares his moral dominance. The bland adjective *good* applied to Hannah More, for instance, in itself conveys, by its setting in the context, the discrepancy between More's professed piety and her avid preoccupation with just the stuff of scandal that interests those devoid alike of professions and of piety. "Killing herself" alludes comically to the extravagant emotional vocabulary of society women; *fit* ("a new fit of benevolence") calls attention to More's emotional extravagance and gains comic intensity by its conjunction with that *benevolence* which More has made her professional stock in trade. Thus Walpole's first twelve words communicate his judgment of his subject, hint the judgment's ground in More's implied disjunction of surface and substance, and invite amused response. The sentence sketches a hackneyed fictional plot; its further comic impact hinges on the word *apothecary*, startling and amusing in its sudden specificity and soliciting a snobbish reaction.

The sentences of Walpole's letters, created with conscious or unconscious artistry, repay detailed verbal analysis. The sentences of oral gossip rarely merit comparably close attention. (Commenting on Horace Mann's remark, in a letter to his brother, *"Mr. W.'s letters are full of wit; don't they adore him in England?"*, Walpole observes that his letters' alleged wit does not suggest his possession of any wit outside them. "A thousand people can write, that can't talk" [7 January 1742 O.S.; 17.270]). Writing, however, may solidify commitments more loosely expressed in speech. In a late letter to John Pinkerton, Walpole reflects on a quality that he acknowledges himself to value in writing: *grace*. "I do believe that it is a perfume that will preserve from putrefaction, and is distinct even from style, which regards *expression*; *grace*, I think, belongs to *manner*."[10] Fielding, Walpole continues, lacks grace, and therefore "is perpetually disgusting"; Shakespeare, the Greeks, the Romans, Waller, and Milton possessed it (270). The swan typifies the quality. "The colouring of the swan is pure, his attitudes are graceful, he never displeases you when sailing on his proper element. His feet may be ugly, his notes hissing not musical, his walk not natural, he can soar, but it is with difficulty. Still the impression the swan leaves is that of grace" (271). The long letter concludes with praise of Madame de Sévigné as letter-writer— a subject leading to what Walpole calls "a word of digression": "I hate the cold impartiality recommended to historians" (273).

Here we have Walpole's literary and moral credo. Its use of Madame de Sévigné as culminating example and its condemnation of orthodox history underline the applicability of the standards here partly stated, partly implied, to Walpole's own correspondence. The notion of *grace* elucidates Walpole's moral position; it helps to account for his peculiar stance toward those familiar subjects of sex and money. Grace, an aspect of manner rather than of style, implies the impression of effortlessness, as the swan example suggests. Any straining after effect opposes it. Hannah More, in her fitful and intense "benevolence," lacks grace. So do the ladies who waddle out with large loss of feathers from their encounter with "Jews and brokers"; so does Lord Vane ("the fool"), who acknowledges to his wife that he wants her back and exposes himself to mockery by his apparent blindness to the meaning of Lady Vane's conduct. Admissions of intense sexual feeling; revelations of deep concern for money; indeed, open passion of any kind—all violate the graceful façade that Walpole values: the *manner* defining excellence. But "cold impartiality" of the sort recommended to historians also opposes grace, which connects itself, as the example of Madame de Sévigné emphasizes, with *appropriate* feeling.

At many points, indeed, "appropriateness" and "grace" appear identical. Both standards imply what the letters reiterate: manners, properly understood, reflect morals. Walpole's brilliant letter to Montagu about the burial of King George II, with its description of the Duke of Newcastle standing upon the train of the Duke of Cumberland in order "to avoid the chill of the marble," epitomizes the point (13 November 1760; 9.323). Comedy and judgment merge, as in the sentence about Hannah More: Newcastle both makes himself ridiculous and reveals his moral inadequacy in his violation of the decorum implicit in grace. By this standard Walpole always judges; he assumes that his correspondents share it; he embodies it in his own epistolary performance. His unerring selection of detail typically reveals both Walpole's grace and its absence in the object of his commentary. The reader, lured into complicity by expert interpretive description, may find it difficult to apply alternative criteria of excellence, so profoundly does the writer assume the validity of his own bases for judgment.

The idea of complicity leads me back to gossip, complicitous in essence. The reading of published letters involves at least a simulacrum of alliance as close, and possibly as morally ambiguous, as that of gossip. In this instance, we might not, upon careful consideration, consciously wish to identify with the particular values Walpole exemplifies and assumes. His snobbery, for instance, violates twentieth-century democratic conviction. Leisurely rumination might suggest pity rather than censure as the appropriate response to Lord Vane, willing to condone his wife's flagrant adultery perhaps because he loves her; and there is nothing really funny about two fine ladies forced to make hard bargains with usurers. The letters, however, make such alternative responses, if not impossible, at least difficult. Walpole declares his spectator's distance from the ruck and turbulence of passion, whatever its object; he invites and encourages his reader to enjoy the same protection.

Many who engage in gossip on occasion worry about its complicitousness, and about the seductiveness of its appeal to closeness. Gossip generates its own momentum. Reading a book of letters can initiate a similar snowballing development—less morally dangerous, since presumably devoid of external consequence, but potentially threatening to equilibrium. The power of Walpole's belief in and embodiment of "grace," with its implied emotional distance, its keen sense of the ridiculous, its valuing of ease and elegance of manner over the disorder of uncontrolled emotion—the power of this ideal, vividly realized in the letters themselves, proves difficult to evade. A published letter-writer with a strong voice, an energetically articulated system of values, may dominate the reader in unsettling ways.

Walpole speaks partly in the tone of his social class. A historian might find a microcosm of late eighteenth-century social conflict in the sentence about Hannah More, where the aristocrat conveys contempt not only for those striving to elevate themselves by prudential sexual alliance but for the values associated with More's evangelical fervor. Yet the dynamics of gossip, regardless of class, create a we-them dichotomy: *we* who talk, *them* whom we discuss; and the dynamics of letter-reading parallel those of gossip. The twentieth-century reader finds him/herself drawn into alliance with Walpole as product of his class and culture, as well as with Walpole the highly individual self. All urgency about judging long-dead aristocrats has disappeared; we know little about them, in most cases, beyond what Walpole chooses to tell or his recent editors to elucidate. Still the text invites us to reach conclusions: to share Walpole's conclusions. We are urged, for example, to mock the society's general over-valuation of sex and money, on grounds of taste rather than of morality. People make themselves foolish, the implicit argument goes, by caring too much about flesh and wealth. Fools of lust or avarice populate the world; "we"—the "we" established by the reader's encounter with the letters—remain elevated above them, faintly amused. Our culture (like Walpole's) takes these matters seriously; we, for the space of our reading, take them less seriously. Just so does gossip work, its potential for undercutting always alive, its "seriousness" often manifest in its refusal to value highly what the culture at large assumes or does.

On the other hand—and we come here to yet another version of the crucial paradoxes involved in reading published letters—our interest in precisely these subjects helps to account for our pleasure in the books (as in the gossip). We keep reading partly because Walpole keeps writing about just those feelings he so insistently rises above. The publication of intimate letters often gives the reader permission to indulge in prurience both by offering convenient disguises (we read Walpole, we may say, from concern with social history or with biography) and by providing skeptical commentary. Walpole, declaring his own superiority to "scandal," assures us of ours.

He also provides us with a relatively "cost-free" outlet for feelings we might find unacceptable in other contexts. As with Lady Mary's correspondence, the situation of the reader in relation to Walpole involves at once gossiping *with* and in effect gossiping *about* the letters' author. The double role of the reader generates a kind of moral security: we can identify with and enjoy Walpole's sense of superiority to much of humankind, a feeling corresponding to deep narcissistic impulse but one which the laws of civilized behavior encourage us to suppress and deny; at the same time (or at the next moment), we can contemplate Walpole's moral inadequacies as though we had not shared them, and gain pleasure by judging him. We vicariously enjoy the position of aristocrat even while condemning its intermittent moral shoddiness: a set of responses parallel to those involved in reading about millionaires in *People*. Part of what we buy in buying letters is the moral comfort implicit in our capacity to make the letter-writer both subject and object of contemplation.

Yet the reader's double position also involves a form of entrapment sometimes productive of moral vertigo. We read Clarissa's letters and share her perceptions and judgments; we consider her as a character and recognize her limitations. No great discomfort accompanies the shift because Clarissa *is* a character, manipulated by another consciousness for his own literary purposes. The work of the editor helps to alleviate unease about confronting an actual person as character: bibliographical and explanatory apparatus insist firmly on the historicity—the distance in time—making this exercise morally acceptable. We can consequently allow ourselves to enjoy what Walpole enjoys: the folly and wonder of the human spectacle as perceived by someone so cultivated, so controlled, so much in command that we willingly submit to his guidance.

My vocabulary (*controlled, command, submit*) suggests that the relation of writer and reader reiterates the issue of power. The psychological alternations of that relationship in reading published letters might be described as shifts in balance between the text's power over the reader, the reader's over the text. Walpole vividly asserts his mastery, which declares itself through the narrative structures he imposes on or perceives in experience. The empowering function of the letters as read between covers depends partly on this control, which the reader vicariously shares. By the little stories he tells, Walpole makes sense of the chaos of human passions; he allows us to believe in the possibility of making similar sense, by similar means, of intense feelings about such matters as sex and money when they erupt in our lives. But the reader's experience of power, in the form of control, necessarily exceeds Walpole's: partly as the living dog's exceeds the dead lion's. As we read his letters, volume after volume (even a single volume, even the "selected letters"), we turn Walpole too into an object of contemplation. We have survived him, existing in a new society which provides a new vantage point. The intimacy of verbal association supplying much of the pleasure of reading letters, that intimacy which corresponds to gossip's close association, gives way to a startling solitude of judgment.

More unavoidably than Lady Mary's published letters, Walpole's, because of their concentration on other people's doings, focus attention on the moral problematics shared by oral gossip and the analogous activity of reading correspondence addressed to someone else. The fact of publication, which allows this activity, also legitimates it. The letters, made public, become available to whoever chooses to read them; no individual need feel guilty. Yet the experience those letters facilitate duplicates in many respects that of talk about the absent. Walpole's letters, encouraging their readers to enjoy and share judgments centrally based on style (or "manner"), thus undermine publicly accepted standards, inducting the reader into a sub-society ("official" values would endorse Hannah More's "benevolence" rather than Walpole's wry disengagement). Just so, in gossip, talkers affirming the beliefs of unofficial or unnoticed groups may reconstrue their social universe. Inasmuch as readers feel allied with the letters' writer, they share his protected (because private) position as critic of his society, thus duplicating the situation of intimate talkers. Inasmuch as they dissociate themselves from Walpole's standards, functioning as audience rather than as vicarious participants in dialogue, they disengage from a seductive interpretive alliance. The opposed impulses of engagement and disengagement generate much of the drama of reading the epistolary Walpole.

In claiming that *People* shares with the collected letters of Walpole or Lady Mary a common similarity to gossip, I mean to emphasize differences as well as similarities. Although a gossip magazine may convey a "voice," the relationship that voice invites with the reader depends on no developed sense of personality. The *persona* behind *People* sounds knowing, enticing readers with the lure of feeling on the inside; the pleasure those readers derive depends on the gratifications of voyeurism and of an evanescent power of narrative or of knowledge: appeals of oral gossip at even its least justifiable. Reading published assemblages of letters establishes a fuller relationship with the writer and generates pleasure from consciousness of another consciousness reacting to the human scene, as well as from reflection on foibles of personality and action in the being whose consciousness differs from our own. Good letters heighten awareness, of the self and of others, as good gossip does; popular magazines of the *People* variety reduce everything to the same dead level.

A text so different from the two previously considered that it seems to have nothing in common with them beyond epistolary convention demonstrates yet another aspect of the gossip-letters analogy, reminding us once more of moral ambiguities implicit even in "good" gossip. E. B. White's *Letters*, collected and published during his lifetime, edited by his goddaughter "with the help of the Whites,"[11] might be expected to suffer from excessive discretion in matters of selection and excision, therefore to provide little in the way of voyeuristic satisfaction or of corresponding moral disturbance. (The editor acknowledges that she has made occasional cuts to spare someone's feelings, although never, she thinks, to spare Mr. White's.) Moreover, White does not write a great deal about other people's lives or much, directly, about his own feelings. His letters dwell on trivial anecdotes about unknown characters: two men overheard on the street, one saying to the other, "So she had the whole fucking bedroom suite sawed up and put together again" (174). Often the letters concern animals or contemplate such phenomena as staplers and staple-removers. White tells few stories about people, including himself.

This correspondence, then, constitutes an example at one extreme of the spectrum of personal letters, about as un-gossipy as possible while remaining recognizably "personal." Yet the letters' interest still derives from narrative about human trivia: the substance of gossip. The correspondence extends over some sixty years; it tells a story the writer—who does not know the story's shape or its ending—cannot have been aware of telling. Indeed, the special interest of these letters derives partly from the sense they convey that their writer actively wishes to *avoid* telling his story: because of his acute awareness of late twentieth-century blurring of boundaries between public and private. Yet the correspondence by its nature encourages the reader to ferret out a tale the writer may not desire to tell.

The details of the particular story hardly matter. The volume presents an early episode of aborted love, a later one of love fulfilled; sub-narratives of life at *The New Yorker*, of house-remodeling, of country existence. The main record, though, concerns the growth, commitment, and frustration of a writer: a man deeply dedicated to the perfect sentence who over and over finds himself unable to write, who has developed a literary reputation on the basis of limited productivity, who suffers from the discrepancy between his gifts and his accomplishment (although he would not put the matter thus). A story about literature, in other words, told in a profoundly literary way.

White inhabits a world in which students writing term papers about him routinely request that he reveal "aspects" of himself for their use, advertising copy about his books ignores his desires, editors urge his appearance at book fairs to publicize himself and his work, scientists wish to study his psychic processes. His letters detail his struggle to remain a private man. He refuses, withholds, disguises, evades; he hides behind a brilliantly executed mask; he constructs a fiction of himself. His letters call attention to the consequences of two centuries' commercialization of human privacy.

Here, in its entirety, is White's response to an invitation from Dr. Frank Barron, director of the Creative Writing Project at the University of California Institute of Personality Assessment and Research, to come to California and be studied.

> Thanks for your kind and unexpected invitation to come to California and be investigated. I shall have to decline, although the trip sounds exciting.
>
> I don't suppose I should feel any deep disinclination to be studied, but the fact is I do. Even if you were to find that I had made no recovery from my neurosis, and that my personality was complex (which it may well be), and that I was sound, sensitive, and well motivated, I still don't know that anything would have been added to the field of knowledge. As a guinea pig I would be unreliable and shifty. My tendency would be to get drunk, to escape the embarrassment of being watched, and this unsavory episode would have to go in the record, to be studied for hidden meanings that weren't really there. In short, I feel that my best bet as a writer is to sit still and write. As my time gets shorter and shorter, I feel that more and more.
>
> But I do thank you for the chance [18 September 1957; 444].

The letter reveals a shy man who has perfected his mode of self-protection. Like all White's published writing, it displays an accomplished style. "As a guinea pig I would be unreliable and shifty": the precise choice of adjectives, evoking two levels of discourse and of reference ("unreliable" suggesting the schoolboy with a bad mark for conduct, "shifty" hinting an older street punk); the comic conjunction of adjectives and noun; the calm air of incontrovertible assertion, even in the conditional mode—these elements generate a sentence of unostentatious richness. The precise selection of detail evokes personality and attitude. In the second sentence of the second paragraph, White adapts Dr. Barron's language, conjoining it with his own artful simplicities. Words like *neurosis, complex, sound, sensible, well motivated*, given this treatment, empty themselves of meaning, exposed as jargon. White powerfully asserts himself in courteously declining an invitation.

I said earlier that White tells few stories about people. On the other hand, his style tells its own stories. It evokes a character, a set of relationships, a stance, a way of interpreting and of imagining events. It tells the reader, insistently, how a man chooses to present himself. If that self exists—as, in letters, it must—always in relationship, it nonetheless demonstrates the possibility of constancy. White sounds different, writing to the California doctor and to his niece; yet also the same. Consider the conclusion of a letter to Janice White, his brother's daughter:

> We are awaiting, breathlessly, an influx of grandchildren of assorted sizes. Joe's wife is about to have her third, by Caesarian section in the Ellsworth hospital, and while she is out of the running we are taking Steven and Martha (age 5 and 4) into our house for a couple of weeks roistering with tinker-toys and space ships. And on top of that, we are also taking our oldest grandchild, Kitty Stableford, a blonde starlet age 15, who plans to attend a French school in the morning (2½ miles away by bicycle) and clean up the space ships and bathe the space-tots in the afternoon. The piano is out of tune, my wife and one of my cows have diarrhea, the temperature outdoors is 48, the milk supply is contaminated with strontium 90 from fallout, rain has been falling ever since Memorial Day, our neighbor's boy just held up the Sunday night Bible class with a .22 automatic pistol and abducted one of the girls in the minister's automobile, the asparagus is growing *down* into the ground instead of up into the air, the lilacs look as though they will still be blooming right through the Fourth of July, and I have lost both pairs of glasses. Hope you are not the same [16 June 1959; 460].

In the letter to Barron, White spins a hypothetical story (he would get drunk, his drunkenness would be studied for hidden meanings); in the letter to Janice, he lists small details of his daily life, mixed with more obviously momentous "news" (strontium 90, the Bible class hold-up). In both, he presents himself with self-deprecating irony as inevitable victim of comic catastrophe. In both, irony provides protection.

Protection in a sense extends to reader as well as writer: White's style, like that of other expert letter-writers, generates a stabilizing force to counteract the moral and psychological instabilities intrinsic in the act of letter-reading. This chapter has argued for a complex pattern in the reading of letters. As readers, we imaginatively duplicate the original relationship letters evoke and we generate our own new relationship with the writer; we allow ourselves to receive what that writer gives and we exert judgmental force upon him/her; metaphorically, we gossip both with and about the text's originator. Yet to read letters proves less unsettling than this account might imply because finally the letter-writer, regardless of life's catastrophes, controls the story letters tell. Without more foreknowledge than the rest of us, suffering immediate pain or joy, that writer yet, by putting the day's (week's, month's) experience into words, however fragmentary the narrative those words create, takes command of experience.

We read other people's letters in print partly because, thus collected, thus presented, they affirm the timeless possibility of communication. A self keeps asserting itself by words on a page intended for another; the reader finds sustenance in that capacity of selves and in the demonstrated will to establish and preserve human contact. Finally as readers we may accept, at least for the space of our readership, the reassurance collected letters offer in their claim not to imitate life or to evade or transcend it but to speak about it on paper, with and to another. When the letters we read are "personal," utterances of intimacy, we are reminded by them of the verbal equivalents for closeness, the degree to which the sharing of small things epitomizes the intimate.

As with gossip, where speaking takes place out loud, the sharing of small things establishes bonding, verbal experience declares possibilities of the intimate.

Inasmuch as readers' interest in other people's letters involves a desire to penetrate personal privacies, readers will convert what they read into the stuff of gossip. Gossip at core resembles an *action of knowing*; to read published letters imitates that action. Books of personal letters allow us the illusion of "finding out" about their writers, providing an invitation to unmask their personae by the processes of literary analysis.

White in his letters insists on the vital distinction between a man and his writing. "The man-on-paper," he writes an admirer, "is always a more admirable character than his creator, who is a miserable creature of nose colds, minor compromises, and sudden flights into nobility" (to L. M. Reuvers, 7 January 1955; 402). "The reading public has an unhealthy curiosity about authors-in-the-flesh"; White refuses to gratify it. "I have nothing to say to parents beyond what is in the book" (to Ursula Nordstrom, 4 August 1953; 381). As Walpole parades his superiority to those who over-value sex and money, yet purveys numerous anecdotes about both, so White insists on his passion for privacy and makes public letters inviting invasion of privacy. Perhaps he believes no such invasion possible; and perhaps he is right. Publishers of personal letters, like publishers of gossip magazines, may sell temptation and illusion rather than reality: the temptation and illusion that gossiping conversation also supplies, of interpreting other people's experience. Although letters encourage the fantasy of the window in the bosom which makes inner workings plain, although they assure their readers of the reality of continuity and of communication, the status of the "knowledge" they offer remains problematic. When we analyze the subtleties of E. B. White's sentences, we learn about the subtleties of his sentences: not necessarily about the man. White's ironies, like Lady Mary's protestations of undying love, delineate modes of self-presentation, not simply a self.

Perhaps the urge to participate in gossip comes from knowledge of the impossibility of knowing. We continue to talk about others precisely because we cannot finally understand them, defying possibility. Just so, I would surmise, with letters.

One more surmise. Gossip exists, always, with precarious boundaries, with the known risk that today's gossiper may turn into tomorrow's subject of gossip. Letters too raise special problems about boundaries. Walter Benjamin spoke, in a rather different connection, of the fact that in the twentieth century readers are always on the verge of becoming writers.[12] The democratization of writing becomes particularly vivid when one considers the phenomenon of published letters: a form in which everyone can imagine the possibility of excelling. If E. B. White can publish his own trivial letters, why cannot any of us do the same with our own trivialities? Because the gap between reader and writer in this respect seems narrower in the case of letters than with other forms of published writing, the authority of linguistic control which I mentioned earlier may in fantasy readily extend to the reader. If sex and money, gossip's crucial subjects, provide modes of social power, they also embody threats to the individual when s/he becomes object rather than agent of power. Personal letters by taking possession of explosive material reassure their unintended readers. They encourage one to believe in human continuity and human capacity for control—continuity and capacity which seem available to everyone. The willing suspension of disbelief they generate possesses more immediacy than do other forms of poetic faith: so much immediacy that the experience of reading them may feel hardly "literary" at all. The problems of aesthetic judgment raised by published letters, the difficulty of fitting them into any canon involve questions about appropriate "distance" in a text—questions analogous to those raised by gossip as a mode sometimes uncomfortably intimate, yet always concerned with other people.

By focusing on letter-writers as different as Lady Mary, Walpole, and White, I wish to suggest the possibility that published personal letters establish a special kind of literary dynamic regardless of specific subject matter. Robert Day, writing of the early epistolary novel (in other words, of fictional rather than actual letters), claims that "epistolary narrative . . . represents a stage in the development of technique for depicting and analyzing emotion, thought, motive, character, and reaction to events—the background and climate before and in which events take place—rather than the events themselves."[13] Literal letters share with their fictional counterparts this predilection for at least implicit personal interpretation. They share the same predilection with gossip; and, whatever their specific content, they share with gossip also the intimacy of dyadic exchange—an intimacy into which published letters necessarily draw their readers.

5

Biography:
Moral and Physical Truth

Telling stories about human lives, biography, like published letters, encourages the temptation to interpret, the lure of "finding out," the fantasy of knowing. Unlike letters, it offers coherent narrative, product of a structuring intelligence other than the reader's. Delineating someone who has actually lived in the world, this narrative claims the status of "truth." Biography has been considered a branch of history, a source of information about politics and about the underpinnings of public events. It has traditionally provided models of conduct, depictions of embodied excellence which readers may aspire to approach in their own lives. More recently, the "debunking" biography has assured us of inadequacies concealed behind public façades. Ernst Kris's demonstration that ancient biographies of artists consistently purveyed the same stories about different subjects suggests that biographies may partake also of fiction ("biography originates in myth," Kris says[1]); yet although the patterns of "factual" narrative derive from legend, from cultural assumption, from individual wish and will, beneath those patterns, readers persistently believe, lies a substratum of facticity. Reading a novel, experienced readers expect to understand the world better for encountering imaginative transformations of it; they do not anticipate learning about actual people in society. Belief that biography affords opportunity for such learning partly explains its ambiguous literary status: if the genre exists primarily to convey information, perhaps it does not merit aesthetic assessment.

One can ignore claims of facticity and treat biography as a literary genre like any other, a verbal structure subject to verbal analysis. (William Dowling's recent exegeses of Boswell, for example, adopt this procedure.[2]) Yet to deny altogether what has long constituted biography's ground of justification seems, if up-to-date, also perverse. An adequate aesthetic, like an adequate epistemology, of biography would take into account the text's claim to relay historical fact, to constitute history of an individual—and would go beyond that claim, to define the art of such history.

The pleasure of reading biography, like that of reading letters, derives from the universal hunger to penetrate other lives. Plausibility, consequently, constitutes biography's fundamental requirement: not necessarily literal accuracy, but the kind of interpretation that "makes sense," a story about human life fitting our convictions about the shapes life assumes. To assess the plausibility of a biographical text thus may involve hidden aesthetic judgment. Decisions about a narrative's likely degree of accuracy often conceal feelings and ideas about appropriateness, beliefs about the form of experience derived as much from fiction as from life.

The narrator in biography functions as source and guardian of knowledge, in ways comparable to novelistic narrators. The novelist, however, invents characters; the biographer only interprets them. The biographical story-teller must convince the reader—particularly the reader aware of more than a single biography of a given subject—of the narrator's right and power to control the story. Such authority and power depend not only on the forms into which narrators fit their narratives but on the distance they maintain: between biographer and subject, between biographer and reader, consequently between subject and reader.

This matter of distance proves complicated in biography. The biographer cannot risk too much coziness. As Frank Brady observes, "If [biography] takes the form of a fictional reconstruction of the thoughts and actions of real persons, it is usually dismissed as a hybrid hardly worth despising."[3] The narrator must not claim to know more than s/he can know; biographical narrators cannot conspicuously indulge imagination, cannot convey the immediate internal specificity of character which their novelistic counterparts provide. The reader's trust will depend largely on the narrator's precise control of plausible distance. The narrator stabilizes both story-teller's and reader's relation to the biographical subject. Authority does not necessarily derive from the preservation of great height: the biographer in a superior position, declaring possession of knowledge that enables interpretation; the narrator may claim, rather, the special awareness of intimacy. Readers' interest in biography as a genre may reflect yearning to grasp how other human beings resemble us or the wish to examine closely an individual specimen of human life, without conscious reference to the self. (Interest in a specific biography, of course, often depends on pre-existent concern with its subject.) We may wish to reflect upon the greatness of the renowned, or to encounter their insufficiencies. The biographer's choices of tone and stance and of detail will determine the relationship established by the text, the boundaries separating subject from reader, the nature as well as the substance of interpretation.

Late in his life, Dr. Johnson verbalized a distinction between physical and moral truth. "Physical truth, is, when you tell a thing as it actually is. Moral truth, is, when you tell a thing sincerely and precisely as it appears to you. I say such a one walked across the street; if he really did so, I told a physical truth. If I thought so, though I should have been mistaken, I told a moral truth."[4] Biographers deal in both kinds of truth; and, as the terms of Johnson's definition imply, they can hardly distinguish between them since in both cases belief informs their telling. Nor, often, can the reader distinguish.

The biographical equivalent of "moral truth" involves issues more important than crossing the street. Interpretation of character and event derives from how things *appear* to the biographer. To call this truth of appearance, as it manifests itself in biography, *moral* directs attention not only to the conviction underlying it, but to the fact that the sub-stratum of interpretation, however concealed, often involves moral judgment. (I am, of course, extending the implications of Johnson's distinction between "moral" and "physical" truth.) The biographer's belief in the subject's human value or meretriciousness informs the life story and shapes interpretations. Dr. Johnson takes a trip to Oxford, Birmingham, Lichfield, and Ashbourne in the fall of 1781. Boswell points out, with a slap at Sir John Hawkins (another of Johnson's early biographers), that "very good reasons might be given [for this trip] in the conjectural yet positive manner of writers, who are proud to account for every event which they relate." He confines himself to quoting Johnson's own comments: the traveler says he hardly knows the motives of his journey, he refers to his love for his schoolmate Edmund Hector, and he claims a desire to show a good example in his native town of Lichfield "by frequent attendance on publick worship" (4.134). Walter Jackson Bate, reporting the same excursion, also quotes Johnson on his doubts about motivation and on his love for Hector. But Bate adds, "The people he wished to see at Lichfield . . . were getting old. . . . It was here, among these people, that his roots had been. He was instinctively turning to them now that he felt himself losing what had been so important in his later life."[5] Bate does not cite Johnson's sentence about wishing to provide a good example.

Boswell's ostentatious refusal to interpret implies his judgment (by no means consistent throughout the *Life*) that Johnson's veracity and integrity make him the ultimate authority on his own actions. Bate's interpretation emerges in declarative sentences, not formally distinct from sentences narrating known events. Such a statement as "He was instinctively turning to them now . . ." exemplifies one kind of "moral truth" in biography: a sincere and precise telling of what to the biographer appears to be the case. It too implies moral evaluation: for Johnson, human ties had powerful meaning. Boswell's inclusion, Bate's omission of the remark about public worship point up their different grounds of judgment. For Bate, as for most twentieth-century readers, no doubt, Johnson's desire to worship in public in order to improve his townspeople sounds like rationalization. For Boswell, the profession of piety heightens Johnson's moral authority.

To come to adequate terms with an individual biography involves assessing—or at least locating—its art, its morality, and its knowledge. All three customarily resemble but rarely duplicate their novelistic equivalents. The *art* of biography, as of the novel, inheres in narrative—the creation of a persuasive story and of characters who make it plausible—but in biography facts restrict narrative form. The *moral assumptions* of a given biography may of course duplicate those of any other genre, though the concern with people who have actually lived and with literal details of their lives often encourages more ethical strictness than do the looser imaginings of fiction. The *knowledge* of biography includes not only the imaginative, interpretive knowledge fiction provides but facts of individual history. In every aspect, then, biography's claimed connection with actuality modifies its manifestations.

Two pairs of biographies will help to elucidate these claims: an eighteenth- and a twentieth-century life of Samuel Johnson, a nineteenth- and a twentieth-century account of Charlotte Brontë. In both pairings, the author of the earlier work, a friend of the subject, claims friendship's special knowledge and functions as apologist. The two twentieth-century biographies share psychological orientations and a technique of analyzing texts as testimony of inner experience. To look at these works under the aspect of gossip will not construct an aesthetic, an epistemology, or a morality of biography; it will not even produce a comprehensive reading of texts. But gossip provides a way of focusing on all three aspects of biography and of demonstrating relationships among them.

No less an authority than Horace Walpole links Boswell's *Johnson* with gossip. "Boswell's book is gossipping," he writes Mary Berry, "but having numbers of proper names, would be more readable, at least by me, were it reduced from two volumes to one."[6] A cryptic footnote, by the modern editors, to this cryptic comment claims that Walpole meant it as a compliment. Walpole's remark seems to imply that, delightful though he finds gossip, too many proper names interfere with readability: less would be more.

I suggested in the previous chapter that gossip resembles an action of knowing, taking *action* in its Aristotelian sense: a unifying explanatory structure for a sequence of events. Gossiping speakers exchange and interpret information in order—for good reasons or bad—to enlarge their grasp of someone else's experience and thus, ideally, better to understand their own. In a more immediate sense, gossip constitutes an action of telling. Without telling, it would not exist.

James Boswell, like all biographers, claims to know a great deal about another person and to tell what he knows. His modes of knowing and of telling connect *The Life of Samuel Johnson, LL.D.*, for all its dignity, with gossip.

Boswell distinguishes himself from other writers about Johnson (Hester Thrale Piozzi and Sir John Hawkins) and associates himself with his mentor by claiming absolute veracity. He works endlessly, he says, to verify allegations; he seeks material everywhere. Implicitly he differentiates his work from Hawkins' by suggesting his own superiority to gossip: "Sir John Hawkins's ponderous labours, I must acknowledge, exhibit a *farrago*, of which a considerable portion is not devoid of entertainment to the lovers of literary gossiping . . ." (1.28). On the other hand, Boswell incorporates into his own text versions of Johnson supplied by such others as Bennet Langton and Joshua Reynolds; he records in detail stories he will subsequently deny, thus satisfying his (and the presumed reader's) pleasure in a good anecdote without damaging his claim of accuracy; and, as he frequently acknowledges, he reports the tiniest details about his friend.

"Much pleasant conversation passed," Boswell writes (of a meeting of The Club on 30 April 1773), "which Johnson relished with great good humour. But his conversation alone, or what led to it, or was interwoven with it, is the business of this work" (2.241–2). Johnson suggests the moral function of his own talk when he justifies himself for refusing to respond to demands for more writing by claiming the same efficacy for his conversation and his writing: only the size of the audience differs. "Now, Sir, the good I can do by my conversation bears the same proportion to the good I can do by my writings, that the practice of a physician, retired to a small town, does to his practice in a great city" (2.15). Boswell, as he promises, makes it his business to record what Johnson says. Rarely does the reported conversation resemble gossip. Indeed, the operative definition of *conversation* implies stress on ideas. When Boswell asks Johnson if good conversation occurred on a given occasion, the doctor replies, "No, Sir; we had *talk* enough, but no *conversation*; there was nothing *discussed*" (4.186; Boswell's italics). By *discussing* issues moral, philosophic, political, social, and literary, Johnson reveals the dimensions of his mind and justifies Boswell's hero-worship. Conversation, in Johnson's view (apparently in Boswell's as well), is combat. It involves competitive self-display, in which one person necessarily emerges triumphant. Johnson talks for victory, as he acknowledges; he will assume a position he does not hold so as to demonstrate his capacity to defend it. The object of conversation is to win. Johnson usually wins.

The value system implicit in this model of conversation utterly opposes the one I have declared characteristic of gossip. To interpret other participants as audience or metaphoric patients, passive recipients of the great man's wisdom, as Johnson does in claiming the "good" he can do by his conversation, or to see talkers as combatants neglects the possibility of fruitful mutual exchange, more likely to occur in what Johnson calls "talk" than in what he calls "conversation." As even Boswell stresses (less emphatically than Bate), Johnson demonstrated vast capacity for loyalty and concern, valuing his affectional ties. But for him conversation belonged more to the realm of war than of human love; gossip, despite its possible animosity toward the absent, asserts the participants' closeness.

Given this fact, and the equally obvious truth that Boswell's *Life* centers on combative conversation, it may seem odd to associate it with gossip. True, the biography contains many names and many stories about the people those names designate; it tells even more stories about unnamed "gentlemen" or "clergymen." (Only Johnson, however, becomes the object of what Clifford Geertz calls "thick description.") True, as I pointed out above, it reports hearsay evidence and dwells on minutiae of conduct and appearance, with the sanction of Johnson himself, who believed as firmly as Boswell in the illuminating power of detail. But more important than any of these facts is the dominant myth of heroism informing this biography: and the implications of heroism, like those of Johnsonian "conversation," do not readily associate themselves with gossip.

Boswell rarely misses an opportunity to declare his subject's virtually superhuman stature. Even before he meets Johnson, he confesses, he feels for him "a kind of mysterious veneration" (1.384), which only increases upon close acquaintance. "During all the course of my long intimacy with him, my respectful attention never abated, and my wish to hear him was such, that I constantly watched every dawning of communication from that great and illuminated mind" (2.357). The very house Johnson inhabits appears to

Boswell's imagination "to be sacred to wisdom and piety" (2.427). "I cannot help worshipping him," Boswell says to the historian William Robertson, who has expressed anxiety lest excessive admiration "spoil" Johnson, "he is so much superior to other men" (3.331). The assumption of categorical superiority controls the entire work, which concludes with the vision of all the world revering Johnson as Boswell does: "Such was SAMUEL JOHNSON, a man whose talents, acquirements, and virtues, were so extraordinary, that the more his character is considered, the more he will be regarded by the present age, and by posterity, with admiration and reverence" (4.429–30).

Yet *The Life of Samuel Johnson, LL.D.* would inhabit the imagination less powerfully if it comprised simple hagiography. Two obvious aspects of the book, to both of which the text itself calls attention, emphasize its actual tensions of purpose and attitude: the constant intrusion of Boswell as a character, and the frequent exposures of Johnson as at least briefly unkind, petty, fearful, or self-absorbed. One can incorporate both Boswell's insistent presence and Johnson's feet of clay into the dominant pattern of stress on the heroic: Boswell deliberately makes himself a foil to his subject's grandeur, playing the fool, we might say; and Johnson's comparatively minor weaknesses only underline his achieved strengths. Such explanations, however, though true as far as they go, fail to do justice to the biography's effect. Despite its claims that Johnson provides an appropriate object of veneration, the book reveals him as a struggling human being; and it insists on the drama implicit in telling the story of such a man. Its narrative, in other words, involves Boswell the writer and Johnson the fallible man. Boswell makes both himself and his hero into subjects of gossip: intimate anecdote, intimate speculation. And he demonstrates that gossip need not preclude glorification.

Vivid consciousness of biography's moral problematics informs the *Life*, with its implicit generic questions: why write, why read, biography? Although Johnson himself, in his *Rambler* essay on the subject, had offered moral justification (biography, by conveying intimate knowledge of other lives, helps us to know ourselves), he did not resolve all ambiguities. Boswell several times worries in print about whether a biographer should expose his subject's frailties. Johnson's precedent—he reported Parnell's and Addison's alcoholic excesses—justifies his biographer, but does not alleviate anxiety. After alleging Johnson's youthful sexual indulgence, the narrator remarks, "I am conscious that this is the most difficult and dangerous part of my biographical work, and I cannot but be very anxious concerning it. I trust that I have got through it, preserving at once my regard to truth,—to my friend,—and to the interests of virtue and religion" (4.398). This threefold obligation suggests high-minded justification for biography. But problems remain. Boswell's anxiety, one may speculate, rises partly from self-suspicion. Maybe, despite his protestations, he wishes to reduce the stature of an uncomfortably gigantic figure. Perhaps people read biography not to confirm but to challenge the moral grandeur of larger-than-lifesize public figures. If a life story uncovers weakness and folly, does it not serve leveling impulses, the desire to emphasize the limits of human possibility so as to avoid the necessity of aspiration? The writer and the reader of biography may gratify malice and envy in the guise of serving truth, virtue, and religion. Where are truth's proper limits? Should everything known be told; should one seek knowledge no matter where the search leads? Need biography respect no privacies?

The issues implicit in such questions, the ambiguity of all possible answers, may remind us of similar issues, similar ambiguities, in discussions of gossip through the ages. Gossip too may seek and circulate truth—or, like biography on occasion, fiction in the guise of truth. Gossip, too, often purports to serve morality, to reinforce communal standards. It declares human interest in human beings, but it violates privacy and punctures pretensions. Enlarging knowledge and understanding, it yet may arouse uncomfortable doubts in its practitioners about the motivation and the propriety of their behavior. Moral ambiguity dogs it.

Boswell invites his reader into a relationship with similarities to the tie expressed and generated by gossip.

> Some time after this, upon his making a remark which escaped my attention, Mrs. Williams and Mrs. Hall were both together striving to answer him. He grew angry, and called out loudly, "Nay, when you both speak at once, it is intolerable." But checking himself, and softening, he said, "This one may say, though you *are* ladies." Then he brightened into gay humour, and addressed them in the words of one of the songs in "The Beggar's Opera."
>
> "But two at a time there's no mortal can bear."
>
> "What, Sir, (said I,) are you going to turn Captain Macheath?" There was something as pleasantly ludicrous in this scene as can be imagined. The contrast between Macheath, Polly, and Lucy—and Dr. Samuel Johnson, blind, peevish Mrs. Williams, and lean, lank, preaching Mrs. Hall, was exquisite [4.95].

This randomly chosen episode epitomizes Boswell's typical mode in relating a verbal interchange of no obvious intrinsic significance. Dr. Johnson is seventy-two years old at the time, Mrs. Hall (John Wesley's widowed sister) and Anna Williams (a longtime pensioner of Johnson's) two or three years older. As the *London Journal* reveals, Macheath, the dashing highwayman of *The Beggar's Opera*, had been a favorite fantasy-model of Boswell in his youth. Now, grown-up, Boswell perceives and gently exposes the discrepancy between imagining and reality. There is no time in the unconscious, Freud has told us; Dr. Johnson can fall into Macheath's role without feeling its incongruity. Boswell evokes not only the ludicrous contrast between the literal and the imagined cast of characters, but the subtler comedy of Johnson's movement (anger—softening—brightening) from impatient anger to self-reminder of the rules of gallantry to discovery of a literary allusion that makes rebuke of ladies morally tolerable to him.

The art here involves more than that dramatic rendering often noted as one of Boswell's literary gifts. Intimately connected with the biographer's capacity for moral perception, it derives also from his ability to perceive significance in the trivial. Not only his precise observation of what Johnson does and says but his sensitivity to the psychic movement underlying shifts in speech and action, his own emotional responsiveness, his ability to specify sources of comedy—all contribute to the scene's rhetorical and dramatic effect. Boswell tells a story, even (or especially) a tiny story, well and interprets it well. If these embody the biographer's skills, they also epitomize the gossip's. Boswell's narrations heighten the reader's hunger for every detail about Johnson. The biographer provides a banquet of idiosyncrasy and urges us to savor it. Johnson rarely gossips; but Boswell's reports of his discourse, however dignified, become the substance of gossip by being incorporated into the pattern of intense concentration on, and implicit or explicit interpretation of, verbal and visual minutiae.

What I have said about Boswell applies, in varying degree, to biography in general. Not all biographers possess Boswell's descriptive or dramatic expertise or his memory, his obsessiveness, his analytic dexterity. But many biographies, like Boswell's, invite their readers to dwell on and to seek significance in human detail. The pleasure of biography can involve not only delight in finding out, but delight in the *process* of finding out, a process bearing striking resemblances to that of gossip.

Because the narrator bears primary responsibility for any intrusion, reading biography feels less like violating privacies than does reading letters. But biography too has liminal status, on the border between "literature" and "history," uncertainly justified by the quality of its narration or the degree of its accuracy. Boswell's version of biography involves another borderland as well, which many, but not all, biographies evoke: that between public and private. The two special aspects of the *Life* I noted previously, the narrator's constant intrusion into the narration and the combination of recurrent debunking with insistent idealization, both illuminate the special relation of public and private in this text. They also have their bearing on gossip.

Invoking "the present age" and "posterity" as sanctions for his own obsession, Boswell indicates—as he does repeatedly throughout the biography—his conviction that Johnson's status as public figure justifies detailed attention to his character and personality. As author of the *Dictionary*, which accomplished for England what academies of learned men had done for Italy and France, as the moral philosopher of *The Rambler*, as writer, finally, of the *Lives of the Poets*, which solidified new standards for biography and articulated a partial canon of English poetry, Johnson indeed belonged to the ages. The religious language of "worship" and "reverence" implicitly claims Johnson's superhuman stature. From one point of view, the biography exists to substantiate this stature and to gratify readers' yearnings for objects of idealization. Like Greek tragedy, this kind of biography shows someone elevated above mankind in general and demonstrates how his character becomes his fate.

The desire to worship and the desire for intimate knowledge oppose one another. As Boswell reveals Johnson scraping bits of orange peel, caressing his cat, losing his temper, fearing death and loneliness, appearing in public with shabby clothes and undersized wig, upholding untenable positions, abusing innocent bystanders and insulting Boswell himself—the reader, encountering emphatic evidence of human frailty, can no longer understand Johnson as saint or monument. As private man, the hero resembles other men. Intimate specificity modifies the myth of heroism. Gossip emphasizes what people hold in common, dwells on frailties, seeks the hidden rather than the manifest; heroism thrives on specialness and on public manifestation. Boswell proclaims his intimate relation with his subject. For the reader's attention to hundreds of pages of data and interpretation, he promises the reward of knowledge that will undermine public pretension. The intimacy he establishes with the reader parallels that he has won with Johnson. With Johnson, he feels himself the inferior: thirty-one years younger than his mentor, infinitely less accomplished. In imagined association with his reader, he assumes the superior position, source of information and interpretation. He also demonstrates the special sense in which he can claim superiority even to Johnson.

Boswell depicts himself in the text mainly as naïf, always deferring to Johnson's superior wisdom and experience. But increasingly also he presents himself as author, specifically as intending biographer, asking Johnson questions about his past, copying extracts from his diary, criticizing the inadequacy of friends who fail to write down what they hear. On page 380—fifty pages before the end—of the final volume of the *Life*, he remarks, "I now relieve the readers of this Work from any farther personal notice of its authour, who if he should be thought to have obtruded himself too much upon their attention, requests them to consider the peculiar plan of his biographical undertaking." He has just reported his own indisposition during the final months of Johnson's life and his consequent inability to correspond, has transcribed Johnson's final letter to him and complained about Johnson's rebukes to him for the melancholy the older man shared, and has assured his readers that Johnson "spoke of me on his death-bed, with affection, and I look forward with humble hope of renewing our friendship in a better world."

Boswell, of course, continues to "obtrude." The first-person-singular pronoun occurs regularly, even in critical observations; the biographer reminds us at every turn that all judgments and perceptions issue from his mind. He professes once more his "sacred love of truth" (4.397) and declares his anxiety, in a sequence I have already quoted, about "the most difficult and dangerous part" of his work. He reports having read, without Johnson's knowledge, in his diary and sets down the subsequent dialogue ("apologizing for the liberty I had taken, [I] asked him if I could help it"; 4.405). He bestows approval on William Windham, the statesman, for visiting the dying sage (407). He declares his own inability to express his feelings adequately: "I trust, I shall not be accused of affectation, when I declare, that I find myself unable to express all that I felt upon the loss of such a 'Guide, Philosopher, and Friend' " (420). Once more, he emphasizes the difficulty of his biographical task, after pointing out that the reader, by this time, "may be considered as well acquainted" with Johnson (424–5). In short, Boswell remains as much on hand as ever after he announces his disappearance.

The "peculiar plan" which Boswell invokes concentrates on developing the reader's intimacy with the subject. "Indeed I cannot conceive a more perfect mode of writing any man's life, than not only relating all the most important events of it in their order, but interweaving what he privately wrote, and said, and thought; by which mankind are enabled as it were to see him live, and to 'live o'er each scene' with him, as he actually advanced through the several stages of his life" (1.30). He thus announces his intent of focusing both on the public and on the private. He does not, however, explain why double focus involves insistent self-presentation. Perhaps he would claim that he brings the reader into relation with the subject partly by representing his own relation. But my citations from the final fifty pages, all of which directly or indirectly concern Boswell's role as biographer, suggest another reason for the biography's partial concentration on its author. "To write the Life of him who excelled all mankind in writing the lives of others, and who, whether we consider his extraordinary endowments, or his various works, has been equalled by few in any age, is an arduous, and may be reckoned in me a presumptuous task" (1.25). So the *Life* begins. However arduous, however presumptuous the task, Boswell performs it. However unequaled Johnson's attainments, Boswell takes possession of them in prose. He assumes the power of representation, he tells the story, he assigns the meanings.

The stability thus achieved opposes gossip's essential insecurity. But inasmuch as Boswell makes his search for such stability a subject of his narrative, dramatizing the struggle for verbal control between a champion talker and a brilliant recorder of talk, he calls attention to moral issues at gossip's heart. I have suggested before gossip's function as resource of the subordinated. Those to whom society allows no power retain the possibility of talking—perhaps only in whispers, behind closed doors—about people who run things. Always feeling Johnson his superior, characteristically subordinating his immediate desires to his mentor's, Boswell reasserts himself by collecting and setting down stories: an activity comparable to gossip.

The concept of "meaning" in a human life implies meaning *to* someone. Gossipers generate meanings, which they may choose to keep within their group. Boswell encourages his readers to share the long process of reconciling his perception of Johnson's moral and intellectual grandeur with his own assertion not only of autonomy but of mastery. Showing himself as manipulator of social encounters (the famous meeting with Wilkes, for example) and of conversation ("If, Sir, you were shut up in a castle, and a newborn child with you, what would you do?"; 2.100), but most of all as controller of significance, Boswell raises questions about what personal narrative means to the narrator and to the subject of narration. His self-exposure becomes his authority. The impossibility of his disappearing from the text demonstrates his presence at the narrative's center: the interpretive consciousness declares itself integral to the story's import. At the narrative's heart lies Boswell's discovery of his own power in an asymmetrical relationship with an overwhelmingly powerful man. Here too, public and private intersect. The biographer shows what precedes the public act of writing. One can play the fool, he demonstrates, without being one. His consistent self-subordination in day-by-day intercourse with Johnson allows him the verbal mastery of his book: a pattern paralleling the contrast he shows in Johnson, whose private inadequacies make his public performance more astounding. The art and the communicated knowledge of *The Life of Samuel Johnson, LL.D.* involve the interplay of two lives as well as the twining of public and private in each of them.

The matters I have been discussing—the narrator's relation to text and audience, the nature of meaning in story, the use of story as mastery—belong to fiction as well as to biography and gossip. Boswell's mode, obviously, does not dominate all biographies. But the problems to which it calls attention, of the narrator's connection with subject, audience, and text, resurface in biographies quite unlike *The Life of Samuel Johnson, LL.D.*

Such as, for example, W. Jackson Bate's late twentieth-century *Samuel Johnson*, a magisterial work which, like Boswell's, assesses the man and his achievement, but emerges with rather different conclusions and employs utterly different techniques. Some of the differences derive from greater distance in time, lack of personal knowledge—some, but not all. In Boswell's biography, the process of interpretation that preoccupies the narrator comes to absorb the reader. Bate provides consistent conclusions rather than a view of the process leading to them. His interpretation appears to have preceded the writing of the biography; Boswell, who starts with an attitude of "worship" toward his great subject, only gradually works out the meaning of his text— a meaning which obviously includes himself. Bate rarely uses the first-person-singular pronoun. He prefers the plural: a "we" invoking the community of cultivated readers, implicitly claiming for Johnson that universality which Boswell too assumed. Bate's Johnson takes on moral and intellectual stature comparable to Boswell's, but Bate emphasizes pain, privation, and struggle: the inner life of suffering rather than the public life of triumph. He claims complete continuity between "public" and "private." And, unlike Boswell, he never deviates from a confident, authoritative tone—although one informed with passion.

Psychic life, in the twentieth century, provides almost as rich material for speculation as sex life. That elegant form of gossip called psychoanalysis, in which a patient supplies a fertile flow of intimate data and the analyst collaborates in constructing a story from it, has deeply influenced twentieth-century imaginations. Bate in his biography eschews vulgar psychoanalytic speculation, calling attention to the ease with which minds informed by Freud leap to sexual explanations for psychological peculiarities, and providing more careful hypotheses himself. Yet he invites and helps the reader to see even in trivial episodes of Johnson's life evidence of a painfully divided man.

In an essay entitled "Literary Criticism and Methodology," the linguist

Thomas Pavel, trying to distinguish between two kinds of literary criticism ("optimistic," which assumes the possibility of saying something about a text, and "apprehensive," operating with opposed assumptions), compares "optimistic" criticism with gossip. He means nothing pejorative: "one can recognize," he points out, "that there is such a thing as 'good' gossip; gossip that correctly applies the rules of the game." "Good" gossip demands that the speaker "stay within the limits of the subject matter and . . . tell the truth"; also "that gossip-hypotheses be as specific as possible and that the evidence for them be a matter of common knowledge. . . . Thus gossip (good gossip) is an informal exercise in hypothesis devising and evidence finding. . . . Its purpose is the understanding of the person or the situation discussed." "Basic gossip" reports facts and constructs simple hypotheses about them; "sophisticated gossip" involves "the devising of elaborate, unexpected hypotheses, often supported only by tenuous evidence." In the equivalent kind of literary criticism, "purpose is not purely cognitive. The reader does not expect to learn only true facts and correct explanations about the literary work, but, more important, to be put in the literary mood, to appreciate the atmosphere of a specific work or, even more generally, of a given literary group or period. One expects this type of criticism to familiarise its reader with the prevalent literary climate in the same way that gossip adjusts people to the surrounding social climate."[7]

Much more than Boswell, Bate (who admires Boswell, but implies his own greater interpretive power) appears to consider biography and criticism intimately related activities. Pavel's comments about criticism apply precisely to the biographical technique of *Samuel Johnson*, which assumes the possibility of saying something illuminating about an actual person. The book's hypotheses rest often on ambiguous evidence, yet they persuasively elucidate Johnson's nature and context. For example:

In January (1740) Johnson was back at Lichfield, again visiting Walmesley and seeing Molly Aston. But even if he continued to delay returning to London, something had to be done about money. Lacking any other alternative, he and his mother made arrangements to mortgage the house. . . . There is no indication that Sarah herself needed to do this. Living very cheaply, she seemed able to survive on the small income that the bookshop still brought her. The mortgage was certainly made at Johnson's own urging, and the request could hardly increase his self-respect. He was now thirty-one. He had earned nothing for over half a year. Owing to his own indolence,

he and—because of him—Sarah were now capitalizing on the sole
asset that remained to them [186].

Neither Hawkins nor Boswell mentions this episode. Bate, interpreting the
bare fact of a mortgage on the Lichfield house, makes much from little. His
vocabulary hints tentativeness: "There is no indication," "seemed," "certainly" (implying considerable uncertainty), "hardly." His general hypothesis
of Johnson's mental distress at this period subsumes the financial transaction,
which then becomes further evidence for it.

I do not mean to quarrel with the interpretation or with its method: Bate's
capacity to make the most of small detail creates his book's richness, and his
reading of events, like his reading of texts, sounds unfailingly plausible
although rarely indisputable. Lives, like texts, demand rereading as time
passes; what Bate sees in Johnson's career epitomizes twentieth-century vision. My point is simply that this kind of interpretation, like that of the
criticism Pavel cites, belongs to the repertoire of gossip.

The point becomes clearer in relation to the kind of biographical material
traditionally associated with gossip: for instance, the matter of Johnson's
marriage. Hawkins hints that he married for money, suggesting that Elizabeth
Porter's first husband "left her, if not well jointured, so provided for, as made
a match with her to a man in Johnson's circumstances desirable"; he says
that "little can now be remembered" of her "personal charms," but that
since Johnson probably didn't see well enough to notice, any deficiency of
beauty would hardly have mattered to him.[8] Boswell describes Mrs. Porter
(inaccurately) as "double the age of Johnson," adding that since "her person
and manner, as described to me by the late Mr. Garrick, were by no means
pleasing to others, she must have had a superiority of understanding and
talents, as she certainly inspired him with a more than ordinary passion."
The marriage, Boswell says, "was a very imprudent scheme, both on account
of their disparity of years, and her want of fortune" (1.95). Four pages later,
he quotes Garrick's grotesque description.

Both these accounts (like all biographies before Bate's) evade the erotic,
with Hawkins hinting prudential motivation and Boswell hypothesizing intellectual appeal ("superiority of understanding and talents") as the most
plausible explanation for Johnson's "passion." Bate confronts the issue more
directly. He notes Mrs. Thrale's testimony about Johnson's extraordinary
awareness of female appearance and dress: however bad his eyes, Johnson
could see his wife. He adduces evidence from another observer (William
Shaw, a clergyman whom Johnson helped and who subsequently wrote a
memoir of the great man) that at the time of the marriage Tetty "was still

young and handsome." And he offers his own explanation, beginning with
a general demonstration of Johnson's unusual capacity for gratitude and
moving to the particular. "Certainly gratitude was for Johnson a powerful
element in this marriage of seventeen years, which was the first of the three
or four things (the next was the new career he was to start in London, largely
because of the responsibility he felt for Tetty) that really pulled him out and
saved him from the self-destructive state into which he had been sunk for
so long. From the start, . . . Elizabeth Jervis Porter had given him help and
confidence" (152). In other words, Bate accounts for an emotional fact in
emotional terms: a kind of feeling we know Johnson to have demonstrated
in other situations may explain the intense feeling he attached to his wife.

Again, the hypothesis rests on little direct evidence. Bate recalls Boswell's
report that Mrs. Porter valued Johnson's conversation, declaring him the
most sensible man she ever saw, and ignored his grotesque appearance: thus,
presumably, she gave him confidence. Johnson worked as a tutor for two
months before his marriage and reclaimed the books he had left at Oxford
five and a half years before: slender proof that "things had made a turn for
the better" as a result of Elizabeth Porter's faith in him (148). Like Bate's
interpretation of the mortgage episode, his understanding of Johnson's marriage derives from his vision of the sage as a man in recurrent (almost chronic)
psychic crisis, ever needing to be "pulled . . . out." Mrs. Porter's apparent
capacity to relieve that crisis becomes, therefore, the ground of Johnson's
feeling for her.

From a twentieth-century point of view, Bate's explanation sounds more
plausible than Hawkins' and more convincing than Boswell's. But all three
accounts conform to the model of Pavel's "sophisticated gossip" and appeal
to the reader's interest not only in facts of human experience but in meanings
attributable to these facts. Bate's capacity to provide a single, complex, coherent interpretation for Johnson's human diversity energizes his biography.
It also answers one of the same human needs as gossip.

Bate understands Johnson's life as a "parable"—that is to say, he *makes*
it a parable—and Johnson's writing as continuous with his life. "Hence in
the moral writings—as in all of his greater writing or as in the parable of his
life generally—we always sense two fundamental values, not because they
are preached but because they are coming to us with the force of example.
One is the potential freedom of man. . . . The second value, sustaining and
rendering practical the first, is expressed in the simplest and finest of his
maxims: 'The first step in greatness is to be honest' " (314). To write a critical
biography implies not only specific belief in the connection between the
individual subject and his or her work but general faith in the intimate

connection of life and art. Boswell assumes that the greatness of Johnson's moral writings testifies to the grandeur of his moral being; Bate uses the complexity of Johnson's moral experience to discover the intricacy of his published prose. Although he does not reduce the mass of published writings to a single model, he finds everywhere supporting evidence for his sense of Johnson's struggle against his own "self demand," his unceasing effort to keep himself psychically afloat. One example, in the *Preface to Shakespeare:* "Here we have continuing for pages what before we found more often in particular sentences or paragraphs: a grasping, against strong internal pressures, for certitude, control, balance, and order. We sense the whole body being involved, as though he were trying to pull himself above the surface. Hence the tamped-down finality as he phrases convictions based on a lifetime of experience" (399). Taken out of context, these observations, except for such specific references as "pages," might as plausibly concern the "parable" of Johnson's life as the nature of his work. The work itself now dramatizes the process of being "pulled out" that the life reiterates. The interpretive act involved in Bate's criticism duplicates that of the purely biographical portions of his book. Both draw from assumptions about discourse which also govern gossip. Both, like gossip, try to win assent by assuming it ("We sense . . .").

Bate includes stories which Boswell omits: for example, the vignette about Johnson's imitating a kangaroo on the journey through the Hebrides. He provides a chapter on "Wit and Humor," emphasizing Johnson's comic gifts. The Johnson he presents does not spend every minute in melancholy, though Bate insists on the melancholy strain underlying all else. But this biography earns its epigraph (from Pythagoras): "What is your warrant for valuing any part of my experience and rejecting the rest? . . . If I had done so, you would never have heard my name." Bate shows Johnson as one who valued his own experience in its entirety, taking everything seriously (comedy, of course, being one mode of taking things seriously), and he shows himself as likewise valuing the entire experience of his complicated, awe-inspiring subject. The biography thus implies for its readers the desirability of understanding, valuing, interpreting their own lives.

All good biography illumines every reader's life by generating intimate awareness of another. Bate's insistent "we" encourages intimacy, suggesting his own identification, allowing the reader's, with his subject. His emphasis on the necessary difficulties of middle age and on the problem of loneliness, particularly that of increasing age, calls attention to the universality of dilemmas he understands Johnson to have faced. If Boswell generates complexity and power by separating himself from his subject, insisting on his role as witness and recorder, reminding his readers of the mastery implicit in acts of interpretation, Bate achieves his effects by virtually opposite means. In conviction and attitude, he finally almost merges with his subject. His empathetic grasp of Johnson's suffering and triumph invites readers too to see themselves in Johnson, Johnson in themselves. By accretion of small detail and by contemplative dwelling on detail (Johnson's mother took a mortgage on her house . . .), Bate constructs a myth of heroism different from Boswell's. Boswell reveals the discrepancy of private fallibility and public achievement. Bate insists that private and public, life and work, participate in a single meaning. His vision of heroism represents not an alternative to fallibility but a mode of life both containing and transcending fallibility; he makes of that vision an aesthetic construct and a moral statement. Affirming shared humanity and demonstrating that sharing by examination and inter-pretation of detail, Bate embodies in yet another way the positive values of gossip, as a process of interpretation and as a humanizing activity.

Elizabeth Gaskell, like Boswell, claims personal knowledge as foundation for her *Life of Charlotte Brontë* (1857). Writing more than sixty-five years after Boswell, a woman whose life demonstrates conventional female virtues (wife of a Unitarian minister, mother of many children, worker among the poor), Mrs. Gaskell shows herself acutely conscious of moral issues implicit in the life story she tells. Her way of communicating a value system that she would not explicitly endorse recalls the subterranean messages of gossip.

"Gossip" is a bad word in this book. Gaskell claims her subject's supe-riority to the taint of "petty local gossip"[9]; she quotes a letter in which Brontë vehemently disclaims allegations that she has written a novel by observing, "I have given no one a right to gossip about me, and am not to be judged by frivolous conjectures, emanating from any quarter whatever" (2.50); she complains about an early review in the *Quarterly Review*: "the Quarterly reviewer goes on into gossiping conjectures as to who Currer Bell really is, and pretends to decide on what the writer may be from the book" (2.71). Gossip implies unwarranted conjecture. Gaskell's own biographical problem, as she formulates it, involves the temptation of saying too much. "The difficulty that presented itself most strongly to me, when I first had the honour of being requested [by Charlotte's father] to write this biography, was how I could show what a noble, true, and tender woman Charlotte Brontë really was, without mingling up with her life too much of the personal history of her nearest and most intimate friends. After much consideration of this point, I came to the resolution of writing truly, if I wrote at all; of withholding nothing, though some things, from their very nature, could not be spoken of so fully as others" (2.225).

The tension between the desire to tell and the desire not to dominates the book. Without telling too much, Gaskell communicates a great deal. From a twentieth-century point of view, she could hardly be accused of indiscretion in her account of one whom she sees as possessing "extraordinary genius" and "noble virtue" (2.269). She appears to "withhold" quite a lot in her version of Brontë's life in order to preserve a myth of female heroism. We cannot, of course, know precisely how much *she* knew. She reports, in decorous terms, the catastrophic liaison of the single Brontë boy, Branwell, with his employer's wife, but she never hints Charlotte's erotic interest in Monsieur Héger, her employer in Brussels, much less the novelist's subsequent ambiguous attachment to George Smith, her publisher. Gaskell's version of Charlotte's late marriage sounds idyllic; she quotes letters asserting Brontë's utter marital happiness rather than those that suggest inner conflict. Emphasizing the woman's devotion to her father and her siblings and her extravagant sense of responsibility, she makes Charlotte into a paragon of Victorian womanhood. She reports, for example, how the old Brontë servant, Tabby, in her increasing blindness, would fail to cut the eyes out of potatoes she peeled. "Miss Brontë was too dainty a housekeeper to put up with this; yet she could not bear to hurt the faithful old servant. . . . Accordingly she would steal into the kitchen, and quietly carry off the bowl of vegetables, without Tabby's being aware, and breaking off in the full flow of interest and inspiration in her writing, carefully cut out the specks in the potatoes, and noiselessly carry them back to their place. This little proceeding may show how orderly and fully she accomplished her duties, even at those times when the 'possession' was upon her" (2.7–8). The dainty housekeeper who accomplishes her duties "orderly and fully," in this account, justifies the novelist. To refuse to break the flow of inspiration would betray female inadequacy.

Far more contextual than either of the other biographies examined thus far, *The Life of Charlotte Brontë* dwells extensively not only on the people surrounding its central character but on places and happenings that might seem to have little connection with her. The book opens with detailed description of the Brontës' physical surroundings in Haworth, emphasizing restriction and gloom. It includes episodes with little obvious bearing on Charlotte's life: for instance, a "specimen of wild stories" told by local folk, about a girl seduced by her brother-in-law (1.46). Gaskell offers apparently random bits of characterization, about people with no direct connection to Charlotte (e.g., 1.100). She tells stories about an unnamed northern minister, to suggest what northern ministers are like (1.101). On occasion, one can understand the justification for including local scandal, as in the anecdote about a man who marries a governess while keeping a first wife concealed, a tale obviously related to the plot of *Jane Eyre* (1.124); but often the stories seem told for their own sake.

Anecdotes and descriptions of this sort establish an imaginative setting. Indeed, they covertly justify lurid aspects of Brontë's fiction by suggesting affinities of melodramatic plot with realism rather than with romance. (Brontë's own life, of course, had its melodramatic aspects.) But they also do something never overtly acknowledged: they delineate a realm of oppression that women inhabit. When a rich brother-in-law seduces a local girl, her parents condemn her and condone his conduct. The scandalous story about the man with a secret wife centers on his taking advantage of another woman. Gaskell reports many specific instances of irascibility and brutality in Charlotte's father ("He did not speak when he was annoyed or displeased, but worked off his volcanic wrath by firing pistols out of the back-door in rapid succession"; 1.43), concluding that his character must remain a mystery, yet emphasizing his destructive effect on his daughters: "It is true that he had strong and vehement prejudices, and was obstinate in maintaining them, and that he was not dramatic enough in his perceptions to see how miserable others might be in a life that to him was all-sufficient. But I do not pretend to be able to harmonize points of character, and account for them, and bring them all into one consistent and intelligible whole. The family with whom I have now to do shot their roots down deeper than I can penetrate. I cannot measure them, much less is it for me to judge them" (1.45). The biographer stresses the distinction between expectations for Branwell, supposed to "do," and his sisters, destined only to "be" (1.167–8); she points out the burden of such hopes for the young man and says nothing explicitly about the corresponding weight on women deprived in advance of the pleasure of accomplishment. Her narrative, however, makes the reader acutely conscious of female burdens. Her sense of women's victimization perhaps emerges most sharply in an incidental comment connected with Branwell, for whom Gaskell displays relatively little sympathy. "The case [his liaison] presents the reverse of the usual features," the biographer observes; "the man became the victim; the man's life was blighted and crushed out of him by suffering, and guilt entailed by guilt; the man's family was stung by keenest shame" (1.265). *The reverse of the usual features*: for women to suffer is *usual*.

Far from seeing Charlotte Brontë's life as continuous with her work, Gaskell, even while recognizing autobiographical elements in the novels, makes a sharp distinction between "woman" and "author." "Before I return from the literary opinions of the author to the domestic interests of the woman . . ." (2.170). To the author belongs genius; to the woman, virtue. The "virtue" of the writing has been thought problematic: Rochester's dubious character (*Jane Eyre*) and Jane's choice of passion over piety, the excessive emphasis on love that Harriet Martineau deplored, the episode in *Villette* when Lucy Snowe confesses to a Catholic priest. Robert Southey, in a famous letter to young Charlotte Brontë, who had written asking literary advice, informed her that the hunger for fame implicit in writing for publication would interfere with her performance of womanly duties; the potential reproach (to which Brontë responded by affirming her dedication to domesticity) underlies Gaskell's stress on Charlotte's capacities as housekeeper. Gaskell defends the writer by emphasizing the woman's conventional virtues. The biographer's final paragraph demands sympathy for Brontë's faults and reverence for her virtue as well as admiration for the writer's genius.

On the next-to-the-last page, however, Gaskell reports an odd anecdote. She has just described Charlotte Brontë's funeral. "Among those humble friends who passionately grieved over the dead, was a village girl who had been seduced some little time before, but who had found a holy sister in Charlotte. She had sheltered her with her help, her counsel, her strengthening words; had ministered to her needs in her time of trial. Bitter, bitter was the grief of this poor young woman, when she heard that her friend was sick unto death, and deep is her mourning until this day" (2.268). The figure of the seduced and abandoned woman has reappeared regularly through the narrative, always unexpectedly, often with little direct connection to Brontë. This final intrusion of the emblematic woman underlines Brontë's Christian virtue ("holy sister"), her acceptance of charitable as well as domestic responsibility. But why this rather than another example of the good woman's good actions? (Gaskell also reports the mourning of a blind girl whom Charlotte has helped, but with less dramatic emphasis.) Perhaps because Charlotte's friendship for this victim of male treachery reiterates the subterranean theme of female victimization.

The Life of Charlotte Brontë preaches no covert doctrine of feminist revolt, but it implies social criticism by its anecdotes from the traditional repertory of gossip, episodes of sex and violence about unknown people; by its tales of paternal outbursts and filial helplessness; in a different vein, by its stories about Charlotte's pathological shyness, based, we are told, on her conviction of her physical ugliness. Explicitly, Gaskell argues that the feminine propriety—indeed, the conspicuous *goodness*—of Brontë's personal life, always subordinated to the needs of others (father, brother, sisters, even servants), compensates for the alleged moral dubiety of her writing. Implicitly, she raises, but does not answer, a feminist question: if female circumstance involves constant self-suppression, may it not become justifiable for a woman to rebel at least in print? I referred earlier to Gaskell's "myth of female heroism." The myth involves two aspects: specifically female virtue (i.e., subordination and service), specifically female genius (assertion through self-expression: passion and will).

Biographies often make one wonder what made the biographer choose a given subject, what the writing of a particular book meant to its writer. Such questions usually remain unanswerable. The title page of *The Life of Charlotte Brontë* identifies its subject as "Author of 'Jane Eyre,' 'Shirley,' 'Villette,' &c." and its writer as "Author of 'Mary Barton,' 'Ruth,' etc." The titles remind us that although Gaskell manifested great gifts as a novelist, they did not include open effusions of passion. "According to Freud," Ernst Kris points out, "the biographer is frequently attached to his subject in a strange manner" (64). Gaskell's attachment to Charlotte Brontë as subject may involve her seeing in the dead novelist an alternative solution—unconventional passion rather than docile conformity—to the biographer's own moral and social problems. The perplexities of Gaskell's emotional situation infuse her discussion of Brontë's; this covert identification lends intensity to the narrative and complexity to the reader-narrator relationship as well as to that of narrator and subject.

Gaskell's use of the first-person-singular pronoun intensifies markedly toward the end of the biography, partly because her friendship with the subject began fairly late in Charlotte's life. Gaskell's "I," unlike Boswell's, declares not verbal dominance but emotional submission. "I cannot measure or judge of such a character as hers" (2.268). "But I turn from the critical, unsympathetic public,—inclined to judge harshly because they have only seen superficially and not thought deeply" (2.269). She herself will not attempt to judge or even to define; she only *accepts*. Gaskell conveys humble admiration of Brontë's capacity to articulate passion and implicitly to criticize female subordination even when describing it (in the characters of Lucy Snowe, in *Villette*; Caroline Helstone, in *Shirley*; the young Jane Eyre). The biographer's gossiplike reports—about her subject, about the Brontë family, about people on the outskirts of their experience—substantiate the need for women to refuse, although she herself rarely did so.

I have not reiterated my earlier points about gossip and biography, but I might have: *The Life of Charlotte Brontë* duplicates aspects of the Johnson biographies. Here too the biographer invites the reader into a complicitous relationship dedicated to uncovering secrets of character; the valuing of small detail recalls the emphases of oral gossip; one learns to take seriously diverse forms of evidence about human nature and to interpret character on the basis of anecdote, and one becomes absorbed in a narrative woven of human experience. But because, I suspect, Gaskell wishes to convey something she will not quite say openly, gossip becomes in this biography also a mode of subterfuge, as so often when spoken in groups.

"All joy or sorrow for the happiness or calamities of others," Dr. Johnson wrote, "is produced by an act of the imagination, that realizes the event however fictitious or approximates it however remote, by placing us, for a time, in the condition of him whose fortune we contemplate; so that we feel, while the deception lasts, whatever motions would be excited by the same good or evil happening to ourselves."[10] Discussing biography, Johnson in this sentence locates the reader in relation to the subject of narrative. His first-person-plural pronouns insist on the universality of his explanation. This model of identification indeed accounts for one kind of response to biography; the gossip model supplements it, to suggest how readers look at as well as merge with biographical subjects. A narrator tells us about someone else's secrets, and instructs us what to think about them. If we respond partly by imagining what it would feel like to *be* that someone (a response also possible, incidentally, in oral gossip), we also enjoy a looking-through-the-keyhole reaction. However formal or chatty in tone, however carefully or loosely constructed, biography solicits such emotion—emotion that solidifies the reader's connection with the narrator and establishes a vague superiority to the subject without destroying the sense of common experience to which Johnson alludes.

Helene Moglen's twentieth-century rendering of Charlotte Brontë resembles Gaskell's nineteenth-century one less than Bate's Johnson resembles Boswell's. Her biographical method accounts for the difference. Assuming the continuity of life and work, Moglen uses Brontë's fiction to illumine her experience instead of (like Bate) interpreting work by life. She observes, "Literary biographies interest me least when they set out to tell exhaustively and 'objectively' the history of an individual, tallying dates, genealogies and events, friends and lovers, geographical locations, and the titles of books written and read."[11] The interaction of life and work, Moglen concludes, best defines Charlotte Brontë. "The events of the life could no longer be melodramatically recounted, as they have so often been. The novels could not simply be examined as quirky stages in a developing genre. . . . [My study] places chronology at the service of causality, . . . risks partiality in the interest of emphasis" (14).

Two observations quoted earlier from Thomas Pavel's essay seem relevant: "gossip (good gossip) is an informal exercise in hypothesis devising and evidence finding. . . . Its purpose is the understanding of the person or the situation discussed." Moglen makes literature a subject for hypotheses of the same order as those about non-literary human experience. With severe selectivity, she adduces fewer facts than Gaskell does about Brontë's life. (The facts, however, frequently differ from those Gaskell knows, or chooses to tell: Moglen analyzes Brontë's erotic feeling for Monsieur Héger, using letters as evidence, details her psychic distress in Brussels, suggests her sentiments about George Smith, and investigates the dynamics of her marriage.) She treats fiction as a kind of fact, assuming the possibility of specifying the connection of experience and work. Her book, consequently, consists mainly of hypotheses and of evidentiary claims, both designed to further "understanding of the person . . . discussed": by Pavel's definition, "good gossip."

Moglen's treatment of the Héger episode exemplifies her method, its value and its limitations. Like Bate, this biographer offers interpretation in the guise of fact. After providing documentable biographical detail about the Belgian schoolmaster Héger, Moglen adds, "Not least of all, he was a gifted teacher: knowledgeable and insightful, appreciative of his serious students, responsive to their intellectual and emotional requirements. He exploited the teacher-student relationship, with its undisputed hierarchy of power, its always latent sexuality, its allowance for dependence—even idolatry—without humiliation. All of this provided a channeling of psychosexual forces acceptable within the Victorian culture. The friendship with Héger provided Brontë with a viable transition between her relationships with her father and brother and the more mature heterosexual interaction of which she was becoming capable" (63). For Héger's pedagogical gifts, Brontë's letters provide at least arguable evidence. For his exploitation of the teacher-student relation, Moglen draws more largely on her own assumption. The last two sentences, about Victorian culture and Brontë's sexual transition, carry the passage's argument and derive from the writer's political, social, and psychological convictions. In diction and syntax, these sentences belong to formal academic discourse. No note of the speaking voice clings to them. The sequential structure, on the other hand, duplicates a pattern familiar in intimate conversation: imperceptible and unacknowledged movement from information to assessment.

Moglen quotes from several letters to document Brontë's attachment to Héger and her efforts at once to assert and conceal it—from herself as well as others. Continuing the narrative of the relationship, the biographer observes, "There seems to be little doubt that Brontë's schoolgirl attachment to M. Héger was perceived by his wife, who deftly but surely saw to it that Brontë would not be misled about the degree or nature of her husband's interest" (66). Using the same kind of evidence—Brontë's letters (although

probably not the same letters)—Gaskell concludes, "One of the reasons for
the silent estrangement between Madame Héger and Miss Brontë, in the
second year of her residence at Brussels, is to be found in the fact, that the
English Protestant's dislike of Romanism increased with her knowledge of
it, and its effects upon those who professed it; and when occasion called for
an expression of opinion from Charlotte Brontë, she was uncompromising
truth" (1.243). Although Gaskell declares this only "one of the reasons" for
Madame Héger's apparent disapproval of the young Englishwoman, she
never supplies others. Did she too feel "little doubt" that the woman perceived
Brontë's interest in the schoolmaster? "It is impossible to deny the romantic
and fundamentally sexual nature of Brontë's interest," Moglen flatly asserts
(67); Gaskell, then, does the impossible in her effort to evoke a woman
virtuous as well as passionate. (Charlotte's letters to Héger appeared in print
only in 1913, as Moglen points out; Gaskell probably had less compelling
evidence available to her.)

Moglen's case about Héger goes through two further stages. First she
raises the question of how far one can generalize from Brontë's experience,
relying on emphatic rhetorical questions: "How many students, more or less
masochistic than Charlotte, but subject still to similar social and psychosexual
pressures, might have created fantasies equally disturbing if less consuming
and not so naïvely tested? In short, how unique was Brontë's response? To
what extent was her infatuation, accepted for so long at face value, simply
another manifestation of the sexual politics pervasive in Victorian society:
more insidious because it was socially validated?" (70). Such questions reflect
the writer's conviction that Charlotte Brontë epitomizes a class of Victorian
young women. (Moglen implicitly acknowledges the answer she assumes by
beginning her next paragraph, "Of course, there was a difference," and
suggesting a rather slight one: Brontë differed from most of her contemporaries in intensity.)

Brontë's first novel, *The Professor,* in Moglen's view provides further
evidence of Brontë's powerful fantasy about Héger. "This fantasy, variously
imaged and developed, recurs in all four of Brontë's novels. Her compulsive
reworking of the same themes demonstrates the degree of difficulty she
experienced in resolving the conflict with Héger. It also suggests the extent
to which that conflict was associated implicitly with attitudes toward her own
sexuality, her father, Branwell, and her work" (83). The novel thus supports
the thesis articulated earlier, about the friendship with Héger as a transitional
stage in Brontë's sexual development.

"*Do not,*" the late eighteenth-century French writer Joseph Joubert advises in a notebook entry, "—Define what is known: gossip."[12] Such a characterization seems to contradict Pavel's view of gossip as hermeneutic device. The thrust of my argument thus far obviously supports Pavel's version—yet a slightly subversive interpretation of Joubert also fits my thesis and helps to clarify Moglen's undertaking. Given the problematic status of "what is known" (what I "know" may contradict what you, with equal certainty, "know"), if gossip defines the known, it reveals the knower. Moglen claims, on the whole, to deal with familiar facts of Brontë's experience. She wishes to *re*define what is known—to understand "physical truth" by bringing to bear "moral truth" (in the sense that I earlier used these terms). Real gossip (i.e., oral gossip) rests on shared group assumptions, but it also provides opportunities to test, clarify, and interpret those assumptions, partly by bringing them into conjunction with various individual moral positions. It too redefines. Moglen in her role as narrator single-handedly performs comparable operations. She tests the significance of such facts as Charlotte Brontë's death in early pregnancy by locating them in relation to her own (not uniquely her own) psychological and political assumptions. The hermeneutic act derives from this conjunction; the hermeneutic power of gossip depends on similar intersections of "fact."

In Moglen's interpretation, the inner life becomes the sole locus of reality. Notions of privacy and propriety that controlled Gaskell's promulgation of information disappear; an ideal of understanding takes precedence, with implicit moral resonance. Indeed, the moral weight of psychological knowledge (as in "Ye shall know the truth and the truth shall make ye free") finds clear articulation in the text. "For Charlotte Brontë, the creation of Angria initiated a long and painful process of self-investigation which did finally yield to discovery and knowledge: to a true if tragic freedom" (33). Moglen interprets Brontë's development as centered on growth in self-understanding and her death as resulting from her final failure. "Never having resolved the traumas of her own childhood, . . . Charlotte Brontë conceived a child and fell ill of the conception: sickened, apparently, by fear" (241). *Apparently.* The biography attempts to make apparent to the reader what the writer finds apparent in the life she contemplates. Moglen believes that human lives proceed by iron laws of psychosocial influence. She sees in Brontë's career "a lifetime of failed relationships" (239) with inevitable disastrous consequences. "Autonomy, defined in agony, was threatened everywhere. Her personal independence had not yet been truly won. Her professional freedom was still in question. In her writing and in her experience she had wrestled with the life-defeating forces of romantic mythology and personal history.

She had described them. She had confronted them. But, Antaeus-like, they seemed to reappear—renewed by the social powers by which they had been formed" (240).

Moglen's capacity to formulate a life in this categorical way (compare the tone of Gaskell's "I cannot measure or judge of such a character as hers") suggests her narrative stance. Like Gaskell, she perceives her subject as a paradigmatic Victorian woman, victim of nineteenth-century "romantic mythology" (Moglen discusses at length the Byronic legend) and "social forces." More importantly, like Boswell, although less explicitly, she declares her verbal control of the character she describes; and more: her conceptual control. It would seem more gratifying to identify with Helene Moglen, who offers the possibility of understanding, than with Charlotte Brontë, victim— despite her "wrestling" with life-defeating forces—of psyche and society. The myth of interpretation implicit in *Charlotte Brontë: The Self Conceived* suggests the knowability of intimate patterns of inward experience. Brontë, the biography tells us, struggled to know herself, but didn't quite succeed; Moglen has succeeded, she implicitly claims, in achieving awareness impossible for the suffering novelist herself; she wins in an unarticulated competition with her subject. The art and the morality of the biography stem from the claim of potent knowledge. The narrator's conviction of governing pattern in the subject's life dictates choice of detail and formal structure; belief in the value of the kind of knowledge this pattern embodies defines the book's controlling moral criterion. The narrator invites the reader to share not, as Boswell does, a process of discovery but a process of confirmation, in which every reported event, even death itself, substantiates an elucidating hypothesis.

The four biographies I have discussed provide a sufficient sample to suggest the usefulness of gossip as an interpretive metaphor. To think about gossip calls attention both to the substance of biography and to the relationship the genre establishes between narrator and reader—a relationship necessarily affected by the biographer's attitude toward the subject of narration.

The material of biography obviously resembles that of gossip. In many respects, the subject matter of biography duplicates that of personal letters; in both instances, the reader may feel like an intruder into someone else's private affairs or may delight in a kind of knowledge prohibited in normal social intercourse but made permissible by being published. The narrator's intervention makes reading biography feel less surreptitious and somewhat less intimate than reading letters, but in both cases one achieves pleasure by acquiring data about another person's hidden life.

The matter of relationship is more complicated. As in most forms of narrative, biographical narrators establish with readers a fundamental alliance. The narrator provides the main source of authority as well as information, responsible to make a life's raw material into a story both interesting and convincing. Biographers can draw on almost the same range of narrative possibilities as novelists, but they must seem *reliable*.[13] Reading biography partly in search of certainties about human nature and human experience, we seek in the narrator a stable guide.

In this respect alone, perhaps, the link between biography and gossip differs from that between gossip and other genres. In fiction, we more readily accept various forms of disorientation. But biography, claiming to provide insight into actuality, provides, as gossip does, reassurance about the continuity and the comprehensibility of experience. We gossip partly to remind ourselves of what we share and to assure ourselves that we can interpret happenings and feelings from other lives. A biographer talks about another person, allows us to listen; we hope to encounter facts in which we can grasp a human pattern. Most biographies concern figures who have already achieved fame; we probably want in particular to learn how success in the great world connects with small happenings of everyday life. To gossip about the great is peculiarly gratifying—not to diminish their greatness, but to root it in common experience.

The art, the knowledge, and the morality of biography all involve the reader's experienced relation with the narrator and the subject of a given study. Biography's proclaimed factuality helps to define that relation: our trust of the narrator, our interest in the narration alike depend on our belief in the story's truth. We expect to learn from biography not how human beings might or should be but how they *are*. We learn that by trusting the narrator. The intimacy of our temporary association with the story-teller parallels that of the writer's connection with the subject; the varying stances of biographer toward biographee affect—as I have tried to show—the reader's response as well. Biography directly gratifies our desire for knowledge that will explain what human beings share and how they differ—the desire which gossip also answers, and to which various forms of fiction respond in different fashion.

Yet comparisons among texts call attention to one respect in which biography's security remains illusory. I have suggested our need to believe in the reliability of biographical narrators; but a close look at different biographies of a single subject suggests that biographers fulfill private agendas in their accounts of other lives. Only Boswell, of the writers here treated, makes his personal purposes the partial subject of his narrative, but one can glimpse comparable purposes elsewhere. To explain the divergence between

Gaskell's and Moglen's versions of Charlotte Brontë requires more than reference to historical change. Moglen suggests explicitly her awareness that she is serving her own ends: "But, seeking ostensibly for the 'truth,' . . . I find that . . . I have pursued my own shadow through the beckoning recesses of another's mind, hoping to discover its substance at the journey's end" (15). Gaskell acknowledges nothing of the sort, but she allows room for surmise. Bate, with his vision of Johnson as a man perpetually in need of rescue, creates a drama reflecting his personal, twentieth-century understanding of experience. The "strange" attachment Freud noted between biographer and subject arises from the writer's inner needs, served in factual as much as in fictional narrative. Divergent renderings of a human life may each contain its own truth. The truth they contain, however, like that of gossip, belongs partly to the creating sensibility.

6

"What Would the World Say?"

The last two chapters have made gossip a loose metaphor for narrator-reader and narrator-subject relationships in published letters and biography and used it as an analogy elucidating functions of detail in these peripheral literary genres. But gossip can provide substance as well as metaphors for literature. Turning to the more orthodox genre of drama, one finds in Restoration and eighteenth-century comedy a striking preoccupation with dark fantasies about what people say of one another. The seventeenth-century moral commentary cited in Chapter Two hinted resemblances between loose talk and loose sexual conduct; late seventeenth-century stage comedy draws on such associations. This comedy takes gossip seriously as social threat and as social control; it also suggests both the moral flabbiness of those who indulge in frivolous talk about others and the equivalent flabbiness of those whose sexual indulgence makes them likely subjects of such talk; it explores a range of functions served by conversation about other people. The shift in the ethical status of gossip in the century between *The Country Wife* (1675) and *The School for Scandal* (1777) reflects a corresponding shift in the tone of published moralizing on the subject and calls attention to crucial changes of social assumption.

Early in Sir John Vanbrugh's *The Provok'd Wife* (1697), two women discuss a third in judicious terms that barely disguise their malice.

> LADY BRUTE She concludes all Men her Captives; and whatever Course they take, it serves to confirm her in that opinion.

BELLINDA If they shun her, she thinks 'tis modesty, and takes it for
a proof of their Passion.
LADY BRUTE And if they are rude to her, 'tis Conduct, and done to
prevent Town talk.[1]

Such an exchange constitutes gossip: conversation about the private life of
another, both information and interpretation; talk devoid of ostensible purpose beyond the immediate pleasure of the participants; in this instance as
in many others, derogatory. The "Town talk" to which Lady Brute refers,
its particular substance unspecified, is also gossip. Virtually all female and
many male characters in Restoration comedy worry about it—about what
"the world" might say—although many also delight in hearing what that
"world" has to say about others. "The world" and "the town"—essentially
a single entity—apparently talk mainly about sex.

Why does "Town talk" matter so much in Restoration plays; why do such
plays frequently contain characters with names like "Tattle" and "Scandal"?
How does gossip shape plots? What assumptions dictate examples of and
allusions to conversation about other people's sexual conduct; how does stage
gossip reflect and illuminate the world beyond the stage? I propose both to
establish a context for comedic uses of gossip and to investigate specific ways
gossip works, mainly in three Restoration texts and one later one: William
Congreve's *Love for Love*, Vanbrugh's *The Provok'd Wife*, William Wycherley's *The Country Wife*, and Richard Brinsley Sheridan's *The School for
Scandal*.

The relevant context extends far back in time. The book of James establishes an important theme: "The tongue is a little member, and boasteth
great things. . . . And the tongue is a fire, a world of iniquity: so is the
tongue among our members, that it defileth the whole body, and setteth on
fire the course of nature; and it is set on fire of hell. For every kind of beasts,
and of birds, and of serpents, and of things in the sea, is tamed, and hath
been tamed of mankind: But the tongue can no man tame; it is an unruly
evil, full of deadly poison" (James 3:5–8). This unruly little member, defiling
the body, burning with the fire of hell, untamable by men, may call to mind
another unruly male member to which similar language has been applied.
In *The Dutchesse of Malfy*, as in other seventeenth-century plays, the connection of tongue and phallus becomes explicit. Warning his widowed sister
not to marry again, Ferdinand observes, "woemen [sic] like that part, which
(like the Lamprey) / Hath nev'r a bone in't." "Fye Sir!" the Duchess responds.
"Nay," explains Ferdinand, "I meane the Tongue."[2]

The tongue, like the penis an instrument of seduction and power, and a means of connection, encourages sexual analogies by its physical form: in a 1635 book of emblems, the image of a winged tongue startlingly resembles a winged phallus. But seventeenth-century commentators found female as well as male sexuality relevant to discussion of verbal activity. The *Precepts* of Lord Burghley include this exchange: "*Qu. What strumpet of all other is the most common prostitute in the World? A. Lingua,* that common-whore, for she lies with all men."[3] George Wither's collection of emblems shows a leaking barrel: "The *Tongue,* which every secret speakes, / Is like a *Barrell* full of leakes." After discussing in detail the nature of the tattler who "utters ev'ry thing hee knowes," the verse continues, without transition,

> *This* Figure, *also, serveth to expresse,*
> *The trustlesse nature of a* whorish woman;
> *For, shee to all displays her wantonnesse,*
> *And, cares to keepe her secresies, from no man.*[4]

Sexual and verbal looseness duplicate one another. A 1613 discussion of the adulterous woman alludes to "malice" and "slandering" as essential characteristics of the sexual sinner.[5] A later diatribe against coffee houses describes such a place as "a *refin'd Baudy-House,* where *Illegitimate Reports* are got in close *Adultery* between *Lying lips* and *Itching Ears*"[6]—an etiology of gossip drawing its metaphor from the same association.

If the tongue as phallus suggests speech's power to seduce and to control (with the ear, by long tradition, corresponding to the female sexual organ), the tongue as whore emphasizes speech's possibilities of corruption, its responsiveness to the demands of others. Whorishness involves both indiscriminate giving and indiscriminate taking, on the metaphorical level an intercourse, as the commentator on coffee houses suggests, between lips and ears. The whore metaphor, as opposed to the phallic association, degrades talk and makes its function ambiguous. It suggests modes of discourse outside the socially sanctioned and polite: a hidden life. For these reasons, it adapts itself particularly well to condemnatory discussions of gossip.

But whores have aspects of power too; they readily become objects of fear as well as of desire. The implication of generativity always latent in sexual imagery (explicit in the reference to illegitimate reports got between lips and ears) suggests one mode of power. What issues from the tongue may or may not belong to a legitimate succession, but production of some sort always takes place. The magic of speech inheres in its capacity to create and to destroy; the verses from James, with their allusions to fire and their hints of phallus, stress this double aspect. Seventeenth-century didactic commentary on gossip in its most aggressive form—"detraction"—often conveys something close to terror at the ambiguous possibilities of such speech. Gossips are not only whores; they are, repeatedly, spiders who suck poison and spin entangling webs, or snakes "so venomous, as they infect and poison with their very breaths." They embody forms of sickness: "spreading tetters which eat into our reputations." They use "teeth and claws, to bite, and scratch, and tear innocent soules"; they "kill a Man as sure as a Gun."[7] The phallic snake and gun, the metaphorically female spider and implied cat, the loathsome spreading sickness: these images hint sexual allusions just beneath the surface. They vividly convey the fear and horror typical of response to the idea of gossip—emotions declaring the potency of the detested phenomenon.

When detractors appear as characters on the Restoration stage, however, their roles emphasize this potency's compensatory and dubious nature. Witwoud and Petulant in *The Way of the World,* the only male participants in Lady Wishfort's weekly cabal to murder reputations, make up between them the equivalent of one man, prized by women, like their counterparts in other plays, as purveyors of scandal.[8] When Witwoud gossips of Petulant, exposing the other man's devices for aggrandizing his own sexual reputation, he grasps the only kind of mastery he can achieve: a substitute, not an equivalent, for sexual force. Tattle, in *Love for Love,* similarly reveals his masculine inadequacy as he gossips about women he claims to have seduced, the excess of his protestations undermining his pretensions. Attempting to use the tongue as phallic weapon, such men underline their phallic insufficiency.

One can hardly call to mind a Restoration comedy in which gossip actually does serious harm to anyone. To be sure, comedy's benign energies exercise their transformative effect; the sinister always succumbs. But efforts at defamation in these plays cause trouble so fleetingly that their menace seems factitious. Dapperwit, in Wycherley's *Love in a Wood,* slanders the absent Ranger; he only stimulates contempt in his auditor. Christina's maid, in the same play, reports "base unworthy things" said of her mistress; they do not discernibly affect Christina's peace of mind.[9] The ineffectuality of such talkers as Dapperwit and Tattle denies phallic potency and fiery destructiveness. Whorishness in its contemptible aspect more accurately characterizes their speech: these men adapt themselves to what they understand of other people's demands. Their gossip diminishes their integrity, betrays friends, sacrifices to the yearning for self-aggrandizement. Its immediate ineffectuality relates oddly to the prevailing anxiety about what the world will say.

Such anxiety looms large in many Restoration comedies. "What do the

World say of me, and of my forc'd Confinement?" Valentine asks Scandal, in the first scene of *Love for Love* (220). He has just declared his independence of "the world," announcing that he plans to turn poet and rail at those with more money than himself; yet what those he scorns may say about him still concerns him. In the final act of the same play, Sir Sampson thinks of marrying Angelica. "O fie, Sir *Sampson*," she responds, "what would the World say?" (5.1, 300). The action bracketed by these two questions—questions articulated by the play's hero and heroine—gains impetus from the almost universal concern about reputation. In an early conversation with Trapland, who has come to demand that Valentine pay his debts, Scandal can distract and appease the scrivener by transmitting sexually flattering gossip about him, making him preen about his amorous reputation. Tattle and Scandal gain importance solely as makers and marrers of reputation. Mrs. Frail reminds herself and others of female vulnerability, observing, "I shall get a fine Reputation by coming to see Fellows in a morning" (1.1, 230). And Mrs. Foresight puts the implicit problem most clearly when she asks, "How can any Body be happy, while they're in perpetual fear of being seen and censur'd?" (2.1, 247). The question echoes through the period's comedies, which suggest that this perpetual fear indeed interferes with happiness—partly by impeding gratifying forms of misconduct.

"The world" as an agent of gossip has no obvious sexual aspect. Without face, body, personality, it exists only as a powerful voice articulating opinions of that sociologists' abstraction, "society." Fear of being seen and censured responds to the typical nature of this voice as evoked in Restoration plays: the world functions as enemy of sex, opposed to individual expressiveness in virtually all its forms. Since the world exists by virtue of what it is thought to say, those who fear it attribute vast power to *saying*. Tricked into marriage with Mrs. Frail, Tattle appears to worry mainly about the verbal transmission of what he has done. "Pox on't, I wish we could keep it secret!" (5.1, 310): if no one says anything, it will not have happened. Mrs. Foresight goes to bed with Scandal, then speaks the morning after as though she had not, thus implying that speech means more than action. "You can't accuse me of inconstancy," Angelica tells Valentine; "I never *told* you, that I lov'd you" (3.1, 254; my italics). This social world operates on the apparent assumption that language more significantly than behavior defines actuality. Foresight's plaintive question, "What do you know of my Wife?" (2.1, 242), means "What do you *say* of my wife?" or, perhaps, "What do others say of her?" He himself knows nothing of his wife or of himself, and he accepts verbal counters without testing: if someone tells him he looks ill, he immediately believes himself so, his physical sensations irrelevant. Like Tattle, Foresight calls attention by parody to the world's commitment to words rather than deeds.

Although Angelica and Valentine articulate the play's crucial question, "What does [or would] the world say?", they escape its consequences, more deeply concerned with their own "saying" than with the world's. Angelica briefly resents Tattle's assertion that her love for Valentine is "whisper'd every where" (3.1, 254), but it provides a pretext to rebuke Tattle rather than real cause for anxiety. When Valentine testifies his love by resolving to yield his estate, since money loses meaning without Angelica, Angelica reveals her own devotion by tearing up the legal bond obligating him to such self-destructive behavior. Then, and only then, she makes the verbal commitment which for true lovers follows on emotional commitment. For a Mrs. Frail or a Mrs. Foresight, a Scandal or a Tattle, language may generate the appearance of attachment, thus facilitating temporary sexual alliance. For Angelica and Valentine, speech sanctions pre-existent reality; it does not create reality. Secure in their own integrity, they need not worry unduly about what the world says.

Yet what the world says matters, in this play and others of its genre, and what the world *might* say matters more. Not by accident do Tattle and Scandal preside over the action, threatening and promising their manipulation of reputations. Only Mrs. Foresight's fear of being seen and censured controls her conduct; Tattle's anxiety lest he lose his reputation as a keeper of women's secrets at least diminishes his blabbing. "What the world says" means what people imagine it to say. Gossip articulates cultural values; the world's imagined saying judges individual conduct by social standards.

Love for Love dramatizes with particular clarity the discrepancy between the emotional and ethical quality of what people actually say about one another and the moral weight of what they are imagined to say. No one takes Tattle seriously. His verbal idiosyncrasies entertain both his interlocutors and the play's audience. The whorishly garrulous man marries the whorishly promiscuous woman as appropriate punishment; the union characterizes the futility of his plotting and emblemizes the moral quality of his talk, but it is also a joke. Most characters, on the other hand, take the judgment of the world very seriously indeed. Spoken by no one, it yet exists powerfully in the mind, enforcing itself on the consciousness of audience as well as characters. No one tells us what to think of a woman who deceives her husband or of an old man who wants to marry a young girl; yet we know quite well what the world would say. The authority of its judgment depends upon what Edith Wharton in *The Custom of the Country* calls "that unanimity of opinion that constitutes social strength." Nothing in *Love for Love* proves any such unanimity, yet the social strength implicit in the general anxiety about the world's possible commentary testifies to its reality.

Angelica and Valentine, who articulate the anxiety in words only to deny it in action, exemplify a balanced attitude toward both kinds of gossip, the trivial, self-indulgent, metaphorically sexual kind spoken by such as Tattle, and the weighty, condemnatory judgments of an anti-sexual, severely prudential world. (Both kinds, it should be noted, share a single set of professed values: Tattle's sexual bragging gains its malicious force from the social assumption that women "should be" both chaste and prudent.) They interest themselves in what is or might be said; they can even use the voice of the world for their own purposes. But their conceptions of such virtues as fidelity and prudence valorize action rather than profession. The world threatens true love, as many Restoration plays attest. Its voice may destroy reputation and individual happiness. Yet those economically and emotionally fortunate can defy that powerful voice with the strength of their own integrity and of their informed awareness of what the world can say.

Fear, however, remains a not inappropriate response to the destructive possibilities of gossip as it actually works. The worry Mrs. Foresight articulates, her perpetual fear of being seen and censured, is by no means unique to stage comedy; it expresses itself repeatedly in contemporary treatises on conduct. "There is no Protection against a depraving Tongue, it's sharper than *Actius* his Razor; I had rather stand at the Mercy of a *Basilisco* or *Serpentine*, than the fury of an Outragious Tongue."[10] So writes William De Britaine, whose *Humane Prudence, or the Art By which a Man May Raise Himself and his Fortune to Grandeur*—a seventeenth-century how-to-do-it book—went through ten editions between 1680, the date of its first publication, and 1710. With less lurid metaphors: "Reputation is gained by course of time, and seldom recovers a Strain; but if once broken, it's never well set again. There is no Plaister, in fine, for a wounded Reputation. . . . It's easy to get an ill Name, because evil is sooner believed; and bad impressions are very difficult to be defaced" (39). Equally anxious, Obadiah Walker, writing about a young man's education, warns of the prevalence of calumniating gossip. "Even in *ordinary conversation* men are wont also to defame their neighbours open-fac'd, without any ceremony, design, or remorse. . . . Consider what you say of others, others say of you. . . . 'Tis madness to make enemies without cause."[11] Francis Bacon had observed earlier: "Suspicions that the mind of itself gathers are but buzzes; but suspicions that are artificially nourished, and put into men's heads by the tales and whisperings of others, have stings."[12]

If, as De Britaine claims, we live upon the credit and reports of others, we live always in danger. As Mrs. Foresight knows, only by guarding all visible aspects of conduct can one hope to escape damaging gossip. On the other hand, to restrain oneself from any action that might attract the disapproval of others implies not only inability to follow the promptings of passion but reluctance to innovate or to criticize the established order, reluctance even to live by the laws of personal integrity. Mary Astell puts the problem well.

> It was not fit that Creatures capable of and made for Society, shou'd be wholly Independent, or Indifferent to each others Esteem and Commendation; nor was it convenient considering how seldom these are justly distributed, that they shou'd too much regard and depend on them. It was requisite therefore that a desire of our Neighbours Good Opinion shou'd be implanted in our Nature to the end we might be excited to do such things as deserve it, and yet withall a Generous neglect of it, if they unjustly withheld it where it was due.[13]

In her own life a sufferer from calumny, Astell yet recognizes the regulating value of the human concern with what others think. Like other commentators, she believes that people will more readily say derogatory than positive things of others (142), but she has abstracted the problem of reputation and of defamation to a degree that converts the phenomenon into cause for calm reflection rather than for fear. We have come a long way from William De Britaine's basilisk and serpentine, from direct acknowledgment of gossip's emotional dangers. Desexualized, detoxified, the talk of other people remains, however, an object of fantasy. Astell in effect says as much. She describes human motivation in terms of desire: we want that good opinion we only imagine, the want impels us to act in accord with our neighbor's standards. The tales and whisperings of others, the defamation that takes place "without any ceremony, design, or remorse": these too exist more consistently in the realm of imagination than of experience. The immense power of reputation-destroying talk derives partly from *lack* of experience. Because we rarely know what others say of us, we fear their saying.

Let me return, in this context, to *The Provok'd Wife*. In Act 4, Heartfree finally acknowledges to his friend Constant that he is in love. He adds instantly, "But, dear *Constant*, don't tell the Town on't" (4.2, 155). The town would mock the very idea of true love in one who has proclaimed his imperviousness; it would circulate the news; it might threaten the fact. Darker in tone than *Love for Love*, *The Provok'd Wife* acknowledges love as an ideal and dwells on threats to it. The good marriage, Constant observes, is the "one inestimable lot, in which the only Heaven on Earth is written"; and Heartfree adds, even more pointedly, "to be capable of loving one, doubtless is better than to possess a Thousand" (5.4, 176). Obstacles to love's realization, however, include not only emotional inadequacy, not only the immediate perplexities of relationship, but the voice of "the Town" and the individual voices that suggest the town's nature.

More often than in *Love for Love*, we actually hear people gossip in this play. In the first scene, in the sequence from which I have already quoted, Bellinda and Lady Brute discuss in detail the character of Lady Fancyfull; as the action draws toward a close, Lady Fancyfull attempts to accomplish her ends by inventing and circulating malicious gossip. The two modes of gossip thus represented frame the play's action and define its issues. They reveal how gossip at once expresses and represses desire.

The dialogue between Bellinda and Lady Brute continues in the same vein, to anatomize Lady Fancyfull in her vanity, lasciviousness, and irresponsibility. The two young women—one unmarried and hoping for love, the other unhappily married and hoping to remain virtuous, yet yearning for emotional satisfaction—share their disapproval of Lady Fancyfull's sexual conduct, mainly, it seems, on the ground of her utter lack of self-knowledge. Their exchange receives no dramatic emphasis; it may strike the reader as both trivial and catty. "None should be believ'd but such as are vertuous," Sir George Mackenzie writes, in a work called *A Consolation Against Calumnies*; "and vertuous persons will be asham'd to have it thought, that they spend their time so meanly, as to have leisure to hear or enquire into what does not concern them."[14] The dramatist initially invites one to judge the conversationalists as just such idle talkers, devoid of meaningful occupation and consequently commenting about what does not concern them.

Only gradually does the true importance of this exchange emerge. Lady Brute, Bellinda, and Lady Fancyfull, as the action continues, will involve themselves in the same kinds of game. All will resort to subterfuge and disguise in projects involving men who interest them. But the two who here discuss the third proclaim by the discussion their essential difference from her. In their implicit condemnation of Lady Fancyfull, they reveal not only their discrimination but their determination not to let their own imaginations and longings betray them. Lady Fancyfull, as her name implies, subordinates reality to her dreams of it. Bellinda and her friend refuse to do the same— in the face, it will turn out, of considerable temptation. Bellinda gives up her wish for social status and wealth; Lady Brute resists her need for emotional and sexual sustenance because she understands that she can't have everything: only by dishonoring her marriage can she accept love. Unlike Lady Fancyfull, she acknowledges the necessity of discipline and choice, although the play's ending allows doubt about whether she can long continue to do so. The extended discussion of another woman reveals the interest Lady Brute and Bellinda feel in sexual possibilities and arrangements, hinting longings they will gradually reveal more fully. In this aspect, gossip becomes a vehicle of desire: an outlet for forbidden energies. If women cannot enact their feelings, they can at least find indirect ways to talk about them. Moreover, through such talk as this they come to understand more fully the dimensions of their own desire: what they really want as opposed to what society tells them they want. On the other hand, gossip also encourages desire's repression. The two women, condemning the third, implicitly condemn also in themselves the longings to which Lady Fancyfull has yielded.

Gossip thus becomes a mode at once of moral declaration and of sexual titillation. *The Provok'd Wife* explores precisely these themes, arriving at a reconciliation that unites the moral and the sexual for Bellinda and thus emphasizes by contrast the pathos of Lady Brute's situation: unlike Bellinda, she must choose between morality and sexuality, doomed by her unwise marriage. In this circumstance of extreme tension, Lady Brute uses her fantasies of what the world might say as moral support. She believes that the world judges by appearance rather than fact; yet she cares greatly about her own reputation, softening to Constant when he reveals in action his concern for it (3.1, 143). In the same scene, Constant attempts to discriminate between true virtue and "the thing that's call'd so": "Virtue consists in Goodness, Honour, Gratitude, Sincerity and Pity; and not in peevish, snarling, strait-lac'd Chastity." Lady Brute inquires why, in that case, men so earnestly recommend chastity to their wives and daughters; Constant responds that the importance of continence "lies in the humour of the Country, not in the nature of the thing" (143). Lady Brute, who possesses all the qualities of true virtue, must yet conform with "the humour of the Country." The society she inhabits limits her possibilities, allowing all freedom to her brutish husband, none to her; Vanbrugh demonstrates the hopelessness of the resulting dilemma.

If Lady Brute cares greatly about what people say of her, Lady Fancyfull cares not at all. Free of Mrs. Foresight's fear of being seen and censured, she considers gossip an instrument to manipulate, not a weapon to dread. Although she offers a *pro forma* statement of concern about her "reputation," she readily accepts her French maid's assurance that reputation, once lost, need trouble one no more (an argument also made on occasion about virginity, though Mademoiselle refrains from making the point quite explicit) and that the price of self-restraint is excessive for keeping one's reputation (1.2, 123) (or, presumably, one's virginity). When Heartfree tries to reform her by citing the town's talk about her ("you are become the Pity of our Sex, and the Jest of your own"), she responds that, in the face of Heartfree and of the "World," "I should still have Charity enough for my own Understanding, to believe my self in the right, and all you in the wrong" (2.1, 126).

Careless of her own reputation, Lady Fancyfull tries to exploit other women's concern with theirs. She welcomes and encourages her maid's gossip as a means of gaining information and control; she circulates gossip to serve her own ends; and she grasps at self-invented gossip as the means to frustrate an intended marriage. "If I can but defer the wedding four and twenty Hours, I'll make such work about Town, with that little pert Slut's Reputation, he shall as soon marry a Witch" (5.3, 174).

Only briefly does the misinformation Lady Fancyfull promulgates deter the lovers; the play ends with all its important characters joining to mock her in her malice. Truth triumphs, permitting at least one possibly successful marriage. As punishment for her gossip and for her sexual vanity and self-deception, Lady Fancyfull suffers mockery, isolation, frustration. Bellinda's behavior and Lady Fancyfull's define poles of sexual conduct; their gossip exemplifies equivalent extremes of verbal conduct. Indulgence in mendacious malignities of gossip, like Sir John Brute's gross physical indulgence, turns on itself, ending in the spiritual isolation of the indulgers. Lady Fancyfull, again like Sir John in his sphere, may be too besotted to know her own deprivation, but the play's action judges her. Conversely, the moral discriminations of the kind of gossip engaged in by Lady Brute and Bellinda parallel the discrimination they attempt in their sexual lives. Through speech and through action, these women try to know themselves and to behave with the responsibility self-knowledge entails. Their way of talking about Lady Fancyfull prepares for their subsequent behavior.

The Provok'd Wife makes marriage its subject in a serious and far-reaching way. Heartfree and Constant sketch an ideal of fulfillment which both understand as precarious and difficult to attain; like his bride, Heartfree knows what risks he takes in marrying. The horror of Lady Brute's marriage, entered into by her for wealth, by her husband for brief sexual gratification, is enacted on the stage: we witness Sir John's crudities, his refusal to be placated, his deliberate provocations, and the uselessness of Lady Brute's efforts to appease him. Marriage, the play insists, is a socio-sexual institution, an involvement in the community as well as a union of two individuals; the difficulties of maintaining it derive partly from implications of "the humour of the Country." Because Sir John can express his sadistic impulses without penalty in the outer world, he feels the freer to indulge them at home; because Lady Brute knows the social sanctions against adultery, she refrains. If marriage involved only the desires of its participants, Sir John and Lady Brute would separate.

In a play centrally concerned with social aspects of sexual expression, gossip provides a useful emblem of ambiguity. Individually expressive, yet resting on a structure of social assumption, capable of moral discrimination or of conveying the most primitive feelings, it supplies a verbal equivalent for other complex modes of functioning. *The Provok'd Wife* supplies more specific detail about gossip than does *Love for Love*, but it investigates the same question: how gossip works simultaneously as sexual expression and as social control.

The connection between the verbal and the sexual finds its most vivid Restoration expression in *The Country Wife*, a comedy as richly preoccupied with talk as with sex. Horner, the play's most important male character, has perceived precisely the double aspect of gossip that concerns me: its capacity to serve simultaneously as enemy and proponent of desire. He puts that duality to work in ways which also shed new light on the discrepancies between language and fact apparent in *Love for Love*.

The Country Wife opens with a dialogue between Horner and the dubious doctor, Quack, about gossip they have deliberately set circulating. Quack assumes the direct equivalence of words and meaning: "I have undone you for ever with the Women," he proclaims. The comedy will, of course, demonstrate the precise converse: to declare impotence intensifies potency.

Horner knows how sexual news circulates—through females and the powerless.

> HORNER But have you told all the Midwives you know, the Orange
> Wenches at the Play-houses, the City Husbands, and old Fumbling Keepers of this end of the Town, for they'l be the readiest
> to report it.
> QUACK I have told all the Chamber-maids, Waiting-women, Tyre-women, and Old Women of my acquaintance; nay, and whisper'd it as a secret to 'em, and to the Whisperers of *Whitehal*;
> so that you need not doubt 'twill spread [1.1, 11].[15]

The secret has titillating force for such purveyors of news because it concerns the alleged downfall of a potent man. Horner has conceived his story skillfully, with a parodic tragic structure: the sexually dominant male overthrown by the consequences of his sexuality, made impotent by venereal disease and unskilled treatment of it. Women react to this news, as Quack predicts, with disgust. The situation depends on the conventionally assumed extreme lasciviousness of the female: since women care only about sexual gratification, although they also know the social necessity of protecting their reputations, they cannot tolerate the company of a man incapable of satisfying them.

The education of Margery Pinchwife in the ways of London, like that of Prue in *Love for Love*, indoctrinates her in the social uses of language. Margery too must learn to relinquish the literal, learn that meaningful events take place mainly in the gap between assertion and actuality. Her husband's inability to confine his utterances to meanings he wishes to convey, Harcourt's capacity to communicate opposed meanings to two hearers of a single speech, the *doubles entendres* about china—all emphasize language's instability. Success in the play's social world depends on a gift for exploiting language's apparent referentiality while understanding its factitiousness.

In the play's central verbal device, referentiality reverses itself. Language literally converts presence (of Horner's active phallus) into absence, then makes that absence an overwhelming fact; action, denying language, transforms the meaning of the asserted absence. The women who profit from Horner's alleged impotence thoroughly understand the verbal game they agree to play. They also understand language's sexual possibilities. "Be continent in your discourse, or I shall hate you," Lady Fidget admonishes Mrs. Dainty (2.1, 30). Continence in discourse substitutes for continence of desire. Only Margery fails to understand the advantage of false assertion, of gossip whose meaning differs utterly to the comprehension of husbands and of wives.

Although much of *The Country Wife* predicates a fundamental war between the sexes, Horner's "dear secret" makes antagonism vanish. Women talking with one another, like men in male company, reveal a sense of outrage approaching disgust for the opposite sex. Men, the women agree, treat women badly. They fornicate with women of lower rank, neglecting their social equals; they mistreat their wives; and they spread gossip about women of quality. "To report a Man has had a Person, when he has not had a Person, is the greatest wrong in the whole World, that can be done to a Person," Lady Fidget complains (2.1, 30). Men's view of women sounds equally dismissive. Females are pleasant to lie with, but they have no further value. They do not go well with wine; they are not good company. "Who

would disappoint his company at *Lewis's*, for a Gossiping?" Dorimant asks
(3.2, 38), alluding clearly to a female gathering. No man, he implies, would
prefer female company to male, except for sexual purposes.

As women come to know Horner's secret, however, they become his
allies because they feel him to be on their side. His sexuality promises
gratification without danger, reversing the terms of the gossip Lady Fidget
complains about. Now the world will report that a man has not had a person
when he in fact has: ideal for reputation and for the satisfaction of desire.
The play's audience, like its female participants, enjoys the brief therapeutic
illusion of escaping cultural restriction. Horner, of course, seeks only his
own unrestricted gratification in conceiving the scheme of asserted impotence, but the removal of restriction for him implies equivalent freeing for
women. Allowing the voice of the "nasty World" (2.1, 29) to say what it
will about him, he helps women escape their fear of that voice. To enable
his sexual freedom, he takes advantage of the social mode traditionally dedicated to opposing such freedom. Gossip, the world's talk, keeps people
decorous, providing an imagined collective voice of conscience. The profound comedy of *The Country Wife* depends on this function's reversal: here
gossip allows what ordinarily it prohibits.

When Lady Fidget worries that other women may find out the truth
about Horner and therefore gossip about her ("oh, 'tis a wicked, censorious
world, Mr. *Horner*"), Horner reassures her: "Nay, Madam, rather than they
shall prejudice your Honour, I'll prejudice theirs; and to serve you, I'll lie
with 'em all, make the secret their own, and then they'll keep it" (4.3, 60).
To translate the verbal secret into physical expression makes gossip's menace
disappear; women keep the secret of their experience if not of their verbal
knowledge. Horner has constructed a world within "the world," a world
devoid of social inhibition; and he has virtually literalized the equation of
tongue with phallus, as the gossip he originates makes possible his phallic
vigor.

In reading *Love for Love*, I have implied, one censures sexual misconduct
as the world censures it (although, like the world, perhaps laughing even
while blaming); in reading *The Provok'd Wife*, one endorses the gossips' view
of Lady Fancyfull, the conventional social view. *The Country Wife* creates
a more complicated relationship between the reader and the world. Inasmuch
as the play encourages our approval of sexual expressivity which the world
would condemn if it knew, it places us for a time in opposition to social
convention. Real superiority seems to belong to the alleged eunuch.

That superiority consists not simply of heightened sexual opportunity; it
derives from the attitude toward society implied in Horner's means for achiev-

ing opportunity. The false castrato in effect takes a satirist's stance. He locates himself outside the conventional, scorning the appearance of sexual success excessively valued by his society. His strategy has aggressive as well as defensive force: it implicitly criticizes ready acceptance of appearance as equivalent to reality, words as equal to things. The fiction Horner conceives satirizes female hypocrisy and male pretension. Its satiric implication and impulse draw the reader toward its inventor: one identifies more readily with satirist than with satiric butt, and the world, in this instance, serves as butt.

Yet this account does not adequately describe either the emotional or the narrative structure of the play. Margery Pinchwife, not Horner, fills the title role. When Margery insists on her real attachment ("I do love Mr. Horner with all my soul" [5.4, 85]) and on Horner's potency, the other conspirators agree in their judgment of her idiocy. Yet in fact her comments, like that of the child who notes the emperor's nakedness, shed fresh light, revealing how fully Horner is implicated in the world he criticizes. By choosing to rely on the discrepancy of word and fact, he partakes of the universal contamination. He becomes the women's victim instead of their exploiter. When Mrs. Squeamish demands more "China" of the exhausted Horner and he responds, "Do not take it ill, I cannot make China for you all" (4.3, 63), the play begins to expose his entanglement in his own web. As the action moves to an end, with Horner compelled to lie about Alithea as well as about himself (confessing as he does so that to "wrong one Woman for another's sake" is "no new thing with me" [5.4, 83]), his meretriciousness becomes increasingly vivid.

Harcourt, motivated by love rather than lust, emerges as Horner's moral superior specifically in his attitude toward gossip. Not for an instant does he believe allegations of Alithea's impropriety; and he will himself promulgate truth rather than falsehood to that world whose voice is gossip. "I will not only believe your innocence my self, but make all the World believe it" (5.4, 83). Harcourt's straightforwardness and simplicity, its impression intensified by contrast with the duplicity of his earlier verbal play, stand, like Margery's, in sharp contrast to Horner's intricacies. When Horner speaks the play's last words, "But he who aims by women to be priz'd, / First by the men you see must be despis'd" (5.4, 87), they carry more than sexual meaning. He has allowed himself to become despicable in his commitment to self-serving falsehood and to the purely physical, divorcing sex from feeling. The gossip designed to increase his phallic freedom has turned him into a whore.

The intimate involvement between gossip and sexuality extends beyond metaphor. To be sure, gossip employs the tongue in both its phallic and its whorish aspects. Particularly as the dreaded, fantasized voice of the world, it possesses the dangerous generativity, the uncontrollable power, the unsettling authority of phallic force. In the trivialized form of sexual tattle, it reveals its whorish side. The degree to which all gossip, both rendered and imagined, in Restoration comedy obsessively concentrates on sex points to another, more ambiguous, connection between gossip and sex: the relation of gossip to fulfillment. At once agent and enemy of desire, gossip allows the individual expression of hidden wishes. People talk about sex because they care about it; they work out for themselves, or remind themselves of, the limits of the permissible by discussing other people's activities; they satisfy themselves vicariously by dwelling on what others have done. Such satisfaction makes room for the other side of gossip: its repressive force, its insistence on social norms at the expense of individual expressiveness.

The Country Wife reveals clearly the emotional ambivalence behind this duality, as the action both affirms and denies the value of free sexuality. Restoration comedies find their substance in the material that people—within and outside the play—gossip about: shifting sexual alliances and how they happen. Certain commentators on gossip noted the analogy between gossip and stage comedy. Richard Allestree, for example, inveighs against the custom of visiting for the purpose of finding conversational material. People who engage in such visiting seek the ridiculous, "and least [sic] the Inquest should return with a *non inventus*, they will accept of the slightest discoveries; the least misplacing of a word, nay of a hair, shall be theme enough for a Comedy. But if a poor Country Gentlewoman fall within their circuit, what a stock of mirth do's she afford them, how curiously do they anatomise every part of her dress, her meen, her dialect?"[16] (The countrywoman, of course, figures as a stock comic butt in Restoration comedy.) Gossip's purpose, this account suggests, is to generate a comedy, finding in observed trivia material from which to manufacture entertainment. A slightly later treatise on conversation tells a detailed story about what two women say of one another, how and why their gossip develops. Each woman alleges the other's sexual misconduct and eye to the main chance. A man immediately comments on this narrative, "This Comedy is pleasant enough, although the matter of it be neither new nor rare; these are Farces we see every day acted."[17] The terms bear precisely on the subject: gossip deals with what is every day acted, with the old and familiar rather than the new and rare; and it creates pleasant comedies.

The metaphorical and literal ties between gossip and sex should not obscure the truth that gossip is, after all, not sex but *meta*-sex, a mode of control, a way of containing contradictory feelings. If it lacks the shaping energy of art, the possibility for literary revision, it may yet partake of the spirit of play, the delight in human possibility that inform comedy. Bellinda and Lady Brute—to return to my starting point—hint their own sexual feelings and their determination to control them in their discussion of Lady Fancyfull, but they also make their subject into a *character*, imagining as well as perceiving her, demonstrating their wit. Even less witty gossip, even the fantasized talk of the world, dramatizes the possibility that the unruly tongue may master the unruly phallus by telling stories about it.

The unruly tongue itself can also supply subject for moral speculation. The title of *The School for Scandal* suggests that gossip has moved from the periphery to the center of dramatic action. The play concerns itself with three kinds of "spending" as opposed to corollary forms of "saving": the monetary extravagance exemplified by Charles Surface, contrasted with the pecuniary prudence of his brother, Joseph; the linguistic extravagance of scandalmongers, countered by Maria's verbal discretion; and, in the background of possibility although never actually realized, the fantasy of sexual "spending." Several male and female characters entertain themselves with versions of this fantasy, conceived as means for revenge or for self-aggrandizement; no one indulges in the slightest actual impropriety.

The prologue to *The School for Scandal* suggests that scandalmongering had by the late eighteenth century come to comprise a real social problem: not only the oral transmission of malicious gossip, but the rise of magazines and newspapers (notably *The Town and Country Magazine*, founded in 1769 and specifically referred to in the play, and *The Morning Post*, dating from 1772) containing printed equivalents for the most libelous tea-table conversation. The prologue begins,

> A *School for Scandal!* Tell me, I beseech you,
> Needs there a school—this modish art to teach you?
> No need of lessons now;—the knowing think—
> We might as well be taught to eat and drink;
> Caus'd by a dearth of scandal, should the vapours
> Distress our fair ones—let 'em read the papers.[18]

As early as 1714, *The Ladies Library*, edited by Sir Richard Steele, had suggested the proliferation and the social danger of slander. "I believe there is hardly a Man living, who is the least conversant with Men or Things past and present, either in Life or in History, but will acknowledge that *Detraction* was never carry'd to such an Extravagance as it has been lately with us in

England."[19] Sheridan's play evokes a world in which the kind of "cabal" over which Lady Wishfort presided in *The Way of the World* has grown to monstrous proportions, its members spewing pronouncements that multiply and change form as the audience listens, but that possess vitality and force giving them power despite their manifest instability. "Detraction is always attended with great mischief, which is at most times irreparable," a French commentator wrote early in the eighteenth century, "because it is almost impossible, that he who did it, should be able to destroy it, whatever retraction he may make of it."[20] It has a life of its own.

Yet malicious gossip has hardly more effect in *The School for Scandal* than in earlier plays. Sheridan's comedy moves through a conventional plot with affinities to folk tale and to eighteenth-century novels as well as to earlier stage comedy—a plot in which "scandal" plays only a subsidiary role. An essentially good though misguided and misjudged younger son triumphs, by virtue of his magnanimous feeling, over his prudent but hypocritical elder brother, Joseph. Rich, visiting Uncle Oliver acts as *deus ex machina*, making moral discriminations of which others have been incapable—except for Maria, the young woman who loves extravagant Charles all along and who, in addition to the wealth he can anticipate from his uncle, constitutes his reward in the play's resolution. One thinks of *Tom Jones* (early reviewers thought of it too), although as a hypocrite Joseph Surface seems far less dangerous than Blifil and Charles lacks Tom's sexual gusto. The machinery of disguise and concealment recalls countless earlier plays; *The School for Scandal* displays more sentiment than its Restoration predecessors, but it proceeds by similar means to its happy ending.

But Joseph's relative innocuousness, in comparison with Blifil, calls attention to the lack of obvious threat in the world of Sheridan's play. No apparent counterpart exists here for the rage that explodes in the baffled father of *Love for Love*, no equivalent even for the more comic rage of Lady Wishfort in *The Way of the World*. When a husband in this play believes that his wife may cuckold him, he prepares to settle more money on her. Fainall, in *The Way of the World*, in anger holds Marwood so tightly that she accuses him—of course with rhetorical exaggeration—of breaking her hands; no one grabs anyone in *The School for Scandal*. The play contains no figure so sinister as Sir John Brute, no suggestions so ominous as the implied socially accepted alternatives to the marriage contract Mirabell and Millamant work out in the proviso scene of *The Way of the World*. The "scandalous society" dedicated to spreading slander accomplishes nothing of lasting significance in the plot.

What, then, should we make of the play's title?

The School for Scandal opens with a scene closely paralleling the first scene of The Beggar's Opera. In Gay's play, Filch and Peachum start the action by tallying recent receipts from their gang of thieves and discussing the prowess in thievery of individual members of the gang. The first song establishes that at every level of class and wealth, professions and people abuse one another in a universal pattern of suspicion and treachery. Lady Sneerwell and Mr. Snake—she at her dressing table, he sipping chocolate— begin Sheridan's comedy with a dialogue about their recent accomplishments in circulating scandal. They praise Mrs. Clackitt as a retailer of damaging gossip: she "has a very pretty talent, and a great deal of industry" (1.1, 25). Then Snake suggests that Lady Sneerwell herself achieves more than any competing gossip, and the scene ends with revelation of her amorous interest in Charles—an interest which she hopes to gratify by the same devious means she employs for other purposes.

The dramatic reminiscence of Gay covertly introduces money as a theme even before the talkers mention Charles's extravagance. To suggest an equation between slander and thievery draws on orthodox moral doctrine. "The human Species . . . [regards] a malevolent Babbler with a worse Eye than a common Thief, because Fame is a Kind of Goods, which, when once taken away, can hardly be restored."[21] "The very Signification of the Word [detraction] shews 'tis a sort of Robbery committed on your Neighbour; it signifying the withdrawing or taking off from a thing; and as it is apply'd to the Reputation, it denotes the imparing and lessening a Man in point of Fame, rendring him less valu'd and esteem'd by others."[22] The subterranean metaphor in Sheridan's text suggests a kind of danger in malevolent gossip that the play never fully substantiates. If fame, or reputation, "is a Kind of Goods," those dedicated to depriving others of it commit a serious crime. Although several characters in The School for Scandal say precisely this, the action demonstrates nothing of the sort. Moreover, Lady Sneerwell and Snake (rather like Peachum and Filch) sound almost innocent in their plotting: they imagine serious consequences from what they say and cause to be said, but those consequences seem only imaginings, not conceivable reality.

When Mrs. Candour comes on the scene, to utter one libel after another, her uncontainable exuberance suggests a new explanation for indulgence in slander.

> To-day, Mrs. Clackit assured me, Mr. and Mrs. Honeymoon were at last become mere man and wife, like the rest of their acquaintance. She likewise hinted that a certain widow, in the next street, had got rid of her dropsy and recovered her shape in a most surprising

manner. And at the same time, Miss Tattle, who was by, affirmed, that Lord Buffalo had discovered his lady at a house of no extraordinary fame; and that Sir Harry Boquet and Tom Saunter were to measure swords on a similar provocation.—But, Lord, do you think I would report these things?—No, no! tale-bearers, as I said before, are just as bad as the tale-makers [1.1, 31].

Mrs. Candour's verbal extravagance, her delight in the scandalous vignette without regard for its truth or falsity, hints a rudimentary interest in fiction-making. That useful repository *The Ladies Library*, after offering various hypotheses to explain the prevalence of detraction (malice, pleasure in news, desire to establish confidential relationships, etc.), acknowledges, "Others there are, who use defamatory Discourse neither for the Love of news nor Defamation, but purely for Love of Talk, whose Speech, like a flowing Current, bears down indiscriminately whatever lies before it" (1.388). The torrential flow of Mrs. Candour's speech has a comparable effect.

The "good" characters in *The School for Scandal* speak emphatically against the circulation of scandal. Maria flees a prospective lover because of his malice: "For my part, I confess, madam, wit loses its respect with me, when I see it in company with malice" (1.1, 29). Sir Oliver Surface uses metaphors of murder as well as robbery to convey his condemnation: "Aye, I know there are a set of malicious, prating, prudent gossips, both male and female, who murder characters to kill time; and will rob a young fellow of his good name, before he has years to know the value of it" (2.3, 51). Sir Peter's terror lest he become a subject of gossip indicates the pernicious force of personal talk: "Yes, yes, I think being a standing jest for all one's acquaintance a very happy situation. Oh, yes, and then of a morning to read the paragraphs about Mrs. S——, Lady T——, and Sir P——, will be so diverting! I shall certainly leave town tomorrow and never look mankind in the face again" (5.2, 105). But Sir Peter receives instant reassurance from Rowley: "Without affectation, Sir Peter, you may despise the ridicule of fools"; and nothing objectively justifies Sir Oliver's dire imagery.

Although malicious talk has no prolonged bad consequences in the play, the resolution which nullifies its temporary damage (Sir Peter and his wife reconcile, Joseph is exposed, Charles wins the wife of his choice) by no means cancels the energy of Mrs. Candour or Lady Sneerwell or even Lady Teazle. Their activity, however, resembles thievery less than squandering. As far as the audience can see, it takes away nothing. On the other hand, it provides an expressive outlet. When Lady Teazle describes Mrs. Pursy ("Yes, I know she almost lives on acids and small whey; laces herself by pulleys; and often in the hottest noon in summer, you may see her on a little squat pony, with her hair plaited up behind like a drummer's, and puffing round the Ring on a full trot"; 2.2, 46), the hearer can hardly fail to enjoy her gusto—the expressive energy equally manifest in the other gossips, and in no one else in the play except for Charles Surface cheerfully selling portraits of his ancestors. The text provides abundant directives for disapproving of Charles's financial and the gossips' verbal extravagance; yet in action such extravagance seems often attractive.

The social world evoked by *The School for Scandal* appears less dangerous than that summoned up by Restoration comedy, but more full of pointless activity. Charles's benevolence and Joseph's knavery prove equally futile. Charles spends indiscriminately, full of good feeling but devoid of judgment and neglecting claims of justice. He gains thoughtless fellowship but little respect; although he promises reform (given the love of a good woman), his verbal vagueness indicates no clear moral insight. Joseph plots and plots and accomplishes nothing. He seduces no one, foils no one. Frustration follows frustration. "Sure Fortune never played a man of my policy such a trick before. My character with Sir Peter, my hopes with Maria, destroyed in a moment!" (5.1, 94). Charles's spending wins him no lasting pleasure, Joseph's efforts at self-aggrandizement produce none. Sir Peter's attempts to live harmoniously with his wife break down repeatedly in quarreling, despite genuine good will on both sides. Maneuvering for sexual or financial gratification—standard activity on the Restoration stage—takes place here too, but no one seems to have much at stake. Unlike Lady Wishfort, Lady Sneerwell conveys no libidinal feeling in her confession that she longs for Charles. People go through the motions of their lives, their roles—except for manic bursts of energy from the gossips, from Charles auctioning his ancestors, and, briefly, from Joseph trying to extricate himself from his own hypocrisies.

At the very beginning of the play, the gossips proclaim their power to make things happen in the world: literally to control other people's lives. Snake, praising Mrs. Clackit, remarks, "To my knowledge she has been the cause of six matches being broken off, and three sons disinherited; of four forced elopements, and as many close confinements; nine separate maintenances, and two divorces" (1.1, 25). Sir Peter's later expression of fear lest the world mock him, by talk and by paragraphs in the papers, until he would feel unwilling to show his face, alludes to another traditional social function of gossip: by generating shame in those who violate social standards, it helps to enforce agreed-upon values. I have mentioned both these purposes of gossip in other connections: as power and as social sanction, gossip often serves important public functions. Sir Richard Steele, in an early attack on scandalmongers, had complained, "What they would bring to pass is, to make all good and evil to consist in report, and with whispers, calumnies, and impertinences, to have the conduct of those reports."[23] He articulates the fantasy of the gossips themselves, and the fear of their potential victims.

Snake's boasts, however, like Steele's warning, correspond to nothing that actually happens in The School for Scandal. When Marwood, in the last act of The Way of the World, threatens Lady Wishfort with the kind of publicity Sir Peter dreads if she resists Fainall's accusation of his wife, Lady Wishfort agrees to comply with Fainall's demands: the threat is both potent and real. Sir Peter, on the other hand, told not to worry, promptly stops worrying. The most extended scene of the "school for scandal" in operation does not suggest that gossip affects either lives or reputations. After Joseph has exposed his hypocrisy to Sir Peter and Lady Teazle, Mrs. Candour, Sir Benjamin Backbite, Crabtree, and Lady Sneerwell discuss the matter with delighted energy. The audience hears how the story expands and develops, taking on ever richer fictional form. The identity of Lady Teazle's hypothetical lover, the degree of her culpability, and the outcome of the revelation all shift with the speaker. Finally attention focuses on the imagined duel between Sir Peter and—depending on the imaginer—Charles or Joseph. Swords or pistols? What actually happened? Crabtree produces the most circumstantial account: "Sir Peter forced Charles to take one [pistol], and they fire, it seems, pretty nearly together. Charles' shot took place, as I tell you, and Sir Peter's missed; but what is very extraordinary, the ball struck against a little bronze Pliny that stood over the fireplace, grazed out of the window at a right angle, and wounded the postman, who was just coming to the door with a double letter from Northamptonshire" (5.2, 101). Not a single word of this detailed narrative corresponds to actuality (no duel at all has taken place)—but it has high entertainment value.

Nothing that I have said yet suggests clearly why the "school for scandal" has sufficient importance to give the play its title. One might argue that the tension between the asserted power and demonstrated ineffectuality of malicious gossip reveals corresponding tension in the play's author, that he writes to exorcise fears which he at once confirms and denies in his comedy, that such fears constitute the play's true subject. Perhaps that explanation is accurate (certainly it could be elaborated); but another possibility occurs to me. If the "good" characters in Restoration comedy face the problem of how to lead virtuous yet vital lives in a world of complicated corruption, their counterparts in The School for Scandal must discover how to preserve energy in a world dominated by elaborate rules of conduct. Joseph substitutes superficial good manners for good feeling when a petitioner appeals to him for money. His negative example suggests the ideal he violates: of forms of courtesy corresponding to substance of genuine concern for others. (Charles, who demonstrates the substance without preserving the forms, illustrates the same point by a less serious violation.) Among the accepted rules of conduct, many concern conversation. A group of recommendations for "young ladies" will exemplify their nature:

> When they Visit, or receive a Neighbouring Visit, where the Tea-Table is the first thing that offers, let their Conversation be free from Scandal, Envy or Detraction; for there are several Ways to keep up Discourse upon indifferent Subjects, besides the common Topicks of Congratulating with their Friends upon any Advantages that have happened to them, or any good News that they have heard; or otherwise Condoling with them upon some Misfortune or Affliction; or else returning Thanks for some Favours received of Respect, Civility and the like, with a thousand other Things which may be said, rather than to talk of what may happen to be prejudicial to any Body. [24]

Advice to gentlemen had a similar tone.

> Now, since it is from the Use and Custom of intermeddling in the Affairs of other Men, that this perverse Practice of being a busybody grows up into such a vicious Habit, we ought gradually to bring ourselves to an utter Disuse of enquiring into, or being concerned at any of those Things that do not pertain unto us: For Men suffering their Minds to rove inconsiderately at every Thing they see, are inured to a foolish Curiosity in busying themselves about Matters impertinent. Persons of an inquisitive Temper ought to restrain the wanton excursions of their Curiosity, and confine it to Observations of Prudence and Sobriety. [25]

The suggestions to young ladies about appropriate subjects for conversation evoke a mode of informal discourse rather like that practiced by the Houyhnhnms in the fourth book of *Gulliver's Travels*. The noble horses confine themselves to such matters as friendship, benevolence, order and economy, the bounds and limits of virtue, the rules of reason: unlike decorous females, they can transcend the personal. But the two kinds of conversation, like that suggested by the recommendations to gentlemen to avoid roving minds, share an atmosphere of restriction. Generations of readers have felt dubious about taking the Houyhnhnms as ideals for human beings; they sound, among other things, *boring*. The exclusionary prescriptions of eighteenth-century conduct books may arouse equivalent dubiety. The advice both to ladies and to gentlemen hints high psychic costs for refraining from the circulation of scandal, which seems implicitly associated with intellectual and psychic freedom.

One could hardly connect anything intellectual with the gossip exemplified in *The School for Scandal*; and *license* rather than *freedom* appropriately describes it. In no sense at all do the gossipers represent models of conduct: if their talk proves less dangerous than they think it, that fact only makes it the more ridiculous. They exemplify the folly which Sheridan's satire attacks, as Joseph exemplifies the play's limited imagining of vice. On the other hand, much of the entertainment this comedy provides for readers or audience derives from its interludes of verbal extravagance: the fiction-making of the scandalmongers, the self-indulgence of Charles, skeptical of and eager to puncture other people's proprieties.

The word *extravagance* calls to mind the metaphorical connection of verbal, financial, and sexual "spending." All three violate the social standards evoked by Sheridan's comedy; all three must be tamed for the play to fulfill its didactic function. The possibility of sexual indulgence hardly exists in the play: only Joseph, the ineffectual villain, seriously pursues it, with little promise of success. Charles can achieve triumphs of financial indiscretion without apparent difficulty, but they accomplish nothing beyond brief gratification; presumably he will give up such satisfactions in committing himself to marriage and sobriety. Like sexual freedom, financial freedom becomes excessively dangerous. Linguistic indulgence, on the other hand, as I have said, appears to do little real harm (although warnings about its harmfulness abound in the text). If it entertains the reader/audience, it also entertains its practitioners. Explicitly declared A Bad Thing (Lady Teazle gives it up to signal her moral reformation), it nonetheless, as realized onstage, embodies energy, imagination, the exploratory, the realm of possibility. To conjure up in vivid detail a duel that never occurred brightens the world. Such fictionizing may damage others; it unquestionably reveals the malice of its makers. But it also reveals the paucity of other emotionally satisfying occupation. When Mrs. Candour observes that "the town talks of nothing else" but Charles's extravagance, Maria responds, "I am very sorry, ma'am, the town has so little to do" (1.1, 30). She is quite right: the town has nothing better to do, caught in its web of social restriction.

Gossip in Sheridan's play takes the place sex fills on the Restoration stage.

In late seventeenth-century comedy, uncontrolled sexuality proves finally unsatisfying; adulterers and rakes suffer by comparison with such couples as Millamant and Mirabell, who eventually find loving and disciplined outlets for sexual expression. Sexual conduct has consequences rich in moral implication. By sexual behavior, men and women reveal their capacity or incapacity for love, fidelity, trust; and for discipline and discretion. *The Provok'd Wife, Love for Love, The Country Wife*: all reveal how much is at stake in the sexual maneuvering that preoccupies virtually everyone.

The School for Scandal substitutes verbal for sexual behavior, and rules of conduct for moral imperatives: a safer, more confined, less serious world. Its action implies a more benign view of human nature than that conveyed by the earlier plays, with their hints of genuine depravity. Neither Sir John Brute nor Mr. Horner could conceivably inhabit the society of the Surfaces, with its abundant exemplars of folly, its absence of real vice. But if this comedic world contains less evil than that of Restoration comedy, it also allows less possibility. Talk is the most important action here, but it has almost no significant consequences. The possibility of controlled yet vital verbal expression, equivalent to the controlled and loving relationship achieved by Angelica and Valentine, is never realized. Verbal energy and imagination do not mark the speech of Rowley and Sir Oliver, the play's moral models. Such qualities manifest themselves most clearly in uncontrolled talk: gossip, outrageous exploits like Charles's auction, Sir Peter's quarreling: only on the edge of the dangerous.

The shift in emphasis in the prevailing moral discourse about gossip between the seventeenth and eighteenth centuries corresponds to the changing implications of stage comedy. As Chapter Two demonstrated (and as the quotations in this chapter substantiate), gossip changed character in moralists' perception: from a moral violation related to pride, envy, anger, and lust, a manifestation of Original Sin, to a failure of social responsibility. Eighteenth-century conduct books provided rules for everything, defining "social responsibility" in concrete but relatively trivial terms. They taught people how to talk, how to attract a husband, how to pray in public, how to dance. Learning proper behavior, they imply, one learns all that the world demands.

The education of Charles Surface, the chastening of Joseph suggest just such a view. Everything works itself out easily, without serious consequence; education requires relatively little effort. A century earlier, Valentine, in *Love for Love*, had to learn, with pain, a new way of being; Charles Surface only has to give up a few bad habits. The lack of real weight in the scandal circulated by frivolous talkers exemplifies the less arduous ethical implications of the later play.

The "school for scandal" encourages people to talk as though something were really at stake, but in fact little of any significance can happen. *The School for Scandal* displays less open anger, less obvious danger, than Restoration plays because it severely limits the moral scope of its world. Its action rests on the assumption that people, usually good at heart, need only have their errors pointed out; that bad behavior can be readily controlled—in contrast with the darker implications of the Restoration stage. The verbal explosions of scandal in Sheridan's play, however, declare that not everything can be controlled, that people will create excitement for themselves in talk if forbidden exciting action.

7

The Talent of
Ready Utterance

Women have always chattered, leaving to men the realm of serious discourse: so the myth goes. In seventeenth- and early eighteenth-century England, while men allegedly pondered philosophy and history, women read romances: fanciful accounts of beautiful heroines fulfilling exciting fates. Then, in the eighteenth century, came the novel. Women both read and wrote novels: about life in the social world and in the home, about disastrous and beatific consequences of passion. Men worried, about the reading as well as the writing. This new fiction, claiming to imitate life, developing for itself conventions less safely restrictive than those of romance, might threaten the moral and psychological stability of its readers, presenting, as it did, characters of mixed motives, attractive villains, flawed heroes. Women and the young risked contamination by reading it. (Men, presumably, were made of sterner stuff.)

This primer version of literary history ignores the fact that men too wrote and read the new fiction; but eighteenth-century commentary indeed concentrated on dangers novels presented to their most "vulnerable" audience—dangers in some respects resembling those attributed to gossip. The novel from its beginning drew on published letters, biography and autobiography, and stage drama: genres discussed in my preceding chapters. Like those genres, perhaps even more obviously than they, it drew also on gossip.

I have already cited eighteenth-century denunciations of gossip; now I want to focus more sharply on commentary addressed specifically to women, trying to locate the moralists' concerns and to speculate about their occasional uneasy hints of gossip's conceivable value. This chronologically limited test case will particularize Chapter Two's hypotheses about reasons for the traditional association of women with gossip.

As the commentary cited in connection with eighteenth-century stage comedy indicated, detailed and restrictive prescriptions for social behavior, including conversation, abounded in this period. Less careful rules governed written narrative. The early novel encouraged precisely the exploration of human possibility that the century's principles of verbal decorum forbade. To think about what women could *not* do respectably in talk calls attention to the surprising latitude they allowed themselves in writing fiction.

To consider novels in relation to moral commentary also permits investigation of how the import of doctrine changes when it is incorporated into a fictional context. Social scientists and historians on occasion assume that they can extract ideas and social detail from novels without considering the force imaginative settings exert; even literary critics have made similar assumptions. But in fact fiction often exercises subversive pressure on the very standards it apparently upholds. On the surface, eighteenth-century novels usually support accepted proprieties. Fiction by women explicitly preaches doctrines long enforced in female lives. By plot and technique, on the other hand, it often suggests quite another message: a problematizing of moralistic doctrine. Two important novels by women, Fanny Burney's *Evelina* (1778) and Jane Austen's *Emma*, published in the nineteenth century but echoing eighteenth-century tradition, will illustrate what I mean. I shall concentrate on the relation between these novels' direct statement and the implications of their fictional procedure in order to investigate why gossip was vigorously suppressed by moralists, yet exploited as a novelistic resource.

First, the moralists, whose statements provide a context for the novels. Upright middle-class citizens in the eighteenth century, even upright aristocrats feared the contamination carried by what they called "the world"—meaning roughly what is implied in the phrase "the world, the flesh, and the devil"—but they glorified "society." Society consists, one commentator explains, in "a polite intercourse, which unites us to each other—in friendly visits, which cannot be dispensed with;—in letters of civility, which we ought to write;—and in that necessary familiarity which we mutually stand in need of for the purpose of relaxation."[1] The increasing stress on necessity and obligation typifies much commentary on social life. The view of society just quoted, concerned with manners and with communication, belongs to a work entitled *Advice from a Lady of Quality, to Her Children; in the Last Stage of a Lingering Illness.* On her deathbed, as it were, the lady insists both on the dangers of "the world" and on the obligations of "society." "The love of society," she concludes, "constitutes a part of our duty; the love of the world makes us forgetful of every duty" (78).

The felt distinction between "society" and "the world" depends partly on differentiation between internalized and externalized pressures. Everyone belongs to "society," that network of human connection declaring our necessary interdependence. Eighteenth-century fiction by and about men occasionally permits a fantasy of retreat to a confined society: the miniature civilization of the country estate. *Tom Jones* and *Humphry Clinker*, for example, resolve in their heroes' return to such relatively limited environments. Novels by and about women, on the other hand, assume the necessity of living in the context of a larger human community: living, therefore, by that community's rules. Those rules, increasingly complex and well defined, in the eighteenth century involved even the most minute aspects of behavior—the forms as well as the fact of conventional visiting and letter-writing, and of conventional conversation. Abundant conduct books promulgated the rules, but the truly well-bred woman—to confine myself to the sex toward whom the heaviest barrage of advice about conduct directed itself—carried those rules in her head and heart. The ideal of feeling socially an "insider" glimmers through the large literature about social ascension. *Pamela* (1740) sets the model for many successors in its account of how a humble country girl wins acceptance by her social betters. Her right to *belong* depends not only on her marriage but on her knowledge of such matters as how to carve at table, how to sing for company. To feel "inside" society, one must contain society's standards inside oneself.

"The world," on the other hand, remains always outside, as in Restoration and eighteenth-century stage comedy. It both judges and corrupts; unlike "society," it implies no structural order or harmony. "The world" provides a locus for fear and anxiety. The dying lady's distinction between love of society as duty and love of "the world" as violation sums up the moral weight attached to each concept. "The world" consists always of other people— other people holding out lures for prospective victims and condemnation for those who have violated social standards. Both temptation and threat, the idea of "the world" expresses the tensions implicit in living among other people; the notion of "society" evokes the reassurance of such life.

Love of society implies love of talk; love of the world encourages the wrong kind of talk, as well as of action: among other things, sexual action. As conversationalists and as sexual beings, women require more warning than men: so eighteenth-century thinkers still believed. Sexual warnings focus on female vulnerability; they assume that women readily become victims.

In conversation, on the other hand, women function as agents. They "have this talent of a ready utterance in . . . much greater perfection than men," Addison points out; he speaks, as usual, for many of his contemporaries.[2] Women like to talk. Their volubility demands control. What they might say, lacking external discipline, threatens the order of things.

As for what they might say, it will come as no surprise that many commentators worried about the alleged female propensity to gossip. The *Spectator* essay from which I just quoted examines four modes of what its author calls "female oratory." Its description of practitioners of the second and third modes epitomizes the century's sentiments; I shall quote it, therefore, at length.

> The second kind of female orators are those who deal in invectives, and who are commonly known by the name of the censorious. The imagination and elocution of this set of rhetoricians is wonderful. With what a fluency of invention and copiousness of expression will they enlarge upon every little slip in the behavior of another! With how many different circumstances, and with what variety of phrases, will they tell over the same story! . . . The censure and approbation of this kind of women are therefore only to be considered as helps to discourse.
>
> A third kind of female orator may be comprehended under the word gossips. Mrs. Fiddle Faddle is perfectly accomplished in this sort of eloquence; she launches out into descriptions of christenings, runs divisions upon an head-dress, knows every dish of meat that is served up in her neighbourhood, and entertains her company a whole afternoon together with the wit of her little boy, before he is able to speak [*Spectator*, 3.376].

After thus suggesting the folly, malice, and triviality of female speech, Addison offers further contemptuous generalization about women's discourse, concluding with patronizing remarks about the female tongue: "I must confess, I am so wonderfully charmed with the music of this little instrument, that I would by no means discourage it. All that I aim at by this dissertation is to cure it of several disagreeable notes, and in particular of those little jarrings and dissonances which arise from anger, censoriousness, gossiping, and coquetry" (379).

If Addison's tone, with its simple ironies, conveys a clear moral message, his vocabulary invites speculation. From some points of view, the imagination and eloquence of the gossip really *are*, as he ironically says, "wonderful," quite literally "helps to discourse." The fluency, copiousness, variety which characterize the gossip's speech embody values which the writer, in other contexts, would readily acknowledge. How can women talk so much about so little? The question haunts the commentator, who reiterates the word *little*, yet cannot conceal his wonder at the sheer abundance of female talk. Addison's description of the varieties of female oratory conveys emotional power as well as moral weakness. Women display remarkable fertility of utterance, but their words lack substantial content, the writer claims. The essayist utilizes all his rhetorical skill in a program of reduction, attempting to convert female speech into mere sound—or "music"—and thus to limit its conceivable power.

Many statements about women's gossip more or less explicitly emphasize that disturbing power, which derives, certain moralists recognize, from female minds as well as female tongues, and which potentially threatens the order of society by investigating what should remain veiled. One may call the special women's gift "curiosity" or "penetration": James Fordyce, a well-known sermon-writer, does both. "Curiosity" he, like his contemporaries, finds reprehensible. "To what shall we chiefly impute that female curiosity, which has been so long, and in most instances so justly, a topic of satire? Is it possible, that women could show such amazing eagerness to be acquainted with every minute particular in the life, character, dress, fortune, and circumstance of others, did they possess a fund of domestic entertainment and liberal conversation?"[3] Like other moralists, Fordyce thus finds a possible excuse for female limitation in the lack of fruitful occupation readily available to upper-class women. But he also in effect re-interprets the vice of curiosity, although he does not appear to notice the connection between what he considers female vice and what he finds an intellectual virtue. "Of this I am certain," he writes, "that amongst women of sense I have discovered an uncommon penetration in what relates to characters, an uncommon dexterity in hitting them off through their several specific distinctions, and even nicer discriminations, together with a race of fancy and a fund of what may be strictly termed Sentiment, or a pathetic manner of thinking, which I have not so frequently met with in men. It should seem that Nature, by her liberality to the female mind, in these respects, has seen fit to compensate what has been judged a defect in point of depth and force" (167). Women make up for lack of intelligence by being nosy.

In this speculation about the special strengths of female minds, Fordyce by no means typifies his period. The frequent eighteenth-century indictments of women's curiosity duplicate one another in language as well as thought, but the complainers do not typically think about the relation between this traditional female vice and other aspects of women's minds. Yet awareness like Fordyce's, of special female gifts, may explain the insistent efforts to keep women from saying what they think about other people. If females in fact possess "uncommon penetration" about character and "uncommon dexterity" in characterizing, if their emotional sensitivity (what Fordyce calls "Sentiment, or a pathetic manner of thinking") combines with a capacity for "nicer discriminations" than men can make—if these things are true, then women potentially possess dangerous powers of accurate commentary. The prevailing emphasis on the "littleness" and triviality of gossip may reveal anxiety about the possibility that gossiping women see and tell important truth.

So moralists warn women against associating exclusively with one another. "In mixed companies alone," John Bennet pronounces, ". . . conversation has its proper interest, flavour, of improvement."[4] Women do not improve each other; in all-female company, they are far too likely to gossip. Only men protect women, in Bennet's apparent view: from one another and from the vacancy of their own minds. And men protect mainly by enforcing a doctrine of repression. Women want to find out about other people and to articulate their knowledge; men attempt to control in them these dangerous aspects of desire. The fantasy that women, left to their own devices, would say destructive things recalls the fear that only constant vigilance by protective males prevents women from indulging their insatiable sexuality. But the persistent association of "curiosity" with gossip hints a more specific fear: that females, attentive to the minute, might uncover everything—Samson's secret, Cupid's—and betray it to other females. The possible assembly of only women—or only women with the company of one or two "half men," as Congreve has it in *The Way of the World*—troubles the male imagination.

Female curiosity bears fruit in stories about other people—stories which might under different circumstances take literary form. In a *Spectator* essay about "the inquisitive," Steele condemns their "temper of inquiry," which stems, he surmises, "from a vacancy in their own imaginations." Although he does not refer specifically to women, his indictment sounds familiar from other statements about the female. But as he continues to muse about "the insatiable desire of knowing what passes," he remarks that the mind gratified by such knowledge is formed, *"like myself,* to be a mere spectator" (my italics). Curiosity, he acknowledges, serves social ends. "This curiosity, without malice or self-interest, lays up in the imagination a magazine of circumstances which cannot but entertain when they are produced in conversation. If one were to know, from the man of the first quality to the meanest servant, the different intrigues, sentiments, pleasures, and interests of mankind, would it not be the most pleasing entertainment imaginable to enjoy so constant a farce, as the observing mankind much more different from themselves in their secret thoughts and public actions, than in their nightcaps and long periwigs?"[5] The subversive implications of such observation readily attach themselves to gossip, but Steele here implicitly connects talk with authorship. The enterprise of a periodical called *The Spectator* doesn't greatly differ from that of the dedicated observer of and talker about other people; and what about a periodical called *The Tattler?* Abstracted from the link with malice, gossip's trivia can generate literary power.

Why do commentators value written forms of observational narrative but at best only joke about gossip which shares such narrative's values? Dr. Johnson, in his familiar exposition of biography's importance, insists on the significance of trivial detail and on the imaginative power of specific knowledge about other people. In a less well-known *Rambler*, on the other hand, he deplores narrative about others as an element of conversation. People enjoy it, he admits; but they shouldn't.

> He who has stored his memory with slight anecdotes, private incidents, and personal particularities, seldom fails to find his audience favorable. Almost every man listens with eagerness to contemporary history; for almost every man has some real or imaginary connection with a celebrated character, some desire to advance, or oppose a rising name. Vanity often cooperates with curiosity. He that is a hearer in one place qualifies himself to become a speaker in another; for though he cannot comprehend a series of argument, or transport the volatile spirit of wit without evaporation, he yet thinks himself able to treasure up the various incidents of a story, and pleases his hopes with the information which he shall give to some inferior society.
>
> Narratives are for the most part heard without envy, because they are not supposed to imply any intellectual qualities above the common rate. To be acquainted with facts not yet echoed by plebeian mouths, may happen to one man as well as to another, and to relate them when they are known, has in appearance so little difficulty, that every one concludes himself equal to the task.[6]

Narrative in speech requires no intellectual gifts; moreover, Johnson goes on to imply, it tends to reduce its subjects to the same level as its hearers, encouraging the pernicious myth of equality.

The *Rambler* essay on biography argues that small facts provide the biographer's best material, since they compose the texture of human life. Johnson emphasizes how much we all share as human beings; biography, he believes, should stress this truth. In the biographical text, he finds such concern not reductive but instructive. Nothing is too little for so little a creature as man, he told Boswell. Yet the talker who reports man's littleness out loud wins only his reproach.

The biography essay insists that a "judicious and faithful narrative" of *any* human life would be useful.[7] A few months earlier, however, Johnson had argued that writers of novels—a genre based, in his view, on imitation rather than invention—must take care choosing specific lives to delineate because of their writings' imaginative potency. "If the power of example is so great as to take possession of the memory by a kind of violence, and produce effects almost without the intervention of the will, care ought to be taken that when the choice is unrestrained, the best examples only should be exhibited; and that which is likely to operate should not be mischievous or uncertain in its effects."[8] Why should novels prove so much more dangerous than biographies? Perhaps because they involve the imagination more intensely; their readers, Johnson tells us, include "the young, the ignorant, and the idle," all susceptible to the lures of fancy. He does not tell us who reads biography.

Let me recapitulate this series of observations. Stories about other people reported in speech attract ready audiences because everyone feels some connection to well-known people, because the hearers can anticipate their own subsequent roles as narrators of the same stories, and because those hearers feel no envy of the narrator's gifts: he needs no gifts, they believe, and Johnson appears to share their conviction. Such tales falsify experience by simplifying it and by suggesting that those talked about have the same flaws as those talking. Stories about other people presented in the guise of printed fiction attract the gullible; the novelist therefore must take responsibility for making characters and actions in fiction instructive, for presenting positive models of conduct. Stories about other people in biography cannot be too trivial; they illustrate the ways in which small actions define character and comprise experience.

The implicit differentiations here involve both author and audience, different kinds of authority, different kinds of receptivity. Johnson appears to imagine oral narrative as communicated in coffee houses: a limited public setting. Novels reach a larger, more indiscriminate public; biography appeals to a group which Johnson fails to define but which he apparently trusts. The transmitters of narrative take their places in a posited hierarchy of authority, a hierarchy which illuminates the subjects of women and of gossip.

The biographer's authority exceeds the novelist's because of the weight of didactic tradition accruing to his genre (I use the masculine pronoun because Johnson entirely assumes it) and because he grounds his narrative in fact. Johnson takes for granted both the didactic intent and the didactic effect of a life story in writing. The biographer imposes pattern on experience to declare the comprehensibility of human existence. Learning of other people, we learn of ourselves. Lacking a long formal tradition to authorize his enterprise, the novelist, with more dubious purpose than the biographer, risks contamination by association with the morally suspect mode of romance: as Johnson reproachfully observes, novels too often make love the spring of action. And novelists rely, of course, on the dangerous power of imagination: to put it bluntly, they *lie*.

Both novelist and biographer, however, by assuming the responsibility and the power of the written word, exceed in authority the conversational narrator for whom Johnson expresses patronizing contempt. Johnson imagines this narrator too as male; he does not even bother to discuss those jabbering females evoked by his dictionary's striking definition of *gossip*, which I quoted earlier ("One who runs about tattling like women at a lying-in"). Such women, in Johnson's representative view, would lack all semblance of authority. Conversing only with one another, they confine themselves to a more private sphere than that of the male story-teller who circulates in coffee houses to relate the foibles of public men, existing therefore at least on the fringes of the public life that tests human worth—*male* worth. Women share secrets, hiding from scrutiny. And—Johnson doesn't say this, but many others do—they deal in scandal, thus raising questions of motive and the possibility of fanciful exaggeration. Critics implicitly grant the biographer moral motivation; they allow its possibility for the novelist, despite suspicion that the fiction-writer may stress pleasure more than instruction. The coffee-house story-teller, Johnson suggests, wishes to make himself important and to reduce the stature of those greater than he. But in the eyes of their critics, female gossips, their specific utterances only hypothesized, conceal destructive purposes, existing thus at the bottom of the moral hierarchy as well as of the closely connected hierarchy of authority.

Public writing on the whole enjoyed higher status than did private talk. Eliza Haywood, writing early in the century specifically about gossip, suggests a possible justification for the oral mode by raising the question, "Will the Knowledge of what other People do make us wiser or happier?"—only to answer it, without further explanation, by insisting that abundant examples, both positive and negative, exist already in writing.[9] Examples in writing of course possess the stability necessarily lacking in oral utterance; their implications can be more sternly controlled. Women's gossip seems dangerous not only because it belongs to women but because it belongs to the unpredictable realm of talk, talk made more unpredictable by taking place in domestic rather than public settings. When Addison speaks of "female oratory," his irony focuses on just this aspect of women's conversation: he considers such talk negligible precisely because it is *not* oratory, not public performance.

Explicitly, the body of moral doctrine I have been citing draws on an acknowledged standard of social decorum to sanction disapproval of gossip. The implications of the doctrine, however, go far beyond propriety. To summarize: the eighteenth-century attack on gossip suggests the superiority of the verbal mode epitomized by those who can read Latin and consider public matters; it hints the inadequacy of female understanding as well as of female talk; it declares the reprehensible nature of concern with human detail if such concern issues in speech; it preaches a doctrine of repression in the service of communal welfare, in the interests of that "society" generally assumed to define value. If the moralizers leave a few loose ends in such comments as Steele's connection of authorship with curiosity and Fordyce's recognition of female insight, they yet display a striking unanimity in their distaste for gossip and in the grounds of that distaste.

Women can write as well as talk, of course, although Dr. Johnson barely acknowledged the fact; and they wrote novels beginning early in the eighteenth century, sometimes anonymously or under pseudonyms, but sometimes attaching their own names. Curiosity; avid interest in other people, their lives, the small manifestations of their personalities; close observation and nice discrimination—the qualities alleged to account for the nature of women's conversation now fueled their writing (as well as that of their male contemporaries) and apparently interested readers male and female, old and young. Even the malice supposed to underlie gossip could provide energy for the novel. In deeper ways than Dr. Johnson may consciously have realized, the novel embodied troubling possibilities.

Let me turn now to *Evelina*.

About two thirds through the novel, the heroine experiences difficulty finding material for a letter. "You complain of my silence, my dear Miss Mirvan," she begins a communication to her female confidante—"but what have I to write? Narrative does not offer, nor does a lively imagination supply the deficiency."[10] Evelina feels a problem about narrative because the story she wants to tell—the story of her own fulfilled love—refuses to take shape. Indeed, she has thus far acknowledged this love not even to herself. The drama of her unarticulated desire informs all she writes, but it generates no story she can perceive. She finds nothing to write because nothing much has happened recently; specifically, the absence of her beloved Lord Orville from the immediate scene deprives her life of narrative interest. She lacks the power, or perhaps the courage, of invention to "supply the deficiency"; she claims only a reporter's gifts. Thus, she fills the letter at hand with an account of a conversation with her guardian—not "narrative," from her point of view, because it frustrates the story she yearns to complete: she and Mr. Villars discuss Lord Orville's apparent misconduct toward her and conclude that it makes him, in effect, ineligible. Finally Evelina begs her correspondent to keep the letter secret even from her mother: "Lord Orville is a favourite with her, and why should I publish that he deserves not that honour?" (268).

Like most domestic epistolary novels, *Evelina* finds its material largely in accounts of conversations and actions by people other than the writers of the letters and in speculative judgment about the import of such talk and action. Evelina reports Lord Orville's doings and her conversation about them because of her own direct involvement, but she recognizes the risk of scandalmongering: her injunction to Miss Mirvan not to tell reflects both her lingering tenderness for Lord Orville and her awareness of the potential social danger of such an account as she has offered. In other letters, she often finds occasion to narrate in the most trivial detail, and not without malice, daily actions and speech of those around her, happenings utterly unmomentous but of absorbing interest to her and her correspondents. With what meticulous specificity does she report the conversation of the disagreeable Branghtons, foppish Lovel, caddish Sir Clement Willoughby! We come to know their turns of mind more exactly even than Lord Orville's. The Branghtons trying to figure out what door to go in at the opera or where to sit for tea, Mr. Smith unwillingly dancing with Evelina's grandmother or explaining a painting of Neptune ("they're all generals"): vignettes of this sort generate the narrative vitality of *Evelina*, as even the earliest readers perceived.

One may wonder what relation exists between trivia about other people—I might as well call it gossip at once—and Evelina's obsession with completing the narrative of her love. I'd like to postpone that question for a bit in order to point out another conspicuous element of *Burney's* narrative: the stuff of scandal in a larger sense than mere allegations of social misconduct. Birth, copulation, and death figure in the background of this genteel fiction. Elopements, secret marriages, questions of legitimacy, a deathbed letter—these create the context for Evelina's well-behaved existence. Even her immediate experience supplies material for scandal. She encounters an aristocratic seducer who absconds with her in his coach, two prostitutes who try to take possession of her, nameless men who accost her when (as happens twice) she loses the rest of her party, a youth with two pistols who appears on the verge of suicide. That youth has a juicy story of his own—real instead of apparent illegitimacy, near-patricide, a romantic and apparently hopeless love. Finally there is the servant's daughter who has pre-empted Evelina's place as heiress of a nobleman: yet another lurid tale, although this one largely suppressed. Such stories and sub-stories, the substance of much eighteenth-century fiction, belong also to the traditional material of gossip. The relevance of these situations to Evelina's love manifests itself more readily, since they provide the blocking forces of the action; yet they generate tonal anomalies which may raise further questions about the nature of this narrative.

A third element in Burney's narrative and Evelina's alike is Evelina herself—"a book," Mr. Villars observes in the conversation reported in the letter with which I began, "that both afflicts and perplexes me!" The account continues:

> He means *me*, thought I; and therefore I made no answer.
> "What if we read it together?" continued he, "will you assist me
> to clear its obscurity?" [263]

The realization that her foster father has defined her as subject makes Evelina mute. She has obscured from herself the complexities of her consciousness as well as the specific fact of her love, insisting on her own passivity and instrumentality. When Villars proposes collaborative interpretation of the young woman as text, she reluctantly agrees to participate. To interpret the text of the heroine comprises a large part of her task and of the reader's: the development of Evelina's consciousness defines Burney's story and generates as much narrative movement as either kind of gossip.

Mr. Villars' efforts to interpret Evelina as text issue soon in a recommendation of suppression—not for her talk (Evelina is hardly a loose talker) but for her imagination. Her propensity for narrative, in Villars' view, specifically endangers her: she has allowed herself to figure as heroine in a version of the Cinderella story, ignoring hard facts. The attempts to suppress gossip in women exemplified by the moralistic passages I have quoted also bear on narrative. People gossip not only because they want to talk but from a need for the specific kind of talk which takes a special shape in story. My question about *Evelina* is, what produces *its* story? The story of the novel does not altogether coincide with the one the heroine wishes to tell, although the novel too could be described as a version of *Cinderella*. I have already suggested three components of its narrative: the material of trivial gossip, the data of scandal, and the heroine herself. Let me complicate the issue slightly more by contemplating the place in *Evelina* of gossip as a literal fact.

The power of gossip as a force in the events of this novel inheres largely in its imagined possibility as the voice of "the world": that threat familiar from Restoration comedy. Joyce Hemlow long ago pointed out the book's relentless stress on proprieties, its potential didactic weight for young female readers. The implicit sanction enforcing good social behavior within the fictional world derives from fear of scandal, socially circulated disapproval: gossip. From the moment of Evelina's arrival in London, she feels the eyes of the world upon her, making her experience panic, shame, desire to sink through the floor, in her "perpetual fear [of] doing something wrong" (30)—meaning not something morally reprehensible, but something socially incorrect. Although twentieth-century common sense may suggest disproportion in the girl's terror, the novel supplies no standard by which to deprecate her response. The terms of condemnation in the overheard male conversation about Evelina's improprieties draw on a serious moral vocabulary, using words like *weak* and *vile*. Lord Orville suggests that she must be either "ignorant, or mischievous" (36). At stake in the opinion of Evelina's dancing partners is her status as a moral being.

But the gossip that might ostracize the heroine involves more important matters than behavior at an assembly; it floats about the unsolved problem of Evelina's lineage. Although her father and her mother, her guardian insists, went through a legal marriage ceremony, the father subsequently refused to acknowledge the validity of the marriage. Through much of the novel, Evelina possesses no avowed parent. She would have had splendid offers in London, Lady Howard assures Mr. Villars, "had there not seemed to be some mystery in regard to her birth," a mystery which "the town" (here as in Restoration comedy essentially identical with "the world") attempted assiduously but vainly to fathom (124). When another alleged daughter of Evelina's true father, Sir John Belmont, appears on the scene, Mr. Villars worries about the influence of this development on the mother's reputation. Earlier, he has refused to consider a lawsuit to restore Evelina's rights, on the ground that such a method would "subject her to all the impertinence of curiosity, the sneers of conjecture, and the stings of ridicule"—eventualities merely verbal, but intolerable (128). When he warns Evelina that she must learn to judge and act for herself, his argument against passivity rests on the assumption that Evelina's lack of determined purpose may "risk the censure of the world" (164): a risk far too great. Evelina anxiously anticipates the emotional consequences of her father's acceptance or non-acceptance; her elders concentrate on the social consequences that gossip might generate or consolidate.

Gossip retains its power, however, only at a distance. Imagined gossip can destroy reputation; the gossip we actually hear in the novel only trivializes. (This pattern too is familiar from stage comedy.) Evelina's vulgar relatives want to know, and to talk about, Sir Clement's income, Evelina's height, the intimate details of her history. Lovel speaks fashionable nonsense, Lord Orville's sister reduces all personal details to the same level of vapidity. Madame Duval, Evelina's lower-class grandmother, attacks the girl with a prying curiosity which she does not know how to forestall, but its purposes seem more frivolous than sinister. Lord Orville, the normative figure of the novel, on the other hand, feels horrified at the very idea that he might wish to know something about the poor Scot, Macartney; he restrains all curiosity even about Evelina herself. Restraint largely defines his excellence, as it does Evelina's: both avoid loose talk. Evelina praises the quality of Lord Orville's conversation, but offers few examples of it. She herself spends much of her social time in silence—a reiterated fact underlining the implications of the moralists' emphasis on the dangers of female talk. The *really* good woman says nothing.

In its manifest treatment of gossip, in other words, *Evelina* confirms the moralists' strictures and emphasizes how such strictures support the assumed importance of "society." The heroine's silences, her conscious refrainings define her good breeding by contrast with the unbecoming verbosity of others; and to defend Evelina against the devastating charge of ill breeding appears to be the book's central enterprise. The heroine proves her right to high rank by her impeccable goodness, despite her social errors in the beginning, and despite her vulgar grandmother, once a barmaid. As letter-writer, Evelina dwells insistently on her cousins' solecisms and her grandmother's to support her own moral and social superiority—the self-esteem that, more fundamentally even than her propriety, protects her from the blandishments of the would-be seducer Sir Clement Willoughby. She comes to know that she behaves better than most of her associates; she sustains that knowledge by commenting on the minutiae of her inferiors' behavior.

Such commentary, as I have already suggested, comprises the material of gossip: if it figures in speech rather than in writing. Oral gossip serves the same functions as Evelina's written communications: as we have already seen, it fosters the gossiper's sense of superiority, provides the illusion of control by narrative possession of fragments of other people's lives, constitutes an oblique moral discourse. Like much oral gossip, moreover, Evelina's written observations belong to a modality of trust. She shares them only with her beloved guardian and with a single female contemporary, knowing that neither will betray her confidence or mock her inadequacies. On the other hand, exchanges in writing differ fundamentally from "real" gossip because of the lack of immediate response, the absence of interchange at the time of utterance. Evelina's letters, therefore, like personal letters actually sent, comprise an analogue to gossip, not an instance of it.

The story of the novel does not altogether coincide with the stories Evelina tells; her definition of narrative does not merge with the author's or, in all probability, the reader's. The narrative we read includes the one Evelina writes, but also includes her as character in a way quite different from that in which she includes herself. Evelina's consciousness enlarges partly by her telling stories. But the book's energy derives also from the clash of values between announced and implied doctrine. Social behavior in this fiction has both metonymic and literal signification: manners stand for moral substance and they create the texture of social experience. Since good manners proscribe expressed curiosity about the affairs of others not present, propriety demands a social rhetoric of exclusion and control in verbal exchange, a rhetoric embodying a morality of non-intervention. On the other hand, intimate correspondence as exemplified by Evelina's letters implies a different system, privileging the fluid and exploratory, risking instability, allowing aggression. Although Evelina occasionally apologizes for her harsh judgments of her grandmother or of Mrs. Selwyn, the middle-aged woman of "masculine" intelligence who takes her to Bath, she displays in her letters a freedom of utterance quite foreign to her social behavior. That freedom involves only her commentary about other people; her direct presentation of self in the letters closely resembles her reported manner in face-to-face exchange, self-deprecating, seeking external authority, passive. Yet the reader perceives that self developing precisely through its exploratory observations and judgments of other people.

Lord Orville rewards Evelina for good behavior by marrying her. "Good behavior" approximates silence. The talk of lower-class characters and of misguided aristocrats in the novel deserves the moralists' castigation: superficial, insensitive, malicious, and tedious, it reveals human insufficiency. Conversely, Evelina's decorum of restraint declares her worth. The heroine's rhetoric of desire directs itself toward Lord Orville; her story can find its happy ending only in his ratification of her social value. On the other hand, the novel also articulates a more hidden version of desire, expressed in her will to *tell* her story. In the shaping and telling of her own romance, a romance which in its narration includes her derogatory characterization of those around her, Evelina reveals her active capacity to judge, to assert, to define. Gossip becomes the very means of the central narrative to which it at first appeared irrelevant, the narrative of Evelina's love. By the exercise of those female gifts of curiosity and penetration, the heroine establishes and confirms her personal power, not for aggression but for self-affirmation. Her written equivalent of gossip has provided her private education.

The novel *Evelina* in effect juxtaposes the young woman reporting— observant, confident in her values, intermittently malicious, judgmental, highly verbal—with the young woman she describes: often silent, fearful, always avoiding offense. And the novel thrives on the juxtaposition, which calls attention to all that polite conversation eliminates, such matters as birth, appearance, wealth, emotion: the personal. The contrast between oral repression and textual liberty implies no necessary criticism of the social mode, but it calls attention to the incongruity of social and literary values. The Spectator conveying his observations in print can indulge curiosity; the spectator in the drawing room must not. The coffee-house narrator earns Johnson's contempt; the biographer who reports detail wins praise. Evelina in playhouse, assembly, or garden, keeps her mouth shut; on the page, she indulges herself. And Burney as novelist exploits in her readers the kind of interest they presumably suppress in their everyday lives, generating her text from the material of domestic scandal, creating her heroine from the simultaneity of repression and expression made possible by the epistolary mode.

For the reader, the disjunction between Evelina as originator and as subject of her own discourse resembles the pattern discussed in Chapter Four in relation to published letters between real people—the pattern I described as an alternation between "gossiping with" and "gossiping about" the letter-writer. Readers may assess a newly wed couple in church as the describer of that couple, Lady Mary Pierrepont, directs them to do; but they will also arrive at opinions about Lady Mary on the basis of her accounts of self and others. Just so, we both share Evelina's contempt for Lovel and think about what such a feeling tells us about her.

The difference between Evelina's expressivity as letter-writer and her restraint as conversationalist calls attention to the contrasting social decorum of familiar letter and polite conversation. "Rules" govern both; but in one case "the world" watches; in the other, it does not. Evelina writes her letters for an audience of one. Mr. Villars does not share her words with others, and he judges by moral rather than social standards. His paternal role makes him a kind of confessor, to whom Evelina can acknowledge errors and doubts without fear of categorical rejection. Writing constitutes Evelina's most authentic action. With the eyes of the world upon her, she must guard her social behavior, constantly deflecting the possibility of self-directed action. Lord Orville promises to take care of her; she happily anticipates a lifetime of his guidance. Under such protection, she can perform in socially sanctioned ways; Lord Orville's rank and his wisdom will make the world less threatening.

The value of imitated letters as fictional devices in the eighteenth century depends partly on the comparative freedom of the epistolary mode. In an urban society with rules predicated on an almost total split between affective and behavioral life—that split which Norbert Elias has postulated as the result of the "civilizing process"[11]—private letters offer greater expressive possibilities than do other forms of conduct. The attentive and censorious "world," mythic embodiment of the threat implicit in the existence of unknown other people, inhibits social behavior. In letters, commenting on one's own behavior and that of others, one partially escapes. As a novelistic resource, the form of private correspondence permits fictional commentary on the individual's efforts to function authentically in a restrictive society. To embody the doctrine of conduct books in a narrative composed of letters alters the doctrine. *Evelina* thus undermines as well as supports the social values it affirms.

I have avoided, mainly out of sheer bafflement, the question of how familiar letters imitated in fiction differ from their literal counterparts. The expectation of artistry in a novel may draw the reader into a process of interpretation which ends by making sense of every rendered detail, understanding each minute happening or observation as part of a coherent meaning. But bringing the same expectation to bear on the collected letters of Lady Mary Wortley Montagu would produce comparable results. They too appear to tell a story of coherent meaning, and a story involving the same issues as Evelina's. One might note the contrast between the ease and freedom with which Lady Mary addresses her daughter in writing and the relative stiffness of more socially constricted letters to Lady Pomfret or Lady Oxford; and one could understand the "story" of the collection as involving a woman's struggle toward self-assertion, the marriage to Wortley one of her several false starts.

If collections of actual letters read like fiction, the reading of fictional correspondence resembles in complexity the experience of reading published personal letters, with their demand for alternating perspectives. The control of the fiction-maker substitutes for that of the editor to give the reader security; the narrative thrust of fictional letters often emerges more forcefully than that of communications between real people; extraneous details crop up in real letters more often than they do in novelistic imitations. And the experience of reading letters which we know to be fictional differs from that of encountering actual correspondence because of the different relation of reader to text. Pondering Lady Mary's plaintive or desperate letters to her lover, we read something not originally intended for us. Evelina's correspondence, on the other hand, relies on the *fiction* of privacy. "Evelina writes for an audience of one," I asserted earlier. True: but *Burney*, the actual creator of Evelina's letters, hopes for an audience of thousands. J. Hillis Miller has commented on the curious pretenses by which fiction typically claims to be something it is not: biography, history, whatever. [12] The claim of a novelistic text to comprise private letters solicits the reader's discomfort, emphasizing his/her status as eavesdropper—but the claim's fictionality converts the guilt of eating stolen fruit into yet another fiction. ("The epistolary novel . . . gives readers the rare pleasure of reading someone else's mail." [13]) Like the gratification of seeing tragedy, which legitimizes our interest in other people's suffering by assuring us of its characters' irreality, the delight of fictional letters includes that of guilt transformed into aesthetic satisfaction. Despite such distinctions, however—all matters of degree rather than of kind—similarities remain more striking than differences, if one takes Lady Mary and Evelina as test cases.

Of course, Walpole's letters differ from Evelina's more than Lady Mary's do; Lord Chesterfield's would differ yet more, Dr. Johnson's more still. As the purpose of a correspondence diverges from the establishment and main-tenance and expression of intimacy, its letters diminish in resemblance to the fictional. The closeness of letters like Lady Mary's to letters like Evelina's, analogous to the closeness between some autobiographies and some novels, reminds us that fiction imitates not only life but life's written records, and reminds us how much fiction concentrates on intimate relations.

One reason novelists draw on the epistolary form—to return to the subject of society and "world"—is that letters provide a way of focusing on the tension between self and world. That tension always shapes literal gossip, which expresses the outlook of defiant individuals or sub-groups or speaks with the voice of social authority, thus representing or opposing (usually doing both in alternation) the world. Another version of the tension emerges in personal letters, to be exploited by their fictional counterparts. Letters articulate ver-sions of the self—portrait or mask. [14] But they also describe the self in society, thus calling attention to discrepancies between personal impulse and social restriction. Society has always allowed in personal letters at least some of the verbal latitude it deplores in gossip. I suggested earlier that private talk pro-vided for eighteenth-century women a means of agency; personal letters serve precisely the same purpose—in fiction as well as in life.

.   .   .

Jane Austen's *Emma*, dealing with village existence, evokes a society without a "world." The people who talk about one another in Highbury all have faces; reactions from neighbors and friends respond promptly to social deviation. The knowing narrator of the novel, who understands the kinds of restriction implicit in a tiny, intimate society, helps to locate the missing term in her heroine's experience, calling attention to the limitations of Emma's consciousness as well as of her society.

The relation between gossip as social prohibition and as narrative resource becomes explicit here: *Emma* articulates a grammar of gossip. Slightly past the mid-point of the novel, Mr. Knightley explains an important truth to Emma and Mrs. Weston. "Another thing must be taken into consideration too," he observes—"Mrs. Elton does not talk *to* Miss Fairfax as she speaks *of* her. We all know the difference between the pronouns he or she and thou, the plainest-spoken amongst us."[15] The entire novel glosses that difference, and elucidates the further distinction of the first-person pronoun from the others. When Emma violates decorum by talking *to* Miss Bates as she might have spoken *of* her—as a dullard—she prepares the way for a sequence of insights which ends by establishing her in a new relation to the first-person pronoun.

People talk a great deal about other people during *Emma*, for one main reason: to alleviate or forestall boredom. The lack of occupation to which some moralists had attributed the female propensity to gossip afflicts male and female characters alike. Only the male Knightleys partially escape, John working as a lawyer in London and unable to comprehend the Highbury delight in trivial conversation, and George busy about his estate, willing to gossip with the others but less dependent on gossip as a resource. Unlike Austen's other novels, this one dwells on its own sense of confinement. "Imaginist" though she is, Emma faces a real, not an imaginary, problem in the lack of possibility her community affords. No new people: hence the sensational impact of Frank Churchill. No new things to do or see: hence the momentousness of an expedition to Box Hill or even to Donwell. Emma can play backgammon with her father, she can visit the few familiar people who surround her, she can shop for gloves or ribbons, do needlework or read or practice her music. Repeatedly the text emphasizes Highbury's limitations. At the very beginning, we learn that Emma, "with all her advantages, natural and domestic, . . . was now in great danger of suffering from intellectual solitude" (7). Like everyone around her, she yearns for "news." "Oh! yes, I always like news" (172). The only news available, the only kind relevant to her concerns, involves people she knows or those associated with them.

Her impoverished world supplies little else in the way of delight. Walking to the door of a shop while Harriet vacillates over muslins, she seeks

> amusement.—Much could not be hoped from the traffic of even the busiest part of Highbury;—Mr Perry walking hastily by, Mr William Cox letting himself in at the office door, Mr Cole's carriage horses returning from exercise, or a stray letterboy on an obstinate mule, were the liveliest objects she could presume to expect; and when her eyes fell only on the butcher with his tray, a tidy old woman travelling homewards from shop with her full basket, two curs quarrelling over a dirty bone, and a string of dawdling children round the baker's little bow-window eyeing the gingerbread, she knew she had no reason to complain, and was amused enough; quite enough still to stand at the door. A mind lively and at ease can do with seeing nothing, and can see nothing that does not answer [233].

"A mind lively and at ease." The phrase appears to come from Emma's consciousness; her self-congratulation may recall dreadful Mrs. Elton's talk of her "resources." The liveliness and ease of Emma's mind get her into trouble, as her imagination goes to work on limited raw materials to create gossip which produces false expectations and pain for others. The "he" and "she" who inhabit Emma's imagination belong to the realm of fiction. She constructs shapely plots, domestic romances, about the unmarried; and when she figures as an actress in her own fictions, one begins to understand her difficulty with the first-person pronoun.

From some points of view, Emma seems all too completely at ease with what Virginia Woolf calls the vertical pronoun. Accustomed to rule in her small domain, suffering only the "real evils" of possessing "the power of having rather too much her own way, and a disposition to think a little too well of herself" (5), unchastened by fears of the world, Emma functions insistently as an "I." Yet her version of "I" bears a troubling similarity to her notion of "he" and "she." She sees herself too, repeatedly, as a fictional character, imagining the audience that the village cannot adequately supply. Her entire relationship with Frank Churchill derives from and depends on her capacity to perceive herself from the point of view of admiring spectator. When she and Frank first dance together, "she found herself well-matched in a partner. They were a couple worth looking at" (230). Dwelling as she does on the idea of being looked at, she neglects to recognize what she feels, thinking, rather, of what she might, or should, feel. When Frank reappears, after an absence from Highbury, she concludes that she has not, after all, really fallen in love with him. She gives him, however, "friendly encouragement, . . . which now, in her own estimation, meant nothing, though in the judgment of most people looking on it must have had such an appearance as no English word but flirtation could very well describe. 'Mr Frank Churchill and Miss Woodhouse flirted together excessively.' They were laying themselves open to that very phrase—and to having it sent off in a letter to Maple Grove by one lady, to Ireland by another" (368). This preoccupation with what might be said about her, with, in fact, the gossip she may generate by her self-presentation as well as by her imagination—this preoccupation helps to make possible her thoughtless insult of Miss Bates. She has become so involved in her immediate social role, in her fantasy of being perceived as powerful, witty, and attractive, that she has lost awareness of others' feelings.

Harriet Smith, for all her stupidity and indecisiveness, parodies Emma. She too keeps constructing fictions round herself, less imaginative fictions than Emma specializes in, but constructions in the same genre. She too has trouble knowing her own emotions and accurately assessing other people's. Her failure to function as a full center of consciousness stems from intellectual inadequacy, Emma's, from more complicated sources; but both alike fall into gossip's trap of objectification. Gossip deprives other people of reality; it ends, the novel implies, by doing the same to the self.

Harriet's fictions, of course, in the neat structure of *Austen's* fiction, bring an end to Emma's. When it darts through Emma with the speed of an arrow that Mr. Knightley must marry no one but herself, she moves rapidly from self-dramatization to self-knowledge, toward the marriage that will chasten the excesses of her imagination. She starts now to concentrate on her feelings rather than her performance: to know herself as "I" rather than "she."

Gossip has provided not only an obstacle to the happy ending but a means toward fruition. In the penultimate chapter, Knightley offers Emma a brief account of how the engagement between Harriet Smith and Robert Martin finally came to pass. "This is all that I can relate," he concludes, "of the how, where, and when. Your friend Harriet will make a much longer history when you see her.—She will give you all the minute particulars, which only woman's language can make interesting.—In our communications we deal only in the great" (472). Despite the ironic overtones of Knightley's commentary, he speaks literal truth: woman's language *can* make the trivial and mundane interesting, it can create histories of its own, and it differs from man's language, although men may also employ it. The history Austen has spun out of the daily experience of Highbury precisely demonstrates the point.

Homer Brown has observed, "Traditionally, two of the ways the novel has had of at once disguising and validating itself have been as letters and as gossip. . . . It is probable that part of the pleasure we derive from the classic novel is a pleasure similar to that derived from gossip."[16] Gossip's hermeneutic power generates the internal dynamic of *Emma:* we see its heroine interpreting minute particulars of her own and other people's experience; her acts of interpretation create the plot. Emma exists so completely as an "insider" that "outside" has virtually no existence for her. Her tiny society enables her to function with utter authority; no amount of experience convinces her of her final incapacity to know the meanings of other people's actions within that confined setting. Knightley's condemnation of her rudeness to Miss Bates also derives from the insider's position. In Highbury, one cannot judge people—as, elsewhere, the world does—on the basis of their social performances: one knows too much. Emma should have remembered Miss Bates's history, her personality, her emotional and economic situation. To operate always from inside carries its own penalties—not least of them Emma's inability to distinguish among the pronouns. Her self-objectification declares her yearning for an audience that *will* assess her performance, instead of one for which her performance merges with her history. She yearns, in other words, for a version of that world so threatening to Evelina and other novelistic heroines: the world that would, paradoxically, make her feel more real by fictionizing her.

Gossip carries particularly complex meanings in *Emma* because of the reader's implication in its patterns. The novel consistently invites us too to participate in acts of interpretation. Revealing again and again Emma's interpretive mistakes, giving us the grounds to judge them and her, it may lure us into believing ourselves more competent than she to understand particularities. Guided by the knowing narrator, we can feel ourselves *super-*insiders. The text offers many particularities to understand. When Emma calls on Jane Fairfax shortly after the delivery of her new pianoforte, a gift which, Emma has decided, must come from Mr. Dixon, Jane does not at once sit down at the instrument. "That she was not immediately ready, Emma did suspect to arise from the state of her nerves" (240); and Emma of course believes herself to understand the proximate cause of nervous tension. The reader possesses the same data as Emma. If we have become, by this point in the novel, wary of Emma's hasty explanations, we face the problem of providing our own. Like a detective novel, the book keeps offering raw material for interpretation, the raw material of gossip, and requiring us to do something with it. The "correct" interpretation for many previous events emerges finally, in the revelation of the secret engagement between Frank and Jane. At this point, we must assess the quality of our own interpretations, realize the degree to which we, as readers, have participated in the making of the fiction—and realize, perhaps, that such participation belongs to a continuum with Highbury's endless speculation. Instead of the pleasure of reading other people's letters, we have been offered the gratifications of complicity—only to have our satisfaction in it repeatedly undermined. Women or not, we have been lured into acting like the women of moralistic stereotypes: lured into rewards and betrayals of speculative gossip. We do not talk out loud, of course; but our inner voices ask gossip's questions, make its judgments.

As usual, Austen provides a conservative text and a challenging sub-text. Emma will presumably settle down and behave herself and stop interpreting so wildly; Harriet will stop interpreting at all. The "longer history" of her engagement that Harriet might provide would surely prove tedious in the extreme. Highbury's gossip substitutes for meaningful life; the village's confinement limits growth and pleasure. Although Knightley jokes when he asserts that men "deal only in the great," his superiority to those around him indeed derives partly from his consistent stress on moral rather than merely social judgment. All these facts argue for a view of the novel as supporting values embodied in the moral commentary cited earlier: trivial and malicious talk reflects impoverished minds as well as experience, male talk about ideas communicates more meaning and value than female talk about people; by extension, the male realm provides the standard by which females can judge themselves and know themselves wanting. On the other hand, the vitality of *Emma* as a fiction, like that of Emma as a character, depends on insatiable interest in personality and its individual manifestations. The reader who has found herself or himself amused, entertained, and impressed by the vagaries of Emma's imagination, by her will to make interest where little obvious stuff of interest exists—such a reader must feel the loss involved in Emma's settling down under Mr. Knightley's exemplary tutelage. Emma has kept herself alive while all around decayed, kept herself alive with the energies of gossip. The novel has lured the reader into direct knowledge of the same energies. Talking of "he" and "she" must not substitute for knowing the self as "I" or for valuing the sensibilities of others as "you." On the other hand, the exercise of imagining "he" and "she" and dwelling on the possibilities of their experience enlivens the mind. And recognition of that fact implies at least temporary acceptance of a set of values and assumptions associated with the female and opposed to the usefulness of dealing only in the great. Fully accepting the standards of "society," *Emma* yet declares the need to evade them.

In both *Evelina* and *Emma*, female gossip—literal gossip in the later novel, its written counterpart in the earlier one—functions as a language of feeling, as a mode of personal development, as an evasion of external restriction. Indeed, it becomes a means of discovering selfhood, of declaring the self an expressive, judging consciousness. As a sub-text for the major line of narrative, it supports the imaginative and improvisational, valuing the private, implying the saving energies of female curiosity and female volubility, celebrating the possibility and the importance of a narrative of trivia. It exemplifies the subversive resources of the novel as genre. The official criticism of gossip derives from and depends on a realm of public value; it assumes the dominance of "society" as standard and sanction. Novels too declare the importance of society, but they value the individual. Inasmuch as eighteenth-century fiction delineated and defended the private, it often implicitly defended also what public moralists attacked. In fiction if not in didactic texts, the "talent of ready utterance" found its supporters: supporters who managed successfully to uphold the values of a women's sub-society even while articulating those of traditional social conformity. Fiction reveals more clearly what didactic texts only hint: that gossip, "female talk," provides a mode of power, of undermining public rigidities and asserting private integrity, of discovering means of agency for women, those private citizens deprived of public function. It provides also often the substance and the means of narrative.

8

Social Speculation

Speculation: from Latin *specula* (lookout, watch tower), derivative of *specere* (to see, look). Beginning in the late fourteenth century, according to the *O.E.D.*, it meant "contemplation or profound study"; from the late fifteenth century, "the faculty of seeing." The metaphorical sense elaborates the Latin root: really to *look* amounts to "profound study." By the late sixteenth century, a new meaning creeps into English usage: "conjecture, surmise." In 1796, the word means "conjectural consideration or meditation"; less than a quarter-century earlier (1774), it had taken on commercial implications: "engagement in any business enterprise or transaction of a venturesome or risky nature, but offering the chance of great or unusual gain."

The word's shift toward epistemological uncertainty miniaturizes a movement of Western thought; its relatively recent connection of intellection with finance may remind us how much of what we think about in modern times involves money and its meanings. Both recent senses bear on gossip, at least metaphorically an economic transaction, as I suggested in the first chapter, and an activity utterly dependent on "conjectural consideration." Nor does gossip's connection with financial risk-taking depend only on metaphor. Not infrequently, literal gossip serves financial ends.

The word *speculation* implies multiple connections. It simultaneously evokes the public world, in which people work with money, and the private, the inner life, realms utterly separate in modern consciousness. It recalls a historical process of change by which poor men became rich, establishing for themselves a new social class, at the same time that it designates the life of imagination, which has no necessary connection to history. I propose to take a look at—indeed, to speculate about—a group of novels that explore links between talk about people and action about money.

Abundant possible texts for such an exercise date from the late nineteenth or twentieth century, when the consequences of "new money" became apparent. Four novelists suit my purposes particularly well: Elizabeth Gaskell, Anthony Trollope, George Eliot, Edith Wharton. Wharton, the latest of the group chronologically, makes most explicit a connection which the others variously disguise. Gaskell's *Cranford* insists on the *un*importance of money; Trollope's fiction concerns itself with power rather than wealth; Eliot dwells on the moral metaphysics of money and gossip. All the novels treated in this chapter use gossip as raw material for fiction and suggest how gossip as subject may influence narrative method. Speculation about the speculation they depict clarifies the interpenetration of private gossip, public affairs.

Gossip, in these novels, supplies an instrument not of subversion but of control. Intimate talk about other people can, as we have seen, challenge assumptions of the powerful; on the other hand, such talk also serves interests of governing classes. Narrative, interpretation, judgment: all three register group alertness to threats from without—threats, often, from below. Both friendly and malicious anecdote can purvey information useful in preserving dominance. Gossip—verbal speculation—derives from and reflects a way of seeing; it confirms the vision of its group.

Raymond Williams suggests the association of gossip (although he doesn't use the word) with seeing and with society in remarks on *Middlemarch*. Conscious examination of other people, he observes, "is the mode of an anxious society—an anxious class preoccupied with placing, grading, defining: the sharp enclosing phrases about others as they leave the room, and a kind of willing forgetfulness that it will happen to the phrasers as they also leave. It's the staple of a familiar—sometimes witty, sometimes malicious—minor fiction, and of a whole world of small talk. . . . [It is] a mode in which we are all signifiers, all critics and judges, and can somehow afford to be because life—given life, creating life—goes on where it is supposed to, elsewhere."[1]

In the novels that at present concern me, the distinction between human signifiers and signified is always at least potentially one of class. Dominant classes (in Wharton, the wealthy; in Gaskell, the impoverished upper class; in Trollope and Eliot, the solid middle class) protect themselves against interlopers by talking about them, asserting their own status as sole signifiers. The interlopers can, if sufficiently clever, use the same resource; and they can negate the power of verbal classification by asserting that of money:

Wharton explores these possibilities too. The relation of talk and money often involves intricate conflict.

As these remarks suggest, to think about speculation finally challenges the separation of "public" and "private." Although gossip, in these novels, preserves the forms of intimacy, its content insistently declares the identification of individuals with their social groups. Most of the important people in these books care desperately about money, or claim not to care at all: a version of the same thing. The dominance of money unites all characters; unable to escape it, they can only speak from shared assumptions. Only Ladislaw and Dorothea, in *Middlemarch*, manage finally and precariously to evade presuppositions of class.

Edith Wharton's novels dramatize how money works and how talk helps it. Like George Eliot's *Daniel Deronda*, Wharton's *The House of Mirth* opens with a man speculating about a woman. Lawrence Selden, seeing Lily Bart unexpectedly in Grand Central Station, wonders "what was Miss Bart doing in town at that season?" He entertains various possibilities; the paragraph summarizing them concludes, "he could never see her without a faint movement of interest: it was characteristic of her that she always roused speculation."[2]

If Lily Bart provokes speculation, she also (again like Gwendolyn Harleth in *Daniel Deronda*) engages in it. Her existence depends on a sequence of gambling moves with survival at stake: first, social survival, requiring appropriate marriage; later, bare physical survival. For risky speculation in the matrimonial market as well as for the "conjectural consideration" of society conversation, language supplies currency. Talk between and among men and women accomplishes society's "business."

The pattern I have sketched governs not only *The House of Mirth* but many other realistic novels. Society, like "the world," constitutes a buzz of voices; the difference between the two collectivities depends on the distance of the buzz. Society envelops everyone. People's talk about one another may create narrative foreground or background; their reliance on words as venture capital for exploitation of self and others in the effort at marriage shapes novelistic plots. Both uses of language—for gossip and for gain—embody tensions of desire and uncertainty.

The House of Mirth with unusual explicitness examines the operations of a money-dominated society. Lily, who says of herself, "I must have a great deal of money" (8), tries to employ her resources of language and beauty for matrimonial prosperity, operating in the terms of her world of appearances. She makes the mistake of believing that her beauty and her skill at using it give her strength; but only money's power endures, and her ambivalence about that fact weakens her.

"Why could one never do a natural thing without having to screen it behind a structure of artifice?" Lily asks herself, having been "caught" coming out of Selden's apartment building after taking tea with him (13). Instantly she makes up a story to explain her presence. *Truth* and *falsity* are only marginally meaningful. Late in the novel, in another encounter with Sim Rosedale, the Jewish financier who intercepted her after the tea-taking episode, Lily confronts the damaging effect of stories currently being told about her. Rosedale points out that these tales have diminished her value in the marriage market. "If they are not true," Lily inquires, "doesn't *that* alter the situation?" Rosedale responds, "I believe it does in novels; but I'm certain it don't in real life" (250). *The House of Mirth* proclaims its affinity to real life by insisting that moral distinctions have no force in social existence. Society relies on "structures of artifice"; Lily's impulse to lie declares her membership.

The scandalous stories that make Lily's wealthy aunt disinherit her niece, stories distorted by the malice of the purveyor and by lack of explanatory detail, yet accurately report the bare substance of what Lily has done and how she is perceived. The stories to which Rosedale alludes, which have ostracized Lily from the realm of the rich, issue mainly from the imagination of an unscrupulous rival. Virtuous Gerty Farish asks Lily for "the whole truth" about Bertha Dorset's allegations. "What is truth?" Lily responds. "Where a woman is concerned, it's the story that's easiest to believe." And, a little later: "You asked me just now for the truth—well, the truth about any girl is that once she's talked about she's done for; and the more she explains her case the worse it looks" (220). As usual, Lily accurately specifies social actuality. She also hints gossip's financial importance. No one in this society would say that who steals a purse steals trash: on the contrary, money measures worth—including the worth of a good name. The economics of gossip becomes literalized.

A mid-nineteenth-century American moralist, elaborating the ancient analogy between slander and theft, inadvertently describes the situation in *The House of Mirth*. "There is in society," he observes, "a great deal less averseness to evil speaking than to theft. If one have his money or his goods stolen, he no sooner makes it known, than his neighbors join with him in searching for the thief, who, if found and convicted, is sure to be punished; because common zeal, as well as common consent, takes sides against the culprit. But the pilferers from character fare less hard; or rather, they are tolerated, provided they manage with art and address, and mingle some wit with their malice or their levity."[3] Thefts of character, more socially tolerable, yet may prove more damaging than thefts of money.

The moralistic tone of such an utterance bears no relation to that of *The House of Mirth*. Ethical rather than economic standards govern descriptions of actuality and warnings about conduct in didactic texts; the financial analogies that moralists use for emphasis take on life of their own in Wharton's novel. Lily, in a moment of crisis, hears the wings of pursuing furies. The next morning, she feels calmer. "The winged furies were now prowling gossips who dropped in on each other for tea" (165–6). Gossips, less portentous than furies, have hardly less power.

Gossip affects dollars-and-cents value. When Lily acquires a wealthy suitor, everyone talks about the fact, her stock rises. Losing him, she loses capital. As she declines in social stature, she becomes a safer and a more vulnerable target for gossip, her decline consequently ever more precipitous.

Manacled by the system, Lily accepts its necessities, her occasional inadvertent rebellions more or less disastrous. She understands all about gossip, but unfortunately not about money. Knowing her own need, she obscures to herself the consequences of allowing a man to alleviate it. When Gus Trenor demands the sexual payment to which he feels entitled, Lily hears the furies and counts her losses—which already amount to more than she can tally. She can figure out how much money Gus has given her, but not how much she has compromised her own integrity.

In *The House of Mirth*, endless restless talk about human behavior establishes and limits possibility. "Mattie Gormer *has* got aspirations still; women always have; but she's awfully easy-going, and Sam won't be bothered, and they both like to be the most important people in sight, so they've started a sort of continuous performance of their own, a kind of social Coney Island, where everybody is welcome who can make noise enough and does n't put on airs. *I* think it's awfully good fun myself—some of the artistic set, you know, any pretty actress that's going, and so on" (HM, 226–7). Mrs. Fisher narrates the Gormers' affairs to Lily with a particular purpose in mind; but gossip in *The House of Mirth always* has a purpose, although not necessarily that of influencing immediate action (the narrator's goal in this scene). Mrs. Fisher's account combines specific social observation with interpretation (Mattie has aspirations, the Gormers like to be important) and generalization ("women always have"). It betrays the speaker's snobberies, most obviously in the Coney Island metaphor, less blatantly in "any pretty actress that's going." Although Mrs. Fisher declares the existence she describes awfully good fun, her condescending tone insists on her superiority. She has recently tried to shepherd the Gormers through the social maze; now she wants Lily to assume the same role. But in fact her summary suggests by indirection precisely the kind of social judgment that will exclude one who links her fate to the vulgar.

Wharton's narrative skill in *The House of Mirth* manifests itself partly in her ability to reveal purposeful undertones in even trivial examples. By speculation about its members—sometimes speculation disguised as declaration—this society assesses value in the marriage market and in the less clearly defined market of general social exchange. Risk-takers—those who venture themselves as social commodities—rarely coincide with assessors, who operate from a position of security. (Hence Lily's infrequent indulgence in gossip herself.) Once worth is firmly established, by prosperous marriage or irreproachable (i.e., wealthy and aristocratic) parentage, its possessor, not needing to speculate in the social marketplace, can indulge in the verbal speculation that guards the walls of privilege.

The shifting rhythms of gossip, reported and imagined, in the novel epitomize the patterns of the society that depends on it. "Even those who *are* too fond of discussing their neighbors, indulge their propensity, in general, with no ill intent," a nineteenth-century instructor of young ladies observes. "They do so, often, from the mere love of talking, and because, when they have exhausted the weather and the fashions, they are somewhat at a loss for subjects."[4] Much of the social talk in *The House of Mirth*, among men as well as women, sounds as though it emanates from this kind of idleness: from understocked minds of limited energy. The apparently aimless movements of consciousness work to deadly effect.

> "When a girl's as good-looking as that she'd better marry; then
> no questions are asked. In our imperfectly organized society there
> is no provision as yet for the young woman who claims the privileges
> of marriage without assuming its obligations."
> "Well, I understand Lily is about to assume them in the shape
> of Mr. Rosedale," Mrs. Fisher said with a laugh [154].

Both participants in this dialogue (the first speaker male, the second female) articulate social convictions in the guise of authoritative pronouncement, innuendo, and rumor. Such statements, reiterated, ever more certainly exclude Lily.

The emotional power of *The House of Mirth* derives from the fully specified tension it evokes between a struggling individual and her community: a tension expressed partly as internal division. The level of anxiety is as far as possible from the enervating harmony of *Emma*. Speculation, in both its modern senses providing means for success in the social world, reveals that world's powerful beliefs. Its determinations of worth, within its own context, prove precisely accurate. When Bertha Dorset tells Percy Gryce that Lily has borrowed money from one man and has had dubious relations with other men, she uses distorted versions of reality to "prove" Lily's inappropriateness as a mate for Percy—the inappropriateness that Lily has in fact demonstrated by spending the day with Selden rather than with more suitable matrimonial quarry. Later, alleging Lily's sexual misconduct with George Dorset, Bertha lies to save her own reputation; but again she expresses truth: of Lily's ever decreasing moral discrimination, her increasing willingness to adopt dubious means of survival. As whispers about Lily's conduct multiply, they ignore her moral and physical struggle to remain uncontaminated yet solvent, insisting that her contamination ever increases—and so it does. Gradually, by its often ugly moral speculation, society shuts Lily out. It thus acknowledges in its own terms what the narrator has revealed in quite different language: unable wholeheartedly to participate in the world for which she was bred, Lily cannot belong. This society allows, at least for women, no partial commitments. Corruption proves commitment. Keeping something of herself in reserve, trying to separate herself from her society, as she ventures in the marriage market, Lily must lose.

Although it allows one to imagine that Lily loses all else but gains her soul, the novel goes beyond this perception. The reader's moral position in relation to Lily's pathos in some respects resembles Selden's. Like Lily's aunt, Mrs. Peniston, Selden constitutes himself an onlooker at life, from the *specula* of financial sufficiency contemplating without penalty the social spectacle to which Lily, at dreadful cost, struggles to belong. His posture of disengagement does not prevent him from entering at will into the community's festal life, free also, he believes, to remove himself at will. (Men, in this book, as primary controllers of wealth, in general have more freedom than women—a fact which in no way ensures their moral superiority.) Selden, a collector of books and of sensations, enjoys penetrating appearances and watching their play. Lily perceives him, rightly, as "different," but fails to understand his difference as only of degree. Selden flatters himself about his powers of discrimination in seeing behind Lily's facade. "He was aware that the qualities distinguishing her from the herd of her sex were chiefly external: as though a fine glaze of beauty and fastidiousness had been applied to vulgar clay. Yet the analogy left him unsatisfied, for a coarse texture will not take a high finish; and was it not possible that the material was fine, but that circumstance had fashioned it into a futile shape?" (3). These "specu-

lations" (Wharton's word for them) engage Selden in his first intimate encounter with Lily; he pursues them to the extent of confirming his suspicion
about the fineness of the underlying material—only to give up all interest
in the young woman because of a false appearance. Seeing her at night
leaving the Trenors' New York mansion at a time when he knows Gus
Trenor to be there without his wife, Selden allows Lily no chance to explain;
he departs on a cruise, relinquishing his vague intention of marriage. By the
time Lily, in her final social degradation, returns to his apartment, she seems
his moral superior, having "passed beyond the phase of well-bred reciprocity,
in which every demonstration must be scrupulously proportioned to the
emotion it elicits, and generosity of feeling is the only ostentation condemned" (301). He focuses for her a fantasy of moral and emotional authenticity, a vision she has accepted too late, but she understands more about
the society both inhabit than he does.

Like Selden, the reader has been led to engage in a series of speculations
about Lily Bart, understanding her sometimes as suffering consciousness,
sometimes as object of social adjudication. Like Selden's, our easiest final
response is pity—a reaction blatantly encouraged by the narrative introduc-
tion of the imaginary infant in Lily's deathbed. That infant, an interpretable
appearance like so many others in the text, challenges speculation. (Selden,
of course, knows nothing of it; the reader's privilege extends further than
his.) The image of Lily falling asleep comforted by the baby's felt presence
gives way to a scene in which Selden examines Lily's effects, raging with
suspicion at the sight of Gus Trenor's name on an envelope, finding a check
within, and finally using memories of old gossip to reassure himself ("old
hints and rumours came back to him, and out of the very insinuations he
had feared to probe, he constructed an explanation of the mystery"; 323).
His re-interpretation generates his self-exculpatory and grandiose understanding of the transaction between him and Lily. "It was this moment of love,
this fleeting victory over themselves, which had kept them from atrophy and
extinction; which, in her, had reached out to him in every struggle against
the influence of her surroundings, and in him, had kept alive the faith that
now drew him penitent and reconciled to her side" (323).

But the novel demands more of the reader. Its demonstrations of the
constant process of speculation and of the frequency with which speculation
produces misinterpretation emphasize ambiguities of the observer's position.
Even the privileged observer—and the reader knows more than anyone on
the scene—makes mistakes. The comforting view that Selden has kept alive
his faith, that he and Lily have avoided atrophy and extinction, protects its
originator from confronting his implication, and hers, in what he euphe-

mistically calls "her surroundings." Selden's much earlier perception of Lily as "evidently the victim of the civilization which had produced her" (5) comes closer to the narrative's import. To separate self from surroundings, in the world Wharton evokes, defies logic. Surroundings make selves. Selden and Lily, through all their waverings, attempt to differentiate themselves from their society, but their "victories" are fleeting indeed. Lily dies with the comforting illusion of a child-companion; Selden lives with the illusion of having kept the faith. The reader can accept Selden's illusions, or Lily's idealization of him, but the text has made it difficult to believe in such easy answers.

On her downward social course, Lily works for a time as a maker of hats. Milliners in the workroom gossip about their social betters; their talk has no effect on those they discuss. The terms characterizing their discourse apply equally well to that of their social superiors, who also generate a "current of meaningless sound," provide their own "fragmentary and distorted" images, display the same mixture of curiosity and freedom (280), but whose talk exercises power over such victims as Lily. Gossip epitomizes social discourse. "Social" conversation takes the form either of speculation about the behavior of others or of advice and commentary about female financial speculation. The current of sound recapitulates the current of desire: directed to social self-advancement or self-preservation, associated more often with money than with love. Constant assessment of the social marketplace constitutes a serious activity. The hat workers, parodying it, call attention to its ubiquity and its importance. They also reveal the objectification involved in such talk. Made objects of discussion by one another—in Williams' terms, *signified* rather than *signifier*—people lose human reality, figuring as pawns in the social game. The tableau in which Lily objectifies herself as a woman in a portrait, hoping to make her beauty so impressive that it will get her a man, epitomizes the novel's social processes. Gossip, treating everyone as representative of a social position, universalizes those processes. Assessing, placing, speculating, the socially secure (and, in pathetic imitation, those with no social aspirations) demonstrate how their world dominates its inhabitants by verbally destroying personal reality and separateness.

In a minor episode toward the middle of Wharton's later novel *The Custom of the Country* (1913), a character peripherally involved in the action comments on a woman's conduct in a way suggesting his sympathy for her. Another woman accuses him of taking sides. "Are there sides already?" Bowen inquires. "If so, I want to look down on them impartially from the heights of pure speculation."[5] "Pure speculation": a luxury of aristocrats, a class quite unable to cope, as the novel makes clear, with the energy of "impure" speculators who relentlessly get what they want. Telling the success story of Undine Spragg, who rises from Midwestern obscurity to wealth and power, Wharton reveals the moral distastefulness and the imaginative force of Undine's speculation as well as that of the men who earn the money that she marries.

Along the way, Undine chooses Ralph Marvell, aristocratic but not wealthy, a young man of aesthetic inclinations. In one brilliant episode, Ralph finds himself involved in a business deal through which he hopes at least temporarily to satisfy his wife's insatiable financial demands. Unpracticed in all varieties of "impure" speculation, he seeks enlightenment from Elmer Moffatt, whose rapid rise in the world testifies to his speculative skill. "As Moffatt talked [Ralph] began to feel as blank and blundering as the class of dramatic students before whom the great actor had analyzed his part. The affair was in fact difficult and complex, and Moffatt saw at once just where the difficulties lay and how the personal idiosyncrasies of 'the parties' affected them. Such insight fascinated Ralph, and he strayed off into wondering why it did not qualify every financier to be a novelist, and what intrinsic barrier divided the two arts" (CC, 169).

To connect financial as well as social speculation with the novel (and with acting) underlines also the link between gossip and finance exemplified in Wharton's novels. Gossip belongs symbolically to women, finance to men. (Men in fact gossip a great deal in these novels, and women concern themselves obsessively—if not always expertly—with money.) Business deals and social maneuverings, like novels, depend on imaginative grasp. The obligation to imagine the environment one inhabits, an environment including other people and their money, imposes itself on everyone. It energizes novels; it motivates readers. People talk a lot in Wharton's fiction. Their talk of people and of money, substituting often for direct revelation of emotion, attempts to assert their power. Often it assigns too much reality to money, too little to people. Ralph cares about his visions more than about money. His straying attention as Moffatt talks of financial affairs destines him to failure.

In *The House of Mirth*, as in *The Age of Innocence*, gossip largely defines the environment which permeates its inhabitants. It seems the product of inertia—the powerful force that keeps things moving in the same direction without involvement of conscious will. In *The Custom of the Country*, gossip becomes compelling action, the product of individual energy. Undine Spragg and Elmer Moffatt ("Invaders," in Ralph's view), determined to succeed in a society which they do not understand, concentrate on information that will help them. For Elmer, such information typically concerns money.

Undine, deprived by her sex of Elmer's opportunity for direct action, explores social and financial advantages of various sexual connections. Mrs. Heeny, professional masseuse and gossip, guides her, supplying social news that initially substitutes for real life. "Mrs. Heeny knew how to manipulate [Mrs. Spragg's] imagination as well as her muscles. It was Mrs. Heeny who peopled the solitude of the long ghostly days with lively anecdotes of the Van Degens, the Driscolls, the Chauncey Ellings and the other social potentates whose least doings Mrs. Spragg and Undine had followed from afar in the Apex papers" (CC, 8). Undine finally triumphs over the Van Degens and their kind (for her, mere images of social success), partly by the power of Elmer's wealth, sacrificing her first husband, who commits suicide, and her emotionally deprived son to her achievement.

All Wharton's New York novels treat gossip as a social force and link it with the operations of finance. They reflect, of course, a specific social situation of the late nineteenth and early twentieth centuries. The English novel from its beginnings had acknowledged connections of other sorts between love and money. Given a social order in which neither women nor men of social standing could work for a living, choices of marriage partner involved decisions about the degree to which money mattered. The connection between the getting of money and the forms of social conversation, that connection epitomized in the word *speculation*, belongs to a new order: one in which caste continues to count, but which allows social mobility: down as well as up. Speculation—both kinds—creates power. But, like novels, it makes people into characters, subject to the dominance of money or of discussion. The pessimism of Wharton's fiction expresses itself in the difficulty, the virtual impossibility, of preserving spiritual autonomy in a money-controlled world.

At the very end of the eighteenth century, in England, the minor didactic novelist Jane West published a work of fiction called *A Gossip's Story*. Its plot does not concern me at the moment: that plot belongs to the older tradition, in which whether or not to marry for money constitutes a problem but the possibility of financial speculation does not exist. On the other hand, it is worth noting that here a gossip functions explicitly as the originator of compelling fictions. The narrator characterizes herself at the outset: "I enjoy some inherent qualities, which I flatter myself render me a very excellent gossip. I have a retentive memory, a quick imagination, strong curiosity, and keen perception. These faculties enable me not only to retain what I hear, but to connect the day dreams of my own mind; to draw conclusions from small premises; in short, to tell what other people think, as well as what they do."[6] A bit later, she complains about the dullness of her neighborhood: "I have often lamented the situation of many good ladies, who like myself may be said almost to subsist upon news, and are often forced to devour very unwholesome aliment. The events which *really* happen in a small neighbourhood, are not sufficient to furnish the supplies conversation eternally requires, without the aid of fiction" (1.35).

The gossip thus typifies the novelist. As the plot begins to develop, the narrator's tone of self-deprecatory irony dominates her report of initial community speculation about new local residents. But that tone vanishes as interest in the action takes over and the narrator becomes fully involved in the story she tells. Her claims of memory, imagination, curiosity, and perception justify themselves. Jane West does not prove an expert creator of fictions, but she demonstrates the link between eighteenth-century versions of romance and the concerns of ordinary life: both the reliance of romance plots on universal tensions between parents and children and universal concern with the opposed values of security and excitement, and the importance of romance for satisfying needs of neighborhoods in which nothing "*really* happen[s]."

More than half a century after A *Gossip's Story*, and slightly more than half a century before *The House of Mirth*, Elizabeth Gaskell published *Cranford* (1853), about a village in which nothing really happens. The novel concerns mainly the middle-aged and elderly. Although three characters (one of them a family servant) achieve happy marriage, their stories occupy the periphery. The main love story concerns a woman who rediscovers her youthful lover a few months before his death; no explicit declaration takes place between them. The principal local excitement rests on an imaginary foundation: for a time, the residents believe in the likelihood of robbery and murder. A long-lost brother returns from India just in time to solve his sister's financial problems: the climax of the novel. *Cranford* invites the reader's imaginative participation in nostalgically unmomentous concerns.

The extreme psychic and social confinement of Cranford life derives partly from poverty, but poverty appears a natural state, not a disaster of human greed or blindness. Bank failure in a neighboring town introduces concerns of a larger world; it also emphasizes the impossibility of separating large world and small. Money and class control possibility in Gaskell's Cranford as in Wharton's New York. Gaskell miniaturizes these issues, translates them into the terms of an all-female universe ("In the first place, Cranford is in possession of the Amazons; all the holders of houses, above a certain rent, are women"[7]), suggests their insignificance by telling her story in the voice of a self-deprecatory female narrator whose tone faintly resembles that of Jane West's narrating gossip. The detoxified version of vast social problems, with little, apparently, at stake, allows moral exploration which, among other things, clarifies relationships between the two kinds of speculation.

The narrative encourages mild amusement as a response. An early episode epitomizes much of the tone and content of the whole. The story of the cow who fell into a lime pit, lost her hair, and "came out looking naked, cold, and miserable, in a bare skin," rests on a foundation of fact: Gaskell gives a one-sentence version of the same happening in an 1849 essay called "The Last Generation in England," reprinted as an appendix to the Oxford edition of *Cranford.* In the novel, the report occupies a full page. It helps to characterize Captain Brown, a male interloper ultimately accepted by the female community because of "his excellent masculine common sense, and his facility in devising expedients to overcome domestic dilemmas." One such expedient solves the problem of the naked cow: the captain advises the weirdly masculine garb of "a flannel waistcoat and flannel drawers," and the cow lives out her natural span "clad in dark grey flannel." The account concludes, "I have watched her myself many a time. Do you ever see cows dressed in grey flannel in London?" (5).

Captain Brown does not fully endorse the advice he offers. After suggesting the waistcoat and drawers, he adds, "But my advice is, kill the poor creature at once." Only a woman, one feels, would follow so ludicrous a suggestion as the captain offers—and only in a tiny community. Who sees cows dressed in gray flannel in London? The reference to the metropolis (similar questions recur several times) makes the reader reflect on the contrast between urban and non-urban, men's and women's, worlds. The narrator obviously realizes the comic effect of a cow in gray flannel. But the women's willingness to manufacture outdoor garb for a cow, their capacity to tolerate being ridiculous in expressing their compassion, their inability to entertain the suggestion of killing the poor creature at once: these facts reveal the inadequacy of amusement as total response. If London cannot accept such an expedient, so much the worse for London.

Verbal speculation occupies much time for Cranford women. The narrator, a woman "past thirty" named Mary Smith (the name suggests her role as almost anonymous chorus), observes of herself, "In my own home, whenever people had nothing else to do, they blamed me for want of discretion. Indiscretion was my bugbear fault" (111). Indiscretion implies both imagining and saying too much: a fault attributable to more than Mary Smith, but one with virtually no bad consequences in the novel. Miss Pole, the most assertive lady in Cranford after Miss Jenkyns' death, gains her supremacy by her penchant for "adventures." "Miss Pole was always the person, in the trio of

Cranford ladies now assembled, to have had adventures. She was in the habit of spending the morning in rambling from shop to shop; not to purchase anything (except an occasional reel of cotton, or a piece of tape), but to see the new articles and report upon them, and to collect all the stray pieces of intelligence in the town. She had a way, too, of demurely popping hither and yon into all sorts of places to gratify her curiosity on any point; a way which, if she had not looked so very genteel and prim, might have been considered impertinent" (82). Her "adventures," this description implies, occur mainly in her imagination: the seat of vivid life for all the Cranford group. The women make the most of small facts. A cat steals a piece of meat: within a day or so, the town believes in the presence of a sinister troop of robbers. A man prints a woman's name as patroness of a public event: the ladies conclude that he proposes to marry her. The reader chuckles over the ways these women surmount the restrictions of their lot by making the minute momentous. So little is at stake in all their concerns.

So little, so much: money, class, manners. Manners cope with exigencies of money and class. Arthur Schlesinger, in his little book on American conduct manuals, suggests a historical sequence of definitions. Courtesy has been justified in turn, he claims, as morality, law, art, and pragmatism.[8] All four terms apply to the Cranford system, derived from a morality of communal concern and discretion, comprising a set of laws or conventions to conceal personal difficulty (the maid brings the loaded tea tray out from under the couch where people sit, having no place else to keep it; everyone pretends not to notice), an art of small contrivance (the ladies agree on the vulgarity of lavish spreads of food, serving one another thin slices of bread and butter on elegant old china), a pragmatic mode of confronting poverty and preserving class distinctions. Norbert Elias refers often to a gradual "advance in the threshold of embarrassment" as a mark of the civilizing process.[9] He alludes also to development of an "invisible wall of affects which seems . . . to rise between one human body and another, repelling and separating" (69). But in fact the Cranford ladies, although they demonstrate the elaborate systems of self-control marking the civilized, use those systems not to separate but to link human beings; and they avoid embarrassment by conventions devised to forestall it. The two examples cited above illustrate this point: a hostess need not feel embarrassed by her poverty because of communal agreement about how to deal with it. A medieval host, one may fancy, in the unlikely case of being faced with utter inability to bestow lavish hospitality, would suffer embarrassment if not humiliation. These ladies give each other what they have, but the rituals of their giving mean more than the substance.

Rituals of courtesy help preserve distinctions of class, a central concern of Cranford ladies' gossip. Lacking money and occupation, the women rely on social differentiation as substance for talk. When Captain Brown helps a poor old woman carry her dinner home from the bakehouse, the ladies expect him to make a round of calls to apologize for "lowering" himself. The Cranford doctor, Mr. Hoggins, becomes more interesting—his very name more tolerable—because he may be related to the Marchioness of Exeter. Mrs. Fitz-Adam generates much conversation about her precise social standing. "I remember the convocation of ladies, who assembled to decide whether or not Mrs. Fitz-Adam should be called upon by the old blue-blooded inhabitants of Cranford. She had taken a large rambling house, which had been usually considered to confer a patent of gentility upon its tenant; because, once upon a time, seventy or eighty years before, the spinster daughter of an earl had resided in it" (63). The problem of social gradation preoccupies Cranford gossips not only because it provides something to talk about (no negligible function) but because it helps them preserve a sense of their own importance. Cranford conversation emphasizes the exclusionary function of class distinctions. In order to be "insiders," the ladies must posit an "outside." They lack money, prestige, power, but they belong to the gentry: an important fact in every evoked female consciousness of Cranford. (Mary Smith, the narrator, only visits, she does not belong.)

Cranford female society deprecates the power of money. Its members happily wear (and establish conventions for valuing) outmoded fashions; they walk everywhere and declare their pleasure in walking; they offer and receive scanty refreshment and scant entertainment. Convinced that they do everything exactly right, the ladies appear to have circumvented the power of wealth. One may wonder, therefore, why a failed financial speculation intrudes into the plot. Matty, victim of bank failure, remains convinced that money matters little, and her unworldliness has its reward. Her servant figures out how to help her, her neighbors secretly contribute to a fund for her support, her friends establish her tiny tea-selling business. Although these events illustrate the necessity of money to survival, Matty herself hardly grasps the point, giving away candy to children at a rate calculated utterly to destroy her profits.

In effect, providence provides for Matty, by human agency. The bank failure and its Cranford consequences from one point of view illustrate the irrelevance of wealth to virtue. Matty continues her benevolence even in straitened circumstances, and her friends act benevolently from their own tiny resources. Cranford need not depend on banks.

Yet the bank-failure episode has more ambiguous implications than this benign summary would suggest; so does the novel as a whole. An excursion into *Cranford's* emphasis on verbal as opposed to financial speculation may clarify the book's emotional and ideological complexities. (I shall return to the question of money after this detour.)

I have already said something of what the Cranford ladies talk about and why. Discussing minute behavior in relation to standards of class and of social decorum in order to affirm their own importance, they exemplify gossip as a resource of the deprived and subordinated. Like women in a harem, they demonstrate verbal freedom when their circumstances preclude other freedoms. Oppressed not by men but by economic and social stringencies, they yet lead and communicate lively imaginative existences, in which traveling conjurors become glamorous figures, robbers and ghosts threaten domestic tranquillity, and the proposed marriage of Lady Glenmire creates even more excitement than did the prospective arrival of that lady on the Cranford social scene. As these examples suggest, Cranford gossip not only approximates freedom and power for its participants, it also manufactures the interest sadly lacking in literal details of their daily lives.

Austen's *Emma* also involves herself in personal speculation to make interest in a severely circumscribed existence. Unlike the Cranford ladies, she possesses beauty and wealth as well as social standing, but she too suffers from the inherent deprivations of village life. But although Cranford and Highbury have much in common as social environments, and although Emma's response to restriction resembles that of the Cranford group, Austen's novel and Gaskell's resemble each other hardly at all. Unlike Emma's fantasizing, that of the Cranford ladies has no significant consequences beyond themselves: Cranford gossip generates no plot, though it participates in one. The level of Cranford speculation remains almost as trivial as the subject matter. No ironic consciousness broods over Gaskell's narrative. As narrator, Mary Smith retains sufficient emotional distance to feel amused or pitying or both as she contemplates the local scene, but she offers no serious criticism of the sort frequently implied by the Austen narrator's tone. The two novels take for granted and question very different things.

Emma assumes a class system in all its consequences: had Harriet Smith married a gentleman before being revealed as a nobody's daughter, Emma and her community and the narrator would have shared a sense of impropriety. Emma's social distinctions attract none of the narrator's ironic commentary. Similarly, the novel takes for granted the association of wealth with social position and the desirability of both. *Cranford* raises questions about just these matters. When the ladies debate Lady Glenmire's precise social standing once she marries Mr. Hoggins, the narrator in effect smiles—and so, presumably, does the reader. The discrepancy between Cranford society's utter lack of power and its dwelling on distinctions of rank and decorum, source of much of the fiction's comedy, demands the reader's uneasy attention to the meaning of class and courtesy. Both function as tools of power; yet class, in the novel, seems a form emptied of content, and courtesy bears rather too much weight in this virtually moneyless female realm. As for money, in *Emma* a source of difficulty only to Jane Fairfax, it too generates troubling questions in *Cranford*. *The Custom of the Country* shows Ralph Marvell's innocence about financial speculation weakening and finally destroying him; Matty Jenkyns' innocence causes her no difficulty whatever. Even financial exigency shrinks to manageable proportions, *Cranford* suggests, by exercise of Christian and social virtues. Yet the bank failure insists on the reality, within the fictional context, of just those concerns the residents of Cranford resolutely reject. The large world impinges on the small; man's business affects woman's privacies. *Cranford* celebrates the unworldliness of the village and its residents; it also stimulates awareness that the exclusionary existence implies dwelling in fictions. Cranford's verbal speculations produce less exciting plots than Emma's, produce, as I have already suggested, virtually no plot at all. Yet they generate their own kind of fiction: the private realm these speculations assume in itself constitutes a fiction. Only acts of imagination posit it; reality allows no such isolation from financial uncertainty and genuine want.

The Wharton novels show women participating, more or less effectively, in complex financial speculation. Their verbal maneuvers often involve hidden financial goals. To ignore the demands of money—as Lily Bart on occasion does—invites disaster; only from a position of absolute financial security can a woman afford to forget her subjection to money as social force. Gaskell's novel, on the other hand, locates profit in the verbal rather than the financial domain. Women ignore money; if they speculate, the book's single instance suggests, they will lose. When women suffer financial need, men must rescue them: Mary Smith's father and Matty's brother reorganize Matty's life for her. Female lives pass in trivial talk; that talk creates interest and protects against pain, although not even the narrator takes it altogether seriously. But the bank failure reminds the reader of the frailty of fiction as well as the need for it. The women of Cranford make the most of their verbal resources, but verbal resources do not suffice against the consequences of other people's financial manipulations.

The story-teller emphasizes the urgency of narrative by her own involvement in creating the story she tells. She "collect[s] evidence" about Peter Jenkyns, Matty's long-lost brother, by asking the ladies for "some clear and definite information as to poor Peter's height, appearance, and when and where he was seen and heard of last" (111). Her inquiries elicit not facts but fantasies: Peter has become great Lama of Tibet, llamas may be carnivorous animals, Miss Matty once wanted to see an elephant. Unable to learn anything relevant, Mary nonetheless sends a letter to the "Aga Jenkyns" of whom the conjuror's wife has told her; as a result, Peter comes home to rescue his sister.

Mary's intervention generates the novel's emotional climax; it also underlines her need to make excitement for herself by functioning as more than an observer. When she hears the "astounding piece of news" that Lady Glenmire will marry Mr. Hoggins, she comments, "I must recover myself; the contemplation of it, even at this distance of time, has taken away my breath and my grammar, and unless I subdue my emotion, my spelling will go too" (113). Although she solicits the reader's amusement, allows herself a faint tone of superiority, and hints self-mockery in the remarks about breath and grammar, her emotional involvement repeatedly manifests itself; she needs to feel that something important can happen even in confined lives. She too "speculates," to more purpose than the ladies of Cranford, and she invites the reader's speculation by asking questions calculated to produce involvement: "have you seen such things in London?"

Of course, Mary presupposes the negative answer to such questions. Asking them, however, calls attention to the novel's most serious preoccupation: what can be made of a diminished thing? Londoners, lacking cows and lime pits, share more conventional sources of interest and pleasure; they require less inventiveness, less responsiveness. Ralph Marvell, in *The Custom of the Country*, has a brief vision of the imaginative force involved in financial speculation. Wharton's novels illustrate imagination's perversion as urban men and women concern themselves with financial and social self-advantage, using imagination to reify one another. Lily Bart's pathos stems from her capacity—unusual in her social setting—dimly to imagine more self-fulfillment than she can imagine how to realize. The residents of Cranford express no awareness of insufficiency, nor does Mary Smith comment directly on the psychic limitations of their, and even her, existence. The novel makes one feel the imaginative triumph of these lives: the degree to which women create themselves by making stories of virtually nothing. But their triumph is fragile: banks collapse; only a conspiracy of decorum and of fiction-making staves off acknowledgment of harsh contingency. Newland Archer, in *The Age of Innocence*, reflects about his own upper-class urban society: "they all lived in a kind of hieroglyphic world, where the real thing was never said or done or even thought, but only represented by a set of arbitrary signs."[10]

"The real thing" manifests itself in *Cranford* through expressed impulses of benevolence. But, like all societies, Cranford also relies on hieroglyphs. Archer's family and friends—none of whom, it is safe to say, has ever seen a cow in gray flannel—spend much of their time in gossip, a deflected mode of expression for their deep concerns, a way of asserting their unity. For comparable reasons, the Cranford ladies gossip, declaring their interest in human relationship, avoiding their justifiable anxieties and fears, making of themselves a *society*. The response of affectionate amusement which Mary Smith exemplifies and which the reader readily shares does not fully answer to the situation: Gaskell invites awareness of the fragility and the courage of female structures of self-protection, but also of their exclusionary force. Utterly without malice, the women of Cranford still fictionize those who don't belong; and fictionize themselves.

By yoking heterogeneous ideas violently together—speaking of *Cranford* and of Edith Wharton's New York novels in the same breath—I hope to emphasize that speculation about people as well as about money provides underpinnings for social functioning in diverse fictional works. (And in diverse social contexts outside fiction.) Wharton and Gaskell, in dramatically different settings, both delineate speculation, whatever its object, as exercise of imagination. In yet other social settings—of English clerical society or English gentry and aristocrats—Anthony Trollope plays variations on these themes. Wharton makes gossip an instrument for preserving class distinctions and assessing status and gain; Gaskell shows how it asserts status and denies the importance of gain. Men and women alike, in Trollope's evoked society (*Barchester Towers* and *The Eustace Diamonds* will serve as representative texts), employ talk to measure other people's advancement and to achieve their own.

Two questions govern *Barchester Towers*: who will succeed to the deanship; whom will Eleanor Bold marry. The corresponding questions in *The Eustace Diamonds* are what will happen to Lizzie Eustace and what has become of the diamonds. None of these issues involves much suspense for the reader; the narrator informs us that Eleanor will marry neither of the unattractive aspirants for her hand; we know before anyone in the novel (apart from Lizzie herself) that the diamonds are not stolen in the first robbery; in both novels, the narrative tone assures us that everything will come out all right. But the four questions occupy many people much of the time and provide splendid subjects for gossip. Gossip serves its usual purposes: it makes people feel important, it declares moral and social allegiances, it fills time. At the very end of *The Eustace Diamonds*, the ancient Duke of Omnium

goes off to bed, "quite fatigued with his fascination about Lady Eustace."
Lady Glencora remarks, "I call that woman a perfect God-send. What should
we have done without her?"[11] Lady Glencora means, of course, "What should
we have *talked about* without her?" Lizzie has provided conversational fodder
for servants and aristocrats and everyone in between; just as, in *Barchester
Towers*, Eleanor's problematic marital intentions sustain conversation for the
idle.

To say that Trollope's novels contain a lot of gossip says nothing very
interesting about them. Nor does detailed examination of how the gossip
works shed much light on the novels as wholes. On the other hand, Trollope's
intrusive narrator implicitly calls attention to the relation of written and oral
story-telling, thus enlarging the implications of speculation's imaginative
origins. Unlike Gaskell's Mary Smith, this narrator does not reveal his name.
Like Mary Smith, he invites the reader into a situation of narrative intimacy.
Trollope's fictions encourage thought about the value of gossip as a model
for the writing of fiction.

> What novelist, what Fielding, what Scott, what George Sand, or
> Thackeray, or Dumas, can impart an interest to the last chapter of
> his fictitious history? Promises of two children and superhuman
> happiness are of no avail, nor assurance of extreme respectability
> carried to an age far exceeding that usually allotted to mortals. The
> sorrows of our heroes and heroines, they are your delight, oh public!
> their sorrows, or their sins, or their absurdities; not their virtues,
> good sense, and consequent rewards. When we begin to tint our
> final pages with couleur de rose, as in accordance with fixed rule
> we must do, we altogether extinguish our own powers of pleasing.
> When we become dull we offend your intellect; and we must become
> dull or we should offend your taste.[12]

The dullness of tastefulness, the intellectual dubiousness of the not-dull:
the novelist cannot escape such oppositions. People enjoy knowing other
people's weaknesses, not their strengths. Happy endings, assurances of respectability resolve novels but supply no compelling interest. Trollope's characters talk obsessively about one another's dubious behavior: Lizzie Eustace
keeps everyone busy and happy for years by her reprehensible conduct. In
precisely the same way, she provides the reader of *The Eustace Diamonds*
with occupation and pleasure.

The novelist enjoys less freedom than the gossip. The reading public,
says the narrator of *The Eustace Diamonds*, has "taught itself to like best the

characters of all but divine men and women. Let the man who paints with pen and ink give the gaslight, and the fleshpots, the passions and pains, the prurient prudence and the rouge-pots and pounce-boxes of the world as it is, and he will be told that no one can care a straw for his creations. With whom are we to sympathise? says the reader, who not unnaturally imagines that a hero should be heroic" (ED, 1.318–19). Literature, unlike gossip, has didactic pretensions; the novelist may aspire (or claim to aspire) to make mankind wiser and better by exemplary fictions. The incompatibility of the two accounts of the reader just quoted reflects an apparent uncertainty in Trollope's novels about whether attempts at realism in characterization and action will please or displease readers: whether fiction should more resemble hagiography or gossip, opposite forms of objectification. Minimal introspection would probably reveal to most readers their own incompatible wishes for fictional satisfaction. We yearn for fairy-tale fantasies (sufficiently plausible to encourage suspension of disbelief) about flawless beauties and dashing adventurers whose lives work out precisely as we would wish; and we respond to the opportunity for dwelling on life's seamy side, imaginatively fulfilling forbidden desires. Gossip, of course, satisfies the latter needs.

Fielding's novels and Sterne's long before Trollope acknowledged awareness of possible reader response: awareness, but rarely anxiety. Fielding's narrator in *Tom Jones* evokes himself as innkeeper or stage impresario or god, metaphors implying connection with other people; but if travelers don't like his bill of fare, they can go elsewhere—he will not change the menu. Tristram Shandy as teller of his own story imagines, often, a hostile reader, who becomes part of the drama of the narrative in process. Trollope's narrators employ formal diction and syntax, but they claim a more intimate link with readers. The reader's sympathies, the narrator observes, "are in truth the great and only aim of my work" (1.319); his effort to play on those sympathies involves increasingly complex consciousness of perplexing coincidences and divergences between art and "real life" ("in real life we are content with oats that are really middling"; 1.319).

The moral ambiguity of fiction, as we have already seen, roused Dr. Johnson to a ringing plea for clear distinctions, good characters unambiguously opposed to bad; such ambiguity connected fiction from the beginning with gossip. But the addresses to readers in Trollope's novels suggest another kind of link: not only the material of the novel but the relationship it establishes with its readers approximates that of gossip. The reader's confusion about what s/he wants and the narrator's corresponding doubts raise the problem of legitimating the human propensity for telling stories about other people.

The nature of that propensity, and of the difficulties it implies, emerges in the novels as fictional characters tell stories about one another. The clerical politics of Barchester and the social politics enveloping Lizzie Eustace generate and thrive on anecdote—anecdote often elaborated to the point almost of myth. Some of Trollope's characters seem mythical in conception: Lizzie herself, Bertie Stanhope in *Barchester Towers*, his yet more spectacular sister, Madame Neroni. By virtue of other people's talk, less flamboyant characters acquire comparable glamour. Mr. Slope seeks information from a maid:

> He had been told that the archdeacon and Mrs. Grantly and Mr. Harding and Mr. Arabin had all quarrelled with "missus" for having received a letter from Mr. Slope; that "missus" had positively refused to give the letter up; that she had received from the archdeacon the option of giving up either Mr. Slope and his letter, or else the society of Plumstead rectory; and that "missus" had declared, with much indignation, that "she didn't care a straw for the society of Plumstead rectory," and that she wouldn't give up Mr. Slope for any of them. Considering the source from whence this came, it was not quite so untrue as might have been expected [BT, 2.71].

Not altogether untrue: truth heightened, intensified, cast into the form of popular fiction. Nor do servants alone engage in this glamorizing activity. Mrs. Grantly declares that Mr. Arabin, in company with Madame Neroni, "looked and acted and talked very unlike a decent parish clergyman." She has witnessed the scene she reports, but her interpretation converts the episode into something far more momentous than others might have perceived.

> At first the archdeacon had laughed at this, and assured her that she need not trouble herself;—that Mr. Arabin would be found to be quite safe. But by degrees he began to find that his wife's eyes had been sharper than his own. Other people coupled the Signora's name with that of Mr. Arabin. The meagre little prebendary who lived in the close told him to a nicety how often Mr. Arabin had visited at Dr. Stanhope's, and how long he remained on the occasion of each visit. He had asked after Mr. Arabin at the cathedral library, and an officious little vicar choral had offered to go and see whether he could be found at Dr. Stanhope's. . . . It was too clear that Mr. Arabin had succumbed to the Italian woman, and that the archdeacon's credit would suffer fearfully if something were not done to rescue the brand from the burning [BT, 2.279].

Life becomes more dramatic as innocence gets interpreted into vice: life takes, in short, novelistic form.

Within the narrator's embracing fiction, other fictions develop, results of individual or communal perception and interpretation. Trollope imagines characters imagining one another. "The German lives in order to live, the Englishman to represent," a German visitor to England wrote in the mid-nineteenth century.[13] Trollope's characters show an inordinate interest in representation. Some—the most flamboyant, such as Madame Neroni and Lizzie Eustace—occupy themselves in constant self-representation, with ever changing versions of self at their disposal. They more or less deliberately generate gossip about themselves: being talked about constitutes not only reassurance but power. If they can create social speculation, maintain themselves as centers of attention, they affirm identities which, however unstable, manifestly have meaning in the world.

Trollope's characters "represent" not only themselves but one another, constantly creating fictions about those temporarily out of sight. The stories they tell create and re-create people they know well or slightly. Fiction-making within the novels consists mainly in manufacture of characters. The stories told by residents of Barchester or London represent others as enemies or traitors or (less frequently and less stably) paragons and generate drama from such representations. Interpretations of character within the embracing fiction derive from self-interest: from fear, anxiety, hope, or simply desire for excitement.

The narrator's representations of character, avowedly fictional, also stem from particular motivations, some of which he specifies. Those motivations, he claims, often involve awareness of the hypothetical reader. Although in life the reader values the imperfect, in literature he wants something more. The fiction-maker hopes to "show men what they are, and how they might rise"; to accomplish this end, he must defy what readers think they want and give them what they should have (ED, 1.320). But: "Our doctrine is, that the author and the reader should move along together in full confidence with each other. Let the personages of the drama undergo ever so complete a comedy of errors among themselves, but let the spectator never mistake the Syracusan for the Ephesian. Otherwise he is one of the dupes, and the part of a dupe is never dignified" (BT, 1.179). So the narrator assures his readers that Eleanor ("my Eleanor") will not marry unwisely—thus allowing readers to share with him foreknowledge impossible for anyone within the world of the novel. "My Eleanor" would not marry foolishly because of her sterling character: the narrator thus claims for her a kind of reality. And she will do nothing foolish because of the narrator's control: he won't let her.

Addresses to the reader thus at once insist on the fictionality of the novel and suggest that such fictionality partakes of its counterparts in everyday conversation. We, as readers, speculate about Eleanor; so do the people who know her, within the fiction. Only the narrator need not speculate: he *knows*.

But he also feels uncertain. Readers speculate, characters speculate, and the narrator . . . well, the narrator claims to have chosen among alternative possibilities. Consequently, such a work as *Barchester Towers* involves a reader in ways very different from, say, *Emma*, in which the reader becomes implicated in the processes of interpretation, but the narrator, coolly ironic, not only knows what has happened and what it means but implicitly insists on the *necessity* of created happenings. Trollope's narrator, claiming the relation of fiction to life, acknowledges the multiple forms such a relation can take. His heroes might have been more or less heroic; he has chosen to make them what they are. The reader, intermittently confronted with asseverations about the nature and desires of readers, is invited to become aware what responses and interpretations and wants s/he brings to the text: part of the novel's drama.

Speculation seeks something new: new meaning or new money, "great or unusual gain." The profit for which Trollope's characters compete consists not in money but in prestige, status as power and fulfillment. Verbal speculation, in Trollope's fiction as in Gaskell's and Wharton's and Austen's, attempts stable understanding of others and endeavors to discover or declare patterns in human lives. Such understanding or discovery involves less risk than investing in a savings bank: nineteenth-century novelists rarely allow ontological uncertainty. But the intensity with which Eleanor's and Lizzie's friends, relatives, and acquaintances try to figure out what the women intend, or what their intentions imply, suggests that they believe something real is at stake. There is no direct connection between understanding what Eleanor is up to and controlling the disposition of wardenships or deanships. Yet characters avidly interested in such understanding make it a metaphor for mastery. Eleanor's goodness becomes clear; her fiancé wins the deanship— the two events almost simultaneous. Gossip in Trollope's fictional universe does not bring people within social norms or exclude them, but by imaginative representation re-creates them into comprehensible meaning. Lizzie's wickedness proves as reassuring as Eleanor's goodness in this respect: both make the substance of a comprehensible society, existing more coherently in linguistic rendering than in itself. Lizzie Eustace, with herself as capital, makes words instruments of speculation in her effort to consolidate her social position and power. Mr. Slope, in *Barchester Towers*, does exactly the same thing. Both fail. But the people who talk *about* them succeed, incorporating them into verbal structures of meaning. Power is profit; gossip helps create it. And so does fiction, allowing narrators and readers alike the illusion of mastery. The good of verbal speculation, in Trollope, is to understand every character as rich in meanings. But all complexities of individual meaning must fit into a stable, predictable social totality. The reader and the other characters enjoy contemplating the machinations of Lizzie Eustace or Bertie Stanhope; yet such contemplation finally provides the means of social exclusion: its most important function.

This world, observes the narrator of *Middlemarch*, is "apparently a huge whispering-gallery."[14] The word *speculation*, in George Eliot's novel, applies often to such lofty concerns as Lydgate's contemplation of the mystery of living tissue. Speculation in its less elevated senses, however, has powerful effects in the web of human connections composing the community of Middlemarch and its environs. To think about the world as whispering-gallery and about the financial manipulation that may preoccupy the gallery's visitors calls attention to Eliot's brilliant use of characters and details on the periphery of her main action.

Take Mrs. Cadwallader, for instance, a figure with a mind "active as phosphorus, biting everything that came near into the form that suited it" (45), whose role in the action consists mainly of soliciting and spreading gossip. As community matchmaker, she watches everyone and everything, lavish in interpretations from her own narrative perspective. Her power operates only on the weak. When she encourages Sir James Chettam to think of Celia rather than Dorothea as prospective bride, he readily takes the suggestion; Dorothea, on the other hand, never succumbs to her hints. In her capacity to bite everything into the form that suits her, in her confidence, in her objects of influence, Mrs. Cadwallader precisely represents the community to which she feels superior. The form that suits her does not always correspond to that suiting Middlemarch, but her kinds of assessment and interference speak for the community.

Mrs. Cadwallader gathers and relays gossip. Gossip speaks in the voice of the community. But, as even the cursory summary above will suggest, Mrs. Cadwallader's gossip has nothing speculative about it: like a novelistic narrator, she *knows*. The gossips of Middlemarch, whose voices echo through Eliot's novel, convey equivalent certainties. Although they may wonder about what has happened or will happen, they experience no doubt about applicable judgments.

Nonetheless, gossip in *Middlemarch* occupies a context of speculation. Its apparent certainties analogize the kinds of financial certainty that all too often evaporate under the pressure of actuality.

"We are all of us imaginative in some form or other," the narrator comments at the beginning of Book Four, "for images are the brood of desire" (237). Speculation, involving a play of images, betrays the dimensions of desire. Lydgate's high-minded speculation and Bulstrode's financial manipulation both conform to this description. Old Featherstone remarks of Bulstrode, "And what's he?—he's got no land hereabout that ever I heard tell of. A speckilating fellow! He may come down any day, when the devil leaves off backing him" (82). "I like neither Bulstrode nor speculation," Fred Vincy responds. Featherstone's characterization has uncanny prophetic force: the devil will soon leave off backing Bulstrode, and he will indeed fall. (He will also acquire land: Featherstone's land.) As D. A. Miller acutely observes, in a commentary bearing on the question of gossip in *Middlemarch*, Bulstrode professes to be "in essence a man without a past, without a story."[15] Yet his story, like other people's stories, unalterably defines him: a *speculator*, a man possessed by an image of possibility creating its own demand for realization. Bulstrode has long seen himself as a man specially favored by God. God could not wish money to go to those who might dissipate it; God must want what Bulstrode wants. Bulstrode's speculation does not risk money for money, but ventures integrity for status and wealth.

Bulstrode cares about public opinion. "Who can know," the narrator inquires, "how much of his most inward life is made up of the thoughts he believes other men to have about him, until that fabric of opinion is threatened with ruin?" And, a few sentences later, "Foreseeing, to men of Bulstrode's anxious temperament, is often worse than seeing; and his imagination continually heightened the anguish of an imminent disgrace" (504). Bulstrode's imagination has always focused on his position—in the world and in the universe. The fantasy of special favor in the eyes of God and of man creates a man who will commit perjury and murder in the service of his self-representation: speculation for high stakes indeed.

Images are the brood of desire. The novel dwells on images of two kinds: those people hold of one another (the substance of gossip) and those treasured self-images that motivate conduct. Lydgate's lofty speculations involve a vision of himself as scientific hero and assume other people's respect. Rosamond's complacency derives from her image of herself as flawless in conduct. Fred claims to dislike speculation, but, believing in his own cleverness, he risks money at billiards or horse-trading in dreams of easy profit. Mr. Brooke's efforts to enter Parliament reflect a view of himself utterly at odds with what others see. Casaubon's plans for a key to all mythologies and Will Ladislaw's vague projects for artistic or political achievement declare their desires and the pleasing pictures desire creates.

Although *Middlemarch* pays considerable attention to money, few individual characters center their "speculation" on money for its own sake in the same way as the inhabitants of Wharton's fictional world. Featherstone considers Bulstrode a speculator because he deals in money rather than land; but Bulstrode himself believes money only instrumental in consolidating his position of pious power. Mr. Brooke, notoriously reluctant to spend money improving his tenants' lots, in his failures as landlord expresses only another form of his general vagueness. He does not care particularly about money; he only fails to think. Mrs. Cadwallader bargains for everything she buys, thus expressing her will to control all about her. Rosamond never seeks or considers money; she takes it for granted, as, until reality intrudes, does Lydgate. Even Fred, directly conscious of his need for cash, envelops that need in fantasies about his own happy destiny. Various kinds of speculation necessarily depend on money: Lydgate, Rosamond, Fred, Brooke, Ladislaw, Bulstrode, Featherstone—all must have and use financial resources to fulfill their visions of self. Money functions as an instrument of imagination: for the model of virtue, Caleb Garth, as well as for the pattern of iniquity, Bulstrode. Money too, therefore, subordinates itself to desire. Only for Featherstone's grasping relatives does it prove desire's fundamental object.

The novel fashions itself from the discrepancy between self-image and the perceptions of others. Its repeated images of self-absorption—the pier glass whose scratches order themselves in circles in the light of a single candle, the world as udder for the supreme self—insist on the importance of this discrepancy. "Let any lady who is inclined to be hard on Mrs. Cadwallader inquire into the comprehensiveness of her own beautiful views, and be quite sure that they afford accommodation for all the lives which have the honour to coexist with hers" (44). No one manages imaginatively to accommodate all other lives; Dorothea's effort to do so marks her heroism. The meaning of community, as rendered by *Middlemarch*, includes constant clash between self-perceived and other-perceived selves.

Yet the community has communal opinions: which brings us back to gossip. Heroic Dorothea feels indignant that Celia should allow her maid to "talk such gossip" to her. "I see no harm at all in Tantripp's talking to me," Celia responds. "It is better to hear what people say" (26). One measure of the brilliance of *Middlemarch* is the fact that Celia and Dorothea, who invariably understand the world differently, are almost always *both* right, although Dorothea is of course "right" at a higher level. Dorothea's rejection of gossip stems from her admirable determination to find her own way to the good. But Celia knows that it is better to hear what people say because of her practical awareness: other people's opinions not only affect the possibility of action but uncover realities which might otherwise escape one. Tantripp's gossip, in this instance, forces Dorothea to confront what she has denied, Sir James's romantic interest in her: something she needs to know.

Eliot renders the community's gossip by allusion, by summary, and in selective detail. As one would expect, the voice of the community speaks for conformity; gossips fail to perceive Dorothea's rareness or to comprehend either of her marriages. D. A. Miller, providing an analysis of community gossip in *Middlemarch* in terms and for purposes rather different from mine, points out how this talk effects social exclusions. Lydgate, Bulstrode, Dorothea, and Ladislaw have to leave town at the novel's end: "ritual sacrifices to the recovery of social routine" (Miller, 121). "The community's narrative-formation," Miller concludes, "is reduced to its source in the need to protect a fantasized self-image, and on theoretical grounds, the authenticity of every aspect of this formation is put into question" (129). But it is equally true that each examined character formulates his or her own story in order to protect an individually fantasized self-image. The "authenticity" of Mr. Brooke's story of himself, or Mrs. Cadwallader's of herself, no less than Dorothea's or Lydgate's, would be challengeable on the same grounds. The novel encourages awareness of the inevitable, crucial difference between stories and lives. All stories derive from self-interest. Communal self-interest distorts in ways different from individual self-interest, but perhaps no more intensely.

Miller implies that communal stories serve the purpose of leveling. Middlemarch cannot tolerate deviants; hence the exclusion of Lydgate, Bulstrode, Dorothea, and Ladislaw. In fact Dorothea and Ladislaw, although from the beginning objects of gossip, do not leave town because of it. Both go to London in search of wider horizons. As Dorothea explains to Celia, "I never could do anything that I liked. I have never carried out any plan yet" (600). Her dreams may, in London, in a new marriage, bear a closer relation to actuality than they have hitherto. Gossip does not deter Ladislaw from wooing Dorothea, although he suffers from the thought of what people will say. The force of imagination in Ladislaw and Dorothea themselves resists the counterforce of other imaginations directed at them.

Middlemarch makes clear the importance of imagination for all speculation. Lydgate's speculations founder under the pressure of an imagination more powerfully focused than his: Rosamond's undeflectable self-will. Bulstrode's speculative imagination finally divides against itself: the devastating impact on him of exposure to those whom he has morally dominated reflects his fantasies of what they say about him as well as the reality. Fred subordinates his undependable fancies to the will of those wiser than he. Each of these points could be elaborated; I shall confine myself, however, to exploring some connections the novel establishes between speculation and money.

Money, as I have already suggested, fills only a minor function as a direct object of speculation. Featherstone's grasping relatives, all frustrated in the end, gamble for wealth as a self-sufficient goal; everyone else demonstrates more complicated imaginative relations to money. Money becomes, on the other hand, a main *subject* of speculation. To put it otherwise: money is what Middlemarch gossips talk about.

Examples come readily to mind. When people gossip about Fred, they interest themselves in his extravagant behavior. They talk about the Vincys living beyond their means, about Casaubon's will, about the expectations of Featherstone's prospective heirs, about the possibility that Bulstrode has bought Lydgate, about Farebrother's card-playing, about Brooke's miserliness and about the money he's spending on his parliamentary aspirations. "Well, Mrs Bulstrode is Mr Vincy's own sister, and they do say that Mr Vincy mostly trades on the Bank money; and you may see yourself, brother, when a woman past forty has pink strings always flying, and that light way of laughing at everything, it's very unbecoming. But indulging your children is one thing, and finding money to pay their debts is another" (79). The speaker is Mrs. Waule, trying to persuade Featherstone to reject the Vincy family, but her tone only exaggerates that of other frivolous talkers. Money is a conversational subject of obsessive interest. Even high-minded Mrs. Bulstrode, reporting "the town's talk" to her niece Rosamond, emphasizes that Lydgate's profession "is a poor one here"—adding quickly, of course, that "this life is not everything"—but then, medical men are seldom religious either (218).

For people who indulge in light talk about others, money provides the most significant measure of worth. (Caleb Garth, who feels no interest at all in money except as a means of providing for his family's needs, for whom land and the "business" of managing it are far more important, also refuses to talk at all about other people. "As to speaking," he tells Bulstrode, "I hold it a crime to expose a man's sin unless I'm clear it must be done to save the innocent"; 510.) Gossip concerns itself with money as the most convenient form of assessment, the most obvious object of desire. Joshua Rigg, Peter Featherstone's unexpected heir, with his "very distinct and intense vision of his chief good," his intent of using his inherited property as a means "of buying gold" (381), only exaggerates the assumptions of the community at large. When Lydgate confuses the traditional relationship between the physician and money by refusing to sell medicine, he wins the community's distrust (and becomes an immediate subject of gossip). Even the narrator resorts to money as metaphor of value: "When a tender affection has been storing itself in us through many of our years, the idea that we could accept any exchange for it seems to be a cheapening of our lives. And we can set a watch over our affections and our constancy as we can over other treasures" (423). Bulstrode's moral authority derives from his wealth; Lydgate's declining fortunes chart his lessening power. Gossips in this novel (unlike the novel's narrator) rarely indulge in conscious metaphor. But in the abundant reported gossip of Middlemarch and environs, money in fact functions metaphorically, to sum up communal evaluations of individuals. The fact that Ladislaw and Dorothea, for different reasons, need not worry about money (except, briefly, as an apparent obstacle to their union) declares their relative freedom from the punishing force of public opinion in comparison to Lydgate, whose marriage forces him to financial awareness, and to Bulstrode, the other "outsiders."

The gossip about Ladislaw and Dorothea is always "wrong": the community cannot at all comprehend either of these unusual beings. But the money-focused gossip about Fred and Lydgate and Casaubon and Farebrother and Brooke and Bulstrode often touches oddly on truth. I mean by that much the same thing I meant when I pointed out that the stories about Lily Bart, in *The House of Mirth*, although literally false, accurately chart her moral deterioration. Fred and Lydgate *are* in trouble when the community thinks they are, though their deepest trouble is not financial. Casaubon's will *does* call attention to real attraction between Ladislaw and Dorothea. Farebrother's playing cards for money marks a danger point; Brooke's inconsistencies reflect his lack of moral fiber; and so on. Money, the communal object of desire, provides an appropriate metaphor for other kinds of imaginative focus.

The various senses of *speculation* come together in *Middlemarch*. Seeing and perspective, as many critics have noted, comprise central preoccupations of the novel. The moral and psychological vision that the narrator cultivates both derives from and generates conjecture, the conjecture that at a lower level of subtlety and discrimination fuels Middlemarch talk. The taking of risk for the sake of gain literally controls Bulstrode, but also, in less restricted financial senses, Lydgate, Fred, Brooke, even Ladislaw and Dorothea, whose notion of "gain" is highly abstracted. At one level, speculation confines. Bulstrode's morally destructive venturing destroys his freedom; Fred risks comparably disastrous losses; even Farebrother's excursions into minor gambling carry the danger of moral deterioration. And the verbal speculation indulged in by groups of men and women alike, depending on narrow perspectives and limited assumptions, forces its subjects into restrictive molds. In both these forms of speculation, the illusion of certainty creates the potential of destruction. Middlemarch gossips do not realize the questions implicit in their judgments; once they decide, for example, that Lydgate has sold himself, they do not inquire about motives or about other possible interpretations for his actions. Just so, Bulstrode uses his "certainty" of God's special favor to justify corruption; Fred believes that he gambles, over and over, on "a sure thing"; even Farebrother tacitly invokes necessity to justify his conduct. More truly venturesome speculation, exemplified in the intellectual sphere by Lydgate's efforts to understand living substance, in the moral sphere by Dorothea's ardent struggles toward comprehension of living substance in quite another sense—this kind of speculation frees rather than confines. Dorothea grows through it; her sister subsides into contented domesticity by virtue of accepting the given. Nothing ventured, nothing gained; but one must take care about the nature of the venture.

Money and talk: both forms of social control, both matter for speculation, both central issues in novels. Talk creates stories; money, in its multiple human bearings, demands the making of stories. By linking them as loci of uncertainty often possessing the forms of certainty, novelists demonstrate the interpenetration of outer and inner life. I said earlier that money belongs to the "outer," "public," "male" realm; gossip, to the privatized realm of women. But these novels reveal the meaninglessness of such separations. Money, the underpinning of capitalistic society, necessarily concerns men and women alike, however they deflect, disguise, or deny such concerns. And gossip, which takes place in relatively small groups, affects large ones and issues from large social assumptions. Brooke's fate in the parliamentary election is sealed by Middlemarch gossip; Lizzie Eustace becomes important in a large world only to be discarded as a result of the world's speculative talk.

Emma and *Evelina* demonstrated an ideological aspect of gossip and its implications for narrative. Gossip provides for the novels' heroines a means of self-development and of counter-conventional assertion, an escape from social rigidities. It suggests a narrative model of free interpretation. In the novels treated in this chapter, more openly concerned with money or with grander forms of power than Emma's local control, gossip speaks in a harsher voice. No longer exploratory, no longer a function of individualized imagination, it becomes an instrument of social ideology, of class self-preservation. Undestructive in *Cranford*, devastating in *The House of Mirth*, executing rough social justice in *Middlemarch* and in Trollope's novels, in every instance it reifies its objects and supports the collective self-esteem of its speakers. (Dorothea and Ladislaw tentatively escape because of their intense imaginative capacities, focused on their own lives and responsibilities rather than on other people.) As an implicit model for fiction, this kind of gossip hints that interpretation of character and event issues from communal self-interest: the opposite of free imagination. Linked with money as an instrument of control, the gossip of these novels, like the financial speculation, insists on certainties while dealing with what must by its nature be unsure. It becomes a metaphor for the restrictiveness of social discourse; and it raises the possibility that novels emanate from the same discourse and from the ways of seeing it implies.

9

Stepping Down
from the Platform

Having included in his text a disingenuous letter from Becky Sharp to Amelia Sedley, the narrator of William Makepeace Thackeray's *Vanity Fair* feels impelled to suggest his disapprobation of it by declaring his own difference from his characters. "One is bound to speak the truth as far as one knows it," he observes, adding that he feels "sincere hatred" for his villains, not identification with them. "As we bring our characters forward," he concludes, "I will ask leave, as a man and a brother, not only to introduce them, but occasionally to step down from the platform, and talk about them."[1] The two implied narrative postures—on the platform, holding forth; down below, "talking"—suggest a range of resources for the novel and a possible subject of anxiety for the novelist. Some narrators never leave the platform: George Eliot's story-tellers, relentlessly pointing the significance of the happenings they report; Joseph Conrad's, sonorous even in asides. Some novelists avoid dilemmas of distance by hiding behind characters, first-person narrators singular or multiple (as in epistolary fictions with letters by several hands, or as in *Wuthering Heights*, with its series of story-tellers). The problem of intimacy pursues creators of fiction. Should one tell a story to an audience, or should one discuss it with men and brothers (women and sisters)? What tone, what relationship should one seek?

The subject matter of realistic fiction may compound the difficulties of choosing among alternatives. A young woman of dubious parentage, accustomed from early youth to trickery and cheating, sets out to make her way in the fashionable world. After narrowly missing two prosperous marital prospects, she secretly marries an impoverished military man of dashing appearance with aristocratic relatives. Dabbling in adultery for her own ends (more financial than sexual), she finally stands exposed to her husband as well as to society in general. So summarized, the Becky Sharp plot of *Vanity Fair* declares its affinities to the material of common gossip. Other novels lend themselves to comparable summary. *The Great Gatsby*: a wealthy man remains desperately infatuated with a married woman, having had a brief affair with her some years earlier. He urges her to leave her adulterous husband for him; she can't bring herself to do so. Driving the rich man's car, she accidentally kills her husband's mistress, whose widower subsequently murders the car's owner. *What Maisie Knew*: divorcing parents squabble over child custody and subsequently pass their little girl back and forth to serve their own purposes. As the parents embark on new marriages and ever more truncated love affairs, their daughter learns her way through a maze of increasing moral complexities. Eventually both parents discard her; she must choose her own guardian. *Anna Karenina, Madame Bovary, Ethan Frome, Jane Eyre*: many important novels draw plots from the kind of material dear to gossip columnists.

The novelist, often reliant on morally dubious raw material, may wish to justify it in fictional or in ethical terms. Narrative stance provides a mode of justification. The George Eliot method embodies one extreme possibility, purifying the stuff of scandal in its articulation. The woman who marries for money in *Daniel Deronda*, the girl who bears and kills an illegitimate child in *Adam Bede* inhabit insistently defined moral structures. The narrator's high-minded tone subordinates subject to ethical purpose and denies any element of prurience in reader's response or writer's motivation. The reader (to say nothing of the writer) thus has it both ways, free to contemplate the kind of behavior one whispers about, while remaining superior to mere scandal.

But fictional purposes involve more than ethical issues. A writer's choice of "scandalous" subject matter implicitly acknowledges the special intensity of human response to such material, not only because this sort of subject raises urgent ethical questions but because evidence of passion in operation arouses the emotions of readers or auditors. People gossip about sex and money because they care about them; novelists write about these issues because they know people care. Gossip is, as I have argued repeatedly, a mode of relatedness. "Psychological development stops in isolation," a psychologist writes; "it seems unable to forgo the context of other souls. . . . Gossip is . . . a primary activity of the psyche. . . . Gossip provides the psychic ballast of human dirt that keeps us down to earthly involvement."[2]

That ballast freights many a novel; in novels as in talk, it creates a convincing context of other souls. For a narrator to remain immovably planted on a platform opposes the involvement implicit in concern with "human dirt." Weaknesses affirm our brotherhood and sisterhood, generate gossip, initiate plots.

Exploiters of human weakness, on the other hand, fill a role at best problematic. The image of the gossip fattening on other people's woes epitomizes the moral ambiguity of personal talk. The fictional narrator, despite the protection of fictionality, risks a comparably uncomfortable moral position. Emily Brontë displaces the gossip's role in *Wuthering Heights* by making Nelly Dean the type of the gossip and creating Lockwood as a surrogate for the reader in his avid interest. Lockwood hopes "sincerely [that Nelly] would prove a regular gossip, and either rouse me to animation or lull me to sleep by her talk."[3] When Nelly shows some inclination to skip over three years of her story, Lockwood insists on chronological minuteness. Nelly consequently agrees "to follow [her] story in true gossip's fashion," year by year (78). She thus satisfies Lockwood's desires—and the reader's. And the onus of being a judgmental busybody rests on Nelly, whom the reader, in turn, can freely judge. Tristram Shandy, making himself as well as his family the object of gossip, displaces not the role but the blame by accusing the reader of prurient interest in his Jenny—perhaps his mistress, perhaps his child, perhaps his friend—and refusing to gratify that interest.[4] Other narrators use the tone of authority to indicate their own separation from gossip's relative frivolity: not only Eliot's moral insistence, but Austen's ironic acuity functions in this fashion. Forms of narrative authority can make readers forget the association of fiction with gossip; yet the association remains.

Unlike eighteenth-century readers, those of the twentieth century rarely worry about the possible immorality of reading fiction. Moral uneasiness may rise to consciousness when one reads published letters or journals, particularly if they mention the living; records of the dead feel less troubling. Death fictionalizes everyone. Relatively free of guilt, almost as though they were imagined characters, we penetrate the privacies of those who leave personal documents for our prying eyes, those whom our curiosity can no longer hurt. Yet more "innocent" are our readings of the invented stories about invented persons which gratify curiosity at one remove, trading on belief in life's infinite variety, personality's infinite possibility. Our fascination with what goes on in Becky Sharp's bedroom converts into acceptable terms our interest in our neighbor's intimate activities. Fiction not only substitutes for gossip, it effectively transforms it, stabilizing conversation's fluidities, ordering its inconsequence, freeing the reader from the potential moral discomfort of talking about others while satisfying many of the needs that generate such talk.

The techniques of narrative can play on desires gratified by gossip. If we feel superior to Lockwood, with his uncomprehending hunger for detail about his neighbors' lives, and yet more superior to Nelly Dean, in the smugness of her narration, we yet, like Lockwood, take pleasure in Nelly's story. Moreover, Lockwood's satisfaction in his immediate situation—cozy, comfortable, harsh weather and harsh passions shut out—corresponds to the reader's experience as a vicarious onlooker to tumultuous but unthreatening (because fictional) events and people. The position of Nelly and Lockwood as narrators not only emphasizes the solipsism of interpretation; it also calls attention to the ubiquity and the varying forms of curiosity, implicating readers in the pattern of seeking and organizing information—and leaving them baffled by the ultimate mystery of personality. Gossip, taken seriously, teaches the same lessons as *Wuthering Heights:* people endlessly interest one another; but although natural affinities create illusions of understanding, one never grasps the full dimensions of another consciousness.

Nelly Dean openly declares herself a gossip. Few narrators, however, offer such explicit characterization of their own discourse. Many by their procedures suggest a need distinctly to separate themselves from the realm of gossip, a realized possibility within the fiction, a possibility for narrators to play with and play against, but one that they must finally reject. Gossip, in many domestic novels, constitutes the constant unstressed alternative to the dominant discursive mode. The fictional context may evoke it in full detail: characters talking about one another, dwelling on trivia with avid interest. Narrators may toy with it, attempting for short or longer stretches to exploit the note of intimate relationship with the reader. Finally, though, most narrators reject the style of gossip in favor of more comprehensive, more dignified forms of interpretation. Yet gossip remains, in domestic narrative, a shadow discourse, a hypothetical alternative rejected yet always conceivable because so obvious, so easy, as a way of discussing sex, adultery, divorce. To support their rejection, narrators often characterize gossip in the most negative terms: as aggression rather than intimacy, trivialization rather than penetration. The platform remains for many story-tellers the most comfortable locale; but the teller's knowledge of other conceivable places to take a stand informs his or her choice. And sometimes the narrator manages to have it both ways: to declare contempt for gossip while making use of its richness. Domestic novels exploit the universal interest in minutiae of human irterest and suggest for such interest, in the particular instance, moral or psychological or historical justification. They tacitly acknowledge while explicitly denying the links between fiction and gossip.

As one would expect in such a study of society as *Vanity Fair*, Thackeray's monumental novel examines gossip's functions as social instrument and as individual resource. Virtuous Dobbin does "not care much about gossip" (724); virtuous Amelia appears never to hear any. Other inhabitants of Vanity Fair, however, both generate it and listen to it.

> *Mutato nomine*, it is all the same. Don't the barristers' wives talk about Circuit?—don't the soldiers' ladies gossip about the Regiment?—don't the clergymen's ladies discourse about Sunday Schools, and who takes whose duty?—don't the very greatest ladies of all talk about that small clique of persons to whom they belong, and why shall our Indian friends not have their own conversation?—only I admit it is slow for the laymen whose fate it sometimes is to sit by and listen [663].

Men as well as women discuss in detail the conduct of others and draw from their discussions conclusions often affecting the human subjects of their conversation. Amelia's inability to register the meaning of the talk that surrounds her corroborates her powerlessness in all aspects of life. A woman entirely defined by relationships, Amelia achieves her ends mainly by passivity, pining away in a slow decline until someone else brings about her marriage to the man of her choice, allowing her husband to be lured away by another woman and her son to be taken from her by his grandfather, only taking care of people. Her pliancy and helplessness and her remoteness from gossip mark her feminine goodness. She marries at last the man who has long loved her devotedly, and she lives happily ever after. But her husband proves fonder of his daughter than of his wife, and his relationship to Amelia is characterized in passionless terms: "he never said a word to Amelia that was not kind and gentle; or thought of a want of hers that he did not try to gratify" (759). The negative formulation applies appropriately to Amelia, herself the negative of all Becky's force.

Amelia neither gossips nor hears gossip because of her utter separation from the worldly. Even Dobbin, almost equally unworldly, proves capable of using other people's gossip to corroborate Becky's unworthiness. Gossip, the world's talk, delineates the world's shape. That world concerns itself intensely with vanities, its members fighting passionately for their share of goods tangible and intangible. Gossip, a constant activity of assessment, measures precise degrees of social status, often converting social to moral terms, since its language articulates worldly morality. "If Amelia could have heard the comments regarding her which were made in the circle from which her father's ruin had just driven her, she would have seen what her own crimes were, and how entirely her character was jeopardized. Such criminal imprudence Mrs. Smith never knew of; such horrid familiarities Mrs. Brown had always condemned, and the end might be a warning to *her* daughters" (194). To "have a virtuous character in Vanity Fair," the narrator points out, one must avoid honesty and emotional involvement: the Fair runs on appearances. Gossip assigns meaning to appearances in relation to wealth and status. Becky, valuing wealth and status at least as much as any of her fellow inhabitants, accordingly through most of her career fares better than Amelia in the world's discussion of character.

Gossip provides social orientation. When Amelia joins her husband in his army assignment, the major's wife immediately pours out "a thousand particulars" (263) about the sexual, economic, and verbal behavior of women associated with the regiment. She thus emphasizes gossip's importance as a form of knowledge. Such knowledge is, to be sure, always severely selective: participants choose the facts they will dwell on to support interpretations they wish to make. The shifting topography of their social universe, always laced with quagmires, threatens the outsider; Becky's skill at locating hidden chasms in the social landscape guarantees her prolonged survival.

But there are many purposes for gossip in Vanity Fair. It provides reassurance and social compensation. When Mrs. Sedley comes down in the world, to lodgings in a mean street, she spends much of her time gossiping with her landlady about the Irish maid and the other tenants on the street. Such verbal occupation, with the related pastime of watching her neighbors and their servants, keeps her busy and cheerful, sustaining her sense of importance in a diminished situation. Gossip supplies entertainment: Becky caricaturing the departed dinner guests to old Miss Crawley; Stubbles and Spooney and other members of Osborne's regiment indulging in "romantic conjectures" about the lieutenant's involvement with a woman—perhaps a duchess, perhaps "an opera-singer of the worst reputation" (130). Gossip articulates rage: Bute Crawley expressing his fury at Rawdon Crawley ("he's a gambler—he's a drunkard—he's a profligate in every way"; 114) because he fears his aunt's possible financial generosity to a rival. Or it can convey envy: the things women say about the girl with whom all the men yearn to dance (121).

Verbal outpourings of envy and rage, Mrs. Sedley's pathetic speculations, even soldiers' chat: all involve efforts of the situationally deprived to equalize their status by acts of linguistic power. Most allusions to gossip in *Vanity Fair* emphasize its possibilities for social or personal power. Mrs. Bute provides a striking instance, seeking gossip as knowledge for self-aggrandizement, eliciting damaging allegations about Becky and passing them on when they can help consolidate her own position. She talks with Sir Pitt's servants in order to keep track of what happens at the Hall, garnering trivial detail to serve her concentrated purposes. Telling stories to Miss Crawley about Rawdon's and Becky's misdeeds, she "had not the smallest remorse or compunction for the victim whom her tongue was immolating" (203); her gossip's self-righteousness constitutes her moral strength.

Although Mrs. Bute does not inhabit urban society, her stories in their malice partially epitomize the talk of the town. Being talked of maliciously, as well as actively talking, generates power. When Becky and her husband begin to entertain "the polite world," the source of their income gives rise to much conversation. "Some persons averred. . . . Other parties hinted. . . . Lord Southdown, it was said, had been induced. . . . Young Feltham . . . was also cited. . . . People declared. . . . Certain it is, that if she had had all the money which she was said to have begged or borrowed or stolen, she might have capitalised and been honest for life" (557). Society's gossip, in other words, assigns Becky more power and more money than she possesses; the assignment, while it lasts, serves as effectively as real possession to consolidate her position in the world.

Vanity Fair, the narrator observes, lacks charity; when in doubt, it declares its victims guilty. The power of social respect or disapproval affects only those who care about it, but that means almost everyone. For Amelia, it has no force, but she stands alone. Even Dobbin goes out of his way to refute gossip he hears, thus admitting its importance, and he recognizes its value as information. Occasionally gossip serves as moral exposure: servants, the narrator suggests, often know and discuss their employers' secret sins—but even servants speculate on the basis of appearances, in Vanity Fair the most relevant facts (489). Gossip, conversation about private appearances, preserves and circulates society's myths. Its narratives supply social currency. They also, the narrator tells us, originate his novel. Dobbin asks the Secretary of Legation in Pumpernickel if he knows anything about Mrs. Rawdon Crawley, "and then Tapeworm, who of course knew all the London gossip, . . . poured out into the astonished Major's ears such a history about Becky and her husband as astonished the querist, and supplied all the points of this narrative, for it was at that very table years ago that the present writer had the pleasure

of hearing—Tufto, Steyne, the Crawleys, and their history—everything connected with Becky and her previous life passed under the record of the bitter
diplomatist. He knew everything and a great deal besides, about all the world"
(735).

The fiction thus declares itself a transformation of gossip. The narrator's
self-presentation, full of disjunctions corresponding to the syntactical ellipses
of his account of origins, draws on gossip's energies, invites the reader's
interest in personal trivia, valorizes knowledge of the private, and takes
advantage of aspects of gossip dramatized in the narrative. The issues I have
touched on—gossip as expression of personal emotion, as reassurance, as
entertainment, as articulation of individual or collective power—bear also
on the evoked relation between narrator and reader. Sometimes on a metaphorical platform, sometimes at a metaphorical dinner table, the story-teller
shifts position so rapidly as to keep the reader off balance. On at least one
occasion, he makes explicit and emphatic his own connection with "the
world in general" and the degree to which he defines himself as a recorder
of gossip with the extra advantage of omniscience. The passage, with its
shifting tone, demands quotation at length:

> I suppose there is no man in this Vanity Fair of ours so little
> observant as not to think sometimes about the worldly affairs of his
> acquaintances, or so extremely charitable as not to wonder how his
> neighbour Jones, or his neighbour Smith, can make both ends meet
> at the end of the year. With the utmost regard for the family . . .
> (for I dine with them twice or thrice in a season,) I cannot but own
> that the appearance of the Jenkinses in the Park, in the large ba-
> rouche with the grenadier-footmen, will surprise and mystify me to
> my dying day: for though I know the equipage is only jobbed, and
> all the Jenkins people are on board-wages, yet those three men and
> the carriage must represent an expense of six hundred a-year at the
> very least—and then there are the splendid dinners, the two boys at
> Eton, the prize governess and masters for the girls, the trip abroad,
> or to Eastbourne or Worthing in the autumn, the annual ball with
> a supper from Gunter's (who, by the way, supplies most of the *first-
> rate* dinners which J. gives, as I know very well, having been invited
> to one of them to fill a vacant place, when I saw at once that these
> repasts are very superior to the *common* run of entertainments for
> which the *humbler* sort of J.'s acquaintances get cards)—who, I say,
> with the most good-natured feelings in the world can help wondering
> how the Jenkinses make out matters? What *is* Jenkins?—we all know—

Commissioner of the Tape and Sealing Wax Office, with 1200 a-year for a salary. Had his wife a private fortune? Pooh!—Miss Flint—one of eleven children of a small squire in Buckinghamshire. . . . How does Jenkins balance his income? I say, as every friend of his must say, How is it that he has not been outlawed long since: and that he ever came back (as he did to the surprise of everybody) last year from Boulogne?

"I," is here introduced to personify the world in general—the Mrs. Grundy of each respected reader's private circle—every one of whom can point to some families of his acquaintance who live nobody knows how. . . .

The novelist, it has been said before, knows everything, and as I am in a situation to be able to tell the public how Crawley and his wife lived without any income, may I entreat the public newspapers which are in the habit of extracting portions of the various periodical works now published, *not* to reprint the following exact narrative and calculations—of which I ought, as the discoverer, (and at some expense, too) to have the benefit? [394–5].

The persona here evoked, himself a full participant in the affairs of Vanity Fair, falls readily into the idiom of society gossip. His assertions of his own social importance and insider's status ("I dine with them . . . "), his knowing allegations of financial specificities, his contempt for poor Miss Flint with her ten siblings, his heartless wonderings about how Jenkins has escaped outlawing—all recapitulate the kind of talk through which characters in the novel assess one another. The slight exaggerations of the idiom—faintly excessive in its piling up of detail, in its use of italics, in its anti-climactic ontology ("What *is* Jenkins?")—call attention to the moral flimsiness of such discourse. The problematic status of the "I" focuses the unease of the narrative situation. The first long paragraph (in my version slightly truncated), with its apparently unselfconscious fluency of shallow reflection, hardly prepares the reader for the asserted fictionality, the essentially allegorical nature, of the "I," who turns out to be a stand-in for everyone in the social world. The notion of the "I" as personification of society contaminates "I" as novelist in the succeeding paragraph. To know everything (the narrator has made the claim of omniscience before, reporting the secret thoughts of Jos Sedley; 27) no longer seems such a fine matter, given the kind of "knowingness" exemplified in the report of Jenkins' financial affairs and the tone of self-righteousness ("and at some expense, too") that protects the speaker from consciousness of his own human weakness. Indeed, the idea of knowing everything takes on its own emphatic fictionality: the narrator appears to *know* mainly in the sense that the world knows.

The narrative "I" as personification of the world at once claims and disclaims authority. His authority derives from the weight of opinion behind him, the complex structure of assumption and conviction informing perceptions in Vanity Fair. What he sees, contemplating Jenkins, corresponds to what "people in general" would see: hence his strength. But his account of Jenkins also calls attention to the limits of his perceptions. "We all know" what Jenkins is: a commissioner. What we *don't* know reverberates powerfully in the background. Later in the novel, further specifying his sources of information, the narrator locates himself as observer. "It was at the little comfortable grand Ducal town of Pumpernickel . . . that I first saw Colonel Dobbin and his party. . . . Everybody remarked the majesty of Jos. . . . The little boy, too, we observed, had a famous appetite. . . . The Colonel . . . I remember joked the boy. . . . From our places in the stalls we could see our four friends . . . and I could not help remarking the effect . . . " (687). And so on. The narrator forces his reader to accept him as part of the world he satirizes. The logic of his presentation of Vanity Fair demands that the reader doubt him, even though the reader may share precisely the same kind of preoccupation. Like Trollope's narrator, Thackeray's suggests that the ordinary reader "admires the great and heroic in life and novels"—adding that such a reader "had better take warning and go elsewhere" (8). The hope for heroism, and charity, and even ultimate certainty will be frustrated not only by the actors in this drama but by the "character" of the story-teller himself. Only a gossip like other gossips, he points out from time to time, gratifying not the dream of larger-than-lifesize paragons but the opposed fantasy that one can touch pitch without being defiled.

Playing out the implications of the gossip's role, the narrator engages on occasion in malicious speculation: about Maria Osborne, for example, whom he discusses from the position of an ironic outsider (126). It is a paradox essential to gossip that those who engage in it must in the process combine the roles of insider and outsider. Indeed, that combination generates one of gossip's most powerful appeals. The person who talks about others must belong to their world enough to know what is going on; but the gossip speaks, often, as one judging from the position of outside observer. Gossip, as I have said before, creates its own "inside," making a unity of talkers; it creates this unity by thrusting its subject firmly out, into the position of exemplum. Gossip interprets on the basis of unlocated but insistent authority. It often disguises its malice ("she'd as soon marry the old man as the young, it's all a matter of money") as moralizing; it generates the superiority of its speakers from their capacity to condemn what they see.

The satiric tone controlling such summaries as the account of Maria sounds more familiar in novels than in life. Yet it bears affinities to conversational tones, and the pleasure it produces in the reader corresponds rather closely (with important differences generated by the crucial fact that the fictional narrator discusses fictional persons) to that of engaging in malicious but formally judicious discourse about actual people. Gossips live in a world of appearances, but hope and claim always to penetrate them. The novelistic narrator, in at least some of his performances, occupies the same slippery ground, describing appearances and proclaiming his understanding of them.

In other sequences, however, the narrator of *Vanity Fair* assumes not the gossip's ambiguous position, at once inside and outside, but the stance of moral partisan. So he describes Amelia, trying in vain to part with George's letters: "That effort was too much for her; she placed them in her bosom again—as you have seen a woman nurse a child that is dead. . . . His looks and tones, his dress, what he said and how—these relics and remembrances of dead affection were all that were left her in the world, and the business of her life, to watch the corpse of Love" (193). When he shifts from sentimental description to pure satire, his note still differs sharply from that of the gossip. "Be cautious then, young ladies; be wary how you engage. Be shy of loving frankly; never tell all you feel, or (a better way still) feel very little. . . . At any rate, never have any feelings which may make you uncomfortable, or make any promises which you cannot at any required moment command and withdraw. That is the way to get on, and be respected, and have a virtuous character in Vanity Fair" (193–4). These recommendations, like the emotionally weighted description of Amelia, belong unmistakably to the creator of fictions, who has, after all, imagined a paragon of sorts in Amelia, who protests rather too much her inimitable virtue, who turns heavy artillery on other female pretenders to attractiveness in the effort to defend his favored creation. He brings to his account of Amelia not social but authorial authority, but his narrative of the death of Amelia's hopes sounds rather thin. Its perspective seems uncomfortably simple; other sequences offer equally uncomfortable complexities. The narrator gains power over the reader both by embracing and by disdaining the role of gossip. To claim inside knowledge, to understand society as one of its inhabitants, to claim superiority in society's games—to assert dominance on such terms, only to leap outside, suddenly invoking the ethical demands of Christianity:

such verbal maneuvers are more than worthy of Becky Sharp herself. The novel, full of shifting maneuvers, shifting tones, creates its effects partly by its narrator's disturbing disjunctions of role.

Vanity Fair can disturb readers by implicating them in various levels of fictionality and by drawing them to perceive the fictions of their own existence. Amelia Sedley watching the corpse of her love and Maria Osborne stepping into the hypothetical coach of a hypothetical elderly lover both comprise metaphors of emotional and social experience, but metaphors emanating from radically different kinds of assumption and commenting on one another. The difference between the characters as presented stems mainly from the difference in the ways they inhabit the imagination of the narrator. Sometimes he speaks as embodiment of "the world," sometimes as lofty and uncontaminated onlooker. As onlooker, he imagines Amelia; as disillusioned participant, he conceives Maria. And both these roles themselves comprise fictions. The narrator's radical shifts of voice and position call attention to themselves by their diversity. "I" as personification of the world in general and "I" as stern moralist oppose one another. The narrator who penetrates the façade of the Crawleys' public appearance to anatomize their private contrivances relates oddly to the one who, late in the novel, calls attention to his efforts "to submit to the fashion at present prevailing, and only to hint at the existence of wickedness in a light, easy, and agreeable manner, so that nobody's fine feelings may be offended." He has stayed, he says, "above the water-line," showing none of the ugliness below; everything has "been proper, agreeable, and decorous" (703). The insistence with which the narrator calls attention to his own procedures demands the reader's awareness of literary artifice.

Like Trollope's narrators, Thackeray's suggests repeatedly his desire to give the reader what that reader wants. The imagined reader—probably the real one as well—wants both the gratifications of gossip and those of moral uplift, wants to contemplate the sordid with a sense of titillation and to enjoy the more soothing satisfactions of contemplating goodness in action. The narrator, setting out to gratify all wishes, thus makes one realize the degree to which moral poses, like fictional characters, constitute inventions. Gossip itself, with its combination of morally dubious substance and morally superior stance, encourages a certain confusion in its participants. Thackeray exploits the possibilities of this confusion to enforce on his readers the intricate contamination of Vanity Fair and their own involvement in it. Inasmuch as we desire from fiction both titillation and exempla, we ask of the narrator a series of incompatible poses. If he obligingly assumes them, he reminds us of a crucial aspect of that Vanity Fair we all inhabit: the degree to which it demands of its inmates—of us—a shifting sequence of self-creations.

"Everybody was always assuring everybody of something very shocking, and nobody would have been jolly if nobody had been outrageous."[5] In these words, early in *What Maisie Knew* (the first of the novels Henry James dictated rather than wrote), the narrator summarizes the moral and social atmosphere of the world inhabited by Maisie's parents and establishes the novel's theme and tone. The idiom ("shocking," "jolly") belongs to the characters; it suggests the state of emotional retardation in which members of this world exist, perpetual children enacting financial and sexual complexities ordinarily associated with adults. The shocking and outrageous, subsumed under the "jolly," supply the substance of this fiction, which focuses on how a small girl learns to survive the moral confusion and infantile emotion of her elders.

The association of the "jolly" with the "outrageous" locates the ground of social gossip. The level at which Maisie's parents are generally discussed suggests the limitation of their own sensibilities: "it was indeed a great deal to be able to say for Ida that no one but Beale desired her blood, and for Beale that if he should ever have his eyes scratched out it would be only by his wife. It was generally felt, to begin with, that they were awfully good-looking—they had really not been analysed to a deeper residuum" (20). Maisie's problem of preserving her own moral substance in a society preoccupied with such matters involves powerful clashes of value—none the less powerful for the fact that the "value" on one side is highly deliquescent.

Unlike Thackeray's narrator, James's never appreciably shifts his tone. Unlike the society gossips he evokes, he analyzes to the deepest residuum. Here is the novel's opening:

> The litigation had seemed interminable and had in fact been complicated; but by the decision on the appeal the judgement of the divorce-court was confirmed as to the assignment of the child. The father, who, though bespattered from head to foot, had made good his case, was, in pursuance of this triumph, appointed to keep her: it was not so much that the mother's character had been more absolutely damaged as that the brilliancy of a lady's complexion (and this lady's, in court, was immensely remarked) might be more regarded as showing the spots. Attached, however, to the second pronouncement was a condition that detracted, for Beale Farange, from

its sweetness—an order that he should refund to his late wife the twenty-six hundred pounds put down by her. . . . The obligation thus attributed to her adversary was no small balm to Ida's resentment; it drew a part of the sting from her defeat and compelled Mr. Farange perceptibly to lower his crest [15].

Heavy use of the passive voice, prolonged generalization of the characters into "the child," "the father," "the mother," "this lady" rather than named persons, judiciously structured sentences: such devices confirm the narrator's air of dispassionate distance. Maisie, the novel's protagonist, receives no name on the first page; she seems virtually an inanimate object, "assigned" to one parent or another, without wish or will of her own. The narrator betrays little emotion, offers no explicit judgment. His withholding of response, however, has the effect of judgment, contributing to the ironic atmosphere generated partly by the metaphors of appearance (bespattered father, brilliantly complexioned mother, lowered crest) that express the moral condition of people themselves mainly concerned with appearances. Ever so faintly amused, the narrator, avoiding explicit moral response, suggests slightly world-weary acceptance of things as they are. He sounds knowing, although not necessarily wise, and utterly in control of his story. His authority derives not from his participation in the social scheme but from his separation.

This account of the narrator makes him sound far removed from the role of gossip. Gossip, always personal, never dispassionate, full of emotion and judgment, bears little resemblance to such controlled narrative as this. Although divorce, allegations of moral and financial turpitude, and matters of child custody comprise conventional material for verbal speculation, this story-teller goes out of his way to avoid gossip's atmosphere. Yet the insistent rejection of gossip's voice and feeling only underlines the book's preoccupation with gossip's substance—not just its subject matter, but the issues of knowledge, interpretation, and morality that focus gossip as discourse. James transposes these issues into a new key; his avoidance calls attention to what it avoids.

The narrator establishes with the reader an alliance based on the superior knowingness of both. From a height of superior perception, the teller of the story follows his characters' intricate maneuvers and exposes their insufficiencies, inviting the reader to feel "jolly" because others are depicted as acting "outrageous." The novel ironically exploits an analogy between the pleasures of reading and writing fiction and those of gossip. Utterly free of moral culpability, made conscious of our freedom by its contrast with the constrictions of the depicted characters, we enjoy the pleasure of knowing and thinking about people's bad behavior; gradually the narrator supplies us with new ways of judging it. We experience a kind of apotheosis of gossip, purified, sublimated, providing gratification without contamination. The game James plays with Beale and Claude, Mrs. Wix and Maisie, as counters ends by disposing of each personage in appropriate fashion. Inasmuch as we participate vicariously in the same game, we combine (as the narrator combines) the roles of god, disposer of human fortunes, and gossip, discussant of them.

The problem of knowledge, announced by the title, assumes complex forms as the narrative develops. Initially the reader can feel superior (as the gossip feels superior), not only to Maisie but to the other actors in the drama—superior in knowledge but also in sophistication, specifically worldly knowledge, and in interpretive power, the capacity to make good use of knowledge. It is not hard to feel superior: so striking are the limitations of each character's knowledge that it might prove difficult to say who knows *least*.

Most obviously ignorant (and innocent) are Maisie and Mrs. Wix, a governess comically devoid of conventional information. Those who have or acquire social authority in the course of the action know mainly the demands of their own self-interest. They also pride themselves on knowing the ways of the world they inhabit, expert at manipulating its possibilities. Ida and Farange, Maisie's parents, know something of how the world operates, think themselves expert in discovering their own advantage (women pay Farange—pay him money—for his attention), tease or mock or rage at Maisie for her ignorance of what they understand so well. On the other hand, they know almost nothing about themselves, almost nothing about one another, almost nothing about their daughter; and they prove incapable of assessment not based on self-interest. Sir Claude, whom Maisie comes to love more than she loves her parents, knows slightly more than they. He knows, for example, his own feelings, although he fears them; and he knows what people say, or might say, about him and his doings and about Maisie's father and mother. He too, however, has conspicuous limitations. He cannot always grasp the full complexity of Maisie's feelings and instincts; he does not know how to extricate himself from the situations in which he finds himself; he proves oddly passive—apparently from moral and intellectual inadequacy—in the hands of a stronger (although no more knowledgeable) woman. The more we, as readers, come to know about these adults, the more negligible they seem; the unstressed pathos of Maisie's situation derives partly from her dependence on such inadequate guardians.

Limitation of knowledge emerges more sharply as a moral than as an intellectual failing. Beale Farange and his first wife utterly lack moral capacity and perception. Their relations with their daughter depend mainly on their anger at one another; they hope to use her as an instrument of revenge. They do not appear to know what they are doing when they require Maisie to conspire with them in obfuscation, pretending to good purposes in their final rejection of her. Both parents remarry; their second spouses turn out at least to manifest generous impulses (although impulses often closely connected to their self-concern). But they too display singular laxness of personality. Mrs. Wix speaks truly when she stigmatizes her employers as deficient in moral sense.

To connect "moral sense" with knowledge invites reassessment of Mrs. Wix and Maisie. The reader's superiority proves less secure than it initially appears; for the narrator penetrates beneath the gossip's knowledge, the knowledge of appearances, to supply evidence also of the workings of consciousness. Mrs. Wix at the outset appears to know only about romantic novels, the plots of which she relays to her student. Those plots, with their celebration of emotion and their insistence on appropriate resolutions for the good and the bad, tell us what Mrs. Wix values: the life of feeling, the romantic action, the morally satisfying outcome. Unlike the other adults, she knows something about right and wrong—although not so much, perhaps, as she believes herself to know. About a third of the way through the novel, she discusses Ida's maneuverings with Maisie, Ida's daughter. Aware of the names (although not of the significance) of her mother's lovers, Maisie elicits from Mrs. Wix the comment, accurate in ways its speaker does not intend, "Well, my dear, I must say what you *don't* know ain't worth mentioning" (91). Shortly thereafter, the governess dissolves in tears, outraged both at the conduct of Maisie's mother and at the woman's accusations that her employee has been spying and tattling. On the contrary, Mrs. Wix wails, she has "pretended, to him and to her, to myself and to you and to every one, *not* to see! It serves me right to have held my tongue before such horrors!" (92). The problem thus announced, of the proper relation between *knowing* and *saying*, yet more intricately involves Maisie herself, who learns the social advantage of silence. On the other hand, Mrs. Wix's final refusal of silence marks her moral triumph. She knows about a subject Maisie cannot comprehend, the complicated sexual relations operative in this social universe, and she knows quite a lot about the human natures involved in them. Although as a result of this knowledge she precipitates Maisie's final moral triumph, she still does not know all that Maisie knows.

What does Maisie know? First of all, what she is told. More importantly, she knows with extraordinary accuracy other people's feelings and the needs derived from them, even when those feelings do not correspond to the assertions of their possessors. She knows how to manipulate adults with small resources of her own; how to live with and accept insecurity; how to limit her claims. The awareness of others' feelings, of how to manipulate people, of how to accept insecurity, corresponds to Becky Sharp's juvenile capacities. But Maisie differs dramatically from Becky in her lack of desire to participate in the society she watches, and in her concern with her own integrity.

Maisie's capacity for acceptance of the "horrors" around her stems only partly from her lack of full knowledge about what they involve; partly that capacity derives from what her experience has taught her: to retain integrity with little outside help. Finally, Maisie, more truly than any other character in the novel, knows herself: the knowledge that sustains her. "Somehow, now that it was there, the great moment was not so bad. What helped the child was that she knew what she wanted. All her learning and learning had made her at last learn that; so that if she waited an instant to reply it was only from the desire to be nice" (275). Even Mrs. Wix achieves no comparable knowledge: she knows part but not all of what she wants, knows that she wishes to remove her charge from an atmosphere of moral corruption but not that she wants the gratification which another woman in fact receives from Sir Claude.

Maisie's moral triumph comes as something of a surprise. Only a short time before, asked by Mrs. Wix about her "moral sense," feeling within herself "something still deeper than a moral sense," but something she cannot articulate, she has found herself forced back to "the old flat shameful schoolroom plea. 'I don't know—I don't know' " (273). Mrs. Wix appears to possess effective knowledge more powerful than any Maisie can muster; Maisie's capacity to assert her own will seems still far distant. But a long process comes to fruition: Maisie knows what she has learned, having made her elders' inadequacies her means of learning. She has come far since the divorce, when "She was at the age for which all stories are true and all conceptions are stories" (27), progressing by concealments, having early discovered that although "She saw more and more; she saw too much" (28), wisdom consists in not saying what she sees. So her parents think her stupid; and even the reader, despite frequent glimpses into her hidden inner life, may not realize her full achievement.

The novel assumes at last a comic shape. Events usually perceived as tragic or pathetic, interpreted in the perspective of comedy, take on new meaning. An elaborate sequence of adult irresponsibility and amorality has miraculously ended in a happy restoration of order—not on the social level, where chaos continues to reign, but in Maisie's individual fate. She finds a proper mother at last: a woman in many ways ignorant, in many ways foolish, but willing to assume genuine responsibility. Chaotic experience generates the heroine's growth. Never really changing in character or personality, Maisie earns at last the right to be fully herself: a happy ending.

And what about gossip? By the novel's end, neither the narrator's stance nor the reader's expectations have much to do with gossip. Indeed, the book has systematically violated the expectations it established in the beginning. Titillating facts empty themselves of significance; the unseen and unsaid turn out to possess more importance than their opposites. Not events but inter-pretations make meanings. Maisie, having interpreted coherently the inco-herencies of her experience, can say what she wants—what she wants not in some fantasy version of the best of all possible worlds but what she wants given the realities she has come to understand. And the narrator, preserving unchanged his wry and distant tone, has established a new hierarchy of insight and knowledge, one mocking the reader's original expectations.

The reader, in fact, has become, like several of the characters, something of a comic butt. At the outset, although invited to smile at the superficiality of those who find the outrageous jolly, the reader is encouraged to feel interested in the same matters that concern society gossips: the ballet of shifting lovers, an uncomprehending child playing her part in its intricacies. The narrator's dry, cool tone checks any impulse of pity toward Maisie, and the plot, with its bizarrely shifting cast of characters, narrowly avoids catas-trophe for the child. Gradually, though with no change of tone, the narrator allows us to perceive Maisie's inner workings. Learning the inadequacy of standard assumptions about the consequences for children of parental in-stability, we are urged toward a new point of view. Maisie emerges as the moral superior of her parents and their varied lovers, but also as the moral superior of those content with "standard assumptions." The tone that initially promised the gratifications of gossip without the emotional penalty finally enforces the utter insufficiency of gossip's judgments. Like Maisie—indeed, *led* by Maisie—we see more and more, we see too much, and are left with nothing to say.

The nameless narrator of *Vanity Fair* identifies himself alternately as gossiping member and sternly judgmental observer of his society; he hints the fictionality of moral poses and reminds the reader that readers too desire comforting fictions. The equally nameless narrator of *What Maisie Knew* never changes his stance, yet the reader's understanding of his ironic re-moteness will probably change. The novel continually provides the data of gossip and encourages amusement at Maisie's inability to interpret it. In a comic scene at "the Exhibition," for instance, Maisie and Mrs. Beale (her father's second wife) see Beale emerging from a sideshow with a dark lady wearing a scarlet plume "as to the ownership of which Maisie was instantly eager. 'Who is she?—who is she?' " Mrs. Beale, predictably preoccupied with her husband's wickedness, observes that he never went where he said he was going— " 'the hound!' That, according to Sir Claude, had been also what her mother had not done, and Maisie could only have a sense of something that in a maturer mind would be called the way history repeats itself." She inquires once more who the woman is, is told "She's a brand-new one," comments that "She's almost black," elicits the reply, "They're always hideous," and responds, "Oh not his *wives!*" (142). The comedy of conflicting responses allows the child's innocence to torment her un-innocent stepmother and titillates the reader with vague suggestions of licentiousness. But the ultimate revelation of Maisie's wisdom suggests that the clarity and simplicity of her view say more than the angry perception of Mrs. Beale and more than the gossip's interest in Beale's sexual escapades. The apparent license to gossip offered at the novel's opening traps the reader in moral inadequacy.

Or is it that the ground of gossip changes? At the outset, the narrator invites the reader's interest in behavior, but his focus shifts from behavior to consciousness. By the final chapters, one feels the same avid interest in the movements of Maisie's psychic life that another novelist might engender in a couple's erotic arrangements. Lovingly, meticulously, the story-teller weaves his tale of inner life.

This difference was in his face, in his voice, in every look he gave her and every movement he made. They were not the looks and the movements he really wanted to show, and she could *feel* as well that they were not those she herself wanted. She had *seen* him nervous, she had *seen* everyone she had come in contact with nervous, but she had never *seen* him so nervous as this. Little by little it gave her a settled terror, a terror that partook of the coldness she had *felt* just before, at the hotel, to find herself, on his answer about Mrs. Beale, disbelieve him. She seemed to *see* at present, to *touch* across the table, as if by laying her hand on it, what he had meant when he confessed on those several occasions to fear. Why was such a man so often afraid? It must have begun to come to her now that there was one thing just such a man above all could be afraid of. He could be afraid of himself [253; my italics].

Maisie sees, feels, and touches not the tangible but the intangible. The drama of her relationships, until the very end, derives not from visible action but from developing awareness. Sir Claude's fear of himself, in the passage above, contrasts vividly with Maisie's self-confidence and self-knowledge, of which the reader has gradually become more conscious than the child. Maisie's close attention to details of Sir Claude's appearance and behavior, interesting to her only as clues to his inner life, parallels the attention induced in the reader: attention to Maisie in particular, to the subtle indications of her development. This effort to discover the hidden, the effort Maisie and the reader share, duplicates yet utterly alters the gossip's concerns. The quality of muted excitement generated in *What Maisie Knew* transforms the characteristic response to gossip. The surprise of such transformation constitutes one of James's most powerful appeals.

Perhaps the point becomes clearer in relation to such a late novel as *The Golden Bowl*, which builds eloquently on the tension between explosive possibilities of a complex erotic situation and the protagonist's determination that nothing at all should happen. A young woman marries an Italian prince; subsequently her father marries one of his daughter's close friends. The daughter's husband and the father's wife, romantically involved wih one another before their respective marriages, engage in an adulterous love affair. Although both wronged spouses come to know the fact, the father and daughter never speak of it openly to one another; neither reveals the significant knowledge to the adulterous woman; the daughter tells her husband of her awareness, but makes no demand of him. Little, in fact, happens in the novel; the love affair takes place, as it were, offstage. Yet the fiction generates an extraordinary intensity of interest, even of suspense—almost entirely focused on the sometimes nearly opaque consciousnesses of the four persons involved, as well as on that of the gossipy woman who interests herself in their behavior. That woman, Fanny Assingham, wonders what these people will *do*; the reader comes to know the more absorbing interest of what they *feel*. (In justice, it must be said that Fanny too shifts her preoccupation as the drama develops.)

By deliberately choosing such fictional material as that of these two novels, calling his readers' attention constantly to the potential for quite a different sort of narrative, James emphasizes the special character of the kind of story he writes. His narrators' particular mode of intimacy with the reader depends not on a chatty, conspiratorial tone but on the gradually revealed substance of intimate revelation. Indeed, the narrative tone partly protects against awareness of this extreme intimacy by preserving a dispassionate atmosphere. The reader's experience duplicates Fanny's: beginning, perhaps, with a disposition toward fascination with the erotic activities of glamorous people, we learn to forgo crude excitements for more subtle ones, learn how much the inner life too can provide matter for shared and provocative speculation.

The Great Gatsby offers rich material for gossiping speculation and abundant examples of such speculation among its characters, but in a tone forbidding comparable response from its readers. This novel, like James's, emphatically declares the insufficiency of gossip's attempts at interpretation. The things said about Gatsby reveal the sayers' limitations; gossip emblemizes democracy in decay. Nick Carraway's insistence on Gatsby's symbolic stature both denies and includes more trivializing accounts. All that happens in the novel happens in gossip's shadow.

Unlike the other narrators I have discussed, Fitzgerald's has a name and a history independent of the persons directly involved in the novel's action. Nick has abandoned his Midwestern origins partly because of gossip, which alleged his intention of marrying a girl whom he had no wish to marry. "The fact that gossip had published the banns was one of the reasons I had come East."[6] His self-definition depends heavily on his role as confidant— not only to Gatsby, to many others as well—a role depending on his willingness to "reserve all judgments" (1) as his father has advised. Although he does not say so directly, Nick appears to think of himself as an observer at life. His brief involvement with a woman, during the novel's action, peters out; mostly he watches and listens: the child's role in *What Maisie Knew*, the narrator's in *Vanity Fair*. Although Nick participates in the social life he describes, he separates himself from its assumptions as completely as does James's narrator; he remains, for better and for worse, an outsider.

Gatsby and Tom, the principal male characters of Nick's narrative, both inhabit an atmosphere of gossip. Tom becomes objectified in other people's talk because of his incurable womanizing. "The fact that he had [a mistress] was insisted upon wherever he was known" (24). Nick's memories of the Buchanans shortly after their marriage include an episode in which Tom gets into the papers because of a car accident with one of the chambermaids at the local hotel riding with him. Daisy obviously knows at least some of the gossip, and the facts to which it alludes. In the scene where she attempts to leave Tom for Gatsby, she responds to Tom's sentimental assertion ("Once in a while I go off on a spree and make a fool of myself, but I always come back, and in my heart I love her all the time") by alluding to a specific event in the past: "Do you know why we left Chicago? I'm surprised that they didn't treat you to the story of that little spree" (132). Tom's "sprees" turn promptly into stories, but Gatsby (whom Daisy here addresses) does not interest himself in them. Like Nick, he feels unconcerned with and untouched by gossip: he has his unsharable dream.

The novel goes to some pains to reveal gossip's vulgarity. When Nick spends an evening with Tom and his mistress and two neighbors, their talk consistently finds its natural level in gossip: Catherine's sister confides to Nick, "Neither of them can stand the person they're married to" (33); everyone speculates about Tom's marital situation and plans; even talk about the self reduces itself to a version of anecdotal gossip. Such talk makes the universal human interest in other people seem ugly, petty, unredeemable. Indeed, only Nick and Gatsby display generosity of impulse or openness of attention toward anyone but a lover. Gossip does not even, as in *Vanity Fair*, serve important emotional needs—expressing rage or envy or admiration, supplying entertainment. Nor does it fill any obvious social function. It merely fills the air, an almost tangible oppressive presence.

The gossip that surrounds Gatsby at least displays imaginative power and intrinsic interest. " 'He's a bootlegger,' said the young ladies, moving somewhere between his cocktails and his flowers. 'One time he killed a man who had found out that he was nephew to Von Hindenburg and second cousin to the devil. Reach me a rose, honey, and pour me a last drop into that there crystal glass' " (61). This parodic rendition exaggerates only slightly the kinds of thing people say about Gatsby, a figure glamorous because rich and mysterious, demanding talk because unknowable in his ostentatious cordiality and lavish hospitality. Unlike Tom, Gatsby by his actions provides no specific substance for gossip: the talk that clings around him issues entirely from fantasy. When he begins his brief love affair with Daisy, he dismisses all the servants because he "wanted somebody who wouldn't gossip" (114): undisturbed by fanciful conjecture, he cannot tolerate the idea of people making small talk out of what matters so much to him.

Gatsby's self-presentation issues as completely from fantasy as do the various versions of onlookers. Guests at his parties, engaging in "romantic speculation" (44) about him, imagine that he killed a man, that he grew up in Germany, that he can't tolerate trouble with anyone because of his sinister past. He himself imagines yet more fantastically: "After that I lived like a young rajah in all the capitals of Europe—Paris, Venice, Rome—collecting jewels, chiefly rubies, hunting big game, painting a little, things for myself only, and trying to forget something very sad that had happened to me long ago" (66). Gatsby invents himself. "The truth was that Jay Gatsby of West Egg, Long Island, sprang from his Platonic conception of himself" (99). The splendor of his imagining, like the splendor of his dream of Daisy, defies actuality. He dreams himself with the same sense of wonder that transfigures Daisy in his vision of her.

Nick identifies with Gatsby on the basis of the enormous hopefulness they share. Gatsby, innocent as Maisie in a world at least as corrupt as hers, hopes and believes that he can get what he wants. Nick hopes and believes in other human beings: hence his inclination to reserve all judgments. "Reserving judgments," he says, "is a matter of infinite hope" (1). On the next page, he speaks of Gatsby's "extraordinary gift for hope"; the failure of Gatsby's dream urges Nick toward new skepticism about people. If, as the novel's final page encourages us to believe, Gatsby's vision epitomizes the American dream of possibility, Nick's hopefulness about the hidden possibilities in others embodies another version of the same dream.

Gossip, the kind represented in *The Great Gatsby*, expresses the world's irresistible opposition to Nick's hope and Gatsby's. It opposes Nick's effort to preserve faith in infinite human possibility by conclusively demonstrating the pettiness, malice, and moral insufficiency of those who attend Long Island parties and those who drink on Sunday afternoons in New York apartments: the pettiness of the speakers more than of their subjects. To spend a few hours with Myrtle Wilson and her sister or with the lovely girls who drift through Gatsby's parties challenges belief in human dignity. Such people demonstrate by their talk their failure to take life seriously. The kind of gossip here rendered challenges Gatsby's conceptions by its relentlessly trivializing interpretation. Here, as in the other two novels I have discussed in this chapter, interpretation becomes a central issue of the text itself. Nick's narrative openly presents itself as an effort to make sense out of the senseless. Essentially Nick talks to himself, angry over what he has seen, troubled by the difficulty of reconciling himself to any available social context. Unlike Thackeray's narrator, he betrays no awareness of audience; unlike the storyteller in *What Maisie Knew*, he invites no complicity. His exercise in memory implies re-interpretation for his own purposes; he must understand Gatsby's "hope" to understand his own. In this sense a document of self-preoccupation, *The Great Gatsby* implies gossip as a perpetually rejected alternative.

Gossip—so this text has it—issues from the voices of people who deprive experience and personality of meaning to make them into conversation. Nick demands more, without knowing where to find it. He rejects the frivolity and the heartlessness which he associates with the talk he hears about Gatsby and about Tom; gossip functions in his narrative as a failure to take things seriously, a verbal equivalent for the "carelessness" he perceives in Tom and Daisy. The possibility of such an analogy suggests gossip's importance in the novel, as a repudiated possibility, dangerous and fascinating, like the Buchanans. The danger that "the East" represents for Nick is that of carelessness, of responsibility denied. He takes interpretation as his responsibility; the level of his interpretation corresponds to that of his integrity. In a corrupt society, gossip as trivialization constitutes a norm of social discourse. Scorning it, Nick tries to separate himself from corruption. Yet the interpretations gossip supplies, despite their inadequacy to the facts, constitute part of the truth of the narrative. What the community makes of Gatsby and Tom comprises part of their meaning; Nick's need to separate himself from every community he knows bespeaks his failure. He arrives at a *private* interpretation, far more compelling than the "public" interpretations offered, but inadequate inasmuch as it fails to comprehend the need of community. Gatsby, despite his gregariousness, falls into comparable failure: he believes he can follow out his dream alone, take Daisy away alone, deny the power, the necessity, of other people. The American dream of individualism takes curious forms in Nick and Gatsby; the novel exposes the inadequacy as well as the grandeur of both its embodiments.

Two opposed understandings of gossip bear on this discussion. Like the fictional gossip considered in the last chapter, gossip in *Vanity Fair*, *What Maisie Knew*, and *The Great Gatsby* speaks for a community: not for a social class, but for a smaller group implicitly concerned with its own collective power. Often the voices of gossip in these novels have no specific personal identity, a fact emphasizing the communal weight, and the potential threat, of what they say. Sometimes the fiction renders an effort to *constitute* a group by gossip. The chatter of Tom's mistress and her neighbors tries to incorporate Nick into a judging collectivity; Mrs. Sedley's discussions with her servant dramatize her effort to find a new form of society that will contain her. Always the group, whatever its size, defines itself in opposition to others: the subjects of its talk.

Unlike Trollope's novels or Wharton's, however, these books also contain characters depicted as successfully separate from the gossiping community. Amelia and Dobbin, Maisie, and Nick claim, at considerable cost, the right to other standards than those by which their fellows judge them. (Gatsby claims the same right and dies for it: an ominous suggestion.) Despite much painful experience, they preserve a kind of innocence that implies isolation. Each suffers from society's corruption, yet manages precariously to avoid it; each claims a right to privacy, denying the implication of the novels about "speculation," that privacy constitutes a convenient fiction. The reader, educated by the novels, can feel no great confidence in the continued viability of lives led only in terms of personal assumptions, but the works at least raise the possibility of such existence.

Each of the novelistic narrators insistently distinguishes himself from those he critically describes. Thackeray's story-teller, the most problematic of the three, plays games, sometimes claiming to speak as a member of the great world, but the rapid disintegration of such claims declares their factitiousness; they serve to call attention to the sources and the implications of society's judgments. And the emphasized separateness of the narrator—in James emphasized by peculiarities of tone, in Thackeray by frequent explicit discussion of the narrator's role—holds out a kind of hope. Not unambiguous hope: the identity of character and narrator in *Gatsby*, the vacillations of stance in Thackeray, the absence of explicitness in James all make it possible to deny the likelihood of sustained genuine individuality. Yet the chosen role of outsider remains at least a viable hypothesis in these novels, uncertainly exemplified in narrator and character alike.

The novels treated in the last chapter allow no such hypothesis, even in relation to their narrators. In the works I associated with speculation, one narrator, Mary Smith in *Cranford*, stresses her position as essentially *inside* the world she describes; the narrators of Wharton's novels and Trollope's do not raise the question of position except inasmuch as Trollope's story-tellers declare themselves creators of fiction: an evasion of the social issue. Eliot's narrator adopts an elevated moral tone quite at odds with the world described—so much at odds that it too insists on authorial authority while avoiding the problem of authors' involvement in social actuality. The pessimistic overtones of the fiction discussed in the last chapter can be expressed through the metaphor of gossip: the world's talk, described as serving class interests, opposes the notion of private imaginations; and each novel at least fleetingly suggests analogies between such talk and the making of fictions. To pursue the analogy implies fiction-makers' lack of freedom too. These evoked worlds, like Emma's, but more dangerously, supply no "outside": everyone must live within a social context and must speak for the enveloping society.

The narrator's position in *Vanity Fair*, *What Maisie Knew*, and *The Great Gatsby*, on the other hand, invites quite a different metaphor of gossip: one recalling positive meanings for which I argued earlier. In a kind of gossip opposed to the class-oriented, objectifying variety evoked by such novelists as Wharton, talk about other people (not necessarily malicious talk) creates closeness, becomes a means of relationship. Novels, particularly domestic novels, can accomplish precisely the same thing. If, as I believe, the sound of the human voice echoes through fiction, it is appropriate to inquire how that voice functions. Oratory and gossip represent opposed possibilities of speech. Oratory is by no means irrelevant to the novel, which draws often and heavily on the forms of public rhetoric. The novels I have here discussed interest me particularly because they combine a largely "public" rhetoric with concerns declared to be "private," and they insist on the conceivability of the private.

Novelistic narrators must find ways to draw their readers in, to create, often, an almost conspiratorial consciousness: that delicious union of concern that helps to keep one reading all night, compelled to discover, with the story-teller's guidance, how Anna Karenina meets her fate. As in the familiar conversation we call gossip, we seek in novels glimpses, knowledge, of other lives; as in gossip, someone shares information and interpretations with us. Yet the novels I have treated don't *sound* like gossip; and this fact too is important. *Vanity Fair, What Maisie Knew,* and *The Great Gatsby* make gossip part of their subject matter; and in all three novels, talk by people about other people sounds typically dull, contemptible, morally inadequate, destructive, or, at best, priggish. None of these novelists, or novelistic narrators, clearly, would acknowledge gossip as a model; all three more or less explicitly condemn it, in its malicious, objectifying mode. The repudiation of oral discourse about people in works which exist as written discourse about people in effect makes room for the novelist's undertaking. The creator of fictions dissociates himself from the world's talk, and from the world, displacing negative aspects of conversation about other people onto imagined characters. He can then feel free to exemplify an opposed (printed) discourse of intimacy, enacting a relationship with the reader that involves the illusion of shared privacy and assumes the value and the fascination of personal detail—the material and the closeness of gossip. At once public rhetoric and intimate revelation, the novels treated in this chapter both criticize the destructiveness and frivolity of hostile group articulation and testify to the importance of verbalizing shared discovery; they thus dramatize gossip's double aspect.

10

The Living Breath of Event

Nothing else on the face of the earth has the same effect as conversation between human beings.[1]

The mystery of gossip is bound up with the mysterious human need of talking. Talk we must, though we say nothing, or talk evil from sheer lack of subject-matter. When we know why man talks so much, apparently for the mere sake of talking, we shall probably be nearer to knowing why he prefers to speak and hear evil rather than good of his fellows.[2]

I think we can say that men and women do wish to talk about personal matters, *for reasons on which I am not clear.*[3]

She did not read herself, though at the time of her marriage she had been able to read a little. She did not practise it much then and during the last forty years she had lost even that habit, preferring now to be face to face with the living breath of event, fiction or news either, and being able to comment and moralise upon it. So she saw no need for literacy in women.[4]

Gossip retains its mystery. Bafflement or wonder at the necessities and the power of personal talk dominates three of these passages. The fourth, from a Faulkner novel, suggests an explanation. "Face to face with the living breath of event," commenting on it, human beings intensely feel their own reality: reason enough to talk about people.

But not the only reason. In the previous chapters, I have investigated gossip's functions and ways that it generates literary power. Fiction-writers, however, have made more extravagant claims than I, arguing on occasion a view of gossip as myth, expressing a community's principles of continuity and helping to generate its sense of continuity. Serving nostalgia, gossip can dignify it into tradition.

To associate gossip with myth, continuity, tradition, re-articulates the problem of gossip's meanings in diachronic rather than synchronic terms. As a mode of interpretation, gossip, like psychoanalysis, helps people make sense of the past in the light of the present, and of the present in relation to the past. A simple literary example is the detective story, in which the detective uses hearsay and gossip to construct retrospective explanation. Agatha Christie's Miss Marple provides a remarkably pure case in point. Old and more or less immobilized, in *The Mirror Crack'd* she epitomizes limitation, deprived of the conventional detective's obvious resources. The novel demonstrates her capacity to transform weakness into strength. She sits at home, reading movie magazines, listening to servants and visitors, collecting trivial data, putting together an interpretation that explains everything, that reveals the committer of the crime and the necessities of justice. Miss Marple exemplifies the passive woman generating power through female conversation. Taking few risks, assuming no responsibility, only listening or reading, she accumulates information to fit into meaning. "Everything's talked about," a detective inspector remarks. "It always comes to one's ears sooner or later."[5] Miss Marple comments on the *sameness* of what she reads and hears. Of her movie magazines, she observes, "A lot of gossip. A lot of scandal. A great preoccupation with who is in love with who, and all the rest of it. Really, you know, practically exactly the same sort of thing that goes on in St. Mary Mead. . . . Human nature, I mean, is just the same everywhere" (128). The detective story as a mode must assume human nature's universal consistency; one can figure out what has happened because people operate by immutable laws. The same assumption governs gossip, generating interpretations out of shared belief in the comprehensibility of motive and action.

The gossip's role, in Christie's plot, metaphorizes that of the writer. Gossip constitutes information; it becomes *truth*. The power to convert it into a pattern acceptable as truth belongs to the listener, the accumulator of fact and interpretation, who takes command of experience and finally of other people by virtue of her ability to understand and to verbalize: as the writer does.

But the gossip's position needs no analogies to the writer's. Words set down on paper provide permanence, but the more fluid permanence of oral tradition may possess equal or greater power: remaking history in talk. Communal histories partake of the mythic. Heightening the felt significance of detail through repeated tellings, those who speculate about the small happenings of their group create its legends, solidify its values, in speech. Words make communities. Two anthropologists reporting on life in a Trinidadian village write:

> Old and young delight in telling, and hearing told, all the little incidents that go on in the village. To the outsider the speed with which news spreads never ceased to be a source of amazement. Equally amazing was the celerity with which the story acquired a texture that made of the commonplace a thing of meaningful or ironic sequences, often going back to relatives long dead, or at the very least recalling to memory some comparable happening that led to unforeseen climaxes. No story was too trivial to stir an active response from the community, and to set in motion the weaving backwards and forwards in time of tales of supernatural deeds, and of retribution. Repudiating the meagerness of his everyday world, the Tocoan [resident of a settlement in northeastern Trinidad] draws on tradition and wit to fill a canvas with more than life-size figures— and always there is the humorous detail, the grotesque situation, the incisive comment.[6]

Most groups demonstrate the same collective capacity to lend "texture" to the commonplace by placing it in a context of past happenings literal or imagined—or literal touched by imagination.

Such transformative gossip, interpreting a community to itself, of course differs from garden-variety speculation about why Sue suddenly left town. It depends on a relatively stable group of talkers who feel themselves members of a larger collectivity. Everyone knows what a story is supposed to sound like as everyone knows what people are supposed to do, or not to do. Everyone knows what the community's myths affirm and wants to convert experience into new embodiment of familiar patterns. The reassurance of communal conversion counters the transgressive thrust of individual actions.

Unlike the communal gossip evoked in the last two chapters, the force of gossip as myth-making is primarily benign: unifying, reassuring, more often inclusive than exclusive, sometimes defensive but rarely aggressive. As rendered in fiction, the processes of talk that generate myths demonstrate the vitality, intimacy, attentiveness of "good" gossip, despite the fact that this gossip too on occasion has negative consequences. The talk itself, as well as its results in lasting legend, unites its participants.

Gossip of this sort serves individual as well as communal ends, and its mythicizing power operates through individuals. A Jungian psychologist suggests that gossip's stories "express the psyche's myth-making function at the personal level of storytelling, tale-telling."[7] Psyches need myths to locate themselves in their social environment. A myth, *Webster's New International Dictionary* says, is "invented as a veiled explanation of a truth." It embodies, according to the *O.E.D.*, "some popular idea concerning natural or historical phenomena." Myths are explanatory fictions; gossip that relates present to past explains communities to their members.

Novelists and short-story writers know all this. Aware of the mystery of human conversation, of the universal, inexplicable need for personal talk, they realize such talk's creative possibilities. Gossip constitutes a vivid subspecies of personal conversation. I have previously emphasized its reductive power, how it opposes the desire for heroes; but it also includes the opposite potential stressed in the account of Trinidadian story-telling. If talk about the half-surmised activities of other people often attributes petty motives, it may also, especially through often repeated stories and slowly elaborated speculation, enlarge its characters' stature. Talk inhabits a context of talk: oral "intertextuality." Gossipers' knowledge of mutual participation—shared by subjects and objects of discourse—in a community with history, knowledge, standards of its own, heightens the impact of reported detail and can magnify characters into representations of large meaning.

The psychoanalyst Hans Loewald has characterized the psychoanalytic process as resembling the co-authoring of a play by analyst and patient, a drama based on the patient's life experience. "The specific impact of a play," he writes, "depends on its being experienced both as actuality and as a fantasy creation."[8] In the psychoanalytic situation too, he argues, both participants at some level know that they are at once making up and discovering a story. The story-making of gossip shares this double aspect, and the interest in personal drama, if not the therapeutic intent of psychoanalysis. In the psychomachy of the unconscious, figures from childhood enlarge themselves into allegorical roles. Each rememberer reports intensely personal experience, yet elicited memories fall readily into generalizable patterns. Gossip conforms to a similar model. Individual human beings tell ostensibly true stories about other individuals; the compulsion toward meaning subtly shapes anecdotes into comprehensible forms. Dramas of actuality shaped by fantasy develop in the telling. Persons loom larger than in everyday life, their sexual or financial escapades removed from personal emotional consequence, converted into matter of social import.

My evidence for these assertions comes from fiction, a fact which raises an alternative interpretive possibility. Perhaps the truth is not that gossip mythologizes (can mythologize) its characters but that fiction mythologizes gossip. Maybe, as our mothers told us, gossip only trivializes; the novelist's imagination transforms it to an instrument of communal power and dignity. The novelistic act, in this case, inasmuch as it includes rendering of gossip, would involve more invention than imitation. Fiction would in effect employ gossip as a metaphor for more serious forms of creativity.

Gossip in fiction indeed carries rich metaphorical overtones, but I believe that the force assigned to it testifies to more perception than fantasy. Everyone realizes the "mysterious human need of talking"; everyone acknowledges that we can't know fully what people say to one another in private, any more than we can know another single consciousness. The elevation of gossip to an expression of communal myth-making pays tribute to speech's unpredictability. Readers have no apparent difficulty accepting gossip in fiction as an important form of creativity; perhaps we all know already that wonders may emerge from any interchange of human speech.

Sometimes, in fiction, a single voice speaks for the community. Ratliff, William Faulkner's sewing-machine salesman, travels through the rural South: "pleasant, affable, courteous, anecdotal and impenetrable. He sold perhaps three machines a year, . . . retailing from house to house the news of his four counties with the ubiquity of a newspaper and carrying personal messages from mouth to mouth . . . with the reliability of a postal service."[9] From the beginning of the Snopes saga in *The Hamlet*, Ratliff supplies observations and judgments which reflect or become the community's opinion. "He aint naturally mean. He's just soured," the salesman observes of Ab Snopes at the beginning (27). The apparent generosity of this view changes aspect as the reader and the community learn more of the army of Snopes relatives. Flem Snopes, Ab's son, at the outset a faintly ridiculous, vaguely sinister figure, made clerk at Will Varner's store because rumor has it that his father burns barns when displeased with their owners, gradually assumes Satanic stature. He becomes the focus of the community's fears, made a demonic force not only by his actions and attitudes—sufficiently evil though they are—but by the talk people share about those actions and attitudes. Ratliff supplies a center for such talk; gossip radiates from him.

The chorus of onlookers with whom Ratliff talks express themselves mainly by questions, drifting to the veranda of the hotel to discuss the village's events, taking their time to arrive at judgments. Varner's hiring of a clerk demands adjudication. "This evening they were gathered even before the sun was completely gone, looking now and then toward the dark front of

Varner's store as people will gather to look quietly at the cold embers of a lynching or at the propped ladder and open window of an elopement, since the presence of a hired white clerk in the store of a man still able to walk and with intellect still sound enough to make money mistakes at least in his own favor was as unheard of as the presence of a hired white woman in one of their own kitchens" (28). The narrator links gossip's three traditional concerns—sex, violence, money—by his analogies. In fact, Flem Snopes's arrival as clerk, at the outset apparently mainly a financial arrangement (although one already linked with violence, since fear of barn-burning motivates the hiring), in the novel's unfolding turns out to imply sex and violence: Flem marries Eula Varner, object of every male's sexual fantasies, and seizes power, manifested by acts of physical as well as financial violence.

Members of the chorus ask questions (" 'How soured?' one said after a while"; 29). Ratliff answers through stories. His elaborate tale of Ab's horse-trading, the first detailed testimony about the Snopes nature, merges into a third-person narrative of his further encounter with Ab, as though experience and telling inhabited a single continuum. The listeners and inquirers reach no conclusion about what the salesman has told them; only gradually, as the novel continues, does public opinion solidify into fear and loathing of the Snopes family, awareness of a relentless force no one can successfully oppose.

The lack of clear distinction between experience and the telling of experience may remind us of the inherent connection between the oral and the written relaying of stories. Faulkner does on a grand scale, and on the page, what Ratliff does on a smaller scale, with his voice. The vividness of the novelistic narrator and that of Ratliff as story-teller derive from different idioms; Ratliff sounds, as he should, more conversational. The sound of his voice—the written rendering of that sound—dominates the early pages of The Hamlet; his compulsion to acquire raw material for his stories controls his movements. As the Snopes saga develops, by his telling, the telling of others (sometimes undifferentiated as the voice of the community), and the telling of the novelistic narrator, Ratliff gradually becomes absorbed into it, no longer narrator, now victim of Snopesian strategy. As watcher and teller, the salesman has wrongly believed himself more powerful than those he watches. The Snopeses, however, can draw virtually everyone into their web by playing on the universal desire for gain. The Varners, at the beginning, make the mistake of thinking they can outwit Ab Snopes into working the Varner land for no recompense. Ratliff, at the end, makes the mistake of thinking himself cleverer than Flem about a financial transaction. Absorbed into the myth he has helped to create, in the unattractive role of poor schnook,

Ratliff feels the limits of the story-teller's power. Gossip transmits and interprets news of intimate happenings, but it cannot control what happens.

The two figures in *The Hamlet* who attract most mythic enlargement, as stories about them accumulate, share also their utter disengagement from community conversation. Eula Varner and Flem Snopes, whom she marries, are talked about; they do not talk. Eula, unconsciously sexual, appears passive, but entices others into her story. There is, for example, the drummer who briefly courts her. "That afternoon the night station agent told of a frightened and battered man in a pair of ruined ice-cream pants who had bought a ticket on the early train. The train was going south, though it was understood that the drummer lived in Memphis, where it was later learned he had a wife and family, but about this nobody in Frenchman's Bend either knew or cared" (133). What the station agent tells, what is "understood," "learned," known or cared about: these pieces of language, referring to the situation of a man essentially unknown to everyone, incorporate the man into the myth, a shadowy character contributing to the tale of female attraction and community possessiveness. For the community (and for the Faulknerian narrator), Eula embodies the awesome principle of mindless and irresistible attraction. This woman, described as limited in intelligence as well as in consciousness, acquires for her neighbors mythic stature; so does her husband, silently obsessed with getting and keeping, incomprehensible because he never reveals himself in talk, but ruthless, fearsomely successful, like a member of a new species in his entire separation from those who physically surround him but who, from his imagined point of view, might inhabit another universe.

Ratliff's voice sounds distinctively and powerfully only at the outset; he loses linguistic authority as he becomes incorporated in the story. All other voices are subsumed in that of Faulkner's narrator, who, unlike Ratliff and the residents of the countryside, possesses no defined history, no character, no personal involvement. He does not speak; he writes. His authority assembles details, articulates the story which the community—despite all its talk—never states in all its connections, invests the sordid with significance. As Ratliff realizes his victimization, he has an exchange with a fellow victim, Bookwright.

> "I thought you knew," [Bookwright] said. "I thought you knew everything about folks in this country."
> "I reckon I know now," Ratliff said. "But I reckon you'll still have to tell me" [360].

That need to be told, whether or not one "knows" already, unites the community. It also involves the audience of the novel, whose members come to know, as the inhabitants of the fictional country do, Snopes's villainy, yet wish and need to be told, over and over, its specific manifestations.

Ratliff speaks for as well as to his community. The narrator speaks only *to* the imagined community constituted by his readership. Shared receptivity defines this hypothetical group: its members allow themselves to be manipulated. Unlike the almost wordless manipulations of Snopes, the story-teller's written manipulation is relatively innocent. Snopes digs in a field for two weeks, knowing that people, drawing incorrect conclusions, will from their greed act to his advantage. The story-teller seeks only the "advantage" of attention. He too takes for granted greed, the avidity with which human beings hunger for a story's unfolding. But the analogy to Snopes does not go far: the narrator serves as hero, not villain, in *The Hamlet*. No representative of traditional values survives within the fictional context; all succumb to greed or to vainglorious belief in their own cleverness. The narrator alone remains impervious, telling his story forcefully, sometimes conveying wonder, but never relinquishing his aloof contempt for the Snopeses and what they represent, although he acknowledges their power to corrupt.

The narrator's role recapitulates and purifies the myth-making that takes place within the fiction. If the talk of the countryside magnifies Eula's and Flem's stature, that talk in no way protects its participants from the depredations of the relentlessly self-interested Snopeses. No individual makes the myth. The people of the community talk and listen, but, as Ratliff's example indicates, they also participate in the action their stories relate. The community, therefore, remains vulnerable. Ratliff, voice of the community, ends by speaking the insufficiency of his knowledge. The voice of the author's persona speaks only sufficiency.

The narrator draws on a life of speech and listening to evoke the texture of experience-becoming-myth; but he includes that oral life in his own more comprehensive myth. Novelists can devise richer myths than communities can, by incorporating the explanatory fictions people devise into larger patterns. In the myth-making over which Ratliff presides, the Snopes family embodies corruption. For Ratliff, Flem Snopes in his development "explains" a shift in communal power. For the novel, he "explains" by epitomizing the horror of undisciplined capitalism in the post–Civil War South. And part of Flem's meaning in the novel's pattern inheres in the fact that members of the community, helpless to resist him in any other way, tell stories about his gradual assumption and consolidation of power: about how their society changes over time.

The question of gossip's relation to the past becomes yet more immediate in *Absalom, Absalom!*, which realizes Kierkegaard's suggestion about incidents related as though they had happened fifty years ago. Most of *Absalom, Absalom!* consists of stories, told in various ways, of events occurring before, during, and immediately after the Civil War—stories told in 1909 to a young man about to go off to college in the North. These tales belong to the history of the community and, more specifically, of Rosa Coldfield, who begins the telling that comes to an unexpected end in Cambridge, Massachusetts. They mostly concern persons long dead. Yet their flavor, individually and in the intricate web they collectively comprise, has gossip's peculiar deliciousness. Past and present inhere in one another, in the minds of the story-tellers. The fragments filtered through the consciousnesses of several tellers possess immediate meaning for those who relate them. The tellers surmise, interpret, judge; they speak of themselves in the guise of reporting what has happened to others; they create and affirm the group unity, declaring that things endure and can be understood. Within the society where the stories are told, and where the actions they allude to took place, their telling serves the functions of gossip. And, like the story-telling reported in *The Hamlet*, that in *Absalom, Absalom!* dignifies its characters. A young man from New Orleans, Bon, has an octoroon mistress and a child by her; he has gone through a pseudo-marriage ceremony. His closest male friend, Henry Coldfield, kills him to prevent him from marrying the friend's sister, Judith. Sordid enough, the stuff of tabloids; but as Quentin hears this episode, mainly from his father, it sounds more like Greek tragedy, containing a record of and a response to fundamental cultural conflict; and when Quentin uncovers a more profound relationship between Henry and Bon, a deeper reason for the killing, his new story, building on the old, heightens its tragic reverberations.

The story-tellers call emphatic attention to their own processes of interpretation:

> And Judith: how else to explain her but this way? Surely Bon could not have corrupted her to fatalism in twelve days, who not only had not tried to corrupt her to unchastity but not even to defy her father. No: anything but a fatalist, who was the Sutpen with the ruthless Sutpen code of taking what it wanted provided it were strong enough, of the two children as Henry was the Coldfield with the Coldfield cluttering of morality and rules of right and wrong; who while Henry screamed and vomited, looked down from the loft that night on the spectacle of Sutpen fighting halfnaked with one of his halfnaked niggers with the same cold and attentive interest with which Sutpen

would have watched Henry fighting with a negro boy of his own age and weight. Because she could not have known the reason for her father's objection to the marriage. Henry would not have told her, and she would not have asked her father. Because, even if she had known it, it would have made no difference to her. She would have acted as Sutpen would have acted with anyone who tried to cross him: she would have taken Bon anyway.[10]

This bit of narrative by Mr. Compson begins with a question paradoxically affirming the narrator's certainty. The story continues with what "would" or "would not" or "could not" have happened, still declaring its certainties through its conditionals. It draws on a more distant past than that of the reported happenings, the childhood episode in which the sister displayed a kind of toughness impossible for her brother. The idea of family grounds the interpretation: to describe Judith as "the Sutpen with the ruthless Sutpen code" definitively characterizes her.

Surmise in the guise of certainty (or certainty in the guise of surmise) typifies gossip. Mr. Compson as narrator differentiates himself from the "mere" gossip by his purposefulness and by his tendency to convert his retrospection into moral affirmation. "Have you noticed how so often when we try to reconstruct the causes which led up to the actions of men and women, how with a sort of astonishment we find ourselves now and then reduced to the belief, the only possible belief, that they stemmed from some of the old virtues?" (121). As an explanation of Judith's behavior, the theory of simple virtue (a form of saving pride, in Compson's view) does not sound like the usual interpretations of gossip. It is myth-making, talk about other people that builds for a group an explanatory account of its own nature and origins. In someone else's version of the same events, Judith's failure to confront her father might bear quite different meanings. Far from "the only possible belief," the conviction that her conduct stemmed from one of the old virtues seems anything but inevitable. One might, for example, under-stand Judith as like Eula Varner in *The Hamlet*: a girl in a state of subdued consciousness, half aware of her own sexuality, only half willing to confront it. Mr. Compson shapes the story, and insists on the necessity of his shaping, for his own purposes, and in the interests of his class, his region, his history.

Like the other segments of the story in *Absalom, Absalom!*, Compson's narrative exists importantly in the act of its telling. The speaking that narrates the painful, splendid, unrecoverable past constitutes the novel's most sig-nificant present-tense action. When Rosa Coldfield initiates the telling, she says to Quentin, "I don't imagine you will ever come back here and settle down as a country lawyer in a little town like Jefferson, since Northern people have already seen to it that there is little left in the South for a young man. So maybe you will enter the literary profession as so many Southern gentlemen and gentlewomen too are doing now and maybe some day you will remember this and write about it. . . . Perhaps you will even remember kindly then the old woman who made you spend a whole afternoon sitting indoors and listening while she talked about people and events you were fortunate enough to escape yourself." Quentin says, "Yessum," but he thinks, *"Only she dont mean that. . . . It's because she wants it told"* (9–10).

He is only partly right. Miss Coldfield indeed wants it told, but she also wants it heard and remembered, hearing and memory being themselves forms of comparative permanence. If Quentin hears her, he will become one more repository of sacred knowledge, knowledge possessing slightly increased stability by belonging to a second person. If he remembers, the stability will extend in time. And if he writes about it—the novel thus calls attention to the meaning of its own creation—he will further enlarge stability, in time and space, giving the story to a larger audience, preserving it for a longer period.

"Not only do we need someone to get the message," Meredith Skura writes, "but we need someone just to hear it, bear witness to it, give it substance and reality."[11] Like Hans Loewald, whom I cited earlier, Skura refers here to the psychoanalytic situation. Rosa Coldfield's needs, which she expects to satisfy by telling Quentin of what happened before he was born, correspond in some respects to those of the psychoanalytic patient: she yearns to exorcise memories by sharing them, she needs to give memories substance by telling them. But her saying emerges not merely from an individual consciousness but from a representative of a class and a historical era who needs to declare herself and her history, which is also the history of her community. Faulkner's novel, by its structure and its rhetoric, insists that the tellers of its tragic story speak *for* as well as *from* their social histories.

All stories in *Absalom, Absalom!* inhabit a context of other stories (as all talk assumes other talk). The novel's contrapuntal structure emphasizes internal intertextuality; individual narrators, possessed of unique caches of information, comment on other people's tales. In the background of all the stories we hear, as surrogate listeners to this intimate oral history, exist other stories we hear only by allusion. Consciousness of what other people have said about her, the version of her story they have told, informs Rosa Coldfield's account of her brief engagement; Quentin's father, reconstructing a narrative with crucial information missing, draws heavily on the reports of nameless others. Specific items of oral tradition make their way into the text, as when Mr. Compson tells his son of a half-mythical aunt and her feud with another woman, an illustrative story, unsubstantiated, but with the flavor of truth: its meaning precisely fits the occasion. The gossip of Jefferson, mainly from the past, helps to construct the narrative we read; and the fact of that gossip, affirming communal continuity across time as well as space, insisting on the meanings a single family possesses for the society it inhabits, enriches our understanding of the community.

Faulkner seems less uncomfortable than many other writers—indeed, not uncomfortable at all—about the idea that novels, like legends, may develop from gossip. He ignores the possible malice or destructiveness of communal talk, to reveal only its positive aspects. *Absalom, Absalom!* associates the gossip's sleuthing with the historian's: a daring enterprise. Valuing hearsay evidence as a basis for social and historical (to say nothing of literary) understanding, Faulkner demonstrates without apology how the gossip's interests merge with the novelist's. Both concern themselves with story and with its meanings. Gossip extends individual memory, fragile and undependable.

> Do you mark how the wistaria, sun-impacted on this wall here, distills and penetrates this room as though (light-unimpeded) by secret and attritive progress from mote to mote of obscurity's myriad components? That is the substance of remembering—sense, sight, smell: the muscles with which we see and hear and feel—not mind, not thought: there is no such thing as memory: the brain recalls just what the muscles grope for: no more, no less: and its resultant sum is usually incorrect and false and worthy only of the name of dream [AA, 143].

Rosa Coldfield's view, that of someone trying to recapture and to communicate the substance of her lost youth, may not for everyone correspond to reality: Mr. Compson, for example, recalls the verbal as well as the physical. But Rosa's stress on memory's dreamlike fictionality applies to everyone. Gossip collectivizes memory. It may record mistakes: Mr. Compson reports, for example, the community's decision that the mysterious part-Negro boy living at Thomas Sutpen's house is the product of Sutpen's incestuous union with his own slave-mothered daughter. The community is wrong. Yet the fact of its wrongness has its own significance in Compson's memory of an experience intensely private for many of its participants and witnesses, yet collectively important even in its misinterpretations.

As the different fragmentary stories of the past converge, the figure of

Thomas Sutpen becomes increasingly mythologized. For Quentin and his college roommate, Shreve, Sutpen figures as "the demon": a designation conveying his inhuman or superhuman persistence in a plan doomed to failure by his unknowing early marriage to a woman with Negro blood— hence, in the classification of the nineteenth-century American South, "a nigger." Sutpen embodies potent virtues of his class and time and place: courage, unflagging energy, hospitality, an elaborate and undeviating sense of honor. Like others of his class and time and place, he labors for the sake of a family. The idea of a son has for him even more importance than the fact of a son. The son of his second (bigamous) marriage kills the son of his first marriage; the grandfather of the girl by whom he tries to engender a third son kills Sutpen himself, provoked to murder by the man's "demonic" disregard for persons in his pursuit of a visionary destiny. Heroic fighter through the Civil War, heroic builder and rebuilder of his estate—that estate which he has created out of mud by the power of his vision—Sutpen in his tragedy remains at core incomprehensible: a being of another order. The young men trying in a Harvard student room to reconstruct his history in fact consolidate his myth: a personal myth inherent in the larger, more awesomely tragic myth of two races sharing the South in absolute mutual dependence and absolute separation.

The myth of Sutpen is *Faulkner's* explanatory fiction, with mystery at its heart. But as *Absalom, Absalom!* unfolds its intricate patterns, those patterns increasingly emphasize the interhuman processes originating stories of Sutpens and Coldfields and Compsons. Quentin says his grandfather referred to language as "that meager and fragile thread . . . by which the little surface corners and edges of men's secret and solitary lives may be joined for an instant now and then before sinking back into the darkness where the spirit cried for the first time and was not heard and will cry for the last time and will not be heard then either" (251). The joining of secret and solitary lives by the slender thread of language constitutes a central subject of this novel. Crucial joinings often appear in mutually constructed story: Rosa telling Quentin and leading him to enact with her the penultimate chapter of her sad tale; Mr. Compson sharing with his son the vital tradition by which he lives; Quentin and Shreve, in a frozen Northern setting, working out the drama of the South and its meanings.

Quentin already knows the story in full, yet that story creates itself finally only with Shreve's collaboration. "It was Shreve speaking, though . . . it might have been either of them and was in a sense both: the voice which happened to be speaking the thought only the thinking become audible, vocal; the two of them creating between them, out of the rag-tag and bob-ends of old tales and talking, people who perhaps had never existed at all anywhere, who, shadows, were shadows not of flesh and blood which had lived and died but shadows in turn of what were . . . shades too, quiet as the visible murmur of their vaporizing breath" (303). The story, legend, myth of the shared telling (a telling at times amounting to a merging of experience between the speakers and their subjects, two young men imaginatively sharing the pathos, the tragedy, of two other young men half a century before)—that myth derives from the operations of consciousness and of language upon historical and presumably verifiable fact. Shreve recognizes that possession of facts and of interpretations determines understanding. " 'Your old man,' Shreve said. 'When your grandfather was telling this to him, he didn't know any more what your grandfather was talking about than your grandfather knew what the demon was talking about when the demon told it to him, did he? And when your old man told it to you, you wouldn't have known what anybody was talking about if you hadn't been out there and seen Clytie. Is that right?' " (274). He implies that he and Quentin, because of what they know, what they have said to one another, have created the definitive version of the tale—not only because Quentin's final visit with Rosa Coldfield to the Sutpen estate has supplied the last piece of the puzzle but because the combined sensibilities of a Northerner and a Southerner generate an interpretation peculiarly rich in meanings. Much remains surmise, in this as in other tellings of the saga, but the Quentin-Shreve account has narrative authority. Truth inheres in story: *Absalom, Absalom!* finally tells us this.

Story and *gossip* are not identical. *Absalom, Absalom!* constitutes a powerful myth of splendid Southern defeat in which a man who fails at his every significant endeavor plays the demonic role. That myth doesn't sound like gossip, it sounds like *story*: Faulkner's achievement, not the construction of women chattering over the back fence. Yet part of Faulkner's great myth of the South involves celebration of an oral culture, a set of habits and procedures by which people tell and retell, adding details, modifying interpretations, the happenings of a community conceived as an entity in time. Faulkner's fiction includes a fiction of its own making: as an interwoven texture of talk.

The talk of characters in *Absalom, Absalom!* lacks the verbal ring of gossip. Faulkner's fictional persons resemble James's in their apparent inability to converse like ordinary folk. When Rosa Coldfield points out to Quentin the wistaria's penetration of the room "as though (light-unimpeded) by secret and attritive progress from mote to mote of obscurity's myriad components," she makes a metaphysical observation not without its bearing on the narrative that includes her; she does not sound like a maiden lady talking to someone about to matriculate at Harvard. She does not sound like anyone talking to anyone. Writing here has moved far from speech. Nonetheless, the narrative proceeds (and the narrator calls attention to its procedure) mainly by a series of recorded verbal exchanges marked by intimacy (achieved, in the instance of Rosa and Quentin, by the verbal happening itself), by relentless concern with other people and with details of human experience, by preoccupation with interpretation and judgment: hallmarks of gossip in other literary avatars. Faulkner has created something like an abstraction of gossip, a purification of language and tone to meet Kierkegaardian standards. Although his narrative values the texture of human exchange, his art is not, in its renditions of speech, principally mimetic. Emphasizing the myth-making potential of intimate conversation, it eschews verbal realism to reveal the function rather than the form of gossip.

Two women writing from the other side of the racial divide that precipitates tragedy in *Absalom, Absalom!*, and writing of twentieth-century America, also emphasize the link of gossip and myth-making. "An envious heart makes a treacherous ear," remarks a character in Zora Neale Hurston's *Their Eyes Were Watching God*. "They done 'heard' 'bout you just what they hope done happened."[12] The novel consists mainly of a narrative offered by one woman to another explicitly as a means of controlling gossip: she will supply the community with the story she wants it to tell. The events she relates incorporate enlarging fictions others have previously created about her and her husbands; the novel develops a counterpoint of commentary. Toni Morrison, in *Song of Solomon*, telling of a young man's search for his family's past, mingles the realistic and fantastic—a woman without a navel, flying men, a woman who turns into a white bull—as if to suggest that only such heightening extravagances can convey the reality of internal experience. Both novels by their rhetoric and structure insist on the value of talk. "Nothing else on the face of the earth has the same effect as conversation between human beings." One effect, these books reveal, is to preserve and heighten small experience for people whom the dominant culture has deprived of significance.

Their Eyes Were Watching God opens with a scene in which people of the community sit on porches and talk.

> It was the time for sitting on porches beside the road. It was the time to hear things and talk. These sitters had been tongueless, earless, eyeless conveniences all day long. Mules and other brutes

had occupied their skins. But now, the sun and the bossman were gone, so the skins felt powerful and human. They became lords of sounds and lesser things. They passed nations through their mouths. They sat in judgment.

Seeing the woman as she was made them remember the envy they had stored up from other times. So they chewed up the back parts of their minds and swallowed with relish. They made burning statements with questions, and killing tools out of laughs [9–10].

This announcement of talk's compensatory power establishes an important theme. Janie tells Pheoby her story so that Pheoby can tell the others what she says. "Dat's just de same as me 'cause mah tongue is in mah friend's mouf." She claims that the porch-sitters misinterpret experience because they fail to understand life. "To start off wid, people like dem wastes up too much time puttin' they mouf on things they don't know nothing about. Now they got to look into me loving Tea Cake and see whether it was done right or not! They don't know if life is a mess of corn-meal dumplings, and if love is a bed-quilt!" Pheoby responds, "So long as they get a name to gnaw on they don't care whose it is, and what about, 'specially if they can make it sound like evil" (17). With these assumptions, Janie sets out to demonstrate that she has "done right," loving and living. Her tale asserts the possibility of endurance and of joy; by its end, she and her third husband, Tea Cake, represent those possibilities, epitomize the best in the black people, express a version of that victory in defeat that Sutpen embodies in *Absalom, Absalom!* But the story does not emerge in Janie's words: the novel switches to third-person narration, an unidentified narrator intervening so that the text can incorporate also the talk of others even though Janie does not hear it.

Janie's second husband, Joe Starks, becomes a focus of talk and the center of the community. Indeed, he creates the community in which he functions as mayor, postmaster, storekeeper, and central intelligence. Janie has fled with him from an arranged marriage with a much older man, a marriage which suppresses all her capacities, but Joe too proves repressive, making her keep her beautiful hair tied in a rag when she works in his store, enforcing her silence, preventing her from participating in communal life. The town talks about her and her husband, but comprehends neither. Without comprehending, it glorifies, concluding over and over again the impossibility of understanding, and deifying what it cannot understand. "The town had a basketful of feeling good and bad about Joe's positions and possessions, but none had the temerity to challenge him. They bowed down to him rather, because he was all these things, and then again he was all of these things because the town bowed down" (79–80). Once and only once, Janie makes an effort to interfere with the local gossip, intervening when she hears a group of men talking maliciously about a woman. "It's so easy to make yo'self out God Almighty when you ain't got nothin' tuh strain against but women and chickens," she says; her husband responds, "You gettin' too moufy, Janie" (117). So she lives largely in silence; until Joe dies.

The town continues to talk. As Joe lies dying, voices from the community suggest that Janie has poisoned him; after he dies, they speculate about her as a rich widow; when she becomes involved with Tea Cake, they think her behavior scandalous and insist that Tea Cake seeks only her money. After she marries Tea Cake and follows him to work in the muck of the Everglades, a new group talk about her and him: about how much they love one another, about the fact that Tea Cake beats her and then behaves more lovingly than ever. When Tea Cake, mad with rabies, tries to kill Janie, she shoots him dead: "It was the meanest moment of eternity" (273). "All of the colored people" come to the trial. "She felt them pelting her with dirty thoughts. They were there with their tongues cocked and loaded, the only real weapon left to weak folks" (275). Acquitted, she hears men talking at the front of the boardinghouse, accusing her of murder. Their talk does not trouble her; she invites them to the funeral and they transfer their hostility to another woman. By the end of her narrative, she can assert her invulnerability to the talk of her neighbors.

> "Now, Pheoby, don't feel too mean wid de rest of 'em 'cause dey's parched up from not knowin' things. Dem meatskins is *got* tuh rattle tuh make out they's alive. Let 'em consolate theyselves wid talk. 'Course, talkin' don't amount tuh uh hill uh beans when yuh can't do nothin' else. And listenin' tuh dat kind uh talk is jus' lak openin' yo' mouth and lettin' de moon shine down yo' throat. It's uh known fact, Pheoby, you got tuh *go* there tuh *know* there. Yo' papa and yo' mama and nobody else can't tell yuh and show yuh. Two things everybody's got tuh do fuh theyselves. They got tuh go tuh God, and they got tuh find out about livin' fuh theyselves" [284–5].

Janie thus declares the priority of experience to verbalization. She has acknowledged repeatedly the effectiveness of language as the weapon of the weak; now she insists that such weapons cannot hurt her, given what she has seen and done and felt. She tells Pheoby that everything has happened "jus' lak Ah told yuh"; she says she's satisfied to be back: "Ah done been tuh de horizon and back and now Ah kin set heah in mah house and live by comparisons" (284). Pheoby responds in telling terms. " 'Lawd!' Pheoby breathed out heavily, 'Ah done growed ten feet higher from jus' listenin' tuh you, Janie' " (234). The reaction calls the reader's attention to what the intervention of an impersonal narrator may have obscured: the fact that Janie has been telling her own story, creating her own myth, of Tea Cake, "the son of Evening Sun," sleeping royally in his coffin, riding "like a Pharaoh to his tomb" (281), and of "her sacrificing self" (273), her "great sorrow" (274), her fighting something worse than death (278). She has restored her losses in relating them. Pheoby grows ten feet higher in listening because the tale has affirmed the dignity of the downtrodden, making physical circumstance irrelevant to moral triumph.

Janie does not gossip about herself. She tells her story with assurance and power, out of her own need and in response to the desire of her friend. She talks from conviction that "talkin' don't amount tuh uh hill uh beans when yuh can't do nothin' else," and she makes it clear that she has done a great deal else. But everything she says assumes communal gossip as context. Not only do the allegations of other people play a part in her narrative, but she tells her story to Pheoby specifically so that Pheoby can pass it on, to become part of the community's mythology. Having suggested such a purpose at the beginning of the tale, she reiterates it at the end. "Ah know all dem sitters-and-talkers goin' tuh worry they guts into fiddle strings till dey find out whut we been talkin' 'bout. Dat's all right, Pheoby, tell 'em" (284). They won't understand, probably, but they can incorporate her story into their stock and mull over its meanings. Although the novel ends in Janie's private memories and fantasies, its power depends partly on its firm placing of private events in a larger setting. Janie's narrative has more moral grandeur than the customary fare of the porch-sitters, but she offers it to them for their use—offers it partly out of contempt, but partly out of community. With talk, these deprived citizens create their world of meaning.

Song of Solomon makes the same point. At the beginning, the protagonist, still nursing at the age of four, acquires the nickname "Milkman," circulated by gossip throughout the black community, and he can never lose it. At the end, Milkman hears about his ancestor, Solomon.

> "He flew. You know, like a bird. Just stood up in the fields one day, ran up some hill, spun around a couple of times, and was lifted up in the air. Went right on back to wherever it was he came from. . . . It like to killed the woman, the wife. . . . They say she screamed and screamed, lost her mind completely. . . ."

> She talked on and on while Milkman sat back and listened to
> gossip, stories, legends, speculations. His mind was ahead of hers,
> behind hers, with hers, and bit by bit, with what she said, what he
> knew, and what he guessed, he put it all together.[13]

Gossip, stories, legends, speculations: all the same verbal texture. "The living breath of event" blows through the communal memory that provides Milkman's final resource. Gossip links past and present: sometimes the immediate past, as when Freddie wanders through town circulating news of what has just happened, sometimes the distant past. People tell stories of a man who drops dead on his own kitchen floor because he believes himself to be falling off a cliff, or of a baby born when its mother is frightened by the apparition of a woman turning into a bull. Gossip generates the drama of the black people. Its truth or falsity matters not at all. Pilate asks, rhetorically, "What difference do it make if the thing you scared of is real or not?" (41). What matters is *feeling*, which generates itself in talk, in talk's sharing. Pilate, lacking a navel, suffers from the response of those who think her a freak. "Men frowned, women whispered and shoved their children behind them" (148). No one talks with her about her peculiarity; no one wants to risk contact with something so incomprehensible. "Her defect, frightening and exotic as it was, was also a theatrical failure. It needed intimacy, gossip, and the time it took for curiosity to become drama" (148–9). Unlike the apparition of a white bull, a woman without a navel presents herself not as manifestly dangerous or frightening, only as bizarre. People do not talk about this defect in the right way to create drama; an absence rather than a presence, it leaves nothing to say. Pilate's physical peculiarity, static, permanent, generates no drama; she remains isolated because no plausible story forms around her, she does not fit established narrative categories of natural or supernatural.

Milkman's forebears, on the other hand, turn out to provide rich material for gossip, legend, speculation. Discovering that he belongs to a dramatic action, the young man, thus freed from his sense of isolation, literally throws himself into his own hereditary story in a splendid, suicidal leap declaring his participation in the liberating legend of flight. The legend, not the flight, is specifically liberating: Milkman's "flying" presumably ends in his death. "As fleet and bright as a lodestar he wheeled toward Guitar and it did not matter which one of them would give up his ghost in the killing arms of his brother. For now he knew what Shalimar knew: If you surrendered to the air, you could *ride* it" (337). The ambiguity of this "knowing" epitomizes the novel. Only by an act of imagination can one ride the air; but in imagination, one *can*. The story Milkman finally uncovers frees him by giving him a heroic vision of himself and his family.

I have been conflating what is usually called oral tradition with what I call gossip. The merging takes place in the texts themselves: the difference between gossip and tradition, or gossip and legend, depends on the temporal emphasis of their material. Gossip deals with the present, tradition concerns the past. Both involve the working of imagination on the material of experience; both embody verbal freedom. The freedom, playfulness, and power possible in speculative talk about people become crucial resources for those with relatively little control of their own destinies. Hurston's novel and Morrison's both dramatize the pleasure and the liberation involved in making people, living or dead, into entertaining fictions: more wicked, more powerful, more exciting than real-life people, and thereby declaring possibilities closed off by social reality.

Eudora Welty, writing mainly of the experience of white Southerners, uses and merges mythologizing talk about past and present, exploiting both comic and serious possibilities. Reading through *The Collected Stories*, one encounters a series of distinctive and powerful voices, voices participating often in shifting patterns of conversation, voices that sometimes speak directly to the reader, sometimes talk to themselves. The stories contain diverse characters, settings, and events; although theme and character link some, others bear no obvious connection to one another. Yet, reading them together, one feels in touch with a community. The voices comment on one another, weaving a rich linguistic texture and affirming the necessity and the vitality and the creativity of talking about people.

Not that each voice is in itself attractive. "Petrified Man," from Welty's first published collection (1941), begins, " 'Reach in my purse and git me a cigarette without no powder in it if you kin, Mrs. Fletcher, honey,' said Leota to her ten o'clock shampoo-and-set customer. 'I don't like no perfumed cigarettes.' "[14] The vulgarity and self-centeredness of utterance, the coziness of tone dominate the entire story. Leota and Mrs. Fletcher speak mainly of other people; from their conversation emerges the tale of Mrs. Pike ("Honey, 'cute' ain't the word for what she is. I'm tellin' you, Mrs. Pike is attractive. She has her a good time. She's got a sharp eye out, Mrs. Pike has"; 17). Mrs. Pike's "sharp eye" uncovers in the petrified man of a circus sideshow a criminal wanted for raping four women in California; Leota's enthusiasm for her and her small son markedly diminishes when Mrs. Pike collects five hundred dollars' reward. But plot has relatively little to do with the story's comedy. Plot functions to reveal character—which is to say, plot uncovers what voice leaves implicit. Leota's self-absorption, vulgarity, and superficiality play themselves out in her responses to shifting circumstances as she discusses Mrs. Fletcher's pregnancy (and the absorbing question of how she herself found out about it) and her relationship with Mrs. Pike, whom she first admires for her skill at coping with social exigencies and then envies and dislikes for the same skill, expressing her rage finally by paddling Mrs. Pike's little boy, who runs away yelling, "If you're so smart, why ain't you rich?" (28)—a profoundly appropriate question.

Talking about other people, Leota reveals herself. Greedy and heartless, she cannot preserve her façade of amiability. She gets her comeuppance in comically exact fashion: nothing could punish Leota more effectively than missing a chance at money. The story, despite its dazzling precision of detail, makes the beautician representative of her type. Magnified into significance by the exactness of her rendering, Leota in all her triviality plays a vivid part in Welty's drama of the South.

In the culture Welty evokes, people talk constantly about one another, generating legends even of the present. Present and past often merge, for Welty as for Faulkner. Miss Katie Rainey, "the old lady that watches the turn of the road" until her death (428), figures in "The Wanderers" (1949) as one who not only sees but hears. The voices she hears come from her imagination. They tell contemporary truth, yet belong to the past; they speak of human recurrence. She waits for her daughter, past forty now, and she listens:

> Waiting, she heard circling her ears like the swallows beginning, talk about lovers. Circle by circle it twittered, church talk, talk in the store and post office, vulgar man talk possibly in the barbershop. Talk she could never get near now was coming to her.
> "So long as the old lady's alive, it's all behind her back."
> "Daughter wouldn't run off and leave her, she's old and crippled."
> "Left once, will again."
> "That fellow Mabry's been taking out his gun and leaving Virgie a bag of quail every other day. Anybody can see him go by the back door."
> "I declare." . . .
> "Oh, sure. Fate Rainey's a clean shot, too."
> "But ain't he heard?"

> Not Fate Rainey at all; but Mr. Mabry. It was just that the talk
> Miss Katie heard was in voices of her girlhood, and some times they
> slipped [429].

Fate Rainey is Miss Katie's dead husband; Mr. Mabry is courting her daughter. Her own experience and her daughter's merge as she listens to the voices of her community, voices of fantasy. "I been by myself all day," she tells her daughter, Virgie (430): yet this world hardly allows isolation. The community and its voices interpenetrate all experience. Miss Katie expresses truth to herself in the guise of imagined gossip.

The constant impingement on the individual of the community's voices and judgments becomes Virgie's preoccupation when left alone by her mother's death. The account of rituals and ceremonies surrounding the death, of people coming to the house of mourning and of what they say, occupies much of the story. Then Virgie, finally alone, drives to a neighboring village, looks at a cemetery, sits in the rain. Her meditations recall other people's insistent opinions. She remembers a man buried in the cemetery who "lived in another part of the world," leaving for a time, keeping his own secrets, yet never avoiding persistent assessment by those of his home place (458). Virgie avoids an encounter with Mr. Mabry, walking in the rain, who fails to see her because she wishes not to be seen. "She watched him march by. Then she was all to herself" (459). She thinks about the extreme difficulty, perhaps the impossibility, of being all to oneself. Remembering a picture of Perseus with the head of Medusa, she thinks about that too. "Cutting off the Medusa's head was the heroic act, perhaps, that made visible a horror in love, Virgie thought—the separateness" (460). Horror, yet also goal. With a black woman holding a hen, Virgie sits under a tree in the rain. "Then she and the old beggar woman, the old black thief, were there alone and together in the shelter of the big public tree, listening to the magical percussion, the world beating in their ears. They heard through falling rain the running of the horse and bear, the stroke of the leopard, the dragon's crusty slither, and the glimmer and the trumpet of the swan" (461).

Both alone and together at the story's end, Virgie and the black woman "hear" natural creatures—not so natural either, in the rural South: animals of legend, rather, imaginable out of literary tradition—in much the same way that Virgie's mother has earlier "heard" voices of the community. Isolation, separation are temporary constructions at best. In fictive isolation, the woman conjures up the alternative community of an imagined animal creation. Those surrounding Virgie in her everyday life are busybodies, compulsive interferers with and talkers about others; they will not leave her alone. Yet to live alone would be, after all, a horror. The gossip that plagues Virgie, the town's compulsive interest in the affairs of others, also affirms necessary connection: an arrangement of things superior to any imaginable alternative. Even the vision of running animals in their beauty and freedom gains intensity by being shared, if only silently.

In "Kin" (1955), Welty investigates the ties of family. These too flourish in talk about others, talk weaving a web of story that binds relatives and descendants of the story's subjects.

> "On purpose, I think she fell [in the well]," continued Kate. "Knowing there were plenty to pull her out. That was her contribution to Cousin Eva's wedding celebrations, and snitching a little of *her* glory. . . ."
>
> "There's such a thing as being unfair, Kate," said her mother. "I always say, *poor* Sister Anne."
>
> "*Poor* Sister Anne, then."
>
> "And I think Dicey just *thinks* she remembers it because she's heard it."
>
> "Well, at least she had something to be poor about!" I said irrepressibly. "Falling in the well, and being an old maid, that's two things!"
>
> Kate cried, "Don't rock so headlong!"
>
> "Maybe she even knew what she was about. Eva's Archie Fielder got drunk every whipstitch for the rest of his life," said Aunt Ethel.
>
> "Only tell me this, somebody, and I'll be quiet," I said. "What poor somebody's Sister Anne was she to begin with?" [452].

The narrator, Dicey Hastings, a young woman visiting Mississippi from the North, has lived in this community as a child. She comments, early in her story, that "Aunt Ethel and Kate, and everybody I knew here, lived as if they had never heard of anywhere else, even Jackson" (539). The dialogue about "poor Sister Anne" exemplifies the kind of conversation that preoccupies Aunt Ethel and Kate and that fascinates Dicey, even though she does not always know or remember its characters. A steady stream of reminiscence, speculation, and genealogizing recalls past scandals, softens past tragedies, recapitulates lost pleasures. It consolidates the participants' conviction that they occupy the center of the universe.

This talk helps to orient Dicey, a "double first cousin" of Kate. As cultural myths locate their people—Greeks, American Indians, Norse, whatever—

in the universe, explaining why things are as they are, so this chatter locates each individual in a universe of "kin." It tells Dicey where she belongs. When she and Kate go out in the country, to visit ancient Uncle Felix and poor Sister Anne, they go in the knowledge of family story (rumor, gossip, memory). A crowd of people occupy the house; the girls assume Uncle Felix has died. In fact Sister Anne has invited an itinerant photographer to take pictures of all comers in the parlor; as a reward, she will receive a free photograph of herself. The girls talk to Uncle Felix in a cluttered back room. He thinks himself at a battle of the past; he gives Dicey a note arranging an assignation with someone unknown, someone probably long dead. The photographer leaves at the same time as the girls. Dicey comments, "I felt the secret pang behind him—I know I did feel the cheat he had found and left in the house, the helpless, asking cheat. I felt it more and more, too strongly" (564). Then the cousins fall into gales of helpless, unaccountable laughter. Recovering, they agree in a negative judgment of Sister Anne: "She's common" (566).

The "helpless, asking cheat" in the house is Sister Anne, desperately trying to hold what she has never in fact possessed. "We're losing him fast," she says of Uncle Felix, adding, "But oh, I can't stand for you all to go! Stay—stay!" A voice from the porch says, as the girls run away, "It seems to me that things are moving in too great a rush" (562). The effort to make everyone and everything "stay," to arrest the rapid passage of time that has reduced Uncle Felix to senility, helps to account for Sister Anne's interest in the photographer. She tries to make herself beautiful for him, but she has never been beautiful; she tries to keep the girls, but they have never been with her; she insists on her integral share in a family which has long ago, by its humorous, reminiscent gossip, judged her and found her wanting: "common." At the end of the girls' fit of laughter, Dicey says, of "Aunt Beck," to whom Kate has referred, "I don't remember her." Kate responds, "But she wouldn't *let* you forget. She *made* you remember her!" (565). Characters inhabit the family story as though by force of their own wills. But in fact this story, like all gossip's stories, takes shape by the power of collective standards and assumptions. Dicey may claim to have forgotten Aunt Beck, but the aunt is remembered nonetheless: she *belongs*, identifying herself with natural beauty (she gives people flowers) even as Sister Anne connects herself with the artificial scenery of the photographer.

"Kin" hints exclusionary possibilities in what I am calling mythic gossip, the kind that solidifies the traditions of a family or a wider group. Sister Anne emerges as a character unattractive in every way, but the characterization of her as a "helpless, asking cheat" suggests pathos underlying and perhaps generating her unattractiveness. Is she excluded because unattractive, or unattractive because excluded? She epitomizes the decay of a family denying its losses through the stories it tells itself. Dicey feels sufficiently an insider to enjoy conspiratorial laughter with her cousin, but at the end of the story she thinks longingly of her Northern fiancé. She needs, after all, to escape; she feels the airlessness of the myth. In other stories, the confinement of communal myth can seem a horror. "The Whole World Knows," for instance, tells a tragic tale through the consciousness of one of its protagonists—a consciousness including awareness of what "the whole world" knows and says. The summary of town opinion issues from Ran's imagination; these undifferentiated voices resemble those heard by Miss Katie Rainey.

> He walked out on her and took his clothes down to the other end of the street. Now everybody's waiting to see how soon he'll go back. They say Jinny MacLain invites Woody out there to eat, a year younger than she is, remember when they were born. Invites, under her mama's nose. Sure, it's Woodrow Spights she invites. Who else in Morgana would there be for Jinny Stark after Ran, with even Eugene MacLain gone? She's kin to the Nesbitts. They don't say when it started, can anybody tell? At the Circle, at Miss Francine's, at Sunday School, they say, they say she will marry Woodrow; Woodrow'd jump at it but Ran will kill somebody first. . . . He used to be sweet but too much devil in him from Time was, that's Ran. He'll do something bad. He won't divorce Jinny but he'll do something bad [379].

Ran, who has left his wife, Jinny, because of her adultery, tells his own story; the narrative derives from his consciousness. His awareness of how the town incorporates his misery into its legend of itself, a legend in which everyone is pre-classified, by age and kin and personal history—this awareness intensifies his suffering. Although Ran belongs to the community from which the talk issues, he feels excluded by the irrelevance of that community's judgments to his actual feelings. The story constructed by the town's gossip exists side by side with actual events, never touching, in spite of the fact that the story includes things that have really happened. But gossip at this level concerns itself not with emotions, but only with happenings. The very power of its myths can make it intolerable.

The clearest association between gossip and myth emerges in "Asphodel" (1943). Three old maids (Cora, Phoebe, Irene) on a picnic recall the story of the ruined house, Asphodel, near which they eat their meal, and of the

people associated with that house. The language of "Asphodel" has a dignified, distant ring, as far as possible from that of gossip. "They pressed at
the pomegranate stains on their mouths. And then they began to tell over
Miss Sabina's story, their voices serene and alike: how she looked, the legend
of her beauty when she was young, the house where she was born and what
happened in it, and how she came out when she was old, and her triumphal
way, and the pitiful end when she toppled to her death in a dusty place
where she was a stranger, that she had despised and deplored" (201).

The three old maids tell much of the story, their quoted language as
stylized as the narrator's. From one point of view, this tale of loss centers
on mortality rather than the immortality associated with the flower of the
house's name and the narrative's title. Yet it also speaks of permanence, and
the women who relate past events, telling over to each other a story long
known, create immortality they fail to recognize. The story for them "was
only part of memory now" (202), but it is narrative as well as memory: a
form of preservation. Their role has always demanded that they speak the
community's happenings. When Don McInnis is first unfaithful to his wife,
Sabina, " 'We told the news,' said Cora. 'We went in a body up the hill
and into the house, weeping and wailing, hardly daring to name the name
or the deed' "(203). When the three of them hear that McInnis "was running
away to Asphodel . . . and taking the woman" (203), they go together to tell
Miss Sabina. Sabina whips her husband out of the house. That night Asphodel burns; the old maids run and tell Sabina, "and she was gratified—
but from that moment remote from us and grand. And she laid down the
law that the name of Don McInnis and the name of Asphodel were not to
cross our lips again" (204). Naming and telling: these crucial acts belong to
the chorus of women. Thus the women solidify the tradition of their place.
Sabina, as they describe her, only hears and knows news; she does not tell
it. "All news was borne to her first, and she interrupted every news-bearer.
'You don't have to tell me: I know. The woman is dead. The child is born.
The man is proved a thief' " (205).

"Asphodel" concerns itself with power. Don McInnis, from the beginning, embodies a force of nature. Sabina, compelled to marry him, must
also submit to him; but the children born of the union die, as though the
wrenching together of incompatible energies in their parents makes their
survival impossible. Gradually Sabina, despite her subordinate position, develops her own kind of force. She drives her husband away, she dominates
the village. " 'She took her stick and went down the street proclaiming and
wielding her power,' said Cora. 'Her power reached over the whole population—white and black, men and women, children, idiots, and animals—

even strangers' " (204). But she will not come to the post office, that center of ordinary human communication. When finally she appears there, she demands her letter, although "Miss Sabina never got a letter in her life. She never knew a soul beyond the town" (206). Then she seizes and tears to shreds the letters of others, and then she drops dead, having attempted to destroy the emotions and connections she cannot share. As far as the three rememberers are concerned, this episode concludes the story. "Here in the bright sun where the three old maids sat beside their little feast, Miss Sabina's was an old story, closed and complete" (206). But it has not ended after all. The apparition of a naked man, "as rude and golden as a lion" (207), drives the old maids away. They recognize him as Don McInnis. Then a herd of little goats completes their rout. They appease the goats with the contents of an untouched picnic basket; they drive away. Welty's story ends in these words: "But Phoebe laughed aloud as they made the curve. Her voice was soft, and she seemed to be still in a tender dream and an unconscious celebration—as though the picnic were not already set rudely in the past, but were the enduring and intoxicating present, still the phenomenon, the golden day" (208).

This conclusion re-articulates the issue of control. Don McInnis' male power, the old maids' telling implies, yielded to his wife's female equivalent. He continued to act out his impulses, but she assumed ascendancy in the community; McInnis, having disappeared, is assumed to be defeated. Cora, Phoebe, and Irene, functioning mainly as voices, have control of the story, thus defining reality. They too embody female power. Because they preserve communal memory, create communal myth, they serve as repositories of value. But older myths than they acknowledge also shape reality. Don McInnis becomes assimilated with Pan; as embodiment of nature, he triumphs over the confining civilization the old maids represent. Irene denies that they have seen Don McInnis ("it was a vine in the wind"; 207). Cora re-asserts female authority. " 'What Miss Sabina wouldn't have given to see him!' cried Cora at last. 'What she wouldn't have told him, what she wouldn't have done to him!' " (207). Only Phoebe acknowledges the desirability of trying to hold on to this too, incorporating this mystery into the preservations of memory and story.

Like Welty's other stories, this wonderful tale specifies and even glorifies the tattle of a small town, but it also recognizes (like "The Whole World Knows," for example) the restrictive effect of such talk. The exclusionary myths of gossip explain the community to itself. As the tone of "Asphodel" emphasizes, they rapidly become legend. Yet they also limit possibilities of understanding: although they preserve happening and locate it in a rich human context, they barely acknowledge interior event. Welty's stories, celebrating and criticizing small-town gossip, suggest both positive and negative reasons for taking gossip seriously.

"Nothing else on the face of the earth has the same effect as conversation between human beings."

"I think we can say that men and women do wish to talk about personal matters, for reasons on which I am not clear."

The fiction treated in this chapter glosses the mystery of human conversation by suggesting that transformations of "the living breath of event" occurring in and through such conversation generate narrative power and stabilize meanings for communities. This fiction also insists on the collectivity of conversation. The model of verbal functioning it sketches implies a process of interchange and mutual modification.

Speech-act theorists have called attention to the fact that saying something constitutes a meaningful act in itself. To say "I do" in the marriage ceremony amounts to a significant action—an action whose meaning is not adequately defined by the meaning of the words spoken. All speech acts have inherent meaning, exercise force in the saying, and imply consequences or achieve effects through utterance.[15]

These ideas about the significance of saying help to focus attention on an important fact about these fictions: the degree to which all assert the intrinsic power of certain kinds of speech and associate that power with the talk we call gossip—gossip on the edge of legend. The force of speech, as the narratives evoke it, derives less from the nature of language than from the nature of people. Although individual characters display individual verbal modes, what is most importantly said within these fictions draws heavily on consciousness of other people's saying. The story Rosa Coldfield tells emerges from a memory including others' accounts of those who inhabit her imagination; she talks both in conjunction with and in opposition to other remembered speakers. The specific relationship between one person's gossip and another's varies from one fiction to another. But all reiterate the communal element in speech, and suggest that the power inherent in a given act of speaking may come partly from that of other remembered or imagined speech acts. Gossip in its essence exemplifies the communal.

Faulkner's novels make the most ambitious claims for a kind of historical gossip, extending the communal myths formed by "idle talk" into a myth of the American South. Hurston and Morrison emphasize gossip's reparative function for the socially deprived. Welty stresses the sheer joy of story-making, and underlines what Hurston and Morrison also hint: the negative effects potential in even the most splendid myth-making. All four treat gossip as creator and recorder of oral tradition: in itself, a form of art.

They differ in important respects from other works we have encountered that also treat gossip as communal action. In Restoration and eighteenth-century comedy, in *Evelina*, in the fiction of Wharton, Gaskell, Trollope, Eliot and of Thackeray, James, Fitzgerald, gossip as the voice of the world utters the negative, condemning deviation from often restrictive standards, interpreting only in reductive terms. A force impossible to combat, an appropriate object of fear, this gossip exemplifies society as enemy of freedom, individuality, privacy. Although Thackeray, James, and Fitzgerald suggest the possibility of individual defiance or escape, they also acknowledge high costs in the very *effort* to escape.

The community gossip evoked by Welty and by Hurston often operates in comparable ways, but it does not have the same purely negative force, partly because both writers also acknowledge other possibilities: versions of the vision dominating Faulkner's mythic fictions. Emphasizing the importance of *story* as gossip's essential component, these writers acknowledge the difficulty of preserving necessary privacy in a universe of other people, but they also render gossip as fulfilling the ideal suggested by Hannah Arendt in lines quoted in Chapter Two ("We humanize what is going on in the world and in ourselves only by speaking of it, and in the course of speaking of it we learn to be human. . . . Humanness . . . manifests itself in a readiness to share the world with other men"). Gossip may threaten necessities of selfhood, but it does not, as in the darker fiction of Wharton, deny the possibility of individual consciousness. It may, as Welty indicates, make *isolation* a fiction; but to dwell in community does not inevitably threaten separateness just because it obviates aloneness. People in these fictions share experience by sharing stories. The works treated in this chapter celebrate the possibility of understanding achieved through narrative and demonstrate the sources of narrative in speech. They recognize that meanings generated by story may exceed the comprehension of the story-teller (Rosa Coldfield in *Absalom, Absalom!*, for example; the three old maids in "Asphodel"). Yet by stressing the roots of story in human association and human attentiveness, they insist also on not divorcing stories from tellers, and insist that the collaborative oral narratives of gossip by their communal authorship generate special density of meaning.

Epilogue

My favorite letter of those I received when newspapers proclaimed my belief that "gossip is good for you" came from a woman who assured me I would sell more books if I alleged instead that gossip is *bad* for you. She and all her friends thought so, she said, and they would buy no book affirming otherwise.

That gossip has good aspects and bad ones, that it attests to community but can violate trust, that it both helps and impedes group functioning—such observations will not appeal to the woman who offered me friendly warning. Yet even the popular press registers uneasy awareness of gossip's positive energies. *Time, Newsweek, McCall's, Family Weekly* have printed articles suggesting, with comic exaggeration or irony or careful qualification by way of protection, that gossip is fun, that it purveys useful information, that it helps avoid embarrassment (if you know your boss is sleeping with his secretary, you don't complain about her to him), that it enables people to help one another, that it offers opportunities to test moral courage. These articles often express anxiety about the activity they partially endorse, but they imply the possibility of completely separating destructive from useful gossip. "It goes without saying that gossip spread systematically to undermine someone else is neither fair nor kind," *McCall's* warns. "And deliberately trashing people at work is more than trashy: It could get them—and you—canned."[1] *Family Weekly*, under the sub-heading "An Ethic for Gossip," advocates examining "our motives to see whether we intend to do another person good or ill, to demean or inhance."[2] Such demurs deny gossip's essential ambiguity, its mixed and often unconscious motives. Reassuring

258

and connective, troubling and divisive, relentlessly ambiguous, gossip evades easy ethical distinctions.

But I wonder why, at just this moment in history, popular defenses of gossip have begun to appear; why, for that matter, it occurred to me to write this book—a book that would have been, for many reasons, inconceivable twenty years ago. An easy explanation for the *Family Weekly* phenomenon presents itself in the current proliferation of printed and televised gossip. The millions who watch and listen may enjoy reading *about* gossip as well as devouring it. And the articles I have cited all offer at least qualified justification for what may feel like a nasty habit.

The nature of the printed justifications also, however, suggests another possibility. These articles claim the importance of the trivial, the value and the pleasure of talk. They assume that people naturally interest themselves in other people. They say that one can find out things that matter by speculation about others. In simplified fashion, they argue what I have argued in trying to validate a set of assumptions long associated with women. The *National Enquirer,* the kind of television show in which husbands and wives reveal intimate details about one another—these familiar products of our culture claim for the public realm material traditionally belonging to the private. Such eliding of boundaries reveals an upswell of acknowledged interest in private matters at the same time that it effectively denies the notion of privacy.

Women, long relegated to the private sphere, have laid claim to it. By tradition talkers ("In every known culture, men have accused women of being garrulous. . . . The chattering, ranting, gossiping female, the tattler, the scold, . . . is older than fairytales."[3]), they have assumed private talk as their special province. The new "official" interest in gossip pre-empts female territory by making it respectable.

Of course, to say that calls attention to what I have asserted throughout this book: realistic fiction and such uncanonical genres as biography, autobiography, published letters and diaries long ago occupied the same ground. The slightly contemptuous eighteenth-century association of the novel with women retrospectively justifies itself in new terms: even now, the realistic novel concerns itself most often with matters generally assumed to interest women. The forms that novels often imitate—diaries, letters, biography, autobiography—deal with similar material: the stuff of private life made substance for public speculation.

To say that the realistic novel builds itself out of human detail is hardly a fresh observation. At every point in the critical spectrum, commentators on the novel emphasize the form's reliance on detail. Leo Bersani remarks that realistic novelists seem "spontaneously to make patterns of meaning from the most isolated and disparate details"; Martin Price speaks of "the peculiar intensity that the novel can lend a detail, a gesture, an event—not by loading it with symbolic import but by giving us the sense of what it is to see such detail when it is rich with the possibility of meanings, no one of which has yet been precipitated or asserted."[4] To link this use of detail—both the "spontaneous" generation of meaning and the sense of rich potential significance in isolated gestures—with the oral patterning of gossip calls attention to fiction's affinities with intimate talk about people and emphasizes the creative power latent in such talk.

The study of gossip and literature, as I have pursued it, is not in the ordinary sense "thematic": it does not attend solely to subject matter. By understanding the structural affinities between fictional narrative and gossip, as well as by noting the ubiquity of gossip as subject in Anglo-American literature of every period, one can begin to grasp the complexities of a much deprecated oral mode. Extending attention to literary forms for which no clear critical principles have been established (biography and published letters) emphasizes gossip's hermeneutic power as a narrative model. To think about how we feel reading letters in print helps us to understand what we feel in talking about other people. My argument—to repeat what I said in the first chapter—bears on life as well as on literature; and it investigates narrative roles and strategies as well as literary content.

Much literature indeed tells us, as my correspondent would wish, that gossip is bad for you. Restoration and eighteenth-century comedy, with its portrayals of mindless malice in operation; Edith Wharton's New York novels, depicting gossip as social destruction; *Middlemarch*, in which gossip speaks the community's small-mindedness; *Diana of the Crossways*, where commercial and social gossip articulate the worst in the society: all emphasize the restrictive and reductive force of collective talk about people. The central characters in these works, on the whole, do not engage in such talk, but are threatened by it. Yet only the Wharton novels fail to qualify the dark view. In Restoration plays, gossip typically speaks social truth, accurate in judgment if not necessarily precise about facts; *Middlemarch* shows gossip on occasion circulating vital information and making vital condemnations, right about Bulstrode if not about Dorothea and Will, and correct in its perception of a flaw in Lydgate if harsh in its exclusion of him. The narrator's exploitation of the reader's curiosity in *Diana of the Crossways* suggests the human necessity of the kind of verbal action that the narrative deplores.

Such novelists as Thackeray, Trollope, Gaskell, Spark, Austen, and Burney more emphatically demonstrate gossip's ambiguity, elucidating in their plots the social destructiveness, triviality, small-mindedness, or ridiculousness of such talk, but demonstrating also its life-affirming aspects *(Emma, Vanity Fair)*, its essential innocence *(Cranford)*, its educative possibilities *(The Prime of Miss Jean Brodie, Evelina)*. *Evelina* and *Emma* work out in elaborate detail a double pattern of condemning idle curiosity, idle talk, idle speculation, while showing how young women can grow by exercising their perceptions and imagination on other people.

Published personal letters and biography in general suggest how gossip is good for you, not only by using it as information and providing the intimate detail gossips delight in, but by inviting the reader into gossiplike relationships, calling attention to the universal hunger for knowledge of facts usually concealed by acquaintances, sometimes even by friends. To learn about each minute stage of a developing fit of anger in Dr. Johnson, to discover Lady Mary Wortley Montagu worrying about whether she will ever marry, to glimpse Charlotte Brontë surreptitiously cutting the eyes from potatoes satisfy needs which gossip also gratifies—and make satisfaction respectable.

Literature makes gossip acceptable as object of observation, sometimes of condemnation; as educative discourse; as analogue for narrative procedures. We enjoy reading about things we do not allow ourselves to do; gossip, like sex, thrives on the page. About gossip as about other matters, literature heightens consciousness. The arbitrary group of texts examined in this study illumine important aspects of gossip in the world. The texts reveal, for example, the ways it serves class and social as well as individual interests. And they emphasize the degree to which the very conception of gossip implies and clarifies relationship.

Gossip, of course, demands a process of relatedness among its participants; its *I*'s inevitably turn into a *we*. It also helps to define the relationship of its objects to their community. Often such definition takes place without the knowledge of those discussed, almost always without the *full* knowledge. Lydgate knows he is talked about, and that the community disapproves of his procedures, but not the devastating range and effect of its disapproval. Maisie's parents are fully delineated in society talk; Becky Sharp's fictional existence depends on how she inhabits the imaginations of her acquaintances as well as how she is directly delineated by a novelistic narrator. Literary texts can reveal the complexity of a self in its own consciousness and in the consciousness of others, uncover discrepancies between the two views, dramatize the tension of self and society (or "world"). The poignance of Lily Bart in *The House of Mirth* derives from just such complex relationships of consciousness. Literature, in short, elucidates gossip's implications and effect.

The idea of loose talk, like that of loose living, embodies both temptation and danger. Manifestations of verbal and sexual freedom often precipitate strenuous efforts at control—efforts presumably the more strenuous because those who make them feel the temptation they passionately deny. Gossip often presents itself as license, sinister excess, a frightening unleashing of impulse in language, that tumultuous outpouring which, as George Steiner noted, has long been associated with women. Yet—one more aspect of gossip's paradoxical nature—such talk itself often serves purposes of control. The unbridled fantasies Bertha Dorset spins about Lily Bart exclude the young woman from the social group to which she aspires, punishing her for deviation from restrictive norms. The tales spun by the gossips of *The School for Scandal*, riotous explosions of fancy, indices of desire, also express communal conviction about how people should and should not behave. As *The Country Wife* most richly illustrates, gossip possesses a double valence: enemy and agent of desire.

One explanation for gossip's two faces, and for its importance as literary subject, is its liminal position between public and private. Often articulated in intimate association, gossip yet speaks for groups: sometimes small subsocieties, sometimes larger communities. It circulates and ponders facts of private experience. Blurring the boundaries between the personal and the widely known, it implicitly challenges the separation of realms ("home" as opposed to what lies outside it) assumed in modern times. Gossip interprets public facts in private terms: the senator will not run for re-election because his wife will abandon him if he does. It also gives private detail general meaning: the young woman's drinking problem exemplifies the strain on women trying to do everything at once.

Flexibility, narrative energy (gossip always tells stories), moral and social ambiguity: these characteristics of gossip make it substance for literature and urge its interpreter toward literary analogies. The link between gossip as oral text and literature as its written equivalent becomes more powerful when one considers gossip as myth-making and relationship: that vision central in the fiction of William Faulkner and Eudora Welty. Literature often aspires to the condition of myth, generating narratives to help us understand the world we inhabit. And literature depends on relationship. Texts require readers, readers respond to texts. Gossip provides one model of what that response involves.

To insist on the analogy between gossip and literature serves a double hermeneutic function: it both emphasizes the importance of gossip's procedures and insights and illustrates some of literature's roots in ordinary experience. Writing and speech (whatever the laws of priority) generate sister arts. If gossip empowers the subordinated into liberated discourse, imaginative literature similarly frees its practitioners for speculation and invention. Literature is not merely literary. The novel, biography, autobiography thrive on their exploitation of "female values": attentiveness to the minute, the personal, the human. The written mode has by now acquired authority: few commentators any longer castigate the novel for immorality. On the other hand, as we have seen, gossip—more volatile, more secret, more ostentatiously female—has for several centuries been the object of fierce efforts toward suppression.

This recapitulation of my previous argument can be summarized in five words: *gossip will not be suppressed*. It thrives in secret, it speaks what needs to be said. Literature, transforming gossip's preoccupations and dramatizing its operations, testifies to its powerful forms of survival. As a model for narrative exchange, gossip provides an interpretive tool for analysis of texts. Fostering re-descriptions of reality, it allows fiction-makers to utilize its often subversive possibilities. Gossip gives voices to the dominated as well as the dominant; literature lets these voices be heard. Martin Price quotes Henry James, from "The Art of Fiction": "the essence of moral energy is to survey the whole field" *(Forms of Life,* 215). Gossip surveys the field through a peephole, but sees a great deal; its perspective shows the world from a new angle.

Notes

1 Its Problematics

1 Laurie Colwin, *Happy All the Time* (New York: Knopf, 1978), 212. " 'I don't call it gossip,' said Misty. 'I call it "emotional speculation." ' "

2 Barbara Herrnstein Smith, *On the Margins of Discourse: The Relation of Literature to Language* (Chicago: University of Chicago Press, 1978), 44.

3 Leila Ahmed, "Western Ethnocentrism and Perceptions of the Harem," *Feminist Studies*, 8 (1982), 529.

4 Richard Sennett, *The Fall of Public Man* (New York: Knopf, 1977), 18.

5 Salman Rushdie, *Midnight's Children* (New York: Knopf, 1980), 108.

6 Joseph Conrad, *Chance* (Garden City, NY: Doubleday, Page, 1914), 124.

7 Margaret Drabble, "Novelists as Inspired Gossips," *Ms.*, April 1983, 32.

8 Victor W. Turner, *The Ritual Process: Structure and Anti-Structure* (Chicago: Aldine, 1969), 100–1, 178–9; Robert C. Elliott, *The Power of Satire: Magic, Ritual, Art* (Princeton: Princeton University Press, 1960), esp. 3–100.

9 Carl Carmer, *Stars Fell on Alabama* (New York: Literary Guild, 1934), 12–13; Rachel M. Brownstein, *Becoming a Heroine: Reading About Women in Novels* (New York: Viking, 1982), 7.

10 Clifford Geertz, *The Interpretation of Cultures* (New York: Basic Books, 1973), 449, 451.

11 *The Stories of John Cheever* (New York: Knopf, 1978), 147–55.

12 Martin Heidegger, *Being and Time*, tr. John Macquarrie and Edward Robinson (New York: Harper and Row, 1962), 212–13. Heidegger's italics.

13 Sören Kierkegaard, *The Present Age*, tr. Alexander Dru (New York: Harper and Row, 1962), 69, 72, 71–2.

14 *The Rambler*, #4, 31 March 1750, The Yale Edition of the Works of Samuel Johnson, 3, ed. W. J. Bate and Albrecht B. Strauss (New Haven: Yale University Press, 1969), 22.

15 Norbert Elias, *The Civilizing Process*, vol. 1, *The History of Manners*, tr. Edmund Jephcott (New York: Pantheon, 1978), 117.

16 M. M. Bakhtin, *The Dialogic Imagination*, tr. Caryl Emerson and Michael Holquist (Austin: University of Texas Press, 1981), 280, 282, 284.
17 Wolfgang Iser considers interpersonal relations, particularly "dyadic interaction," a model for the exchange between reader and text. See *The Act of Reading: A Theory of Aesthetic Response* (Baltimore: Johns Hopkins University Press, 1978), and "Interaction Between Text and Reader," *The Reader in the Text: Essays on Audience and Interpretation*, ed. Susan R. Suleiman and Inge Crosman (Princeton: Princeton University Press, 1980), 106–19.
18 Walter Benjamin, *Reflections*, tr. Edmund Jephcott, ed. Peter Demetz (New York: Harcourt Brace Jovanovich, 1978), 302.
19 Barbara Herrnstein Smith, *On the Margins of Discourse*, 85.
20 *The Gossip* (Kentish Town: J. Bennett, 1821), #2, 10 March 1821, 13.

2 Its Reputation

1 Norbert Elias, *The Civilizing Process*, vol. 1, *The History of Manners*, tr. Edmund Jephcott (New York: Pantheon, 1978), 188.
2 Leslie Epstein, *Regina* (New York: Coward, McCann & Geoghegan, 1982), 7.
3 Simon Raven, *The Decline of the Gentleman* (New York: Simon and Schuster, 1962). The title of Chapter One is "The Age of the Gossip Column."
4 R. H. Bowers, ed., "A Middle-English Diatribe Against Backbiting," *Modern Language Notes*, 69 (1954), 161; *The Royal Book* (London: Caxton, 1484), 53, 51; *The Book of Vices and Virtues*, ed. W. Nelson Francis, Early English Text Society, 217 (1942), 60 (a fourteenth-century translation of a work first published in French, 1279); *Peter Idley's Instructions to His Son*, ed. Charlotte D'Evelyn (Boston: D. C. Heath, 1935), 2.2679, p. 151 (composed 1445–50); medieval manuscripts quoted in J. R. Owst, *Literature and Pulpit in Medieval England* (New York: Barnes and Noble, 1961), 455–6.
5 Thomas Churchyard, "The Manners of Men" (1594), *Frondes Caducae* (Auchinleck: Alexander Boswell, 1816).
6 Peter de la Primaudaye, *The French Academie*, tr. T.R., 3rd ed. (London: George Bishop, 1594), 157, 123, 434 (first published 1577 ff.); Thomas Elyot, *The Boke Named The Governour* (London, 1557), fol. 211–12 (first published 1531).
7 William Baldewyn, *A Treatise of Morall Phylosophye* (London: Edward Whitchurch, 1556), 3.13 (p. 105).
8 Richard Brathwayt, *Essaies Upon the Five Senses, with a pithie one upon Detraction* (London: Richard Whittaker, 1610), 77–8; Owen Felltham, *Resolves, Divine, Moral and Political* (London: Pickering, 1840), 114 (first published 1620); Sir George Mackenzie, *Moral Gallantry* (London: Hanna Sawbridge, 1685), 46–7; James Cleland, *The Institution of a Young Noble Man* (Oxford: Joseph Barnes, 1607), 190.
9 James Burgh, *The Dignity of Human Nature*, 2 vols. (New York, 1816), 1.14 (first published 1745); *The Ladies Library*, 3 vols. (London: Tonson, 1714), 1.359–60; *The Gentleman's Library: Containing Rules for Conduct in all Parts of Life*, 3rd ed. (London: Mears and Browne, 1734), 306 (first published 1715); James Forrester, *The Polite Philosopher: Or, An Essay on that Art which Makes a Man Happy in Himself, and Agreeable to Others*, 2nd ed. (London: J. Wilson, 1736), 32 (first published 1734).
10 [William De Britaine,] *Humane Prudence, or the Art By which a Man May Raise*

Himself and his Fortune to Grandeur, 10th ed. (London: Richard Sare, 1710), 53 (first published 1680).

11 T. L. Haines and L. W. Yaggy, *The Royal Path of Life: Or, Aims and Aids to Success and Happiness* (Chicago: Western Publishing House, 1880), 301.

12 Edna Lyall, *The Autobiography of a Slander* (London: Longmans, Green, 1894).

13 Richard Le Gallienne, "The Psychology of Gossip," *Munsey's Magazine,* 48 (1912), 124, 126, 123.

14 Samuel C. Heilman, *Synagogue Life: A Study in Symbolic Interaction* (Chicago: University of Chicago Press, 1976), 156; *Roland Barthes by Roland Barthes,* tr. Richard Howard (New York: Hill and Wang, 1977), 169; Jean B. Rosenbaum and Mayer Subrin, "The Psychology of Gossip," *Journal of the American Psychoanalytic Association,* 11 (1963), 829.

15 "The Boke of Curtasye" (c. 1430–40), 11.245–8; "What-ever thou sey, advyse thee welle!", 11.9–16, 25–32, both in *the Babees Book . . . &c.,* ed. Frederick J. Furnivall, Early English Text Society, 32 (London: Trubner, 1863), 306, 356, 357; *Peter Idley's Instructions,* 1.57–60, p. 82; Thomas Wright, *The Passions of the Minde* (London: W. Barne, 1601), 186–7; *The Gentleman's Library,* 320–1; James Burgh, *The Dignity of Human Nature,* 1.18.

16 Barnaby Rich, *Faultes Faults and Nothing Else But Faultes (1606),* ed. Melvin H. Wolf (Gainesville, FL: Scholars' Facsimiles and Reprints, 1965), 13.

17 Francis Quarles, *Enchyridion* (London: G. Hutton, 1641), 4.84.

18 T. L. Haines and L. W. Yaggy, *The Royal Path of Life,* 313.

19 Baldassare Castiglione, *The Book of the Courtier,* tr. Sir Thomas Hoby (London: Dent, 1937), 190 (first published 1561); George Savile, First Marquis of Halifax, *The Lady's New-year's Gift: or Advice to a Daughter,* 4th ed. (London: M.G. and J.P., 1692), 132–3 (first published 1688); *The Complete Works of Geoffrey Chaucer,* ed. F. N. Robinson (Boston: Houghton Mifflin, 1933), "The House of Fame," 11.345–54, 1727–70; *The Book of the Knight of La Tour-Landry,* ed. Thomas Wright, Early English Text Society, 33 (1906), 181–2 (first published in English 1484); William Alexander, *The History of Women, from the Earliest Antiquity, to the Present Time,* 3rd ed., 2 vols. (London: C. Dilly, 1782), 1.460–1.

20 *The Gentleman's Library,* 336.

21 Peter de la Primaudaye, *The French Academie,* 157.

22 [William De Britaine,] *Humane Prudence, or the Art By which a Man May Raise Himself and his Fortune to Grandeur,* 55; Abel Boyer, *Characters of the Virtues and Vices of the Age* (London: Abel Roper, 1695), 44–5; Joseph Hall, *Characters of Virtues and Vices* (London: Bradwood, 1608), 82–5; Sir George Mackenzie, *A Moral Paradox: Maintaining, That it is much easier to be Virtuous then Vitious* (London: J.B., 1685), 8–9; "Sir Walter Raleigh's Instructions to His Son and to Posterity," *Advice to a Son,* ed. Louis B. Wright (Ithaca: Cornell University Press, 1962), 26; William DeWitt Hyde, *Practical Ethics* (New York: Holt, 1892), 57–8; *The Gentleman's Library,* 337; John Evelyn, *Memoires for my Grand-son,* transcribed by Geoffrey Keynes (Oxford: Nonesuch, 1926), 80, 78 (written in 1704); [Edward John Hardy,] *"Manners Makyth Man"* (New York: Scribner's, 1887), 133.

23 Roland Barthes, *A Lover's Discourse,* tr. Richard Howard (New York: Hill and Wang, 1978), 185.

24 Robert Paine, "What Is Gossip About? An Alternative Hypothesis," *Man: Journal*

of the Royal Anthropological Institute, 2 (1967), 283; Samuel C. Heilman, *Synagogue Life*, 161; Susan Harding, "Women and Words in a Spanish Village," *Toward an Anthropology of Women*, ed. Rayna R. Reiter (New York: Monthly Review Press, 1975), 301; Jack Levin and Allan J. Kimmel, "Gossip Columns: Media Small Talk," *Journal of Communication*, 27 (1977), 169; Jerry M. Suls, "Gossip as Social Comparison," *Journal of Communication*, 27 (1977), 165; Rebecca Birch Stirling, "Some Psychological Mechanisms Operative in Gossip," *Social Forces*, 34 (1956), 265–6; Max Gluckman, "Gossip and Scandal," *Current Anthropology*, 4 (1963), 308; Stanley L. Olinick, "The Gossiping Psychoanalyst," *International Review of Psycho-Analysis*, 7 (1980), 440; John Sabini and Maury Silver, *Moralities of Everyday Life* (Oxford: Oxford University Press, 1982), 98, 102.

25 *The Complete Works of Geoffrey Chaucer*, "The Wife of Bath's Prologue," 11.525–42.

26 *The Gossips* (Shaftesbury: High House Press, 1926).

27 *The Comedy of Errors*, ed. Robert Dudley French, The Yale Shakespeare (New Haven: Yale University Press, 1926), 5.1.408–9, 410, 422; p. 66.

28 Mary Astell, *A Serious Proposal to the Ladies* (New York: Source Book Press, 1970), 142. First published 1694, 1697. My italics.

29 *The Gossip* (Kentish Town: J. Bennett, 1821), #2 (10 March 1821), 9–13; Julia C. Byrne, *Gossip of the Century: Personal and Traditional Memoirs, Social, Literary, Artistic &c.*, 2 vols. (New York: Macmillan, 1892), Preface, 1.v–vi; Henry Morley, *Gossip* (London: Chapman and Hall, 1859); John Sabini and Maury Silver, *Moralities of Everyday Life*, 100.

30 F. G. Bailey, "Gifts and Poison," *Gifts and Poison: The Politics of Reputation*, ed. F. G. Bailey (Oxford: Basil Blackwell, 1971), 1.

31 Sir Thomas Overbury, *Miscellaneous Works*, ed. Edward Rimbault (London: John Russell Smith, 1856), 50 (*Characters* first published 1614); John Evelyn, *Memoires*, 70; [Obadiah Walker,] *Of Education, Especially of Young Gentlemen* (Oxford, 1673), 252; *The Looker-On*, #66, 17 August 1793, *The British Essayists*, ed. Alexander Chalmers (Boston: Little, Brown, 1856), 36.21–2.

32 *The Book of the Knight*, 204; George Wither, *A Collection of Emblemes, Ancient and Moderne* (London: John Grismond, 1635), 246; Thomas Fuller, *The Holy State* (Cambridge: John Williams, 1642), 2, 9; *Directorium Cosmeticum or, A Directory for the Female Sex: Being A Father's Advice to his Daughter* (London: George Larkin, 1684); [Richard Allestree,] *The Ladies Calling*, 6th ed. (Oxford, 1693), 12 (first published 1673).

33 [Eliza Haywood,] *The Female Spectator*, 4 vols. (London: T. Gardner, 1745), 3.3–4.

34 [John] Gregory, *A Father's Legacy to His Daughters* (New York: Shoker and London, 1775), 57–8. First published London, 1774.

35 *The Polite Gentleman; or, Reflections Upon the several Kinds of Wit*, done out of French (London: R. Basset, 1700), 25–6. See also [Juan] Vives, *A Very Fruteful and Pleasant Booke Called The Instruction of a Christian Woman* (London, 1557), 2.3 (first published 1529); *A Discourse of Women, Shewing their Imperfections Alphabetically*, Newly Translated out of the French (London: R.T., 1673), 48; *The Whole Art of Converse* (London: Joseph Hindmarsh, 1683), 14, 84.

36 Ezra Sampson, *The Brief Remarker of the Ways of Man* (New York: Appleton, 1855), 325.

37 [Laurent Bordelon,] *The Management of the Tongue*, done out of French (Boston: B. Edes, 1783), 94 (first published 1706); [Richard Allestree,] *The Gentleman's Calling* (London : R. Norton, 1672), 101; *A Farther Essay Relating to the Female-Sex* (London: Roper and Wilkinson, 1696), 97; [Richard Allestree,] *The Ladies Calling*, 10.

38 Immanuel Kant, *The Metaphysical Principles of Virtue* (Part II of *The Metaphysics of Morals*), tr. James Ellington (Indianapolis: Bobbs-Merrill, 1964), 138.

39 Hannah Arendt, "On Humanity in Dark Times," *Men in Dark Times* (New York: Harcourt, Brace & World, [1968?]), 25.

40 Carol Gilligan, *In a Different Voice: Psychological Theory and Women's Development* (Cambridge: Harvard University Press, 1982).

41 *The Book of the Knight*, 96–7.

42 *The Civile Conversation of M. Steeven Guazzo*, the first three books translated by George Pettie, Anno 1581, and the fourth by Barth. Young, Anno 1586, 2 vols. (London: Constable, 1925), 1.68–9.

3 How It Feels

1 J. Huizinga, *Homo Ludens: A Study of the Play-Element in Culture* (London: Routledge and Kegan Paul, 1949), 13.

2 Roger D. Abrahams, "A Performance-Centered Approach to Gossip," *Man: The Journal of the Royal Anthropological Institute*, 5 (1970), 291, 293, 294.

3 Clifford Geertz, *The Interpretation of Cultures* (New York: Basic Books, 1973), 451.

4 Stanley L. Olinick, "The Gossiping Psychoanalyst," *International Review of Psycho-Analysis*, 7 (1980), 441–3; Samuel C. Heilman, *Synagogue Life: A Study in Symbolic Interaction* (Chicago: University of Chicago Press, 1976), 156.

5 Olinick has also pursued this analogy, in ways rather different from mine.

6 Sigmund Freud, *Jokes and Their Relation to the Unconscious*, tr. James Strachey (New York: Norton, 1963), 90.

7 George Meredith, *Diana of the Crossways* (New York: Norton, 1973), 292.

8 *Persuasion, The Novels of Jane Austen*, ed. R. W. Chapman, 3rd ed. (Oxford: Oxford University Press, 1933), 5.155, 156. First published 1818.

9 Muriel Spark, *The Prime of Miss Jean Brodie* (New York: Dell, 1966), 25. First published 1961.

10 Erik H. Erikson, *Toys and Reasons: Stages in the Ritualization of Experience* (New York: Norton, 1979), 88.

11 D. W. Winnicott, "The Location of Cultural Experience," *International Journal of Psycho-Analysis*, 48 (1967), 368, 372.

12 Doris Lessing, *The Golden Notebook* (London: Michael Joseph, 1982), 25. First published 1962.

4 Borderlands

1 Keith Stewart, "Towards Defining an Aesthetic for the Familiar Letter in Eighteenth-Century England," *Prose Studies*, 5 (1982), 179–92.

2 Michel Foucault, *The History of Sexuality*, vol. 1, tr. Robert Hurley (New York: Pantheon, 1978), 107.

3 *Northanger Abbey, The Novels of Jane Austen*, ed. R. W. Chapman, 3rd ed. (Oxford: Oxford University Press, 1933), 5.108. First published 1818.

4 Walter Benjamin, "The Work of Art in the Age of Mechanical Reproduction," *Illuminations*, tr. Harry Zohn (New York: Harcourt, Brace & World, 1968), 222, 225.

5 To Mrs. Frances Hewet [13 February 1710], *The Complete Letters of Lady Mary Wortley Montagu*, ed. Robert Halsband, 3 vols. (Oxford: Clarendon Press, 1965), 1.21–2.

6 4 September 1789, *Horace Walpole's Correspondence with Mary and Agnes Berry and Barbara Cecilia Seton*, ed. W. S. Lewis and A. Dayle Wallace with the assistance of Charles H. Bennett and Edwine M. Martz, vol. 11 of The Yale Edition of Horace Walpole's Correspondence (New Haven: Yale University Press, 1944), 64–5, 66.

7 13 December 1759, *Horace Walpole's Correspondence with Sir Horace Mann*, ed. W. S. Lewis, Warren Hunting Smith, and George L. Lam, vol. 21 of The Yale Edition of Horace Walpole's Correspondence (New Haven: Yale University Press, 1960), 353.

8 23 June 1750, *Horace Walpole's Correspondence with George Montagu*, ed. W. S. Lewis and Ralph S. Brown, Jr., vol. 9 of The Yale Edition of Horace Walpole's Correspondence (New Haven: Yale University Press, 1941), 108–9.

9 23 April 1740 N.S., *Correspondence with Mann*, 17 (1954), 12.

10 26 June 1785, *Horace Walpole's Correspondence with Thomas Chatterton, Michael Lort . . .* , ed. W. S. Lewis and A. Dayle Wallace, vol. 16 of The Yale Edition of Horace Walpole's Correspondence (New Haven: Yale University Press, 1951), 268.

11 *Letters of E. B. White*, collected and edited by Dorothy Lobrano Guth (New York: Harper and Row, 1976), x.

12 Walter Benjamin, *Illuminations*, 234.

13 Robert Adams Day, *Told in Letters: Epistolary Fiction Before Richardson* (Ann Arbor: University of Michigan Press, 1966), 6.

5 Biography: Moral and Physical Truth

1 Ernst Kris, "The Image of the Artist," *Psychoanalytic Explorations in Art* (New York: International Universities Press, 1952), 74.

2 William Dowling, *The Boswellian Hero* (Athens: University of Georgia Press, 1979); *Language and Logos in Boswell's Life of Johnson* (Princeton: Princeton University Press, 1981).

3 Frank Brady, "The Strategies of Biography and Some Eighteenth-Century Examples," *Literary Theory and Structure: Essays in Honor of William K. Winsatt*, ed. Frank Brady, John Palmer, Martin Price (New Haven: Yale University Press, 1973), 246.

4 *Boswell's Life of Johnson*, ed. George Birkbeck Hill, revised and enlarged by L. F. Powell, 6 vols. (Oxford: Clarendon Press, 1934), 4.6. First published 1791.

5 W. Jackson Bate, *Samuel Johnson* (New York: Harcourt Brace Jovanovich, 1977), 561.

6 26 May 1791, *Horace Walpole's Correspondence with Mary and Agnes Berry and Barbara Cecilia Seton*, ed. W. S. Lewis and A. Dayle Wallace with the assistance of Charles H. Bennett and Edwine M. Martz, vol. 11 of The Yale Edition of Horace Walpole's Correspondence (New Haven: Yale University Press, 1944), 275.

7 Thomas G. Pavel, "Literary Criticism and Methodology," *Dispositio*, 3 (1978), 147–8.

8 Sir John Hawkins, *The Life of Samuel Johnson, LL.D.*, ed. and abridged Bertram H. Davis (New York: Macmillan, 1961), 18. First published 1787.

9 Elizabeth C. Gaskell, *The Life of Charlotte Brontë*, 2 vols. (New York: Appleton, 1857), 1.76.

10 *The Rambler*, #60, 13 October 1750, The Yale Edition of the Works of Samuel Johnson, 3, ed. W. J. Bate and Albrecht B. Strauss (New Haven: Yale University Press, 1969), 318–19.

11 Helene Moglen, *Charlotte Brontë: The Self Conceived* (New York: Norton, 1976), 13.

12 "Notebooks of Joseph Joubert," selected and tr. Paul Auster, *The New Criterion* 1:4 (December 1982), 22.

13 Frank Brady offers an interesting counter-case, of Johnson as unreliable narrator in the *Life of Savage*. See "The Strategies of Biography," 252.

6 "What Would the World Say?"

1 *The Provok'd Wife*, 1.1, *The Complete Works of Sir John Vanbrugh*, ed. Bonamy Dobree (New York: AMS Press, 1967), 1.119.

2 *The Dutchesse of Malfy*, 1.1. 375–9, *The Complete Works of John Webster*, ed. F. L. Lucas (London: Chatto & Windus, 1927), 2.46.

3 William, Lord Burghley, *Precepts* (London: Thomas Jones, 1637), 60.

4 George Wither, A *Collection of Emblemes, Ancient and Moderne* (London: John Grismond, 1635), 246.

5 Barnabe Rych, *The Excellency of Good Women* (London: Thomas Dawson, 1613), 28.

6 *The Character of A Coffee-House, with the Symptomes of a Town-Wit* (London: Jonathan Edwin, 1673), 6.

7 The quotations come, in order, from Richard Flecknoe, *Enigmaticall Characters* (1658), 86–7; Richard Brathwayt, *Essaies Upon the Five Senses, with a pithie one upon Detraction* (London: Richard Whittaker, 1610), 77; A *Discourse of Women, Shewing their Imperfections Alphabetically*, Newly Translated out of the French into English (London: R.T., 1673), 69; Abel Boyer, *Characters of the Virtues and Vices of the Age* (London: Abel Roper, 1695), 45.

8 *The Way of the World*, 1.1, *The Complete Plays of William Congreve*, ed. Herbert Davis (Chicago: University of Chicago Press, 1967), 396. Subsequent citations of Congreve will be incorporated in the text, with act, scene, and page numbers from this edition.

9 *Love in a Wood*, 2.1, *The Complete Works of William Wycherley*, ed. Montague Summers (London: Nonesuch, 1924), 1.95. Subsequent citations of Wycherley will be incorporated in the text, with act, scene, and page numbers from this edition.

10 [William De Britaine,] *Humane Prudence, or the Art By which a Man May Raise Himself and his Fortune to Grandeur*, 10th ed. (London: Richard Sare, 1710), 58.

11 [Obadiah Walker,] *Of Education, Especially of Young Gentlemen* (Oxford, 1673), 252.

12 Francis Bacon, "Of Suspicion," *Essays and New Atlantis*, ed. Gordon S. Haight (New York: Van Nostrand, 1942), 138. First published 1597.

13 Mary Astell, A *Serious Proposal to the Ladies* (New York: Source Book Press, 1970), 74. First published 1694 (Part I), 1697 (Part II).

14 Sir George Mackenzie, A *Consolation Against Calumnies: Shewing how to bear them easily and pleasantly* (London: T.B., 1685), 9.

15 All citations of *The Country Wife* come from volume 2 of Wycherley's *Works*.

16 [Richard Allestree,] *The Ladies Calling*, 6th ed. (Oxford, 1693), 77–8. First published 1673.

17 [Pierre d'Ortique, probable author,] *The Art of Pleasing Conversation*, tr. from French (London: Richard Wellington, 1708), 137. First published 1691. The name of Cardinal Richelieu appears as author, but this is almost certainly a false attribution.

18 "Prologue," by David Garrick, *The Plays and Poems of Richard Brinsley Sheridan*, ed. R. Crompton Rhodes, 3 vols. (New York: Macmillan, 1929), 3.23. Subsequent citations of *The School for Scandal*, with act, scene, and page numbers, will refer to this volume.

19 *The Ladies Library*, 3 vols. (London: Tonson, 1714), 1.358.

20 Laurent Bordelon, *The Management of the Tongue*, tr. from French (Boston: B. Eades, 1783), 60. First published 1706.

21 James Forrester, *The Polite Philosopher: Or, An Essay on that Art which Makes a Man Happy in Himself, and Agreeable to Others*, 2nd ed. (London: J. Wilson, 1736),25–6. First published 1734.

22 *The Ladies Library*, 1.359–60.

23 *The Spectator*, #348, 9 April 1712, *The Spectator*, ed. George A. Aitken, 8 vols. (London: John C. Nimmo, 1898), 5.150.

24 John Essex, *The Young Ladies Conduct: Or, Rules for Education* (London: John Brotherton, 1722), 91–2.

25 *The Gentleman's Library: Containing Rules for Conduct in all Parts of Life*, 3rd ed. (London: Mears and Browne, 1734), 337.

7 *The Talent of Ready Utterance*

1 *Advice from a Lady of Quality, to Her Children; in the Last Stage of a Lingering Illness*, tr. from the French by S. Glasse, 4th ed. (Gloucester: B. Raikes, 1796), 78.

2 *The Spectator*, #247, 13 December 1711, *The Spectator*, ed. George A. Aitken, 8 vols. (London: John C. Nimmo, 1898), 3.377.

3 James Fordyce, *Sermons to Young Women* (Philadelphia: Thomas Dobson, 1787), 194. First published 1765.

4 John Bennet, *Letters to a Young Lady, on a Variety of Useful and Interesting Subjects. Calculated to Improve the Heart, to Form the Manners and Enlighten the Understanding*, 6th American ed. (Hudson: William Norman, 1811), 124. First published 1789.

5 *The Spectator*, #228, 21 November 1711, *The Spectator*, 3.28.

6 *The Rambler*, #188, 4 January 1752, The Yale Edition of the Works of Samuel Johnson, 5, ed. W. J. Bate and Albrecht B. Strauss (New Haven: Yale University Press, 1969), 222.

7 *The Rambler*, #60, 13 October 1750, The Yale Edition, 3.320.

8 *The Rambler*, #4, 31 March 1750, The Yale Edition, 3.22.

9 [Eliza Haywood,] *The Female Spectator*, 4 vols. (London: T. Gardner, 1745), 3.

10 Frances Burney, *Evelina, or the History of a Young Lady's Entrance into the World*, ed. Edward A. Bloom (London: Oxford University Press, 1970), 262. First published 1778.

11 Norbert Elias, *The Civilizing Process*, vol. 1, *The History of Manners*, tr. Edmund Jephcott (New York: Pantheon, 1978), e.g., 190.

12 J. Hillis Miller, "Narrative and History," *English Literary History*, 41 (1974), 456.

13 John Vernon, "Reading, Writing, and Eavesdropping: Some Thoughts on the Nature of Realistic Fiction," *The Kenyon Review*, N.S., 4:4 (Fall 1982), 46.

14 See Janet Gurkin Altman, *Epistolarity: Approaches to a Form* (Columbus: Ohio State University Press, 1982), 185.

15 *Emma, The Novels of Jane Austen*, ed. R. W. Chapman, 3rd ed. (Oxford: Oxford University Press, 1933), 4.286.

16 Homer Brown, "The Errant Letter and the Whispering Gallery," *Genre*, 10 (1977), 574–5.

8 Social Speculation

1 Raymond Williams, *The English Novel: From Dickens to Lawrence* (London: Chatto & Windus, 1970), 91.

2 Edith Wharton, *The House of Mirth*, ed. R. W. B. Lewis (New York: New York University Press, 1977), 1. First published 1905.

3 Ezra Sampson, *The Brief Remarker on the Ways of Men* (New York: Appleton, 1855), 322–3.

4 *The Young Lady's Own Book: A Manual of Intellectual Improvement and Moral Deportment* (Philadelphia: Key & Biddle, 1833), 282.

5 Edith Wharton, *The Custom of the Country* (New York: Berkley, 1981), 133. First published 1913.

6 Jane West, *A Gossip's Story, and A Legendary Tale*, 2nd ed., 2 vols. (London: T. N. Longman, 1797), 1.2.

7 The opening sentence of Elizabeth Gaskell, *Cranford*, ed. Elizabeth Porges Watson (London: Oxford University Press, 1972), 1. First published 1853.

8 Arthur M. Schlesinger, *Learning How to Behave: A Historical Study of American Etiquette Books* (New York: Macmillan, 1946), 65.

9 Norbert Elias, *The Civilizing Process*, vol. 1, *The History of Manners*, tr. Edmund Jephcott (New York: Pantheon, 1978), e.g., 116.

10 Edith Wharton, *The Age of Innocence* (New York: Appleton-Century-Crofts, 1948), 42. First published 1920.

11 Anthony Trollope, *The Eustace Diamonds*, 2 vols. (London: Oxford University Press, 1950), 2.375. First published in book form 1872.

12 Anthony Trollope, *Barchester Towers*, 2 vols. (New York: Dodd, Mead, 1893), 2.323. First published 1857.

13 Theodor Fontane, *Ein Sommer in London* (1852), qu. Norbert Elias, *The Civilizing Process*, 33.

14 George Eliot, *Middlemarch*, ed. Gordon S. Haight (Boston: Houghton Mifflin, 1956), 302. First published 1871–2.

15 D. A. Miller, *Narrative and Its Discontents: Problems of Closure in the Traditional Novel* (Princeton: Princeton University Press, 1981), 120.

9 *Stepping Down from the Platform*

1 William Makepeace Thackeray, *Vanity Fair* (New York: Heritage Press, 1940), 88. First published 1847–8.
2 James Hillman, *The Myth of Analysis: Three Essays in Archetypal Psychology* (New York: Harper and Row, 1978), 26.
3 Emily Brontë, *Wuthering Heights*, ed. Hilda Marsden and Ian Jack (Oxford: Clarendon Press, 1976), 40. First published 1847.
4 Laurence Sterne, *Tristram Shandy*, ed. James A. Work (New York: Odyssey Press, 1940), 49. First published 1759–67.
5 Henry James, *What Maisie Knew* (Garden City, NY: Doubleday, 1954), 20. First published 1897.
6 F. Scott Fitzgerald, *The Great Gatsby* (New York: Scribner's, 1953), 20. First published 1925.

10 *The Living Breath of Event*

1 David G. Hays, "Language and Interpersonal Relationships," *Language as a Human Problem*, ed. Morton Bloomfield and Einar Haugen (New York: Norton, 1974), 206.
2 Richard Le Gallienne, "The Psychology of Gossip," *Munsey's Magazine*, 48 (1912), 127.
3 Max Gluckman, "Gossip and Scandal," *Current Anthropology*, 4 (1963), 315. My italics.
4 William Faulkner, *The Hamlet* (New York: Random House, 1964), 97.
5 Agatha Christie, *The Mirror Crack'd*, in *Five Complete Miss Marple Novels* (New York: Avenel Books, 1980), 124. First published 1962.
6 Melville J. Herskovits and Frances S. Herskovits, *Trinidad Village* (New York: Octagon, 1976), 275. First published 1947.
7 James Hillman, *The Myth of Analysis: Three Essays in Archetypal Psychology* (New York: Harper and Row, 1978), 26.
8 Hans Loewald, "Psychoanalysis as an Art and the Fantasy Character of the Psychoanalytic Situation," *Papers on Psychoanalysis* (New Haven: Yale University Press, 1976), 355.
9 William Faulkner, *The Hamlet*, 13.
10 William Faulkner, *Absalom, Absalom!* (New York: Modern Library, 1951), 120–1. First published 1936.
11 Meredith Anne Skura, *The Literary Use of the Psychoanalytic Process* (New Haven: Yale University Press, 1981), 174.
12 Zora Neale Hurston, *Their Eyes Were Watching God* (New York: Negro Universities Press, 1969), 16. First published 1937.
13 Toni Morrison, *Song of Solomon* (New York: Knopf, 1977), 323.
14 *The Collected Stories of Eudora Welty* (New York: Harcourt Brace Jovanovich, 1980), 17.
15 See J. L. Austin, *How to Do Things with Words*, 2nd ed. (Oxford: Clarendon Press, 1975), 100.

Epilogue

1 Mary Ann O'Roark, "A Few Good Words About Gossip," *McCall's*, 110:9 (June 1983), 72.
2 Sam Keen, "Why We Love Gossip," *Family Weekly*, 5 June 1983, 7.
3 George Steiner, *After Babel: Aspects of Language and Translation* (New York: Oxford University Press, 1975), 41.
4 Leo Bersani, *A Future for Astyanax: Character and Desire in Literature* (Boston: Little, Brown, 1976), 52; Martin Price, *Forms of Life: Character and Moral Imagination in the Novel* (New Haven: Yale University Press, 1983), 313.

Index

Permissions Acknowledgments